# Family Genealogy

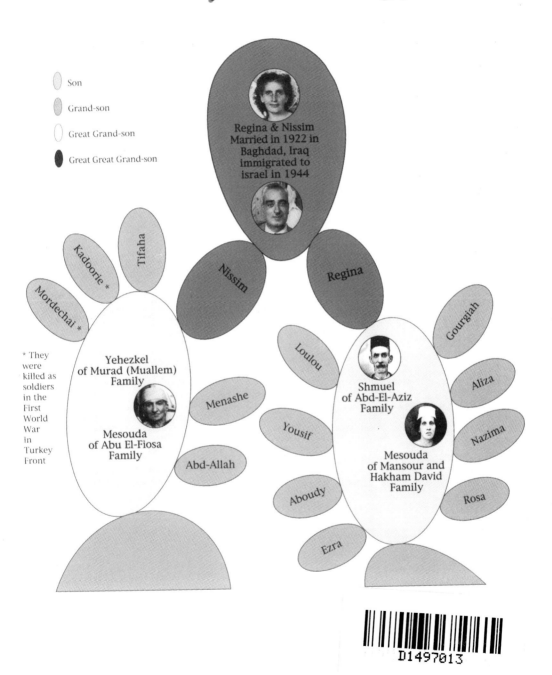

Son

Grand-son

Great Grand-son

Great Great Grand-son

Regina & Nissim
Married in 1922 in
Baghdad, Iraq
immigrated to
israel in 1944

Kadoorie *

Tifaha

Mordechai *

Nissim

Regina

* They
were
killed as
soldiers
in the
First
World
War
in
Turkey
Front

Yehezkel
of Murad (Muallem)
Family

Mesouda
of Abu El-Fiosa
Family

Menashe

Abd-Allah

Loulou

Shmuel
of Abd-El-Aziz
Family

Gourgiah

Aliza

Yousif

Nazima

Mesouda
of Mansour and
Hakham David
Family

Aboudy

Rosa

Ezra

D1497013

# To Baghdad and Back

## The Miraculous 2,000 Year Homecoming of the Iraqi Jews

## Mordechai Ben-Porat

JERUSALEM ♦ NEW YORK

Copyright © Mordechai Ben-Porat
Jerusalem 1998/5758

All rights reserved. No part of this publication may be translated,
reproduced, stored in a retrieval system or transmitted, in any form
or by any means, electronic, mechanical, photocopying, recording or
otherwise, without express written permission from the publishers.

Translation from Hebrew: Marcia Grant and Kathy Akeriv

Typesetting: Marzel A.S. – Jerusalem

Cover: Studio Paz, based on the Hebrew cover design of Michele Optovsky


Edition  9  8  7  6  5  4  3  2


Gefen Publishing House Ltd.
POB 36004
Jerusalem 91360, Israel
972-2-5380247
E-mail: isragefen@netmedia.net.il

Gefen Books
12 New Street
Hewlett, NY 11557, USA
516-295-2805


Printed in Israel

*Send for our free catalogue*

**Library of Congress Cataloging-in-Publication Data**
Ben-Porat, Mordechai, 1923-
[Le-Bagdad va-ḥazara. English]
To Baghdad and back / Mordechai Ben-Porat
    p.        cm.
ISBN: 965 229 195 1
1. Jews—Iraq—History—20th century.  2. Jews—Iraq—Migrations.  3. Israel—Emigration and immigration.
4. Iraq—Emigration and immigration.  5. Israel—Politics and government.  6. Ben-Porat, Mordechai, 1923- .
I Title.
DS135.I7B4513  1998
9563.7'004924—dc21
98-19660
CIP

# CONTENTS

To my dear late wife Rivca, mother and grandmother, who accompanied me with great loyalty in all my public vicissitudes; to her parents, Aliza and Yaacov Gafni; to my late parents, Regina and Nissim, who imbued me with a pride in my Jewishness; to my sisters and brothers, who carried the family's burden when I was busy with public activities; to my daughters, Idit, Tamar and Michal, who accepted my absences due to my various public activities.

To the activists of the Ezra and Nehemiah Campaign and to the Halutz Movement members, who were the pillars of fire directing the camp; to the late Moshe Carmil, an officer and friend; to the memory of the people executed by the order of the authorities, the late Yousif Basri and Shalom Saleh, who paid with their lives for their activities as emissaries of Israel; to the people imprisoned for their Zionism, who tasted the bitterness of prison life, to those who crossed the Iraqi borders in search of freedom and to all those who fulfilled their dream and immigrated to Israel; to the pilots who took part in the enterprise and to our loyal air stewardess, Ilana Marcus (Lilian Nada).

# ACKNOWLEDGMENTS

This book is the product of prolonged research, assembling and collating material. I owe deep gratitude to all those people, without whose help I would not have been able to complete and publish it.

To the Mossad Aliya Bet members, comrades and partners; Haim Yisraeli, assistant to the Ministers of Defence, the custodians of the Israel Defence Forces' Archives as well as the Haganah and the Zionist Archives in Jerusalem; the staff of the Babylonian Jewry Heritage Centre; Editor Eitan Ben-Natan and the Ma'ariv Book Guild; writer and researcher Yacov Habakuk.

To Yehezkel Nathaniel in memory of his wife Mary (Ruth) who made possible the translation; to Mrs. Kathy Akeriv who did the basic translation and to Mrs. Marcia Grant for her dedication and expertise in adding the final touches.

# PREFACE

I am neither an historian nor an academic, who has dedicated time and means to study documents for the purpose of researching specific topics, but I am a practical man. All my life, I have been assigned to various missions dealing with public and political affairs. As a teenager I was active in the Underground Movement in Baghdad; as an officer in the army in Battalion 42; an emissary of the Mossad Aliya Bet in Iraq, a mission which is the topic of my book; as the first Head of the local Council of Or Yehuda, and active in the political sphere of the country, a Member of the Knesset for sixteen years on behalf of Mapai, Rafi and Telem, as an emissary for the country for dangerous missions such as the one to Teheran during the rule of Khomeini; as a Minister who accepted delicate and complicated projects of which the general public was not always aware, as an initiator and founder of the Babylonian Jewry Heritage Centre, etc. This is always how it has been and how I like it to be, in the service of the public and my country.

In the course of the last decade, several books were published concerning the Babylonian Jewish community and the Ezra and Nehemia Operation in particular. Although I was pleased that the subject had been handled in detail, I found myself, not once, reading some events described inaccurately or tendentiously. I would make notes in the margins of the books concerning the latter and often felt like commenting or even criticizing the writers. Only lately have I felt the desire to write my own version of the story.

This is not objective writing. No author can be objective when he writes, nor am I. Possibly other readers will find fault with my book; I am telling the story as I saw and experienced it. I tried to be accurate and faithful to memory and made great efforts to go over the manuscripts several times, scrutinizing documents, letters and telegrams that I wrote and received, many of them to be found in various archives in the country. I even studied documents relating to the subject that I found abroad.

I spoke to colleagues, emissaries and activists to refresh my memory and to hear their stories first-hand. I interviewed leaders of the communities who were living abroad and from whom I received information or taped material which I collected for the Babylonian Jewry Heritage Centre. I feel I have presented what I consider a serious and accurate account of my experiences.

In the Appendices, I chose to reveal the report of the Committee of Inquiry, founded by Isar Harel, the Head of the Mossad, with special instructions from David Ben-Gurion to do so, in order to allay any suspicion that the Halutz Movement itself, its members or agents threw bombs into Jewish centers to frighten the people into leaving Iraq. His report was classified "Top Secret" and acquits the Movement of any involvement and, by publishing it, I sincerely hope that this false information will be put to rest. My original preface in the Hebrew Edition is considerably longer in substance. I have used what I consider relevant to the English reader. Any researcher who wishes to study the original manuscript is more than welcome to visit the Babylonian Jewry Heritage Centre in Or Yehuda in Israel where the manuscript is now housed.

In writing this book regarding my personal experiences that began fifty years ago, my work has been accomplished. It is a testament to several years of intensive public and political activities. A heavy burden has been lifted from my shoulders – its absence gives me much relief. I hope this book will add yet one more chapter to the story of the Babylonian community, will complete the information published until now on the Ezra and Nehamia Operation, and will allow historic justice for the activists who risked their lives with great courage, to assist in the immigration of the Babylonian Jews to Israel.

# Chapter 1

# MOBILIZATION

O n one of those hot sultry days in August 1949, returning to camp after intensive training, my Commander, the late Shema'ya Bareket (Beuknstein), took me aside and told me, in a very secretive manner, that I was to be invited to a meeting at the headquarters of the Mossad Aliya Bet, situated in Rothschild Boulevard in Tel Aviv.

His words took me completely by surprise, and I could feel my pulse racing. When he turned away after patting my shoulder, I felt rooted to the spot where I stood. I thought of all my unfulfilled dreams. The first was to establish, near the Zrifim military camp, a settlement whose nucleus would contain soldiers who had enlisted in the battalion where I and my brother Uri served. My second dream was to join the "Shahar" unit, which was founded in 1942. The aim of that unit, which was based in the south of Acre, was to help infiltrate agents into other countries. Its commanding officer was Shmaryahu Guttman, his deputy was Shimon (Sam'an) Somekh, and the intelligence officer a man called Yaacov Nimrodi. I thought that having lived in Iraq, being well versed in Arabic and familiar with Arab culture, I would be eligible to join this unit.

I arrived at the headquarters of Mossad Aliya Bet, curious and very nervous. At the entrance, I recognized some of the people there, and it transpired that they were also invited to the meeting and didn't seem to know what it was all about.

"Listen, Second Lieutenant Ben-Porat," one of the three persons sitting in an inner room declared. "We have been following your progress since your immigration to Israel. We find that you have settled down well. You have earned a commission rank and become a platoon commander. We would like to put you in charge of a sensitive and dangerous mission with a great deal of responsibility. It's all up to you...."

"What does it involve?" I asked, studying the three men sitting there before me. One of them was Shlomo Hillel, whom I already knew, but the one who had full powers was the interviewer, whom I heard later on was Moshe Carmil (Cherbinsky).

"I don't have to tell you in what a state the Iraqi Movement is now," he continued. "You were there, you came from there. The community is in a bad way. People are being persecuted and are eager to arrange for their emigration to Israel. We want you to fly over there in order to help them leave the country. You are Iraqi by birth, well versed in Arabic and familiar with the Iraqi Jewish dialect. You understand the Iraqi mentality. You are also familiar with the work of the

*Mordechai Ben-Porat with other Cadettes at the first officer's course after the establishment of the State of Israel.*

Haganah. You have a command background. You certainly are the right man for us..."

"But..." I tried to say something, the interviewer interrupted me.

"The fact that you are still a bachelor is to your advantage."

I tried once again to say something, and once more I was interrupted:

"What is your opinion? Do you agree to go back to Iraq in order to help the young generation and the Halutz members who wish to immigrate to Israel?"

"Yes!" I answered swiftly. "I know Iraq, the community and the Movement, and I am ready to help."

For the first time the interviewer smiled. His two colleagues, who never said a word, looked at me and nodded their heads, very pleased with my reply.

I left in a daze, and walked slowly along Rothschild Boulevard. My thoughts were vague. I could see before me the sights of Baghdad, which I had abandoned four years ago. I could see the expression on my family's faces and looked back to my Swearing-In Ceremony when I joined the Movement. I went over (in my

*Mordechai Ben-Porat at Front No. 5 during the Independence war (1947).*

imagination) my escape route and wondered how it would feel to be back again in Baghdad.

Some days later, during my second interview with Moshe Carmil, I discovered that the Mossad was having difficulty in obtaining my release from the army. The Israel Defense Force of those days, barely a well-organized army, could not afford to part so easily with young and experienced officers. Like many of my friends, I also had an offer to continue in regular service. I was promised a good salary and living expenses, and all of a sudden the offer made by the Mossad bothered me.

Then my Brigadier, Yitzhak Pundak, called me for an interview:

"Do you know that the Mossad Aliya Bet asked us to release you immediately?"

I nodded.

"I understand that you were there for an interview and agreed to accept a mission..." Pundak continued.

*Company Commanders of the Regiment, right to left: Yacov Eiges, Mordechai Ben-Porat, Dan Cohen (Colonel), Auzi Rosenberg, Moshe Eshed, Israel Efa'l, In the background from L. to R. the lates: Nathan Lahab, Yacov Vidislavski, David Peleg.*

I nodded again.

"Mordechai, I understand your motives, but I must first think about my unit, and the army, therefore I am against releasing you..."

But as it happened the Mossad did not accept the army's refusal as the final word and approached David Ben-Gurion, the Prime Minister and Minister of Defense, to obtain the order for my release. It arrived immediately: Ben-Gurion instructed the army to release me at once for the benefit of the Mission.

On 15 September 1949, I presented myself to my unit for a discharge. Then I reported to the headquarters of the Mossad for further instructions. They informed me that they were looking for a way to send me back to Iraq as soon as possible. After several discussions, a decision was reached: I was to fly to Iran as a crew member where Sion Cohen, the Mossad emissary in Iran would be waiting for me, and from Teheran I would continue on to Iraq.

I started training myself for the mission. I spent hours going through all the telegrams received from Baghdad, trying to understand the situation, the general feeling, problems, activities. I met Shmuel Moriah and Yehuda Rabinovitz, who had just arrived from Iraq, and told me what was happening in Baghdad, on the state of the Movement, the emissaries – first-hand information. The Foreign Office and the Intelligence Service also gave me further documents to study. With a sense of awe and reverence I read every scrap of paper and report. I understood that the collecting of information was probably the only training the State of Israel was capable of giving me. I did not receive any of those courses or special training described in books and espionage films; perhaps because Israeli Intelligence at that time was incapable of offering such courses, or perhaps that, from the start, I was not meant to be a spy. They gave me the job of information gathering and told me, that in case of an emergency I was to take over command and protect our people. But my main mission was to assist in the emigration of Iraqi Jews and so there was no need for any special training.

On 17 October 1949, a telegram from the Mossad was wired to Goldman (code word for the Mossad Representation in Teheran) where the following message was relayed: "A plane is leaving at dawn with Rony Barnett, nicknamed 'Dror' (an emissary for the emigration of Jews from Teheran and Iraq) together with Moslem pilgrims heading for Mecca." This was the green light....

I said farewell to my family and went to the taxi station in Tchernichowsky Street in Tel Aviv, but was told on arrival that the flight was postponed for a day for technical reasons. The next day I went once more to the station with Rivca, my red-headed girlfriend, who wished to accompany me to the airport. Moshe Carmil was waiting for me there. After an emotional separation from Rivca, with my foot already on the lower ramp of the plane, Carmil took hold of me, put his right hand on my shoulder, his face close to mine and said:

"Mordechai, if you have any regrets, say so now!"

"The moment I made that decision, there was no going back!" I answered him. "If I go back now I will never be able to forgive myself!"

We landed in Teheran airport after a little over a four-hour flight, where three decades later, during the Islamic revolution of Ayatollah Khomeini, I found myself landing for a second time to help save the Iranian Jews. There is no doubt of the similarity between the two missions. During my second mission also my lack of training also left a lot to be desired. In Feb. 1979, when the Chairman of the Jewish Agency and the managers of the immigration department approached me (with the knowledge of Menahem Begin) to assist in the rescue of the Jews of Iran, I informed them that I did not speak Farsi. The answer I received was, "Your task will mainly be to create coordination between the various Israeli groups working there, so you will not need to speak the language." I asked for some time to think it over, and after consulting my family I agreed.

Back to my first mission. In Teheran, a well-known person boarded the plane; he was greatly respected by everyone. His name was Sion Cohen, the Mossad emissary in Teheran. He looked for me, shook my hands and led me out of the plane in a hurry without anyone uttering a word or protest.

My first station in Teheran was in the comfortable home of Sion Cohen, his wife Zipora and their children. I stayed with them for several weeks until I could continue on to Baghdad.

The next day I joined them on a visit to the Jewish cemetery grounds, where a camp was erected for the Jewish refugees who had succeeded in escaping from Iraq and were rescued from the Iraqi police; they were notorious for their relentless pursuit of the leading agents of the Movement. Sion Cohen, as usual, worked with great energy. He tried to procure an identity card for me: that of a

Shiite pilgrim on his way to visit Karbala, one of the sacred cities of the Shiite sect, but this time, unfortunately, he met with many setbacks, and I began to lose patience.

During my stay at the Cohen's house I continued to read the telegrams we received from Baghdad. They were voices crying for help, and their contents broke my heart. I believed I could help, I was sure I could help, but I felt restricted and powerless. My frustration intensified my homesickness and yearning for my parents, my brother and especially my girlfriend Rivca. Again and again I would play the only phonograph record I had with me and which I had brought from Israel. I listened repeatedly to the song "You wait for me and I'll be back," which was written by Simonov and translated into Hebrew by Shlonsky: You wait for me and I'll be back / You wait patiently / You wait for me even in gloom / when the heart suffers from frost…

Even now, I feel emotional whenever I remember the words of this wonderful song. Not long ago, at a surprise party organized by members of my family on my 70th birthday, they told me that my mother would listen to this song, reminding her of me, and start to weep.

The days were passing: A month went by and no papers arrived. I impatiently suggested to Cohen to give up the idea of procuring me an identity card and to find me some other way of crossing the border. Sion succeeded at last. A local agent recruited by Sion accompanied me on a flight to Abadan, where I met Mordechai Bibi, who performed two duties: aiding the escapees from Basra to find accommodation, or some sort of shelter, on their way to Teheran, and recruiting smugglers to assist the Jews escaping from Basra. Two other agents, David Elias and Abraham Eitan, assisted him.

Mordechai Bibi was one of the heads of the Halutz Movement in Iraq since its establishment, and the first Chairman of the pioneering Underground Organization in Israel. Our paths crossed before my immigration to Israel, and also after that, when both of us were active in the Israeli political scene in the Knesset. In August 1949, when the Mossad asked for his opinion on whether I was suitable for the job offered, he wrote; "Personally, I think he is serious enough; but this young man has had little contact with the matter of emigration. As far as I know, the above mentioned has had no experience at all in this field. It is difficult to presume that willingness alone can help the envoy in present conditions such as they are today... Under the current situation there is no possibility that the envoy can attend to the concerns of the refugees whilst he is here since it is imperative that, immediately upon his arrival, he requires experience and a special talent which I believe he lacks."

However, on my arrival in Abadan three month later, I was received by him with benevolence and unlimited help. Bibi helped me once before to leave Iraq, and four years later assisted me in returning. He purchased suitable clothes for me, took care of my needs, and on 20 November 1949 I was on my way to Basra. Dressed in Bedouin robes I crossed the Shatt-El-Arab waterway on a small boat with an outboard motor, accompanied by the smuggler Haj Aziz Ben Haj Mahdi. Neither my friends nor my parents would have recognized me in the black *agal* and *kaffia* (Arab headdress) adorned by a thick mustache on my upper lip.

On the boat, almost twenty passengers were packed together; they were on their way to prostrate themselves on the sacred Shiite graves in Karbala, in southern Iraq. None of them carried any form of identity. I sat at one end of the boat while my escort, Haj Aziz Ben Haj Mahdi, perched on the far end. We maintained visual contact as we wanted to prevent any trouble should the boat came to a halt. During the trip, as the small vessel slowly chugged along its way, the passengers conducted a very lively conversation on the merits of "margarine" new on the market, which gradually replaced butter in the shops. For the first few minutes, I just listened to them, then realized that if I did not take part, they might become suspicious of me. So I started showing off my knowledge about the new product even though, in fact, my information on the subject was minimal. However, the speech I made and the air of self-confidence I exuded did its work: I was certain I had impressed my fellow passengers and convinced them that in some way I had something to do with the production of margarine!

We landed on the west bank of the river, not far from the city of Basra, in the neighbourhood of a local coffee house. On one of the bamboo benches, a policeman squatted, slowly sipping a cup of tea. From his vantage point, he scanned the passengers and of all the people there he singled me out:

"Hey, you, come here!"

I approached him.

"Where is your family?" he roared at me.

"My family lives in Kadhim."

My choice of this city was made to enable me to direct the conversation, if need be, to a topic well known to me. Kadhim is another city, sacred to the Shiite sect and situated to the north of Baghdad. I would sometimes journey there with my classmates. When I mentioned the name of the city, the policeman slowly nodded his head and waved me on; then settled down to enjoy his cup of tea.

The guide, who accompanied me, kept his distance while I conversed with the policeman; he then took me to the contact man of the Movement in Basra, Yehezkel Shlomo Pasha. Yehezkel welcomed me to his home and there I removed my Bedouin disguise (it was immediately burnt), showered, donned a suit and tie and was taken to Zvi Barr Nissim's house. After a stay of two days in Basra, I traveled by train to Baghdad and that was the start of my mission.

*Mordechai Ben-Porat on his way from Abadan in Iran, to Basra in Iraq, November 1949.*

# Chapter 2

# ON THE BANKS
# OF THE TIGRIS

Eleven sons and daughter were born to my parents: Regina, who was a Mansoor on her mother's side and Abd-El-Aziz on that of her father's, and Nessim Yehezkel Murad, the head of our family. As was the custom in those days, when the British ruled the land of the Tigris and the Euphrates, some of my sisters and brothers were given European names and other local ones: I, the eldest, am called Murad (Mordechai), in memory of an uncle who was drafted into the Ottoman army and disappeared during the World War I; after me came Rachelle (Rachel), Nuri (Uri), Bertha, Bahjat (Yosef), Valentine (Varda), Samuel (Shmuel), Marguerite (Margalit), Edward (Yehezkel), Hilda (Hila) and Shlomo.

When they came home from school, my sisters would immediately begin to help mother with the housework, whereas my brothers and I would throw our satchels into the doorway and head for the yard. Rascals by any standard, we would leap fully-clothed into the courtyard pool or splash each other and enter the house soaked through. Constant "warfare" reigned. In the bedrooms, pillows and bolsters, quilts and blankets would sail through the air, and battles often ended with broken windows or shattered pottery, overturned beds and painful bruises. Mother, an organized and strict housekeeper, would fume and scold us, but it wasn't long before we reverted to our mischievous ways.

At first we lived in a spacious house in Taht-El-Takia, Baghdad's Jewish quarter, where some of our relatives also resided. Eventually, my father bought an old house nearby, razed it to the ground and built a new one with four

*Typical alley in the Jewish quarter in Baghdad.*

bedrooms, a large guest room, kitchen, basement and a cistern which the women used regularly as a ritual bath (mikveh). Crowning this structure was a large flat roof, where the family congregated during the summer nights. We would put out our iron beds and sleep under the stars. My parents had a double bed draped with mosquito netting and this afforded them some privacy. Although the days were scorching, the nights were cool and pleasant, and anyone who had a home slept on the roof garden.

In 1934 or 1935, after consulting with mother, my father decided to leave the Jewish quarter and move to El-Adhamiya, a township north of Baghdad and east of the Tigris, facing the Shiite holy city of El-Kathemia on the other side of the river. In El-Adhamiya or, more precisely, in the El-Nassa neighbourhood, my father bought a 1.5 dunam plot and erected a new house surrounded by a large yard and garden. Our rooms were spacious, the guest room was as wide as an entrance hall with quite a large basement below. A staircase led to the roof which served us well on social and family occasions. At the centre of a spacious yard was a pool in which we children larked about, especially enjoying the fountain. A fence of brick and wrought-iron separated the yard from the garden.

El-Nassa offered us a better quality of life than we had had in Taht-El-Takia. El-Adhamiya was considered a resort area and many Jews purchased land and built bungalows on the riverbanks. When father decided to build there, he managed to convince two of my uncles and ten other families to join in the venture; hence, thirteen families simultaneously erected houses in a single area thus, creating a Jewish street. A temporary synagogue was built in one of the courtyards.

Our garden with its date palms and fruit trees, extended over a dunam at least and was enclosed by a stone wall. Father cared for the plants and trees with devotion, and my younger brother Uri would climb the palms with great agility. Our many visitors loved to relax in the garden under an arbour of grapevines. Father would seat them near the canal, fed by the cool waters of the Tigris. This would stream in at fixed intervals from the locks, preceded by the pump owner's stentorious announcements of the flow's beginning and end; he was paid according to the length of pumping time. I remember father and his guests bringing out bottles of homemade arak (distilled from a special gum, apples and the steam emanating from chicken on the boil), withdrawing them from time to time from the chilly canal to take a swig, and gently putting them back. Saucers of *mezze*, tidbits, cucumber strips, quartered tomatoes and pickled vegetables were placed on a faded hassock, and the men passed many hours drinking, singing, reminiscing and conversing about sundry topics.

We studied in a Moslem school, and because our original family name, Murad, was obviously Jewish, we took another, Kazzaz, which means "silk dealer." The choice was not random, for this had indeed been my grandfather's profession.

During that period, the Iraqi educational system was a copy of the local British one: six years of primary schools, followed by three years of intermediate and two years in secondary schools. Examinations were administered at the end of every year and those who failed had to repeat the grade. No exceptions were made. Thus, almost every class had an age-spread of two to three years.

School began daily with assembly in the courtyard where we sang nationalistic songs and raised the Iraqi flag. We then proceeded to our classrooms, walking past our headmaster, a much despised martinet who would wait at the entrance to punish latecomers with staccato blows of his ruler on their fingertips. Painful under ordinary conditions, these strikes were excruciating in the winter cold. One of the teachers in the school, a cheerful Jewish chap, liked to start the day by playing his violin, choosing melancholy or merry tunes according to his mood. It would not be far from the truth to say that the one who most enjoyed the music was the musician himself!

Although we were not strictly religious, my family adhered to a traditional way of life, with all that this implies. My parents insisted on eating kosher meat only, purchased at a Jewish butcher shop. Mother lit Sabbath candles and father ushered it in with the requisite chants. We neither cooked nor lit fires on the Sabbath, and during their conjugal relations, my parents were careful to observe the Laws of family purity (under Jewish religious law, married couples abstain from physical contact during the wife's menses and for some time thereafter). Even as a child, I noted the unique nature of my parents' relationship, although I could hardly understand what it all signified. I observed that mother's behaviour towards father changed from time to time: For example, she would avoid handing him a cup of tea or a pair of socks that he might require, leaving it instead on the table for him. This change of habit took place a few days every month, but was engraved in my consciousness, although I had no idea what it signified.

In Iraq, the rules were clear: The wife was in charge of running the home and her husband's welfare. He was the Head of the Family and, as it were, the "Foreign Minister." The wife cared for the children, cooked, laundered, mended, cleaned the house, etc., while her husband dealt with the outside world, and did the shopping. This division of labour did not imply any contempt for women; on the contrary, in most of the families of my acquaintance, the women were treated with great respect.

My mother, Regina, responsible for eleven children and a pampered husband, was busy from sunrise to sundown. Although she was assisted by a servant and by my sisters, the burden was primarily hers, leaving little time for leisure. Generally quiet and controlled, she could be provoked to lose her patience and raise her voice only by her irrepressible sons.

Father, as mentioned, was used to being indulged; he always wanted clean pressed clothes and a varied menu daily. If the rice he was served was slightly sticky, he would explode; if, heaven forbid, the soup was a bit too salty for his liking, he would burn with rage. The same fury resulted if his suit was not properly ironed or a shirt button came lose. Mother absorbed these criticisms silently and tried as hard as she could to satisfy her husband's whims. Although I know she suffered within, she absorbed the censure and maintained a stalwart and sunny exterior. Through her wisdom and behaviour, she gave us enduring values that contributed to our family's unity and solidarity even today, nine years after her death.

Like all the other heads of Jewish families, my father, Nessim Yehezkel Murad, would go early to the marketplace to buy our daily needs — meat, fruit and vegetables. He insisted on buying fish directly from a fisherman who would stand by his catch on the banks of the Tigris. For a small additional fee, the fisherman would deliver the purchases to our house, and father would continue on towards his store in the El-Midan *suk* (bazaar), in the Moslem section of Baghdad, near El-Sarai, the government compound. The El-Midan *suk*, it should be noted, incorporated very diverse neighbours. At one end were government ministries and courts of law, the central ruling institutions, and at the other, the local brothel, a legally licensed trade providing rapid satisfaction to its many customers.

When I was a pupil in the upper primary school, not far from father's store, I liked to spend time with him and collect my pocket money. The store had all kinds of merchandise, from construction materials to British spare parts, for the horse-drawn carriages which filled Baghdad's streets — you name it, he had it. My brothers and I would love to wait excitedly for the cartons of merchandise that arrived from abroad in order to search them for the gifts hidden within by our foreign suppliers.

The *suk* was always teeming with people. The stores were owned by Moslems and Jews, good neighbours working peacefully side by side.

I'd often stand in the doorway and observe the goings-on: heavily-laden beasts spurred onward by the blows of young green branches or bamboo rods, mustachioed government clerks and police and army officers in starched uniforms, crossing the *suk,* their chests puffed up with self-importance. Sometimes I witnessed more interesting events, such as policemen leading/dragging a prostitute with knife wounds to the station, to file testimony. She would yell, bleed and struggle to escape, but her captors held fast, relentless in their mission. Even injured victims requiring immediate medical care were first taken to the police station to testify; hospital treatment came only after depositions were duly signed.

At the *suk's* centre stood a *hammam,* a large bathhouse frequented by many of the shopkeepers, wholesalers, merchants and even customers. For the men, this was a place to meet and unwind. A visit to the *hammam* took several hours. Bathing was followed by massage, the masseurs being skilled men who spared no effort to release tensions and straighten out knotted muscles. After their massage, the naked bathers would stretch out on mat-covered pallets, noisily sipping dark sweet tea with loud slurps. The Moslem bathers used a special unguent, a mixture of arsenic and gypsum, to remove hairs, especially in the pubic area. Among other things, father stocked this depilatory in his store; it was in great demand.

While relaxing in the *hammam,* spread out on the wooden pallets in the humid rooms, the bathers would carry on interesting conversations, mainly on sex. When talk heated up, tongues loosened and the discourse became more direct and "juicy," father would abruptly remember some errand that needed my urgent attention — somewhere far away.

Father, whom everyone called "Abu Murad," would go to his store daily in Arab dress: a *zboon*, a long straight gown for men, above that a dark *abaya* and a red *tarbush* on his head. His colleagues treated him with great respect. At home, he would exchange these clothes for more comfortable ones and turn to his beloved hobby, gardening. Towards evening, he would dress more elegantly, donning a suit and tie for a visit to the coffee-house. As soon as the coffee-house owner spotted father in the entrance, he would announce Abu Murad's arrival and command the waiter to fetch drinks immediately. There, father and his friends would discuss the seasons, what to plant and when, and how to deal with agricultural pests. Interspersed would be other topics, more earthy and savoury.

Relations between our family and our Moslem neighbours were warm and friendly. This doesn't mean that we had no problems; but such is the way of the world. Once, on a Friday night, a burglar entered and stole all our shoes and those of our guests', that were lined up in front of the doorway between the yard and our home. This was the only theft we ever experienced. Father had two whistles to alert the police. Whenever he sensed anything suspicious, he whistled. The police would hear it, realise that something was wrong, and rushed to our aid. This system worked well for years.

One night, father noticed someone trying to steal leather sheets belonging to our Moslem neighbours that hung out in a field near our house. He grabbed his whistle and blew hard. The police arrived and caught the thief, who, it turned out, was the son of one of father's close acquaintances. After the son was released, his father denounced mine for having called the police and having the boy arrested. But father would have none of it: "Before you attack me for calling the police, get your son to mend his ways."

As often as they could, my parents would try to supply our needs on their own. A goat which grazed in our garden provided fresh milk for drinking and preparing cheese and dairy products. A *tabun* (oven) built in the garden was used by a Jewish baker who came once a week to make our bread. Our fruit trees supplied peaches and apples; other fruits and vegetables came from the nearby market, where local farmers arrived early and, piling high their melons, watermelons, cucumbers, tomatoes, peppers, beets, turnips, squash, grapes, apricots, dates and more, loudly extolling their produce. The customers, mostly storekeepers who came to replenish their stocks, bargained, argued and would make their purchases. Father would often take us children to the market for the experience. The merchandise was delivered to customers by donkey. The driver, used to taking the foodstuffs to commercial establishments, would ask father: "Where is your store, sir?" and be surprised to learn that the stock was meant for a private home.

Because of the distance from Baghdad, we were somewhat cut off from the Jewish community and developed closer relations with our Moslems neighbours. We children would play together, visit one another and get to know each other's way of life. As examinations approached, we would often meet at each other's home and study together. Sometimes we'd wander together in the fields; on other occasions, we would have friendly tussles, and knock our friends about. I must make it clear that only a minority of Jews had good relations with the Moslems. Most of our people were not involved in the society around them. A Moslem's right to harass a Jew was taken for granted; it would not have occurred to the victim to react or to report the matter to the police. This sort of Jewish reaction annoyed father no end; I would often hear him complain about his inability to change it, even to those close to him.

It is impossible to describe our daily lives and surroundings without touching on homosexuality. In Iraq, and throughout the Arab world, a puritanical lifestyle reigns supreme, based in part on the clear segregation of men and women. The severe restrictions on having anything to do with contact between the sexes has produced a special way of life. Moslem women wearing an *abaya* and a *pushi* (a cape covering the head and face) would arouse great curiosity among the males seated in the coffee-shops. The men would lustfully appraise them as they passed, speculating, sometimes aloud, on the female forms concealed beneath the robes and veils. The garment conceals the figure almost entirely. The only parts exposed were the ankles, and these, as if to taunt them, were covered with glittering anklets. Lacking alternatives, the men would try to divine a woman's appearance and skin colour from the ankles. The atmosphere was one of unceasing desire and curiosity; it is no wonder that Arabic poetry is suffused with sadness, fantasy and yearning.

*Baghdad, on the west side of the Tigris river*

This way of life also increased the incidence of homosexual behaviour in the Baghdad I knew: Boys and adults molested children and some deviants even sought sexual release with animals. Quite a few women became lesbians, perhaps because their confinement in their homes and their limited access to men led to boredom and the search for emotional release.

Once, two friends left school with me and went strolling by the river's edge. At a bypass, the two disappeared and entered a small sandy cave that faced the river. I thought they were playing "hide-and-seek" so I ran after them and found them locked in an embrace, their trousers at their feet.

The spectacle was quite strange to me: I had not, until then, even heard of homosexuality.

However, when they saw me, they asked me to come closer.

"Come on!" called the "male" partner, inviting me to sample the experience. I had no idea what he wanted. I didn't understand what the act meant. For a moment I froze, but then moved closer to the "female" and grabbed hold of him rubbing my body against his buttocks in the matter I had just witnessed; then, overcome by nausea, I let go and ran away.

When we lived in El-Adhamiya, surrounded by Moslems, I also tended to seek out Jewish friends. I formed ties with new friends and renewed relationships with others I had known for a while. We used to meet in southern Baghdad, in a coffee-house on the banks of the Tigris, playing *tawli* (backgammon), chatting, dining on *samak masguf* (grilled fish), returning home late at night, they to their homes in the Jewish quarter and I, riding my bicycle, to El-Adhamiya.

On hot summer nights we had more interesting and stimulating pursuits. During that season, when the Tigris was at a low ebb, it would shrink to a width of less that 50 meters, exposing a row of islands. Skipping among them, we would spend most of the nights with girls, around campfires, singing, playing instruments and grilling fish. On the banks of the river were booths built from planks and palm fronds, which, during the day, sheltered the swimmers. At night, these booths became romantic hideaways for trysting couples. This special atmosphere also provided cover for meetings of the Halutz, a Zionist Movement.

Our lives continued in this manner until the Nazis came to power and their influence increased, ably assisted by the German Ambassador, Frytz Grobba. Hatred took hold of the Iraqi people against the Jews, and Moslems became progressively more militant. Members of the Jewish minority reduced the scope of their activities and tried to keep a low profile, to no avail. The Rashid Ali El-Kailani revolt, on 2 June 1941, ignited the flames and exacted a bloody price. Life thereafter would never be the same.

# Chapter 3

# JOURNEYING TO THE LAND OF ISRAEL

W e received warning signs, but we ignored them, because we couldn't believe things could change or perhaps, deep down, we didn't want to believe. In my family, only my mother, Regina, was more farsighted than we were and could see the writing on the wall.

The first indication we had was the *Farhoud*, a pogrom which took place on the Feast of Shavuoth (Pentecost) in the year 1941, when 135 persons were slaughtered, men, women and children. On reflection, those pogroms marked the end of a period of paradise for the Iraqi Jews. I remember, on the Eve of the *Farhoud* our neighbour, Colonel Taher Mohamed Aref, came to our home in El-Adhamiya, when normally we each kept our distances. He tried to warn us of coming events. Father (not in character) took him seriously, strengthened the locks on the door, added stone bricks to a wall in the kitchen, building a sort of double wall to conceal our valuables, stocked our larder and ordered us to sleep in our day-clothes, ready for any eventuality.

On that eventful day, Sunday, 1 June 1941, on the day of the Feast, Moslem citizens had been inflamed by fiery orators and were armed with vicious tools such as axes, knives, and all manner of sticks and clubs. They invaded our neighbourhood, El-Nassa in El-Adhamiya city, as they did in other various Jewish quarters. Their strident voices and calls on Allah to sanction their murder of Jews – *"Allahhou Akbar!"* (God the Almighty!), *"Idhbah Al Yahud!"*

(Murder the Jews!) and *"Mal el Yahud – Halal!"* (Sanction to rob the Jews!) could be heard so clearly.

We barricaded ourselves in our home, locked all the doors, strengthening them with stout beams and dragged furniture and other heavy objects to further bolster our defenses. We then rushed up to the roof garden to follow the proceedings. I watched as our "good" Moslem neighbours, living on the opposite side of the street, those whom mother would offer occasional savoury dishes from her kitchen, participated in the general madness. Neighbourly goodwill had vanished: They guided the raving attackers to our front door. I also spied the wife of Colonel Taher Mohamed Aref. Either he was not at home, or on his specific instructions before he left she decided to help us. Armed with a gun and a hand grenade she stood facing the menacing crowd: She threatened with her weapons if they invaded our home. Her determination and show of arms convinced them of her serious intent and they retreated. This incident remains fresh in my memory to this day: It was an act of bravery and left an indelible impression on my mind.

There were warning signs. At the height of the *Farhoud*, Sasson Naim, my cousin, came to our house. He used to visit us frequently; this time he could not inform his parents where he was, for they lived in the Taht-El-Takia Jewish quarter in Baghdad. Because of the pogroms taking place, my mother wished to assure them that their son was safe and staying with us. As there were no means of phoning them, the only way of making contact was to go directly to their home. My mother didn't think twice about it. Alighting from a bus in Taht-El-Takia, she faced an ugly mob. She was dressed in Arab garb, but the minute she spoke she revealed her origins. One of the youths, brandishing a tar-smeared staff, hit her on her head several times until she fainted. A policeman tried to revive her, then listened to her story and offered to accompany her to my aunt's home. It was yet another instance of a kindly Moslem showing concern for someone not of his faith.

However, political developments caused great hardship for Iraq's Jewish citizens. The behaviour of the Colonel's wife and the policeman in the face of danger proved exceptional: The general mood was ugly and explosive. We, the young Jews in the neighbourhood, felt we ought to do something about it. After much deliberation we organized an underground movement to combat this growing menace with protests and action. Benyamin Yehezkel, Moshe Etzioni, David Fattal (subsequently a Member of the Knesset and Chairman of the Iraqi Immigrants in Israel Union), Yousif Shaul Koko, Yehezkel Shahrabani and myself held meetings, even recorded protocols and made sure to hide them in secret places, but it all came to nothing.

My mother's intuition served her well – she was certain matters would not improve and could only worsen, so she began to talk of leaving Iraq. Father listened to her and said that he too had been thinking of emigrating – to India, following in the footsteps of the great Sassoon and Kadoorie Families, who immigrated there in the 18th century and were now well-established.

My mother refused to countenance this: It could only be the land of Israel for her.

"I am not interested in acquiring wealth – I only want security for my children!" she declared stoutly, "and we can only find this in Palestine, the land of our people!"

*The Iraqi passport of the author's mother, Regina Ben-Porat, where the names of the rest of the family members were included. With this passport the family left Iraq.*

With this announcement she made plans. She contacted a Jewish truck driver whose business it was to transport fish, eggs, fruits, etc., from Iraq to Palestine via Jordan. One day, in the year 1943, she set out with him and after several weeks arrived in Jerusalem. She had an Iraqi passport and wished to learn what she could about the country. She hoped to acquire residential permits for herself and her family from the British Mandate Government. Some relatives of hers, the Bakshis (one of their children subsequently became the Sephardic Chief Rabbi of Israel), obtained the necessary permits for her and she returned to Iraq.

On her arrival in Baghdad she tried, without success, to obtain Iraqi passports for all the family so she asked the help of the Halutz Movement and Salha Hayim (Zvia Ezra). They in turn recruited Albert Shamash, an expert in forgery, and thus succeeded in registering all the family, except myself, on my mother's passport.

I was also a member of the Halutz Movement, and was among the first to join the group, which was created in 1942. I shall never forget the thrill of the Swearing-In Ceremony. It took place one evening at the home of the Sehayik family. The house was encircled by a yard where vines and large clusters of grapes hung almost to the ground, touching my head as I entered.

I was invited into a dimly-lit basement where I could barely discern, in the left-hand corner, a table draped with an Israeli flag. On the table lay a bible on one side and a gun on the other. Two Israeli emissaries, Shmaryahu Guttman and Ezra Kadoorie, were seated there; I had the honour of knowing them better later on. I remember having to "swear on my honour and with all that I held sacred, to fulfil every order given, to guard all secrets well and to protect the lives and properties of my Jewish brothers and sisters. If I ever betrayed them, may their souls haunt me as the saying goes 'If I forget thee, O Jerusalem, let my right hand forget her cunning!'"

After the ceremony I participated, under the guidance of Yehuda Shohet, in several actions of the Movement; meanwhile I was preparing myself for the external matriculation examinations and also worked for a Polish army unit under General Andrus, which was camped in Kizil Rabat, near Khanakin.

On February 1944, my parents, together with my eight brothers and sisters, left Iraq on a hired sea plane. They flew from Lake Habaniya, north of Baghdad,

*The six who made the journey from Baghdad to Israel (1945) from left to right: Eliahu Cohen, Levi Shimshon, Mordechai Ben-Porat, Abraham Solomon, Rahamim Kashi, Nahman Levi.*

and landed on the Dead Sea in Palestine. Two of my brothers, Uri and Yousif, flew to Palestine two days later, whilst I stayed behind to take my matriculation exams. In this I was successful and then tried to obtain a passport in order to join my family in Israel. I wasn't successful in that and approached members of the Halutz to help me escape from Iraq.

On 7 August, 1945, Mordechai Bibi and Avner Shashou, members of the Aliya Committee, came to my grandmother's home where I was staying. They briefed me on their plans for me. I was taken in a rowing boat on the River Tigris to meet my fellow travellers: Nahman Levy, Shimshon Levy, Abraham Nissim (Solomon), Elyahu Zingi and Reuben Kashi, and the organizer of the campaign, Mordechai Bibi. The route that was mapped out for us was to take us from Baghdad to the city of Anah in the north of Iraq, close to the borders of Syria. From there we would cross Syria and Lebanon to reach Israel. This was a newly planned route and we were the first chosen to take the risk. Mordechai Bibi took us to meet our guide, a Moslem smuggler, Hassan Abu Sabri, and we agreed to meet him again the next day at the bus station in Anah.

My fellow travellers spent their last night in Baghdad in a nightclub, where Salima Pasha, a Jewish artiste, used to sing. Shimshon Levy, who was a bit of a daredevil, asked the famous singer to give us a rendering of *Bukra El-Safar* (Tomorrow is the Journey). Salima Pasha, who later married the well-known Iraqi singer, Nathim El-Ghazali (her life story is certainly worthy of a book in itself), understood the significance and obliged them with a lot of feeling and passion, but warned them not to show too much enthusiasm lest it drew unwanted attention.

The next day, we met at the bus station before dawn. Avner Shashou made the arrangements for a minibus to take us to Anah without delay. We arrived there at about 8 o'clock in the morning where we met the smuggler's assistant Nouri, the son of Sheikh El-Dal'ani who welcomed us to his home. His father wished to know who we were and Nouri told him we were Moslems and immediately found us Arab names – Abas, Ibrahim, etc. Those were times when the Allies were victorious over Hitler and the formidable Axis powers: the Iraqis were on the side of Hitler and greatly disappointed with events. Sheikh El-Dal'ani asked my opinion regarding Hitler's failures despite his fame and power. I answered vaguely in order to discontinue the conversation. I did not wish to be caught in a trap causing me embarrassment.

Anah is a region with a Jewish past. As we drove through the city we were aware of its historical associations. Here – between Kufa, where according to tradition the tomb of King Yaknia is situated, and El-Kifil, where it is believed that the Prophet Yehezkel was buried – Jewish settlements were established and here were the beginnings of the Exilarch (rulers of the exiled Jewish community). Here the Nehardea settlement was created: Within its walls, gifts of the Babylonian Jews to the Temple were housed. In this place resided the famous Pumpadita Yeshiva which superseded the Nehardea centre as a school for Torah students. The great Sura Yeshiva, where the Talmud was completed, also stood here and this was where Rabbi Saadia Gaon lived and worked.

In the mid-forties Anah was a city with a moderate climate and a flourishing trade. It was well situated on the road leading to Syria and this contributed to its prosperity. Thousands of Jews used to live there, but in the summer of 1945 only a small number were left, about 300 at the most.

I do not know how my fellows-travellers remember the city, but I shall remember Anah all my life. During our five-day stay there, we were served *bamia* (okra) three times a day in various dishes and this would give me a terrible stomach-ache. Although the food was a problem, the sleeping arrangements were most comfortable. Nouri, who was about to be married, had bought some bedding for his dowry, and we had the pleasure of consecrating it.

One evening, Hassan Abu Selim himself came to assist us on our journey. We boarded a car together with some other travellers. They seemed suspicious of us and asked Hassan where we were going. He lied to them and mentioned some other destination. We left the car and as we advanced along our original route, we could see from afar the border police looking for us. Hassan's suspicions that the travellers would inform on us was a correct one. We marched in the dark and if we saw the headlights of the border police, we'd crouch down of sight. Our guide was worried as we wore leather shoes that clattered on the stony path; his were made of rubber. So he bade us remove them and we continued barefooted. Unaccustomed as we city boys were to this form of travel, we soon found it difficult to carry on as our feet began to bleed and hurt. Now and then we would stumble into one another or trip and fall. We didn't grumble: We'd bite our lips and soldier on. At dawn we reached the Iraqi-Syrian border. To express their delight, some of my companions urinated on Iraqi soil to show their contempt for a country that disappointed us and were treating the Jews badly.

Crossing the Syrian border, the smuggler warned us: "If anyone gets injured or killed, carry on and do not stop to assist him." We were members of the Youth Movement, trained to help a fellow member in distress, and this posed a problem for us. Luckily no one suffered and we were not required to put it to the test.

After crossing a Moslem cemetery we reached the frontier city of Abu Camel. It was during the Feast of Ramadan, when Moslems usually visit the tombs of their dear departed. We tried not to attract attention by merging with the crowd and adopted a "relative" to wail over. If the genuine mourners arrived we'd move on to some other gravesite. We roamed the cemetery area for about an hour until the smuggler advised us to spend the rest of the day on the Euphrates riverbank. We were overjoyed, as this was the first opportunity to bathe ourselves since we left Baghdad.

The next morning, on our way to Dir-El-Zor, a truck carrying bags of sugar and flour awaited us. Its owners profited by this "trade" in smuggling people to the inner areas of Syria. Other travellers who joined us wore village clothes, and so did we, but underneath them, we had on our city suits. These were exposed when our outer garments flapped in the wind and we could see our fellow-travellers whisper among themselves.

Our smuggler, who realized what was going on, averted the danger by saying that we were the sons of prominent merchants who were studying the route. Then he gave each one of them a banknote to buy their silence. All was quiet once again in the fork-lift truck. Arriving at El-Zor, we marched to the meeting place, where another truck was expected to take over. While we waited, a suspicious policeman approached us and asked: "From where do you come?"

We said in unison: "From Aleppo. We are returning to our families."

The policeman seemed satisfied but after about a hundred meters down the road he started to follow us until the truck arrived. We climbed in quickly and pressed the driver to hurry on. He did so although the policeman waved and whistled for him to stop; the driver paid no attention and slipped away from the spot.

We arrived at Aleppo on Saturday night. Looking for a place to spend the night without arousing suspicion, we picked a hostel, where porters used to lodge. It was a red-light district. Each one of us chose a new name. The smuggler, Hassan Abu Sabri, and myself bought watermelons, cheese and bread, just as the porters did and climbed on to the roof garden. After the meal, we slept in our day clothes with our shoes tucked under our heads. The following day Zeev Housni, nicknamed "Dibo," arrived. He was born in Aleppo and had joined the Halutz Movement in his youth; his job was to assist Syrian Jews and those from Turkey, Iraq and other countries heading for Israel. He led us to the attic of the glorious Yoav Ben Zrouya Synagogue in the Jewish quarter. Dibo organized a service in conjunction with other families in the neighbourhood to supply us with food.

Meanwhile two refugees from Turkey joined us, and we were asked to look after them. We stayed there for two weeks. The waiting got on our nerves and we begged Dibo and the Movement to rescue us from this situation. We were taken to a photographer, and our photos were glued to converted passports. Abraham Solomon, aged fifteen, received a passport claiming he was thirty-six. Nahman Levy had one in the name of Naji Levy; Reuben Kashi the identity of a fourteen-year-old and I received a Syrian one in the name of Abbas.

We were sent to Beirut in two groups. In one of them was Shimshon Levy, Eliyahu Zingi, myself and one of the Turks. In the second were Abraham Solomon, Nahman Levy and Reuben Kashi. Our group took off first. At a certain stage in our journey, two Lebanese policemen entered our bus, asked for our passports and enquired from where we came. Our companion, a member of the Movement, sat near the driver, some distance away. The policemen were satisfied with our credentials, but were not pleased with the Turk's. He was not in command of the Arabic language, so he did not understand the questions. To overcome the difficulty we told them that the young person was a deaf-mute, so they left him alone and moved on.

There was another worrying incident. Shimshon Levy sat beside an elderly person and during the long drive struck up an acquaintance. The man asked from where he came, and he said "Beirut."

"And where do you come from?" Shimshon asked.

"From Iraq," the man answered and added: "Do you like songs?"

Shimshon, who subsequently became a teacher of Arabic in Israel, nodded.

Within several minutes, they were in competition with one another in the singing game. Then Shimshon felt himself being carried away by his intimate knowledge of Iraqi melodies, possibly arousing the other's suspicions, so he stopped singing.

After a long journey, the bus reached the coast. It was a lovely sight, for this was my first view of the seaside. I heard a lot about Beirut, the capital of Lebanon, its places of entertainment, gambling houses and theatres, but this did not really interest me. I only considered it a stopping-off place on my way to Israel.

Our companions took us to the synagogue in the Jewish quarter of Wadi Abu Jamil. The following day, they drove us out of Beirut, a two-hour journey, where we joined up with another eighty people, mostly women and children. We, the youngsters, were asked to supervise them. At dusk we left our car and started walking. We marched all night and in the morning we settled down on a hill, using our clothes to shade us from the sun.

We were lucky compared to those who followed us. We heard later on that the other group, that is Abraham Solomon, Nahman Levy and Reuben Kashi, were victims of the smugglers' greed. They provided them with salty cheese and then asked an enormous sum for water in order to slake their thirst.

That evening we continued on our journey lifting young children onto our shoulders. The walk was arduous and the load a heavy one. The child I carried on my back couldn't get to sleep, and from time to time dribbled a warm fluid onto my shoulders, neck and back. I held him close with my two hands and would now and then release a hand to shake it from the cramp. An old woman slipped and injured her head. We had to improvise a dressing from a piece of cloth as we had no bandages. Another old woman, finding the march too arduous, broke down and cried out: "I have no more strength and no wish to go to Israel! I'd rather die here!" We kept her spirits up by assuring her we were coming to the end of our journey.

The smuggler held a stick and would lightly tap the stragglers to hurry them on. At dawn we reached the Litany River. With the guide's permission we went down to the river to bathe, to quench our thirst and to soak the dry bread we carried, in its cool waters. We then took water and bread to our companions and waited on one of the hills until nightfall and the continuation of our journey.

It was the third night of our march since we left Beirut. We were exhausted: our feet bothered us, the distress of the children and the elderly increased. Frequently, our smuggler-guide tried to lift our spirits by saying: "You will soon reach your mother's house." We trudged on wearily – it took a maximum effort on our part.

Two hours passed and someone spotted flickers of light. We looked up and saw searchlights probing.

"The northern kibbutz," I murmured.

This spurred us on and we found new energy.

As we approached we saw someone signalling with a torch and some Hebrew words were spoken. The relief was general. Members of the "link" who

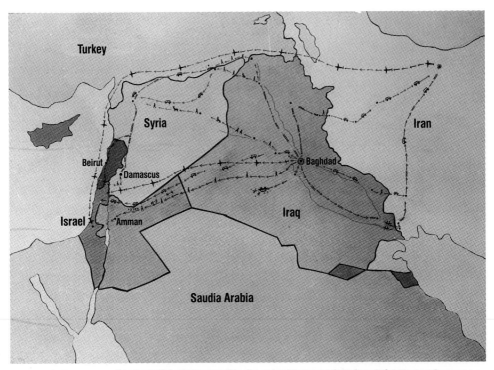

*Escape routes from Baghdad to Israel before the 'Ezra and Nehemiah' Operation.*

were on hand to receive the "Ma'pilim" (clandestine Jewish immigrants during the British Administration of Palestine) from the North, took us through the apple orchards of Kibbutz Kfar Giladi. On this occasion I would like to thank and confess that I couldn't resist picking apples for myself and the child on my back and that they were the most delicious and sweetest I've ever tasted.

We were warmly received in the kibbutz's dining-room. The excited members of Kfar Giladi were thrilled and happy to serve us hot beverages and plates full of cheese and fruits. An hour later, we were driven to Kibbutz Ayelet Hashahar so as to be as far away as possible from the British Army, who were energetically tracking the illegal Ma'pilim.

I reached the Land of our people on 8 September 1945, exactly a month after I left Baghdad. One chapter had come to a close, but not entirely, I thought to myself; that will be when I am re-united with my family.

A month later, on 8 October 1945, the newspaper Davar published the following:

> A group of about 50 Jews crossed the Lebanese border illegally into Israel at 6 o'clock on Saturday morning. At 7 two British officers from Trans-Jordan Frontier Force saw a group of Jews of some such number near Kfar Giladi. When they were about to investigate the matter, they were pushed aside by members of the Kibbutz who had absorbed the group into their settlement. In the morning the Frontier Force surrounded the settlement. At three in the afternoon the settlers of Kibbutz Manara attacked and shots were fired, wounding eight people. Five of them were taken to Shivitzer Hospital in Tiberias. The condition of one of the injured is critical, two are moderately severe and the other two have light injuries. The Trans-Jordan Frontier Force claim that two shots came from the settlement.

Aliza Katan was in the above-mentioned Ma'pilim group. She was one of the oldest instructors of the Halutz Movement in Iraq.

I return to my group's story: Fearing the British Army, we were shuttled to Kibbutz Yagour and from there to the headquarters of the Labour Council in Haifa.

Yitzhak Shiloah met us there. He was the representative of the Aliya Department of the Labour Council. He discussed the various possibilities and jobs that were available to us. In fact, at this stage our group split up. I left the Labour Council's depot in Haifa and drove to Tel Aviv, where my family was staying. Not having their address I wondered how to contact them in the big city.

I left the bus at Central Station, worming my way through the crowd when I suddenly spotted my sister Bertha. No words can describe this chance meeting and my reunion with the family.

At my parent's house which stood on the border of Tel Aviv and Jaffa, I embraced my parents, brothers and sisters, except for two of them, Varda and Shmuel who were absent.

"Where are they?" I inquired, wiping tears of joy from my eyes.

"In Kfar Giladi," they replied.

"In Kfar Giladi?! What a pity! That was our first stop in Israel!"

I decided to go back there to see them. I couldn't relax until I did. Only then would I truly feel that I had come home to Israel.

# Chapter 4

# JUST IN CASE...

I f there happened to be Jews in Iraq who ignored, accidentally or intentionally, the uneasy conditions of the Jewish minority in the country, and the danger inherent in the resentful Moslem population, the pogrom of Rashid Ali El-Kailani jolted them from their indifference. After the pogrom, which cost many lives, they also understood that it was no longer feasible to sit with hands folded, trusting to luck, that they must all be prepared for far more difficult times.

To be able to face it, first and foremost they needed to stockpile weapons for self-defense. The evacuation of British forces from Iraq left the Jews exposed to the mercy of the authorities and local extremists; this only emphasized the danger. An article was added to the Constitution in Iraq, which obliged the Government to protect all its minorities. But no one could promise that the authorities could or wanted to fulfil this duty to protect the Jews in turbulent times.

The situation in Iraq was being watched by the leaders of Eretz Yisrael (the Land of Israel). People like Ben-Gurion, Haim Weizman, Moshe Shertok, Eliahu Dubkin and others noticed a similarity between the situation of the Jewish Communities in Europe before the Second World War and that of the Jewish communities in Middle Eastern countries. Going through the records of the debates of national institutions in Eretz Yisrael of former days reveal an amazing fact: Words like "extermination" and "slaughter" were being used. It is probable that a feeling of remorse, brought on by the realization that not enough was being done to awaken and recruit the Free World against the acts of oppression in Europe, long before the event of mass genocide took place that the leaders in Israel realized that there was an urgent need to act quickly in Moslem countries.

At the meeting of Haganah volunteers in 1943, David Ben-Gurion said: "The Jewish communities in the Middle East are hostages to our Arab neighbours. If there were to be any upheavals here in the Country, we will be alerted, but we have no guarantee whatsoever that Iraqi Jews won't all be massacred by then. I also wonder what would happen to the Jews in Egypt and Yemen even without the present 'riots' (anti-Jewish riots in Mandatory Palestine) in the country. We are not prepared to wait until a disaster occurs." And in another speech given in the same year at the Mapai Centre (Israel Labour Party), Ben-Gurion said: "It is our duty to terminate the Iraqi exile and not await our people's destruction."

Since it was clear that we must be prepared for any development and had to stockpile weapons for self-defense, the question of how to acquire them, where to stock them, where and how to practice using them was raised. And here, the emissaries from Israel entered the picture. Dr. Enzo (Hayim) Sereni, Shmaryahu Guttman and Ezra Kadoorie lived at that time in Baghdad. Sireni stayed in a hotel and the other two, Guttman and Kadoorie, lived at the Sehayik house. They understood that it would be difficult for them to do their job from there, so they decided to buy a house where current underground activities could take place, including the training and absorption of new applicants. After an extensive search, a house in the Jewish quarter was selected, adjoining the Alliance School for girls.

Guttman and Kadoorie moved into their new residence, and immediately began their training program. The first exercise included teaching Ju Jitsu, hand-to-hand fighting with knives, sticks and later on firearms such as guns or grenades. Weapons like these were needed for the well-trained members known as the "Shura," which was affiliated to the Haganah Organization in the Land of Israel. The first supply reached Iraq through the assistance of Moshe Dayan.

Dayan, who later became my friend and colleague, told me that after losing an eye in the war against the Vichy forces in Syria, he lost his job as well. When the Haganah suggested that he helped to transfer weapons to Iraq he jumped at the offer with enthusiasm. Enzo Sireni met him on his arrival in Baghdad and introduced him to Shlomo Sehayik. "Enzo introduced me to the youngsters. I was wearing shorts, was blind in an eye and made no impression on them," he told me after some years. In that same meeting Sereni requested Shlomo Sehayik to organize, for that very night, a car with a Jewish driver in order to pick up three suitcases from Dayan, in one of the British camps on the other side of the Tigris River.

Sehayik approached his friend, the son of the General Manager of a Jewish bank, and drew him into this mission. The young man positioned his car at the fixed time and appointed place; at 10 o'clock in the evening Shlomo Sehayik and Salim Khalifa left Baghdad. After an hour's drive they reached the British camps. When they passed the first camp they noticed a car parked with its lights on. They drew up and Dayan handed them three heavily-loaded suitcases. With these they headed back to Baghdad. A few minutes later they noticed a British policeman warning them to stop. Afraid that he may have witnessed the transfer of the suitcases, the three of them decided to give him the slip and make for the El-Khur bridge crossing.

Arriving at the bridge they joined a long queue of cars. It was obvious they were being held up by a military road block. While waiting, the three of them racked their brains without success, to think of some way to avoid the search. It was clear to them that they would be exposed and condemned. When their turn came, a British policeman approached them and asked for their driving licence. The driver, with a deadpan expression, claimed that his licence was not on him. The three of them appeared calm although they were most apprehensive.

The British policeman popped his head into the car and directed his torch onto a big suitcase.

"Open up," he ordered Halifa who was sitting beside the suitcase. He made as if to unlock the suitcase without success.

The Briton, unruffled yet suspicious, waited for a minute or two and then went to the barrier to call out to his colleague, an Iraqi policeman. The latter looked at the licence plate of the car, held the hands of the British policeman and moved two steps back, asking him to wait there and not to approach the car; then he himself rushed off to alert his officer. The Iraqi officer appeared at once, approached the driver's window, bowed a little and murmured "Sorry!" – and waved them on.

The three continued on their way to Baghdad, wondering why the Iraqi had let them pass. A short while later, the owner of the car understood the reason for this and told his two partners: "Not long ago I bought this car from the District Governor of Baghdad. It seems that the Iraqi officer at the road block did not know of the change of ownership. He surmised from the licence plate that the car belonged to the District Governor and was convinced that the car was being driven under his ownership and did not want to make any trouble..."

The first delivery of arms arrived at the Shura depot but was disappointing. There was a need for many more weapons. These were received in small quantities in other ways, such as by parcel post: Weapons were sent in the name of Salim Halifa. Haim Shamash, Manager of the parcel post office, would set them aside and deliver them to the Movement. There were also weapons bought individually by people such as Eliahu Shami'a, or weapons were purchased by the Jews of Basra, who had excellent contacts with arms traders in El-Zubair city (which was within the limits of Kuwait before its independence). The contact man in Basra was Barukh Daniel, a local merchant, who used to travel in appropriate garments, in order to buy weapons for the Halutz Movement. He was later arrested and sentenced to twelve years. There was also Naim Bekhor, a senior instructor of the Movement, whose house was used as a stopping-off place for various emissaries. Once he travelled to Basra for a trade mission for the Haganah in Israel, but for different reasons the deal did not come through.

The weapons were stockpiled then in small quantities and it took many months to acquire. They were stored in caches in various Jewish homes. Those caches were well hidden and only one or two members in each family knew where they were.

As the purchase of weapons needed lots of cash, and since the funds could not be relayed from Israel, the Movement agents approached wealthy Jews and pressed them to donate money. Some of the donors publicly disapproved of any connection with Israel or Zionism; but what made them pay up and buy those weapons was their realisation that those weapons were meant for self-defense and the settling of difficulties for the whole community in their hour of need.

Dan Ram, a member of Kibbutz Hanita and an old member of the Palmah (striking force of Haganah), arrived in Baghdad in July 1945 in order to reorganize the Shura in Iraq. Simultaneously, Sasson Noobik and Yeruham

Cohen were sent on the same mission to Syria and Lebanon, and Shlomo Habilio to Egypt. At the end of that year, Dan Ram prepared a defense plan and offered it to Yigal Alon, who was in charge of the protection of Jews in Arab countries; he needed his permission. When it was given, Alon advised Ram not to be rash and do anything except what was necessary and vital for self-defense, and stressed the point that: "It is vital that your people not be in a hurry to draw fire. An accident may encourage the schemers who are eager to promote general pogroms; unless they attack, you must be careful to act in such a way as to prevent a massacre." And, in order to warn them further, on the problems of self-defense, Alon wrote explicitly: "Your job is to hold on until we recruit worldwide diplomatic support to help you."

With the increase in emigration, Jewish houses were being emptied and the reason for stockpiling weapons – to guard the Jews in case of a Moslem attack – lost its urgency, so the problem then became a different one – how to dispense with the arms.

# Chapter 5

# EXODUS FROM BABYLON

My job in organizing the emigration from Iraq, or as it was known by its title the Ezra and Nehemiah Operation, was one of the most difficult and complicated assignments I ever undertook in the number of years of my public and state activities. Since December 1955 and for fourteen committed years, I concentrated on the handling of the Sakia and Kfar-Anah transit camps – which later came to be called Or Yehuda – in order to improve the living conditions of the inhabitants dwelling there in tents and wooden huts; I was a Member of the Knesset and a Minister of State serving the Israeli Government; I initiated and founded the Babylonian Jewry Heritage Centre in Or Yehuda – but up until today I realize that my main energies had been reserved for the Ezra and Nehemiah Operation.

It was in itself, according to any standards, a very special and prestigious project, an operation whereby nearly a whole Jewish community of more than a hundred and thirty-five thousand people were uprooted from one country to another within a short space of time. And, in order to perceive how deeply these immigrants have sunk their roots into the earth of the Land of Israel, it is sufficient to observe our general participation in all spheres of politics, law, economics, industry, and occupations both public and private.

## The Government in Iraq – 1949-1952

Iraq in those years was a Kingdom with a boy king, Faisal II. His uncle from his mother's side, Abd El-Ilah, was appointed Regent and received plenipotentiary powers such as the constitution would offer a king. He held office until 1953, and even after King Faisal reached adolescence.

The Government was under British influence and all the public administration departments were managed by them. The British Ambassador, who lived in a big house on the west side of the Tigris River, was called "the 'Mukhtar' from across the river" (meaning in Arabic the head or official representative of the village). The Prime Minister and Ministers of the Interior were frequently changed during that period, but the "big chief" in Iraqi politics was the pro-British Nouri El-Sa'id, whether he held office as Prime Minister or when he was serving with the Opposition. Below is the list of Prime Ministers and Ministers of the Interior in Iraq during the period of the Ezra and Nehemiah Operation:

| Name | Period | Mission |
|------|--------|---------|
| Nouri El-Sa'id | January 6, 1949 until December 10 | Prime Minister and Acting Minister of the Interior |
| Towfik El-Nayib | March 17, 1949 until September 17 | Minister of the Interior |
| Omar Nadmi | September 17, 1949 until February 5, 1950 | Deputy Prime Minister and Acting Minister of the Interior |
| Ali Jawdat El-Ayoubi | December 10, 1949 until February 5, 1950 | Prime Minister; Omar Nadmi continued his assignment |
| Towfik El-Suweidi | February 5, 1950 until September 10 | Prime Minister |
| Saleh Jaber | February 5, 1950 until September 10 | Minister of the Interior |
| Nouri El-Sa'id | September 10, 1950 until July 1952 | Prime Minister and Minister of the Interior |
| Omar Nadmi | February 5, 1951 | Minister without Portfolio entrusted with Interior Affairs |

In the Autumn of 1949, prior to my departure for Iraq on assignment, I spent, as I have already mentioned, many a long day perusing all the reports and telegrams sent from there. I was deeply moved by descriptions of the atrocities that followed – the persecution of the Jews by the Iraqi authorities. It was obvious to me, as to all those before me, who sifted through those telegrams and reports, that the condition of the Jews in Iraq was becoming untenable and could not continue like that for very much longer. Take, for instance, the order given to the Mukhtars by the Iraqi police to prepare a list of those Jews who had quit Baghdad since the population census of 1933, to include the names of those about to leave for Israel and that of their relatives, details of their financial assets and their method of departure, whether they had left legally or illegally. The Mukhtars were requested to supply detailed lists within seven days, otherwise they would be sentenced to three years imprisonment or a fine of a hundred and fifty Dinars, or both.

It is obvious that those instructions put a great deal of pressure on the Mukhtars and caused serious panic among the Jews, especially as they were

*From left to right: King Faisal II, the Regent Abd-El-Ilah, Prime Minister Nouri El-Sa'id.*

subject to scrutiny on the part of the authorities, intent on coercing the Jews, persecuting them and pouncing on their immigration planners.

In the Spring of 1949, three hundred Jews were already in prison, forty women among them; and the Iraqi police continued with the arrests. On May 24, we received information from Baghdad that a group of women prisoners, among them instructors for the Halutz Movement, decided to protest against the terrible prison conditions and declare a hunger strike. Two weeks later the prison authorities decided to apply force-feeding on them.

On 9 June 1949 rumours were spread (and this was confirmed by official sources) that a Bill would be passed stating that the possessions and financial assets of all Jews accused of Zionism would be confiscated: however, the Constitution Committee of the Iraqi Parliament rejected this motion.

On 5 July it was revealed that the Prime Minister Nouri El-Sa'id wrote a pamphlet and circulated it among the ministers and various other people. This pamphlet was restricted to fifty-two copies, and referred to the way Arab countries ought to deal with Israel before its consolidation, the reasons for Arab losses in the war against Israel (even after the State was founded) and the way to handle the Jews of Iraq and their impending departure. The Istiklal Party supported the ideas but the Ahrar Party, including Jamil El-Madfa'i, Nasrat El-Farisi and Sheikh Riyadh El-Shabib, persons of influence, opposed it.

In Israel the concern regarding the situation in Iraq increased. Reports from emissaries and also from foreign sources were thoroughly scrutinized here, and a major effort was made to attract attention in the country and abroad.

On 24 September 1949, a meeting was held in Israel between Rabbi David Shahrabani, Salim Saleh and Yousif Cohen, members of the Babylonian Community Committee, David Kadoorie and Yehezkel Sofer from the Aram Neherayim Youth Union; Nahman Shina from the Bureau of the Babylonian Group of the United Kibbutzim and Dr. A. Nadad and B. Halfon from the Middle East Department of the Jewish Agency. The main issue of the day was to provide information on the situation in Iraq and the action needed to help those imprisoned there for their Zionist activities. After an up-to-date report delivered by Dr. Nadad, the participants expressed their anguish at the way people with means in Iraq refused to help members of their own community from being harassed. The reason, they explained, was fear. At the meeting it was agreed unanimously to approach the Iraqi immigrants in Israel to undertake this task and help their brothers over there, and also to call on the Iraqi Jews living in England and the United States to extend their support as well.

Meanwhile, hard facts continued to emerge from Iraq. On 21 October 1949, Raphael Sourani and David Ben Meir, emissaries residing at that time in Iraq, informed us that more Jews were constantly being arrested. After a series of savage torture, they confessed their attachment to the Zionist Movement and gave the names of some of the so-called "guilty" ones in the Movement, the Shura and the Mossad Aliya. The police searched over twenty homes. The Secret Police examined the agents with full rigour. Sourani and Ben Meir added that their main job at that time was "to smuggle out the suspects connected with the Movement and the Shura, and with this our task will be accomplished, that is if we are still alive."

The various tortures described in their reports were: chaining both the elbows as well as the palms of the hands together with iron chains, whipping all parts of the body, immersing hands and legs in boiling water, burning with hot irons all sections of the body, and more. These tortures contributed to the general alarm felt within the community, and among agents of the Movement in particular, there was utter dismay. There were those who suggested fasting and repentance, and others who advised using weapons to fight it. The emissaries approached the Mossad asking for advice and to advise them on the role to adopt when caught – as Israelis or locals.

At the end of October 1949, Ziama Dibon from the Israeli Foreign Office released information that Aba Eban, the Israeli Representative in the United Nations conversed with his British colleague, Hector McNeal, regarding the Jews of Iraq. The latter was of the opinion that the only solution was to transfer the Jews to Israel, and he promised to approach Nouri El-Sa'id immediately. Aba Eban was about to make an announcement at a press conference on behalf of the Israeli Government.

While Eban was still talking to the British, shouts and cries of despair were heard from the prisoners' relatives in Baghdad who assembled outside the office of the chairman of the community, Sasson Khadourie. He alerted the police who quickly dispersed the crowd.

Two days later, at about 9 o'clock in the morning, numbers of mothers and brothers of prisoners demonstrated before the community offices and from there streamed towards the Palace in El-Rashid Street. Arriving there, police cars shot out of hiding, collected many of them and took them to prison, where they were interrogated and tortured.

Yacov Battat, Member of the Iraqi Parliament, conferred with the Minister of the Interior and asked him to halt the harassment. The Minister replied that applying torture during interrogation was necessary to reveal the truth, and neither fast nor strike was going to help them.

The newspaper Al-Yaktha reported, as ordered from higher sources, that those who were against the Iraqi Government had to be apprehended and decided that "the Jews, many as they were, were not to be trusted." The Al-Istiklal newspaper was also concerned with the problem and described the Jews as "germs to be rid of." Both newspapers demanded that the Government immediately banish all the Jews.

At the time when the chairman of the community sent the Government a note of protest regarding its unfair treatment of the Jews, the emissaries warned their superiors in Israel not to publish details of the tortures practiced but to keep it on hold. The "El-Tahrir" newspaper published reports on the situation in Iraq, relying on broadcasts from Kol Israel, and concluded that there was a definite bond between the Jews of Baghdad and those in Israel. It also stated that Nouri El-Sa'id announced in Parliament that there was even constant telegraphic communication between Iraq and Israel.

The two energetic emissaries in Baghdad, Sourani and Ben Meir, resumed their activities. They succeeded in assembling twenty important instructors from the Movement and the Shura, whom the police were seeking, and hoped to send them across the border soon. Meanwhile reports on the Jews arrested during the demonstration were published: nine were sentenced from two to three years, one for a year and the rest were either fined or acquitted.

On 21 November 1949, an emissary in Baghdad sent the following telegram: "Khadourie has tendered his resignation. As a protest against the helplessness of the community elders to assist the prisoners, the Jews have imposed a ban on the purchase of meat. The yearly tax the community elders imposed on kosher meat amounted to nearly 34,000 Dinars. This money helped to support the community institutes, schools, hospitals, etc. The whole event came about from the growing awareness of the congregation to their plight. We were not involved in any way."

During this difficult period I arrived in Basra on 22 November 1949, and three days later went on to Baghdad. There I fulfilled important speaking jobs and other tasks. I would use the aliases "Dror," "Zaki" or "Habib," each according to the projects I undertook and occasionally adopted other nicknames.

On 27 November we informed Israel that the outgoing committee of the community distributed circulars in the synagogues reporting on the financial losses of the community and explained why the boycott had to stop. Some leading members of the community together with several government officials tried to reinstate Khadourie, but we were against it. The Iraqi Minister at the Foreign Office, Shaker El-Wadi, reasoned that the latest actions taken against the Jews was the result of their affiliation to the Communist Party in Iraq where some Jews directed an underground cell; and that was why the police were forced to bring the leaders to a military court and to charge them with making contacts that were against the country's security. The police action incited the Iraqi Jews to demonstrate: These demonstrations kindled the anger of the Moslem citizens and the police were forced to interfere and arrest some Jews in order to protect them.

The news of the persecution of the Jews in Iraq reached many countries and the Israeli diplomats acted swiftly to publicize the fact, especially in America and Europe. On 7 November 1949, a telegram was sent to the French Minister of Foreign Affairs, Robert Shumain asking him to alert his country to these events and to use his influence in the United Nations to put a halt to these persecutions. Also the Iraqi Ambassador in Paris was requested to deliver a message to his Government. At the assemblies of the International Human Rights Organizations, which were held in France, the Iraqi Government was summoned to honour its international commitments. On 19 December 1949, the Zionist Congress presented to the General Secretary of the United Nations, Trigva Lee, a memo on the persecution of the Jews in Iraq with factual references to the arrests and attacks on synagogues and Jewish homes.

Arising from this deplorable situation, the leaders of the Mossad and its emissaries in Iraq concluded that every effort ought to be made to intensify the awareness of the Jewish community, to the fact that there was no solution to their condition other than to emigrate to Israel. David Ben Meir, who was involved with the assignment before I took over, worked with complete devotion and did his utmost to help those who wished to leave Iraq. They were obliged to relinquish all their savings and possessions to the Movement in order to be rescued from this Iraqi hell. They were mainly those sought out by the Secret Police, or else youngsters who were fed up with life in Iraq and looked for ways to emigrate to Israel.

The moment I took over the job I increased my efforts to expand the departure set-up. One of the accepted routes went through Iran but a problem appeared after crossing the border: The Iraqi Government insisted on the Iranian Government sending all its fugitives back to Iraq. Our people, Shlomo Hillel at first and then Sion Cohen, made great efforts to try and influence the Iranians to leave the fugitives within their borders at a transit station. They succeeded and on 5 December 1949, the Israeli Embassy in Washington sent Michael Kumai of the Israeli Foreign Office the following telegram: "The Iranian Government informed its Embassy in the United States to let us know informally that foreign Jews in Iran will be allowed to leave the country for any chosen destination. All their needs will be attended to."

The operation came into force, but the escape plans were further tightened after the removal of martial law on 18 December 1949. In a report sent to the Mossad on 9 February 1950, I wrote: "Manpower dealing with the smuggling operation is limited. I transferred agents to the South of Iran in order to help Mordechai Bibi absorb the great flow of arrivals via Basra. In Basra itself, the girls and boys are really tired…. I came to a decision to prepare a group of members for training in walking, reading maps, judo and the use of weapons so as to accompany the fugitives effectively in crossing the border. This group will study the border maps and concentrate on the escape routes. I hope three months will be enough to prepare them for this. The usual smuggling routes are: via Amara, via Khanakin and via Basra. We are sending a large number of people via the Basra route despite police operation there."

Shlomo Shina, member of the Aliya Committee in Baghdad, who was sent to be of help in Basra, wrote me on 19 February 1950 the following letter which clarified much of the work of a field man:

> My dear Zaki, I didn't write to you earlier as I was very busy. Our condition is precarious. I am convinced that not once in the history of the Babylonian emigration was the committee in such bad shape. Every day Jews come to us and are arrested by the police. We manage to release some of them in exchange for 10-20 Dinars per person, and those we fail are sent back from whence they came. Today they rarely release anyone on bail. And if required, a guarantor must be found who is wealthy, and this is a most difficult task.
>
> The detective, the police and the officials receive money mainly from those who don't travel via the Movement. We pay the smuggler 5-6 Dinars per person, but we don't know for how long this can continue, as there are others who are willing to pay more.
>
> Those who are dealing with unauthorized smuggling groups and mainly for the money, are endangering the emigrants departure and disclosing facts about the escape routes. On Saturday morning, six members came to us on a slow train from Nasriya, where another fifteen girls and boys also arrived but not through our network. Their clothes were smart and neatly pressed, not in the manner of dressing in these parts. This aroused suspicion on the train. The police in the nearby city of Smawa were alerted. The officer working on our behalf was in a dilemma. He knew about our six boys, but was placed in a difficult position to be able to obtain their release. With a great effort we had them freed on bail except for one boy who was sent back to the capital.
>
> You should know that we are not the government. Yesterday and today, not only those who were on the train were arrested but also those who were waiting for them at the station.

In his letter Shlomo Shina also inquired where to lodge the newcomers until they could leave – a question which perplexed the Aliya agents. There were certainly many families who were willing to accommodate and feed them without asking for money. It was dangerous for them because, whenever the neighbourhood militia spotted new faces, they would inquire "whose guests they were." The lodgers would reply that they were relatives who had come for a family commemoration. Apart from the guards, there were also detectives who ambushed them before they entered the houses, or hooligans scouring the neighbourhood looking for trouble. All of them were alert to any unusual movements or any cars parked near houses. A Jew walking in the street could well be a candidate for assault and robbery.

Members of the Aliya Committee decided to transfer their activities to the region of El-Ashar, where conditions for work were much better. They also decided to act in broad daylight. The shortage of safe houses was a problem. There were also, apart from those who offered help, some who refused to do so. Nevertheless, the Aliya Committee succeeded in taking about a hundred people a day to the banks of Shatt-El-Arab waterway. The transport of the fugitives was accomplished with the help of two vans and various cars rented from Jewish owners.

Many of them were nabbed at the borders and imprisoned. Quite a few succeeded in running away, but around one hundred and fifty people were caught daily. Food was prepared for delivery to various prisons, certified and uncertified lawyers were hired to deal with bail and also to prepare appeals. A wide network of smugglers was formed, and this included police and military men. There were frequent encounters between the smugglers and the Iraqi Defense Force. In one case, a smuggler was killed through the exchange of fire between police and a military officer who was loading fugitives on to a military truck. The officer was sentenced to five years. While visiting the prison in Basra I met him when he was working in the prison office.

On 8 February 1950, the American Consul in Basra reported the following to his Foreign Office:

> The illegal escape of the Jewish minority in Iraq has taken on new proportions. The group of local smugglers, which has been in existence for some time, has now become very competent at their new pursuits – smuggling emigrants across the border. These Jews arrive in Basra from Baghdad, rent a car and travel on the main road from Basra to Faw,

where they are met and transferred into boats, waiting to take them to the lower part of the Shatt-El-Arab.

Lately the authorities have sent soldiers to patrol the main road in order to prevent the smuggling operations. The soldiers, it seems, are happy to have such a golden opportunity to profit on the side and soon became involved in bribery and corruption just as the Home Guards did. A few days ago, some military trucks full of Jews were stopped while on a smuggling trip to the borders, planned by a Major in the Iraqi Army.

In the course of the report, it was stated that local senior civil servants expressed the hope in private that all Jews would eventually leave the country legally and the Government would at last stop the patrol, fight the bribery and take charge of the imprisoned fugitives.

On 15 February 1950, the American Consul received an affidavit from a representative of the Iraqi Government: "The Governor of Basra has started a widespread campaign to stop the flow of fugitives from the Jewish minority illegally crossing the Iraqi borders. In a private chat he suggested that the Government would be better off if it would let the Jews cross the borders legally. Nevertheless, if his superiors wished to stop the illegal traffic, he would do his utmost to deter them and would persist on imposing on them a severe penalty."

In this statement he also corrected his previous one regarding the Major. He was told that he was only a captain who claimed, in his defense, that he owed the Jews money he had lost in gambling and that they pressed him to clear his debt in that way. According to him, he only received 1,000 Dinars for his trouble.

On 26 January 1950, Mordechai Bibi sent a detailed report from Abadan in Iran, situated across from Basra, in which he described the complicated set-up of the escape activities in his region. Bibi was in charge of ten people in the south: three agents who came from Baghdad and were volunteer recruits and another seven Iranian Jews who worked on monthly salaries. The main difficulty, apart from evading the local security people and the tiresome journey from Baghdad to the south, was the question of accommodation for the fugitives. The Iranian Jews in the cities of Ahwaz, Khurmshaher and Abadan were indifferent, not to mention cool, towards the Iraqi Jews who stayed in their cities on their way to Israel. In Ahwaz, for instance, most of the local Jews refused to house the fugitives from Iraq. Therefore the Movement had to organize itself in the city in two main places: the synagogue, which was placed under the authority of the Movement and offered accommodation for about a hundred people, and a vacant house whose owners were unknown and where, in two of its three rooms, around fifty people were housed under the worst sanitary conditions. In Khurmshaher, the Movement members were forced to rent a house in order to accommodate emigrants and the situation in Abadan was even worse, where not even one house could be found for the Movement. As with accommodation, so food was a problem. The members of the Movement were obliged to arrange a ration for the fugitives and not to depend on local Jews, who were unhelpful to say the least. Even when they agreed to provide food they would charge exorbitant prices.

There were also difficulties in the north of Iraq just as in Basra: Naim Barzilay, whom I met in the prison in Baghdad, told me the following story regarding his attempt to arrange emigration in December 1949 for a group of twenty youngsters:

> We met on the outskirts of the city of Karkuk with two Kurdish smugglers. The weather was wet and very stormy. We took off on our journey, and after several nights of trudging, the smugglers provided us with ten donkeys to ease our passage. During the day we hid in caves and ate bread provided by the local villagers. We reached the River Dhiala which was only a meter and a half deep and through which ran a strong and dangerous current. We crossed it in groups carrying our bundles of clothes on our heads. Because of the mist and rain the smugglers lost their way and advised us to turn back.
>
> We were divided into four groups and went on towards the railway station in the village of Kifri. We sat in a local coffee-house where we unfortunately attracted the attention of the police. They summoned us for questioning, promising that they would only ask a few questions and then release us.

We had agreed between us to tell the same story about coming to Kifri for a visit. They took all five of us into a cell and asked us to explain the purpose of our visit and we stuck to our story.

A few days later they transported us to Karkuk by train. The Movement didn't abandon us. Its representatives paid us a visit and received a detailed report on our route. They decided that I should take responsibility for the group and told us to get ready to travel to Baghdad.

We arrived handcuffed at the Secret Police building in Baghdad. They lined us up for an identification parade before Sion "the informer." I must say, to his credit, that he pretended not to know us. The officer pointed me out to him and said: "The father of this boy is called Hagouly Hadad and he was sentenced to three years on a charge of belonging to the Zionist Movement. That means that his son must also be a Zionist!" Sion replied without hesitation that he had never met me before. After the evidence of Sion and our sticking together with the same version of the story the police had to release us on bail.

Another incident concerned Rony Shalem, who was put in charge of the Misgav branch of the Movement in the village of Kifri. As this was near the border to Iran, it was chosen as a transit station for smuggling Jews. Thus Rony said to me:

We looked for smugglers to work on that route. We knew someone of about 22-24 years old, who was in trade with my father and seemed a suitable candidate. For a start, we gave him a letter to send over the border. He did this and also brought an answer back. Then we put him in charge of three boys to take over to the Iranian border city of Kasr Shirin, where there were associates of Sion Cohen.

Cohen posted some of his men along the border of Iraq-Iran and arranged with the Iranian Military Commander that if ever fugitives from Iraq arrived, they would send them to his people who would then transport them to the capital, Teheran. The three boys arrived safely in Ketzer Shirin and the smuggler returned back, giving the agreed signal. The decision was then taken to continue on with that route.

After success with the first dispatch, another group was prepared for departure. They met at the railway station dressed as Arabs and climbed onto the mules provided. During the day they hid themselves and at night they marched towards the border. We waited for the smuggler to bring us an assurance of their safe arrival, but he didn't appear. It was clear that the group had been captured near one of the villages. They lit cigarettes at night contrary to the smuggler's warnings and, as luck would have it, the daughter of the village Sheikh, who was on the roof of her house, noticed some specks of lights in nearby bushes and informed her father.

The village policemen grabbed them. While waiting for the smuggler, the police together with an officer came up to me, put me under arrest and transferred me to the local city of Khanakin. I was interrogated while they whipped and kicked me all over. They hung me by my feet and beat me. I fainted. When I woke up the officer threatened that if I didn't confess he would shoot me and claim that I had tried to escape.

This form of torture continued for three or four days. My parents used their connections, even approaching the Minister of Justice, a Kurd, Jamil Baban, and searched for me all over Iraq. The officer suggested that I made a confession, that I led the boys to the smuggler and I would then be released. I knew he wanted to incriminate me and I refused. I stuck to my version of the story – that I worked with my father in trade and could tell him nothing. I was sure that the police knew nothing of our activities despite my presence at the railway station. They asked me for money. I showed them the three Dinars I had in my pocket and added that I could give them the business address of someone in the city of Khanakin whom the officer knew well. I mentioned his name as I knew that he had already left the country. I suggested the officer approach him and that he would receive a hundred Dinars for his trouble.

I signed an affidavit to say that I wasn't acquainted with the smuggler, and the sergeant then took me to the centre of the city. We sat in a coffee-house, ate and drank something and then met the officer I had sent to the shop of the Jew. He told me that he wasn't to be found. I was taken to Ba'kouba, forty kilometres east of Baghdad. That is where, for the first time, I met the five boys. The smuggler was also present. I understood that they had said nothing about me, rather they declared that some other individual took them to meet the smuggler. They also asked me if I signed any confession. I shook my head. An identification parade was held and the smuggler pointed me out as the one who had led the boys to him.

A series of tortures began once more and this lasted for a month and a half. They beat us on our hands and feet. It was Yom Kippur and we had been fasting. A few days later they took us to the notorious prison of Abu Ghraib in Baghdad, where it was the custom to strip youngsters at the entrance, leaving them only in their underpants and to make them run for some distance with two jailers hitting them from behind. We were taken into a dark small cell, and two weeks later transferred to a larger room with a small window above. At first we were alone but after awhile they brought in another three boys. There were also Communist prisoners present. We were then separated. We dug a channel under the floor tiles and in this way we exchanged cigarettes and various notes we had secretly received from our parents. Occasionally they used to take us out to the yard at night, but never without some sadistic comment.

One morning they bundled us into court. Judge El-Na'sani, a bit of a clown, began at first by cursing us in a manner I have never witnessed before, with references to our dubious past and the immoral behaviour of our mothers and grandmothers. No one escaped his torrent of curses and abuse.

The police who had captured the boys in the fields were brought in to give evidence. It seemed that in the meantime, two policemen had been fired for accepting bribes. They didn't identify me but pointed to someone else. Since they had no evidence to convict me, I was set free, but the rest were sentenced to three years and the smuggler to five, and the mules were confiscated.

After being released Rony Shalem came to see me in Baghdad, utterly worn out. After a brief stop he took to the road again but this time he crossed the border safely and arrived in Israel.

# Chapter 6

# INFORMERS

U p until the crisis of the year 1949, talking in public about the activities of the Halutz Movement in Iraq was almost non-existent among local Jews. Many of them knew about the existence of the Movement, even a little about its activities, but kept silent. The families of the members of the Movement, apparently, were aware that certain things were happening and that their sons and daughters took part in those activities, but never broached the subject with them. Also, when weapons of the Underground Movement were hidden in any of the houses, most of the family members knew nothing about them.

In a wider context, beyond the circle of activists and their families, people heard of the existence of the Movement, and perhaps they were curious as well, but they accepted it as an existing phenomenon – just a part of their existence – and extended it great honour and respect. The Iraqi Secret Police made serious efforts to find collaborators or secret agents by offering them money, but were not successful in their quest. In the Jewish community there was a code of behaviour towards the Movement that no one crossed, or dared to breach. The emissaries from Israel planned carefully to avoid capture and exposure, so as not to endanger members of the community, and from them they received the closest cooperation. The Jewish families who offered accommodation to the emissaries in their homes put themselves in great danger, but considered it a modest contribution to the Zionist Movement.

This is how it was until 1949. In that same year the code of behaviour towards the Movement faltered, and a crisis, among other things, was caused by certain incidents of betrayal. The most notable of those was the episode connected with the Youth Halutz members. But before I tell you the story, it is appropriate to mention something of its background.

The mastermind of the plan was someone called Yehoushua Givoni, a cultured man and a member of Kibbutz Alonim, who was sent to Iraq in April 1944. He introduced a plan by which youths of 15 and 17 years old could be incorporated into the International Halutz Movement. In December 1944, during a second meeting of the Movement, Youth Halutz was inaugurated in Iraq and its main function was national awareness, education, Hebrew and pioneer activities to be integrated later on with the parent body. A separate committee was appointed for the youth department and was guided by Mordechai Bibi. Among the members were Esther Sourani, Yehuda Nahtomi, Rina Dloomy, Yehuda Shohet, Yohanan Towfik (Goral), Shulamit A. (consequently the wife of the writer Michael Murad) and Ilana Bibi. The second meeting of Youth Halutz terminated with the following address: "We have proved to ourselves and others that Middle Eastern and Iraqi Jews are capable, like any Jewish youngsters in the world, of self-reliance, winning respect, courting freedom, working hard and achieving ideals, and, too, of facing a pioneer's existence."

On 8 October 1949, the Iraqi Secret Police succeeded in catching a group of Youth Halutz members. As they were still in training and inexperienced, the imprisoned youngsters cracked after sessions of torture and supplied the names of members of the Movement.

I don't know if it is possible to call these boys "informers," but this isn't the point. The fact remains, and no one can deny it, not even members of the group itself: They talked, they confessed and secrets were disclosed.

There is no way, whatsoever, of estimating the capability of endurance under physical and emotional pressure. It is difficult to blame anyone who breaks down under torture, particularly among the youth. I myself was twenty-eight years old when I was captured and "handled" by Iraqi policemen and their Secret Police. This was the second time in my life that I found myself apprehended. The first was two years previously, in 1947, when I commanded a Hagana post station on the borders of Jaffa and Tel Aviv, near the flour-mill. From our vantage point we could watch all the movements of the Arabs gathering their forces against us. We were finally encircled by British military units and then transported, with our weapons, to Jaffa Police Station in Clock Square, where we were arrested and questioned. One day later a lawyer on behalf of the Hagana obtained our release. We weren't tortured and didn't suffer; it was simply an uncomfortable incident. The second arrest to which I now refer, and will do so further in another chapter of this book, was of a longer duration and rather unpleasant. It was a first experience of loss of freedom, of physical and emotional pressure and a combination of lack of sleep, threats and torture.

The hours between one investigation and another were devastating emotionally. When I was left alone in the cell for a while, free from physical torture, fears and doubts arose and all kind of thoughts seared my mind. My interrogators tried various methods to break my spirit, and to my relief they failed. But I myself am not sure that I could have carried on and kept silent if my interrogators had varied the torture or pressured me further. I cannot judge those who suffered arrest and interrogation with torture, and then caved in.

But the perspective of the Movement activists who were arrested due to the betrayal by the Youth Halutz members was sharper and much harsher, even though a long period had elapsed, and their anger has not diminished.

Yousif Ben-Ezra, who was caught as a result of information acquired, related the story of a boy of twenty-five who died in prison from an infection because the Iraqis refused him medical care. He also spoke of tortured prisoners who had had nervous breakdowns and of others who would cry out in their sleep. Most of the prisoners were young school kids. Yaacov Yazdi, who was sixteen when apprehended in October 1949, was betrayed by information given by Sa'id Khalastchi, who related that his interrogators wanted to know if he was a member of the Movement, and when he denied it they tortured him. "In the interrogation," Yazdi remembers, "Sa'id Khalastchi and Sion El-A'rag (Sion Mattatyahu), who was a cripple, were also there. They tied me to a tree in the yard of the Secret Police station. Several policemen closed in on me and started to beat me with clenched fists, sticks and kicks and also pulled my hair. This went on till 3 o'clock in the morning when I passed out. They left me alone for a day and repeated the treatment once again. They removed my clothes, tied me to a tree completely nude, and plucked hairs off my skin; then they hit me on the face and broke some of my teeth. While torturing me they kept asking for the names of the instructors – 'we want the names of those who arrive from Israel to train you. We are not interested in the officers in charge of the Movement.'"

Yazdi endured the torture without saying anything. He was afraid lest they would connect him with his brother, who was caught whilst on his way to Israel and was imprisoned in another place in Ba'kuba prison. The interrogators did not leave him alone. They continued beating him until he decided to make a so-called "confession." He "confessed" that he was a Yeshiva student in the Zilkha Synagogue. When he was questioned as to who the Principal of the Yeshiva was, he gave the name of Sasson Khadourie, chairman of the community. At one o'clock in the morning they untied him from the tree and returned him to his cell. Two days later, they told him that Sasson Khadourie was a prominent individual, loyal to Iraq and asked him how he dared to slander him. They began to maltreat him again, extinguishing cigarettes on his body, harming his sexual organs and forcing him to curse the Zionists and Israel. At that point, Yazdi was surprised to see Sa'id Khalastchi assisting the brutes.

After a series of tortures he was taken before Judge El-Na'sani.

"How old are you?" the Judge asked.

"Sixteen," Yazdi answered.

"Put him down for eighteen," the Judge ordered the court.

When Yazdi insisted that he was only sixteen and asked them to check with his identity card, the Judge responded swiftly, growling under his breath:

"Eighteen years old. Only then can he be condemned to hard labour!"

The accused stood in three rows and the Judge glared at them severely, and without batting an eyelid or hearing what they had to say in their defense, he passed sentence: "Those in the first row are sentenced to three years in prison; those in the second – two years, and those in the third – one year!" Yazdi, standing in the first row, received a three year sentence.

There were no investigations, no questions from the plaintiffs, no questions for the accused, no witnesses to be examined. The only one who spoke was the Judge. Yazdi went to prison and was not released until 1952.

It is no wonder that members of the Movement who were arrested and tortured, and their families, are still incensed at the Youth Halutz who betrayed them. They are still smarting with anger because they claim that several of the informers gave evidence voluntarily. Some of them would accompany the Secret Police and pinpoint members of the Movement and even attend the torture sessions.

Because of this anger, members were planning how to punish the informers so as to prevent further damage to the Movement. I reported the event to the Mossad on 2 January 1950. We received an unequivocal reply: "If that is so, the anticipation of the Movement and the expectations people have regarding your opinion towards the informers retrospectively, will draw the attention of the public to any act you do and accuse you of taking part. So, we are warning you that we oppose any hasty act of retaliation that may cause or encourage a new wave of persecution, which might interfere with the possibilities of renewing the project."

This was the telegram sent to the Mossad on 29 December 1949 in respect of the damage caused by the informers:

> We gathered details and proof against seven informers [...]. Against the first two there are very serious proofs that they themselves tortured our people in order to help acquire information on the Movement. Against the rest there is less evidence, and the information they handed over was given under stress. They were all released at the beginning of this week. Khalastchi received a job as payment for his involvement and assistance. He was disappointed as he expected a more lucrative assignment for his betrayal. We are posting Shura Members on their trail [...] and the rest are thinking of emigrating to Iran and staying there until a decision on their fate has been taken.

After prolonged meetings between the Aliya activists and the emissaries, we decided to kidnap the young group of informers and keep them under surveillance until their departure to Iran was arranged. Reuben Elias and the main Aliya activists related:

> We put three of them in the house of Naim Bouba, a Shura member. From there, accompanied by escorts, we transported them to a hiding

place. Three weeks later, an escape route was found. The three of them with other Movement members were entrusted to a new smuggler by the name of Abu Arbah. According to him the route was a difficult one and he had trouble with one of the informers, Sion, who was a cripple, and while riding his horse his prosthesis leg came away. All the group were caught and taken to the station of the Secret Police, then released and finally smuggled through Basra. One of this group escaped handcuffed, from the Secret Police. We took him to Mandalawy's house where we dyed his hair and arranged for his eventual escape.

The Aliya activists feared those informers, as well as those who were out of prison. Yehezkel Yona, a talented and zealous worker, joined the Movement when he was twenty-two years old, soon after the pogroms of Rashid Ali El-Kaylani, and was active in the illegal emigration effort. He told us that at one time, when escorting some travellers on behalf of the Movement to board a train leaving for Basra on its way to Iran, he saw Sion the cripple rushing towards him. He asked if he could join the group and quoted Yousif Trumpeldor – "it is good to die for one's country." Yehezkel, fearing a trap, ignored him and hurried on, deviating from the regular route into various side roads in order to avoid the Secret Police, in case they happened to be following him.

Before I end this chapter I have to say that, throughout the years, I have tried many times to make contact with this group. I have also sent friends to obtain their version of the story, but to my regret they absolutely refused to talk. Today, forty-six years later, I still wonder if their refusal was due to the fact that they had something to conceal.

# Chapter 7

# ENIGMA

This is a sad story from any angle that it might be told, or heard from any source or any point of view. It is about three young Jewish lads who lost their lives in Iraq whilst emigrating to Israel. Since those were the days of illegal emigration, they approached the Halutz Movement for help and were referred to a smuggler who was familiar with the long and dangerous route to the borders. They disappeared without trace, as if the earth split open and swallowed them up.

The three were: Yousif Hai Ben David Ovadia, twenty-four years old, born in Arbil, member of the Halutz, and who performed missions on its behalf, including the preparation of arms caches. Daniel Ben Nouriel Distchi, twenty-eight years old, born in Karkuk, a dentist who was known to the Movement and whose house was a meeting place for the members and a lodging place for passers by on their way to the border. Zion Abdu Kassab, twenty-eight years old, born in Arbil, member of the Movement and a butcher by trade.

The event occurred before my arrival in Iraq as an emissary for the Mossad, and on hearing this I was deeply moved. Since then, throughout the years, I did everything I could to solve this puzzle, which remains an open sore that does not heal for the families involved and in the history of the Movement.

They departed for Iran one evening in October 1949 on the route outlined by the Movement. Their smuggler guide was Kaba-Bara. They passed by the city of Halabtcha in the north of Iraq, and from there they were meant to continue on to

Kassawa, the smuggler's village, then cross the River Sirwan towards Fawa where they were supposed to meet with another Persian smuggler, to guide them to Eliahu Mouallem, a representative of Sion Cohen, emissary of the Mossad in Iran. Somewhere on the way, whether in Fawa or near the border town of Kasr Shirin or in the River Sirwan, they disappeared.

A comprehensive debriefing was conducted and the conclusion was that they had had a dispute with the smugglers and quarrelled. One of the three lads carried on him some gold coins, contrary to instructions from the Movement. One smuggler or perhaps both of them, desired the money, robbed the three and murdered them. No one knew for sure who killed them, when, where exactly and where their bodies were to be found. Their families lived with this uncertainty; throughout the years they clung to hope, wrote letters and moved heaven and earth in order to search for their beloved sons.

On 30 December 1949, a few weeks after my arrival in Baghdad and nearly three months after their disappearance, I wrote the following to Moshe Cherbinsky (Carmil): "The disappearance of the three in the north of Iraq has shaken me to the core. No one can be blamed, as there are no witnesses. I have decided to give the matter my fullest attention in order to trace them, alive or dead."

I also tried, in the fifties in Israel, to delve into this affair so as to uncover the missing details. Menahem Aloni, who was responsible for the emigration in the north of Iraq, wrote the following letter on 3 February 1952 to Izi Rice, member of Kibbutz Giv'at Brener and the elders of the Mossad Aliya Bet:

> In accordance with our discussion on 15 January 1952 with the Mossad, I wish to supply your Honours with certain details regarding the three brave lads who lost their lives in 1949 on their way to Halabtcha in the North of Iraq.
>
> 1. Name of the father David Ovadia Arbil, hut 45, transit camp E, Tiberias. the name of their late son was Yousif Hai.
>
> 2. Nouri Nouriel Dishgui [Distchi], hut 145, transit camp Kfar Hasidim, name of their late son was Daniel.

3. Zion Abu Kassab, transit camp Rosh Pinna. The name of their late
   son was Zion. His two brothers, Naji and Salim, live in Jerusalem,
   30/24 Yamin Moshe near the kindergarten Beit Yaacov.

On Saturday 2 February 1952, I met by chance in Haifa the late Daniel's
brother Sammy. He addressed me with shouts and curses and all kinds
of threats. He mentioned that he would file a complaint against me and
Avner Shabtai in court and I am sure he will do so. In no way did he
wish to hear me say that they would be receiving a house-call to clarify
the matter.

with kind regards
Menahem Aloni,
Section of Immigrants Care, Benyamina transit camp

In a letter on 15 January 1958 Menahem Aloni wrote to Sammy:

You must remember the time of the crisis in the Movement and the
decision to send the instructors to Israel. This was done mainly through
Northern Iraq. The route was from Karkuk to Kasr Shirin. It was a
journey on foot taking four days and nights. Every day around 15-20
instructors and Shura members would arrive at Karkuk where they
would be lodged and await their departure. There were also members of
the Movement from the north who were obliged to emigrate for various
reasons, and because of that we looked out for further outlets.

At the end of the year 1949 we succeeded in transporting three
emigrants from the north through the route of Halabtcha near
Slemaniya, to Karmanshah on the Iranian border. On that route they
were supposed to cross the river Sirwan. The route chosen was a
successful one and the first three arrived safely. After some time we sent
another three who were: 1. Daniel Dishgui, 28 years old from Karkuk. 2.
Yousif Hai, 25 years old. 3. Zion Abu Kassab, 28 years old. The last two
were from Arbil. They were sent with the permission of Emissary Yuval
[David Ben-Meir] who was responsible for emigration affairs, and

precisely at that moment Mordechai Ben-Porat arrived to replace him. The three were sent in the company of local smugglers from Halabtcha under the supervision of Mordechai, Secretary of the branch of the Movement there.

They left Karkuk for Slemaniya and then Halabtcha where they were accommodated by members of the Movement for several days for their final preparations. According to the plan, they were supposed to leave Halabtcha on foot until they reached the border and crossed the River Sirwan, which was actually on the border between Iraq and Iran.

Two or three days later which I believe was in January 1950, a member of the Halabtcha branch arrived in Karkuk with a note, given to him by a smuggler and written by one of the emigrants, Daniel Distchi, asking us to try and send them some good cigarettes. Then we tried to discover where they were and the reason why they didn't get to the other side of the border. So we asked those responsible in Halabtcha to check it out and waited for several days but received no reply. We later asked the emissary Aziz, who was David Ben-Meir, to enquire about their fate in Iran, from which place we didn't receive an answer either.

Several days later we had a message that the three, together with the smugglers, were in an Iraqi village near the border and when they were about to leave, the head of the village sent an armed unit to kill the three and the smugglers escaped. The murder took place near the River Sirwan. If they had only succeeded in crossing the river they would have been out of danger. The emissary Aziz received the message at the time of his departure and conveyed the matter to Ben-Porat. A report on this incident was relayed to the families whether abroad or in Israel. Two months later I returned to Israel. When the families arrived in Israel, troubles erupted, the substance of which I reported to you some time ago.

In order to receive more information on the matter, which I hope you will find interesting, I suggest you get in touch with the emissaries Aziz, Ben-Porat and Avner as eight years have already passed and the details are sketchy in my mind. Shanior says that when he was in Kasr Shirin, Sion Cohen ordered him to check on the fate of the three in the region of

Kurdistan near Karmanshah (Khurmshaher). So he sent local people several times to check on it but got nowhere.

Shalom Ovadia, Yousif Hai's brother, wasn't satisfied with the vague replies received. Throughout the years he sent letters addressing one person after another and also sent a letter to the President of Israel requesting information on the fate of his brother. On 22 March 1966, he sent letters once more to the authorities and another to Prime Minister Levy Eshkol with a request to help the family to ascertain the fate of the missing brother, Yousif Hai Ben David Ovadia. On 3 April, Michal Feldman, from the Prime Minister's Office, wrote to me (when I was a Member of Knesset and Head of Council of Or Yehuda) and enclosed a copy of the letter. She wrote back after consulting Moshe Carmil (who in the meantime was transferred to the Foreign Office). He sent her to me and asked me to clarify the matter in writing.

At the same time Shaul Avigur, who was then Adviser to the Minister of Defense, applied to Moshe Carmil and to me requesting a thorough investigation of the matter. We met with nine witnesses, checked the correspondence kept in Iraqi and Iranian files in the archives of the Hagana, were assisted by the Mossad and after four years of investigation we compiled a report which was sent on 10 March 1968 to Shaul Avigur. This report, classified Top Secret, is published here for the first time almost in full:

> To: Mr. Shaul Avigur
> From: Moshe Carmil
> Mordechai Ben-Porat
>
> Re: Report on the disappearance of three young Jews from the North of Iraq on their escape route from Iraq to Iran on Succoth (5-7 October 1949).
>
> [...] When the persecution of the Jews and particularly that of the activists of the Zionist Movement became intense, the Israeli emissaries in Iraq searched for escape routes. In August 1949, David Ben-Meir (Aziz), emissary of the Mossad, summoned together in Baghdad other

activists from the North of Iraq, in order to discuss ways of finding new
escape routes in the North.

Following that discussion and after Menahem went back to the
north, the route from Halabtcha was discovered, a mountainous path
leading to the village of Kassawa inside the border of Iraq and from there
to the village of Fawa in Iran. From that village the fugitives were
supposed to get to Karmanshah in Iran. Mordechai Abrahami (Neftali),
resident of Halabtcha, knew a reliable smuggler guide called Kaka-Bara
who directed Daniel Shabtai (Avner) and Baba Arieh (Arieh) how to cross
the route on their own. They left at 10 o'clock in the morning from
Halabtcha on donkeys and after a ride of three hours they arrived at the
River Sirwan situated on the border of Iraq and Iran. From there the
smuggler was supposed to take them to Fawa. They were convinced that
the route was a good one and advised David Ben-Meir from Baghdad to
adopt the plan. It was then accepted.

Three lads arrived between 5 and 7 October 1949 to Halabtcha at the
house of Mordechai Abrahami, accompanied by Daniel Shabtai and Baba
Arieh. That same evening they left the town and met the smuggler who
was waiting for them as agreed. The fees of the smuggler Kaka-Bara was
fixed at 80 to 100 Dinars. On the morning of the same day he would
receive half the amount and the rest of the money when he brought back
confirmation of their safe arrival. Kaka-Bara was an Iraqi citizen, so in
order to make them cross from Kassawa (Iraq) to Fawa (Iran) across the
River Sirwan he needed the services of another smuggler, an Iranian
called Amin.

The smuggler received the three, who were separated from their
companions, Abrahami, Arieh, Shabtai and other local members of the
Movement and followed the route on mules. The three were supposed to
reach Fawa in one or two days. Therefore confirmation was expected to
arrive in three or four days. Whilst waiting for this, another two boys
arrived on Sunday in the intermediate days of Succoth in order to cross
the border, but as the confirmation hadn't arrive they were sent back to
Karkuk. Another two boys who followed a different route crossed the
border in safety.

Still waiting for confirmation and after a week since their departure, a note written in the hand of one of the three (it seemed to be that of Distchi as he was the only one who knew Hebrew) was received in Halabtcha. Thus it was written – and here there are two versions:

1.  That of Abrahami and Arieh, who witnessed what was written in the note; to say that the smuggler wanted more money and was not satisfied with what had been agreed upon and to send good cigarettes.

2.  That of Daniel Shabtai, who witnessed what was in the note, saw Distchi complain "that the Movement received 80 Dinars and paid less to the smuggler" (the Movement used to collect from the fugitives according to their financial ability and in this way they could afford to send out, without payment, those who couldn't pay; this meant that the sums received were not equal).

The note worried the organizers who decided to look for them. Abraham sent another smuggler called Kader, the brother of the head of Kaba-Bara's tribe. Three days later he came back and told Mordechai Abrahami that when the three reached the border they were supposed to be handed over to a second guide, Amin, to help them cross over to Iran. Amin had a dispute with Kaka-Bara over the money. One of the three, Daniel Distchi, who carried gold coins on him against the instructions of the Movement and inserted them in a lighter, took one out and handed it to Amin. It seemed he still wasn't quite satisfied with what he got and a fight ensued amongst them. Amin stabbed one of them to death then murdered the other two. Their bodies were thrown into the river and when they were cast up on shore, Kader buried them.

Sion Cohen, who was at that time in Teheran, recalls that after receiving the telegram from Baghdad he sent someone to Kasr Shirin to meet the three from Fawa.

Alarmed at their fate and after information from Kader, Abrahami was called to Baghdad by Mordechai Ben-Porat, emissary of the Mossad in Iraq who replaced David Ben-Meir. Ben-Porat asked him to transport

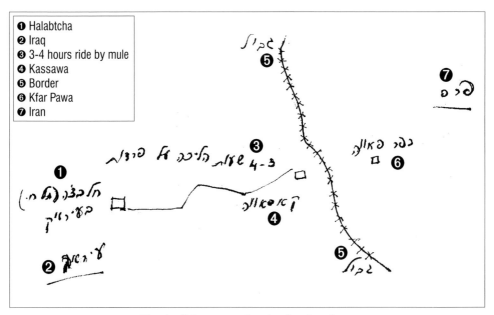

*Sketch of the route taken by the three boys.*

the bodies to Iran and to take vengeance on the murderer. Following this matter Ben-Porat sent this telegram to Israel on 23 January 1950:

We have now received further details regarding the three from Tel-Hai (Halabtcha) who went missing five months ago. They were killed by the smuggler and another two robbers from the village of Massan on the northern Iranian border. I arranged for transport of their remains and the death of the smuggler. It is right that they should be buried in Israel. From our side we can transport the remains of the bodies to Karmanshah of "Goldman" here (meaning Teheran).

Abrahami certified later that he transported the remains to Karmanshah and that the killing of the smuggler was arranged by Hassan Ahmadi. As a witness, Sion Cohen certified that the remains of the bodies were buried in Kasr Shirin.

Three months after the disappearance of the three, Distchi's father received a letter from the instructor Aliza, who emigrated from Iraq to Iran, informing him that the three had been killed.

## Conclusion of the Committee:

1. From the testimonies of reliable witnesses to the Committee Members (Abrahami, Baba Arieh, and Daniel Shabtai), it is certain that the three departed on 3 or 4 October 1949 from Halabtcha with the smuggler, on their way to Iran.

2. The Committee members were unable to collect evidence of the fate of the three (their murder, their bodies). There were no eye-witnesses to certify that the three had reached Iran alive.

3. There is no certainty as to where they were buried.

4. The Committee is of the opinion that someone in authority ought to inform the families of the fate of their sons, because the only information they received from the Aliya activists was that the three had left the country and since then there has been no further news.

Moshe Carmil and Mordechai Ben-Porat

# A NEW POLICY

# Chapter 8

From my first day as an Aliya emissary in Iraq, it was clear to me that the mission was an enormous one and we couldn't make a success of it without the assistance of the leaders of the Jewish community in Iraq and their various connections. I met Yehezkel Shemtob, Member of the Board of the administration of the Community, headed by Hakham Sasson Khadoorie.

Shemtob was alert to the affairs of Israel but a dark cloud hovered over his relationship with the Israeli emissaries. In 1942-1943, when Enzo Sereni lived in Baghdad, under British protection, he was disappointed with the influential Jews in Iraq and felt that they were too busy with their material welfare and not sufficiently concerned with Zionist affairs. He was frequently invited to the home of Advocate Shlomo Horesh, whose sister studied with him in the same group. One day he asked him if he could find for him at least one young member of the wealthier citizens of the community who would want to emigrate to Israel. Despite Sereni's doubts, not only one young person was found but eighteen, who were all smuggled to Israel without the permission of their parents, an act which greatly upset the community. Among the eighteen was young Yousif, Yehezkel Shemtob's son. Horesh related that when Shemtob heard that his son was among the emigres he was furious and threatened to bring him back.

However, Yousif Shemtob went to Israel, stayed for a few months in a kibbutz and then asked to return to Baghdad. Since he was without a passport, he applied to the Iraqi Consul in Jerusalem, who happened to be his father's friend, and claimed that he had lost it. The Consul issued a new one and advised him, with a wink, not to lose it again in the future.

His son's escapade wasn't the only event that darkened his relationship with the emissaries of the Zionist Movement and Israel. In 1938 Shemtob bought lands in Jerusalem in the region Emek Hamatzleba, and the Israeli Minister of Finance decided to confiscate it. Only with Golda Meir's assistance did the family receive compensation, but in my opinion the damage was done.

During the persecution and arrest in 1949 of members of the Halutz Movement, they approached the leaders of the Jewish community in Baghdad for help. When they spoke to Senator Ezra Menahem Daniel, he told them that had they not been Jews, he would have instantly summoned the police (his stern opinion didn't prevent him from showing courage in the Senate and attacking the Government over its attitude towards the Jews). In contrast, Yehezkel Shemtob had better contacts and agreed to meet the Halutz. At the conference I.D. Sofer also participated and constantly assisted the Movement, as did Shemtob's sons, Yousif and Jamil. Shemtob agreed to help them provided they sent him reports of all their activities. The Movement member informed him that they would like to replace the President of the community, Sasson Khadourie, and asked him if he would be prepared to accept the job. His wife was against it, but when Khadourie resigned, Shemtob took his place.

During my conversation with him, I understood that his social and commercial connections with the Prime Minister, Towfik El-Suweidi, were a valuable asset. From a practical point of view it was possible to use those connections to relay suggestions to the Prime Minister, and after a short while to receive some reaction or answer. Later on, these important connections were wrecked, mainly due to the input of some retired Movement members who supplied Shemtob with false rumours; to make him doubt whether the Israeli emissary whom he was meeting was really qualified to speak on behalf of Israel. But this did not damage his great credibility to help smooth the passage of the Revocation of Citizenship Bill and receive confirmation of the business with the airlines. In fact, if it had not been for his contribution, it would have been difficult to envisage how the incident could have progressed.

I was impressed with the personality of Yehezkel Shemtob. Relations between us were always correct, and the differences between us, great as they were, did not obscure our common objectives. He came from a world of dignified men, who loved to have everything done according to their wishes, while I was a young man of twenty-seven and a captive of the Socialist order; in our meetings there was always complete understanding and honesty between us. I introduced him to all the secrets of our smuggling activities and transferred various messages through him, which I hoped would be relayed to the Prime Minister. I asked him to mention two topics to Towfik El-Suweidi – the distress of the prisoners and permission for the legal emigration of the Jews. A few days later he came back with this reply: "Regarding the prisoners, Suweidi promised

*Emissaries and activists in Baghdad, from left to right: Mordechai Ben-Porat, Raphael Sourani Yerahmiel Assa, Yoav Goral, Naim Bekhor.*

to examine the possibility of studying the verdicts once more and, as for emigration, he also promised that there would be further developments to come...."

This answer corresponded well with information I received from a different source. When the leader of the parliamentary delegates enquired what steps the Government was considering in connection with the escape of the Jews, the Prime Minister replied that they were studying the matter seriously and would soon announce their decision. I understood from Jamil Shemtob (one of his sons) that the Revocation of Citizenship Bill would be passed.

On the basis of all the conversations I had with the leaders of the community, and particularly with those who had had dealings with the people who determined the policy of Iraq, I came to the conclusion that there was no way but to increase the pressure on the Iraqi Government. Thus, for instance, I informed Shemtob to convey a message to the Prime Minister that with the approach of Passover a huge demonstration was planned, whereby 5,000 people with their bundles would be heading for the borders and that we intended to make sure that this fact would be published in the international newspapers, an act that would surely embarrass the Government.

On 13 February 1950, after my meeting with Shemtob, I wired Israel that Shemtob wished us to use our influence to try and bolster Towfik El-Suweidi's new government; he suggested that we use the services of Kol Israel to attack certain people such as the Director-General of the Police, Ali Khaled Houjazi, and Naji El-Khdeiri, etc., and accuse them of corruption and bribery. I also added that there were consultations between Suweidi and Nouri El-Sa'id to transfer Ali Khaled Hujazi from his post and appoint him Governor of the Suleimaniya District. Nouri El-Sa'id preferred to keep him in his present job but the moment he left for Rome, on assignment Suweidi had him transferred.

Two days later, Ali Khaled Hujazi invited some men from the Istiklal Party to meet him and they decided to organize a coup d'etat to overthrow Suweidi's people and to seize power. Between Saturday evening and Sunday he and his men captured the radio station, post and telegraph offices and disconnected outgoing telephones lines. Accompanied by some of his assistants and under heavy protection from the police, he crossed the river, called Suweidi and forced him to dismiss the Minister of Interior, Saleh Jaber, or else he would enter and seize Baghdad. Suweidi called the Ruler and Shaker El-Wadi, the Minister of Defense, and after consultation, they decided to arrest Hijazi and so it came about: The army attacked the camp where he was staying and arrested him.

On the night of the bill, I.D. Sofer and Eitan Shamash visited Shemtob, who told them that the Prime Minister wanted to know how many Jews, in his opinion, would seek to emigrate if ever they were free to do so and he replied about 10,000. The Prime Minister said that the Government had come to the same conclusion, then added, according to Shemtob: "Let those troublemakers go and you remain behind with the community."

On 15 February 1950, I sent word to Israel that the Prime Minister informed Yehezkel Shemtob that same morning, when the Government decided to let the Jews depart with travel permits, that a week later an official announcement would be published concerning this matter. "They will let every Jew take out 200 Dinars," I reported, "I request a decision on the larger sums to be transferred. I presume there will be a big rush to transfer money."

A week later I wired the Mossad the following:

> Today I met with our Government contact [Yehezkel Shemtob] and discussed the matter of the emigration of the Jews with their permits to travel:
>
> a) What is the better way for us to send planes from Baghdad to Lod or to arrange for cars to drive via Jordan. I prefer the former method.
>
> b) What will be the immigration quota and what type of immigrant is preferred. Can we discuss costs and the transfer of money.

Two days later, on 4 February 1950, I received the following:

> a) Give us the name of your contact.
>
> b) We are very uncertain about travelling through Jordan. Still making inquiries.
>
> c) We don't understand your question "what is the best way, to send planes from Baghdad to Lod." Find out if they will let American

airlines, such as Trans Ocean, take off from Baghdad and under what conditions, the rest is a simple matter.

d) The Iraqi Government will make a decision on the emigration quota. Our preference is for you to send as many young boys and girls to our country as you can. When we receive your reply we will let you have further details.

e) Check with the Government whether they will accept someone from our side to help direct negotiations, and under what conditions and in what manner they will permit him to enter and leave the country.

# Chapter 9

# THE GATES ARE OPENED

On the evening of 3 March 1950, I hurried to our wireless centre. Yitzhak Sayegh and Shimshon Hubeiba were just closing down the apparatus. I asked them to stop doing so and by the light of a single bulb I sent the following telegram:

> We should cry for joy to be able to witness the results of our work and of those before us. At last we have news of the liberation of our troubled people. The government has decided unanimously to permit the exit of the Jews. Here are the Laws prepared by the Minister of the Interior, Saleh Jaber and presented to the Senate to revoke our citizenship:
>
> a) The Cabinet has the power to revoke the citizenship of any Jew who wishes to leave Iraq on his own volition, after signing a special form.
>
> b) Any Iraqi Jew who leaves Iraq illegally will automatically lose his citizenship.
>
> c) Any Iraqi Jew who has already left Iraq for a period of two months or more will also lose his citizenship.
>
> d) The Minister of the Interior is required to deport any Jew who has lost his Iraqi citizenship.
>
> e) The bill shall be valid for a period of one year but can be annulled by order of the King.

f) This bill will be in force as soon as it is published in the official newspaper.

g) The Minister of the Interior must execute the bill.

There was a big discussion in the Iraqi Parliament over the bill. The Minister explained it by saying that there was a general effort by many of the Jews to flee the country, and since it wasn't a good policy for the country to force those to stay who didn't want to, and since it also affected those members of the Jewish community who wished to stay, the Government suggested we grant them permits to emigrate.

Parliamentary delegates, especially those in the Opposition, claimed that the bill didn't refer at all to the assets of the departing Jews. Members of the Istiklal Party demanded that they confiscate Jewish property and assets to counteract Arab assets impounded by the Zionists in Israel (Faik El-Sameraee); also to banish all Jews from Iraq, not only the young and old (Ismail Ghanem).

In his reply, Jaber divided the Jews into two categories: loyal Iraqi citizens, and those who conspire against the country. In the name of justice, he added, we must not regard all Jews as enemies and deport them, rather rid ourselves of the undesirable ones. He opposed adding to the bill any paragraph referring to the freezing of Jewish assets.

The next day on 4 March 1950, Jaber presented the bill to the Senate. The discussion there was even livelier than that which took place in Parliament. The chief opponent was Muzham El-Pachachi, who claimed that by accepting this Bill they were about to surrender to those who were breaking the country's laws and were doing so without sanction. Instead of punishing the transgressors, the authorities were giving in to the wrong-doers. He protested against producing future soldiers for Israel, raised the subject of the assets and was surprised at what the Iraqi Government was doing to placate the Zionists without making conditions, such as bringing back the Arab refugees.

Jaber stated in his reply that it was precisely during the tenure of office of Ayoubi-Pachachi that the illegal flights of emigrants increased. Senators Mawlood, Moukhlos, Ali Jawdat El-Ayoubi and Moustafa El-Omari supported the Opposition's pleas. The Prime Minister, Towfik El-Suweidi, supported the Minister of the Interior.

In a speech given by the Jewish Senator, Ezra Menahem Daniel, he mentioned that one had to ensure the rights of the Jews who preferred to remain, and to remove restrictions from them. He mentioned to his colleagues in the Senate that the Jews had been living in Iraq for 3,500 years. Our father Abraham was born in Mesopotamia, therefore it wasn't easy for Jews to leave their native land; however, if they wished to leave, it was only because of the repression now in force.

Jaber promised that the remaining Jews would enjoy full equal rights and would remain Iraqis in every sense. The bill was passed by a majority vote and was published in the official newspaper on 9 March 1950 and after the approval of the Monarch, it came into force. The festival of Purim arrived.

The joy among the Jews was evident. A Purim festival such as this had never been celebrated in Iraq before. Spontaneous parties were held everywhere and in nearly all Jewish homes, songs were reverberating: *El-Leila Id El-Dounya Sa'id* (Tonight is a happy feast for the world) by Um El-Kalthoum, and *El-Yom Dounya Zahat* (Today the world rejoices) which was written especially for the Jewish singer Salima Murad by El-Umari. Incidentally, those songs were sung in private homes, in full; over the Iraqi radio station, where Jewish musicians abounded, only the tunes were broadcast.

Compliments also arrived from Israel: "Today we intended to send you our regular greetings for Purim. Now you deserve a double portion. But we have to do everything quietly, with caution and reflection. Do you think we can send an unofficial emissary to Iraq? We think the last pronouncement of the Iraqi Government adds urgency to the fulfillment of this mission. Try and check this."

I wired the Mossad that it was possible to bring an unofficial emissary into Iraq, as though he were any other now working here. Although my joy was great – the impossible had occurred – I had no idea how to cope with such an operation, that of transferring a complete community from one place to another. Suddenly I recalled David Ben-Gurion's words to his daughter Renana on 29 November 1949 in the Kalia Hotel on the Dead Sea. He was in his room and told her that he wouldn't be joining the celebrants, as he was aware that Israel was facing a most difficult war. I ought not to compare the two situations, but at that moment I understood how he felt.

The approval of the Revocation of Citizenship Bill brought a series of pressing questions: who would arrange the exodus? In what way? Who would fly them out and what would happen to their assets in Iraq and other countries? From the start I asked those questions of the Mossad, but those in Israel didn't seem to feel the urgency of the request.

The Iraqi Government was of the opinion that the Jews would depart for Iran on the same routes used for the illegal escape undertakings, only this time with travel permits. We, the Movement emissaries and the community activists, were against it and insisted that the emigration should only leave from the West. The discussions, clarifications and telegrams continued, but until 10 April 1950 neither was an exit route established, nor travelling agents decided upon, nor airlines contacted; and the local personnel had not yet been chosen to deal with the emigrants.

The day after the acceptance of the bill, I met Shemtob and agreed to apply to an American firm to deal with the refugees and, through them, to receive permission from Iraq to let planes arrive and pick up the emigrants. That would help us to open a refugee office where we could register and classify the emigrants, and see to their security, and would also prevent their competing in the queue for places by bribing the clerks. Our interest was also to prevent any conflict between the emigrants and the Iraqi people. I planned further outlets, such as employing Jaber on a percentage basis to establish a regular route from Baghdad to Istanbul and thereon to Israel; or else, a journey by car through Jordan, or by using ships sailing through the Suez Canal.

The Minister of the Interior, who was interested in seeing this bill put into effect quickly, decided to organize two committees, with the participation of the Jewish community, one in Baghdad and another in Basra. The Jews began to sell their movable property. The courtyards of the coffee-houses and garages were used to open markets for the selling of their goods. Extremist factions decided to use this opportunity to cause trouble and acquire benefit from it.

On 5 March 1950, the Mossad informed me:

We are expecting you to tell us how much luggage and cash they will be permitted to take. We are enquiring about various routes; you should also do so. For your information, we may use the services of Near East Airlines, who work in conjunction with our national carrier El Al and then perhaps our connection with Trans Ocean will cease.

That was the first reference to Near East Airlines, a subsidiary company of El-Al; in fact it was a joint venture of the Zim company and El Al.

On the same day another telegram was received:

You must conduct the negotiations and meetings with various factions without giving commitments on any specific exit route, cost, number of emigrants. Keep us informed about everything and we will advise you further.

A few days later the Mossad asked:

Will they permit an exit from Basra port? If so, what are their financial and overall conditions? Will they permit you to cross to Abadan and sail from there? Is it possible to use a train to Turkey to take the emigrants and their luggage? Can Syria prevent the traffic? Check every detail, the length of the journey and prices. Contact railway experts. If they are permitted to take out their possessions, is it feasible to arrange for transport in containers, and what can they bring with them?

On 11 March 1950, I replied to the Mossad:

The army and the police are on standby. Yesterday members of the Istiklal attacked the places where Jews were selling their possessions. The situation is tense and warrants concern. The Government passed the bill without mentioning the exit routes. This puts us in an awkward situation, but they will approve our suggestions if we stand firm. Some foreign person, under the protection of the United Nations or any refugee institute, ought to be invited at once to open negotiations with the Government on our behalf.

At the same time people from the Israeli Government and representatives of the Mossad contacted various organizations in the world in order to speed up the process. For instance, Ephraim Evron, Head of the Bureau of the Foreign Ministry at that time, wrote to the Mossad: "Our representatives in Geneva received instructions to make enquiries with the Egyptian representative, if they would permit the passage of ships holding Iraqi Jews to pass through the Suez Canal on their way to Israel. The Foreign Minister ordered the Israeli Ambassador in Washington to be in touch with the Iraqi Ambassador; to contact his government and examine the difficulties regarding permits of the emigrating Jews from Iraq."

Meanwhile the illegal emigration continued despite the new law. During February 1950, 1,020 people crossed the border with our help and on 9 March, 110 more Jews left. The American Consul reported: "We shall inform our Consulate that the flight has recommenced on 11 March. This new development proves that the Jews have no faith in the new bill."

The ongoing waves of emigration from Iraq following the approval of the Revoking of Citizenship Act was satisfying and remarkable. Moshe Shertok (Sharett) wrote on 10 March 1950, "The permit has been crowned with success and victory. The diligent and daring efforts of the Mossad through years of underground activity, and ever since the arrival of emissary Enzo Sereni in Baghdad, has created a Movement that has infused Iraqi Jewry with a new spirit. Be strong and of good courage." There was no end to the greetings and declarations of praise. In Israel and Paris where the centres of planning were situated, they were forever grappling with this new situation. On that day a message was transferred from the Mossad in Israel to its branch in Paris – "The Minister of Finance, Mr. Kaplan, requests you to make sure that Eshkol also participates in the meeting." They also sent us a telegram asking us to send Yousif El-Kabir, the lawyer, to Israel, Iran or Cyprus (he took part in drafting the bill) for consultation, on how to liquidate and transfer Jewish assets. They also asked for a detailed report on the financial, economical and political situation.

On the same day the Mossad in Israel reported to its branch in Teheran: "Today we held an unofficial meeting with Eliezer Kaplan, Sharett, Shaul Avigur and Giora Yousiftal regarding Iraq. The suggestions were: a) To ask Egypt to let us use the Canal; b) to try and hold direct meetings with people from the Iraqi Government, in order to study the situation and to confirm the order of exit and liquidation and the transfer of assets; c) to check the possibility of establishing a foreign company, American-Turkish-Iraqi, to take upon itself the selling and buying of the assets and to deal with anything connected with the emigration of the Jews."

At the same time, the Mossad in Paris informed the Mossad in Israel: "We are checking the possibility of using non-Zionist international organizations to operate in Iraq on our behalf. Let the emissaries in Iraq check this out as well. Your suggestion to send Shlomo Hillel and Akiva Yafeh to Iraq is a good idea. You should look out for more candidates. It is absolutely necessary that someone should be sent to Iraq without delay."

After a series of meetings held between Shemtob and myself, which excited public opinion, slanderous talk reached me that Shemtob was meddling in our affairs and causing trouble. Meir Basri, from among the members of the community, started these rumours. I decided to act and meet with some of them so as to strengthen the position of Shemtob and also to get some support on what had been done with Shemtob's participation. On 23 March 1950, I met with Abraham El-Kabir, who had parted from the Movement five years ago, ever since his meeting with Shmaryahu Guttman. I briefed him on our political policy and the cooperation of Shemtob, but despite

*Abraham El-Kabir, Director-General of Finance and Member of the emigration committee of the community.*

*Members of the emigration committee of the community in Baghdad,*
*from left to right, above: Sasson Nawi, Sasson Abed (Chairman);*
*below: Moshe Shohet, David Sala.*

the satisfactory atmosphere that prevailed during our conversation, when I asked him to hold a meeting with Shemtob, he refused. He agreed that we could meet on urgent matters and that we could also transfer messages through Advocate Shalom Darwish, secretary of the community.

The connection with El-Kabir continued even after his emigration to London in 1965. He visited Israel with his wife Rene, met with David Ben-Gurion and participated in a party in his honour with important Iraqi immigrants. Although he chose to live in London he couldn't forget his former homeland. Hospitalized in London a short while before his death, he expressed his nostalgia for Iraq. "They took my Iraq away from me," he told me with tears in his eyes.

I continued to look for connections to assist us in transferring our people quickly, and met two new smuggler-guides, Hussein and Karim, in order to consider new routes: one via Jordan following the oil pipeline and the other through Saudi Arabia. Unaware of activities taking place between Israel and Paris, I started looking for ways of organizing a route through the west of the country. We had had enough of hardship, crossing through Iran. The Iraqi Government, somewhat unhappy at the situation, now asked the Iranian Government to permit the Jews to cross through Iran. When I heard of that request, I asked my friend Sion Cohen in Teheran to try and block this route.

On 11 March 1950, Paris wired the Mossad in Israel saying that they had had a long conversation with Levy Eshkol (who was then Head of the Settlement Department at the Agency and also a full partner in decision-making on the subject of immigration) about the new development in Iraq, and in private talks the question of the Iraqi refugees came up. The American Joint (Jewish) Distribution Committee offered the American State Department its services and requested its help.

On 15 March 1950, I reported to Israel:

> When I was in Basra, I took a dangerous step in calling Major T. A. Cayton, Manager of the British company Fowler, and introduced myself as a Representative of the Community. He was the liaison man for British Intelligence. During his military service he worked in the department of transport in Iraq, Iran and Egypt and was considered an

expert in all fields of transportation. We agreed that he should send an official letter to Shemtob and explain to him the importance of transferring the Jews to any part of the world they wished to go. We presented this letter – a part of his general plan to approach the Government – to the Prime Minister and asked him to clarify his attitude.

Cayton is ready to take over the transfer of passengers to Israel by air. He thinks we should be in touch with the Red Cross or the Quakers. He is waiting for an answer from the community and will ask the opinion of the British Minister of Foreign Affairs. Our decision was that on his way back to London, he will go through Tel Aviv and will then deal with the negotiations. For a direct flight to Israel he is asking for an advance payment of 25 Liras per person carrying 25 kilos of luggage for the first 150 people, then 14 Liras for the rest. For a flight through Rome he wants 73 Liras. He is ready to take off from Basra and Baghdad. He will use Swiss planes. I await your reply; even if his offer is acceptable we are not bound by any commitment.

A few days later Cayton brought me up-to-date, that he received from Britain the authorization to take over this project and added that the next day, on 2 April 1950, at noon, he would be in Tel Aviv and asked to be met at the airport. I transferred the message to Israel and gave Cayton a letter, on behalf of the Jewish community, to be forwarded to the Minister of Foreign Affairs, Moshe Sharett, that he was familiar with events in Iraq. I sent a copy of the letter to the Mossad.

Abraham El-Kabir asked me to help the community to answer questions forwarded by the Iranian Government to Iraq, regarding the request to permit Jews to cross through Iran. After filling in the questionnaire we asked our friend Sion Cohen in Teheran to be on the alert: The minute the forms reached the Iranian Government he must do all he can to abort the Iraqi request.

Here are the questions and replies:

Question: How many Jews are ready to leave within a year?
Answer: In the first year between 40,000 and 50,000.

**Question**: What kind of transport will they need?

**Answer**: The Jews are asking to fly direct to Israel and to accept the International Red Cross decision to choose a stopover point on the way out. They are not ready to leave through Iran.

The activities were handled quietly, in private meetings and lots of messages were delivered; there were some in the Iraqi Government who didn't understand what was happening. The attitude of the newspapers was also casual. The papers wrote that there seemed to be a strong hand directing the enterprise, but the radical papers were more outspoken: "Those who stay behind are sure to do as Israel dictates."

Foreign diplomats living in Iraq tried to analyze events as they occurred. On 18 March 1950 the American Ambassador reported the following to the State Department: "Those who submit applications are asked by the representative of the Interior Ministry specific questions, such as whether they are familiar with the emigration routes as well as the Iranian ones: whether Iran agrees to let them enter the country after losing their citizenship; what are the contents of their luggage; details of personal possessions they are carrying with them. The government clerk was not able to be of assistance; therefore only a few applications were submitted." The Ambassador estimated that among many members of the Jewish community and clerks working for the Iraqi Government there were doubts regarding the readiness of the Iranian Government to permit Jewish emigrants to enter their country. According to him, many wanted to leave and had been selling their possessions for more than seven weeks. He added that the young ones should be sent out first, then adults of the lower working classes, the unemployed, craftsmen, small shopkeepers, servants, etc. Those in well-established businesses ought to stay on for a while and study developments before thinking of exchanging their comparatively comfortable lives for an uncertain future in Israel.

On 15 March 1950, an office for registering the Jews for departure was opened. Whoever applied there had to have a certificate stating that all their debts to the government, municipality, etc., were paid. Every Jew was told to provide for his own journey to the border, presuming they were leaving via Iran.

As no Jew had yet registered, the Government representatives tried to make things easier by offering to pay their travelling expenses.

According to a report of 21 March from the American Embassy in Teheran to the American Secretary of State, it was stated that the current Iranian Minister of Foreign Affairs Ardalan informed Richards, of the US Embassy, that the Iranian Government was studying the subject of the transfer of Iraqi Jews and in principal he did not oppose it, but would expect difficulties if a large number should suddenly arrive in Teheran. It was also reported that Iran would see the matter in a more positive light if the Jews did not enter Teheran or other main cities, and suggested they transfer by air from Abadan or any other place near the Iraqi border, so as not to attract too much attention.

On 19 March 1950, I informed the Mossad that we could hasten matters if we suggested to the Prime Minister and the Interior Minister that we would be prepared to exchange part of the Jewish assets left in Iraq to compensate for property owned by the Arab refugees fleeing from Israel. I asked for their opinion and approval but there was no reply.

I became rather frustrated. I acted, directed negotiations, reported to Israel on every step we took but received no reaction, encouragement or objection whatsoever. The representative of the community sent Cayton's plans to the Prime Minister, who approved them, but requested that all flight documents should be issued through a neutral country. I received no reaction from Israel.

In the early days of discussions over exit routes and the technical difficulties involved, Jews continued to leave Iraq in any illegal manner they could. They hired transport lorries, private cars, animals, any movable object and even the likelihood of a strict search at the borders did not deter them.

I enquired of Israel concerning the attitude of the Iranian Government and asked the Mossad to press them to delay giving a positive reply to Iraq until our negotiations with Cayton were completed. I was convinced that the Iranian route was not necessary to our plans. The information from the American Embassy in Teheran reached me later, but the experience we had in smuggling the emigrants through Iran wasn't a joyride. However, I continued to search for other routes.

On 31 March 1950, I reported to Binyamin Jibli of the Intelligence Branch of the Israeli Army that "on 14 March 1950 the Iraqi Government must surely have sent a letter to the Iranian Ambassador in Baghdad, asking if Iran was ready to grant entry visas to a number of Iraqi Jews. Those Jews were about to lose their Iraqi citizenship and Iraq had no interest in keeping them back and was ready to supply them with travel permits to leave the country. Israeli Intelligence had information that until 27 March 1950 no answer was received from Iran."

On 3 April, Israel wired us that Cayton hadn't arrived and asked for details about him – his passport number, flight number, etc. I impatiently sent a telegram to Israel the next day: "This silence of yours is worrying me. It is difficult to work without getting any response, positive or negative, regarding the exit plan. Our people may explode with frustration and decide to register after the Feasts despite our objections."

Since there was no reply to that telegram, I sent another one on 8 April:

> We are concerned about your continued silence. Please answer the following questions:
>
> a) Is Israel ready to absorb the Iraqi Jews and to what extent?
>
> b) Do you approve of the exit plan that we inaugurated; if so, what are your future plans?
>
> c) What is your plan regarding the assets held for the emigrants?
>
> d) Have you started to press Iraq to arrange for an exit route and to direct negotiations seriously?
>
> e) Are we to receive answers to our former telegrams, which I consider most urgent?
>
> Awaiting your reply. In case matters are not cleared up soon, I doubt if we can continue with our plan to provide our people with a dignified exit and our fullest cooperation.

The American Government was informed by its Embassy in Baghdad that Iraq rejected the interference of the Joint or any other agency, as the local Jewish community was dealing with the matter, assisted by the Government. Iraq was very sensitive over this question, especially after the USSR was denied supervision over the exit of the Armenians in Iraq a few years ago. Iraq feared that by giving us permission, it may stir up trouble with the USSR for their having been rejected then.

On 9 April 1950, there was a furious argument took place at the meeting of the Movement activists regarding registration. Members claimed that after the Feasts, pressure from the community was to be expected, so it was desirable to use the opportunity and permit registration. I opposed it and asked for a delay of another week to await the outcome of the travelling arrangements, so that our people could rest assured that we had a safe passage open to them. In the end I was obliged to accept a majority verdict which supported immediate registration. On the same day I sent the following telegram:

> I have reached the conclusion to allow members of the Movement and our people to register, starting tomorrow; to abandon their citizenship, even though our exit plan has not yet been formulated. Here is the reason for our decision;
>
> a) A large number of our people have sold their possessions and are spending their meagre savings on living expenses.
>
> b) We know that there are many Jews who are determined to register tomorrow, come what may, and we fear that we would lose their respect and influence if we opposed them.
>
> c) A mass registration of several thousands would put too much pressure on the organizers to handle it satisfactorily.

The day following Pessah, announcements were made telling our people to register. There was no limit to public excitement, so much so that it created a general impression that the Jewish citizens had serious connections with the Movement. On 10 April 1950, the registration took off on our initiative. I agreed with Shemtob to open six centres to be managed by the Halutz Members who would be employed by the community. In this way I thought we could give priority to members of the Movement and their families, in gratitude for their unswerving services to the cause and hoping their arrival in Israel would strengthen the Halutz efforts to ease the absorption of the Iraqi Jews. On the first day 3,400 registered and on the second 5,700 people.

Meanwhile, in Mossad Headquarters in Israel, they decided on a similar plan to mine, without bothering to let me know, or to stop me from dealing with Cayton. Rony Barnett, who fulfilled various missions on behalf of the Mossad and who was the moving spirit behind every emigration operation, filled me in later on the series of events about which I am going to mention here.

In 1949 Barnett was the Vice President and Operation Manager of the company Trans Ocean Airlines, registered in America and owned by the Maronite Church. He built up a good relationship with Gulhussein Ibtihaj, Chairman of the Iranian Airlines Company and with Ahmed Shafik, Minister of Civil Aviation in Iran and brother-in-law of the Shah (he married his twin sister). On many occasions he flew the Shah in private planes. Trans Ocean also flew Iranian pilgrims to Jedda, and thereon to Mecca. The flights were under the patronage of Iranian Airlines Company and were operating in Damascus, Istanbul and Ankara.

It seemed that the Mossad in Israel, which was aware of his good relations with Iranian personalities, asked him to check the possibility of flying immigrants from Iraq. In one of his meetings with Ibtihaj and Shafik, Barnett asked them if they had strong connections with Iraq and after some time a meeting in Teheran was held with Abd-El-Rahman Raouf, the General Manager and Operation Manager of Iraq Tours, whose Vice President was Towfik El-Suweidi and the active General Manager was Sabah El-Sa'id, son of Nouri El-Sa'id. The conversation was conducted on a business basis only. At the beginning, the two spoke of flying pilgrims to Iran and Jedda and then mentioned flights from Baghdad to Israel. Barnett took him to Marimad Airport in Teheran to show him how Jews were being flown from Teheran to Israel. Abd-El-Rahman Raouf was very impressed and said he would go back to Baghdad and would ring him in two or three days, which he did. A day later he arrived and met with Sabah El-Sa'id. Barnett told them that he lived with his family in Rome, the centre of his operations.

Abd-El-Rahman Raouf and Sabah El-Sa'id consequently went to Rome and invited Barnett to Baghdad, where he also met Prime Minister Towfik El-Suweidi and Minister of the Interior Saleh Jaber. The two officials made it a condition of acceptance that all flights had to be arranged through Iraq Tours. The reasons were obvious: Suweidi and Sa'id were major shareholders in the

*From right to left: Yehezkel Shemtob – acting Chairman of the Community, Rony Barnett (standing), Prime Minister Towfik El-Suweidi.*

company. The latter who was very interested in speeding up the exit of the Jews, as he disclosed to Barnett: "Every Jew who left for Israel would be another nail in the coffin of the Israeli economy."

The Mossad Aliya Bet accepted the arrangement with alacrity and informed them that "Shammai" (Shlomo Hillel) would soon arrive in Rome. James Wouton, who was also one of the members of Near East Airlines, also joined the trip. On 6 April 1950 he returned with a stopping-off permit in Cyprus, from where the plane could then be diverted to Lydda Airport. Barnett promised that the stopover in Cyprus would be used during the first month and then the flight would be directed straight to Israel. He also fixed a price: 12 English Pounds per person from Baghdad and 14 from Basra, and on direct flights the price would be 2-3 Pounds less. The price included: benzine, parking, personnel and 15 kilos of luggage. He hoped later on he could work out an illegal method for the transfer of gold.

All of a sudden, on badgering the "Sphinx" (the Mossad in Tel Aviv), it started communicating. On 9 April 1950 a telegram arrived; the anxiety was evident: "Shammai is leaving for Europe and we hope he will attend you in two weeks time. We agree to your advice to encourage registration. Make sure that at first they register in small numbers and send only the young and the needy. In Israel, talks are being held and plans prepared to receive the huge immigration from Iraq, but the shortage of tents and huts obliges us to tread carefully in the next few months. Shammai will bring you details of the talks and clarify the liquidation and transfer of assets. No commitments or decisions to be made before his arrival."

Not one word or even a hint regarding Cayton's discussion with us.

Arriving in Rome on 11 April, Shlomo Hillel sent a telegram asking Avigur about two problems: the assets of the travellers and their security.

He wrote that one ought not be satisfied with taking personal possessions only (meaning what they could carry with them) and demanded a more thorough attention given to the matter of their financial assets. As for security, he mentioned that even though we assumed that the Iraqi Government would take charge of the travellers' security, there were bound to be those who would want to harm them, such as individuals from the Istiklal Party. Therefore, he suggested authorizing the Shura (a branch of the Hagana) in Iraq to take upon itself the protection of the emigrants.

While Rony Barnett and Shlomo Hillel were "finalizing the deal" in Rome, Cayton knew nothing of this and went back to Baghdad on 13 April 1950. I asked I.D. Sofer to meet him, entertain him at nightclubs and try to sound him out carefully. Cayton met Yehezkel Shemtob twice and Interior Minister Saleh Jaber once. He informed us that there was a good chance of obtaining a permit from the government to fly to Cyprus. Meanwhile I asked Sofer and Shemtob not to mention my name. I stressed that my previous meetings with Cayton were adequate and every rash move might jeopardize my work and the Movement, especially as he had connections with British Intelligence.

Cayton tried several times to discover some facts about me and my position in the community, without success. I maintained my connection with him through Shemtob and Sofer. I made every effort to get him the permit from the government to bring in planes to take our people out. Meanwhile, it was agreed with Shemtob that we must employ an Iraqi lawyer to assist us with all the legal problems occurring and he would receive his fees from the community. I suggested Yehya Kassem, Saleh Jaber's good friend. We also agreed to give priority to the prisoners' families and members of the Movement at the registration centre, which caused a lot of dissatisfaction among the rest of the people and accusations of bribe taking. We checked every registration. Apart from all the preparations for mass emigration, we had to smuggle out those who were unable to fly openly. Thirty-three people crossed the Dhyala River on 16 April 1950 in the evening, accompanied by the smuggler Ja'far. Yehezkel Yona (affectionately called Yehezkel Austin, as he worked for the Austin car agency) and myself accompanied them until they reached the river crossing and then returned in the early hours of the morning. The next day, I flew to Basra and had a meeting with our people there: It was presided over by emissary Uziel Levy. After reviewing the activities, I told them of our meeting with the Prime Minister.

Meanwhile, the American Ambassador in Baghdad reported that the Iraqi Deputy Minister of Foreign Affairs, El-Rawi, informed him that the Iraqis in Teheran were pressing on the Iranians, for several days, to permit the Jewish emigrants to use Iran as an intermediate stop. Pressure was also put on the

Iranian Ambassador in Baghdad. He informed them that Iran had asked Iraq for answers to some questions regarding emigration. The Iraqi Government got the information from the community.

While we were busy with our plans, work was going ahead with an alternative plan in Europe. Rony Barnett wrote to Moshe Carmil on 13 April 1950:

> When Raouf and his daughter arrived, I checked them into the Eden Hotel and invited them to my house for lunch. I told Raouf that if, in Iraq, we could arrange for the direct flight of the Jews to Israel, then we could take them by air. If he could contact the right people in Baghdad, it might turn out to be a very profitable arrangement. Raouf asked if I were doing it for Trans Ocean and I denied it. This was between him and me, I told him. He said he could manage it, all for obvious reasons: Towfik El-Suweidi, the present Prime Minister, is the one responsible for the legislation of the Bill, allowing for the exit of the Jews; he is also Chairman of Iraq Tours whose manager is Raouf. Raouf added that if Suweidi was aware that the matter was not for his own benefit only but for that of the company as well, he would be very cooperative.
>
> Raouf and Suweidi are good friends. On his trip to Rome, he took letters and gifts for Suweidi's daughter, who is the wife of recently arrived Ambassador Mohamed Fakhri El-Jamil. Raouf said that only two days ago he spoke with Suweidi on the matter and he offered to help. I asked Raouf to arrange a permit for planes to land, and to make sure that no problems occurred to prevent direct flights from Baghdad to Israel.
>
> Raouf agreed except for direct flights. He was of the opinion that there would be difficulties regarding official acceptance of direct flights. I insisted, and he agreed, that payments were made according to the results obtained. I told him that I would go to Baghdad together with my assistant (Shlomo Hillel) and would remain there to ensure that all was well. I told him that we would need to employ some local people to work in his office and he also agreed to that. Raouf introduced me to the Iraqi Ambassador Mohamed Fakhri El-Jamil, who had been recently elected.

He is 40 years old, the son-in-law of Suweidi and arrived in Rome with his wife and three children. I invited them all to dinner in my house. We stayed up talking till the early hours of the morning and became good friends. At his office, I received on the spot visas for three months for myself and Shlomo Hillel.

In Baghdad Cayton's plan appeared to have promising results. "There is a possibility of completing the project," I reported to the Mossad on 13 April. "The chairman of the community met the Interior Minister to discuss with him some problems regarding emigration, such as security, organization, traffic, type classification of the people who were registering and the exit route to be adopted. The Interior Minister agreed to Cayton's plan but insisted that we fly through Cyprus. Cayton came to Baghdad to obtain a written permit from the government and will leave for Cyprus and then come to you. We are discussing the transfer of luggage via the Cypriot route."

Encouraging support came from the American Secretary of State, Dean Achison, who wrote to his Embassy in Teheran on 14 April 1950: "Due to the large number of Iraqi Jews who are registering for emigration, if we find that the Iranian Government refuses to let the Iraqi Jews enter the country, you must unofficially inform them of America's hope that Iran will find ways of doing so, on behalf of those emigres on their way to Israel."

Here, too, ropes were extended and knots tied; personal diplomacy did its work, like some benign hidden force; international diplomacy completed the job started by the emissaries in the area, and all the signs pointed to the day, not out of reach, when planes would be able to carry large numbers of emigrants and touch down in Israel.

On 17 April, Shlomo Hillel sent a letter from Rome to Moshe Carmil, informing him that he would leave for Paris the next morning with Rony Barnett and continue on to Baghdad from there at the beginning of the week. He admired Barnett; and also said that there would be a need for many organizers and depots for registration in different places, so he requested for more activists to be recruited.

On 20 April, groups of the Halutz Movement assembled in Baghdad. A report was given on the various smuggling routes and it was discovered that the

Movement was not aware of its extensive range. One of the senior leaders suggested that the Halutz in Iraq would adopt the ideas of Kibbutz Me'uhad. I opposed this and explained the importance of not identifying with any political party. The one who suggested it tried to convince us that the kibbutz wasn't a party; in the end his suggestion was adopted.

The next morning we listened to a special broadcast from Kol Israel on our behalf. There was great jubilation. We felt at one with Israel. We received greetings from the General Chief of Staff and the Jewish Agency and scores of private letters.

Meanwhile Cayton met with Interior Minister Saleh Jaber, who verbally accepted the plan, costs, etc., and promised that in a day or two a written permit should reach us. When he received it, Cayton would then leave for Israel. On Sunday 23 April, I received a telegram telling me that Cayton would arrive in Paris sometime before Tuesday and requested the name of a hotel where he could stay.

That very day the Mossad received information on the financial situation in Iraq: A week before that the banks in Baghdad were closed for seven days. The official reason given was the apprehension caused by the large withdrawal of accounts by Jewish clients who were about to leave the country. The banks suddenly stopped honouring promissory notes presented by their Jewish clients. The immediate result of this was great alarm among the Jews as bankruptcy faced many of them.

This crisis was also to affect non-Jewish merchants, as the Iraqi Government feared for the economy. One of the efforts made to rectify the situation was an announcement that Iraq was ready to grant the Jews import licenses under Category A, meaning the import of any merchandise in the region of 50,000 Dinars. But there wasn't a Jewish citizen able to accomplish such financial transactions owing to the recession.

On Wednesday 24 April, the Mossad wired:

a) Shammai and Rony will arrive on Thursday.
b) Shammai will, at 6 p.m., be present at the bookshop of the Hindu situated below the Regent Hotel.

c)  If the shop is closed on Friday he will be taking a walk on the bridge "Mode" at 3 p.m.

d)  Take great care.

A day later I met with Shemtob in order to outline our plans for publicity regarding our registration policy; by doing this we could avoid malicious gossip. Shemtob told me that Nouri El-Sa'id's son made him an offer to take the Jews by air. He refused to accept the assignment, as many large planes were needed to fulfil the mission, and said that Sabah would not be able to supply them.

I kept the appointment at the selected shop at 6 p.m. accompanied by Naim Bekhor, one of the zealous officers of the Hagana, whose house was often used to lodge emissaries. Rony Barnett was also there and we all went to I.D. Sofer's house. We discussed at length on the most suitable exit plan and only then did they disclose the arrangement they had with Near East. I still felt that Cayton's plan was the better one, since it was supported by the British Government, whose influence in Iraq was still being felt and more so than that of the Americans.

We met the next day and I.D. Sofer spoke of the final stage of negotiations reached with Cayton. We emphasized that Cayton had already prepared the ground for transit to Cyprus and everything was in readiness for the operation. I informed the Mossad on 28 April that: "Cayton has received permission from his government to land in Cyprus. He will reply to the Iraqi Government today." Although Hillel and Barnett came with fixed ideas, I wired the Mossad the following: "We met today with 'Shammai' (Hillel) and Rony. We haven't yet decided which plan to support." Shlomo Hillel gave me a telegram to send to Israel: "Rony and I met today with 'Stanley' (Towfik El-Suweidi) and then with Shemtob. So far Stanley supports our offer and even recommends it to Shemtob. We may be able to start the operation in a few days. Certainly the first planes must come directly from you."

Several years later Rony Barnett explained how his connection with Shlomo Hillel was established:

I was asked if I could take Shlomo Hillel with me to Baghdad. I agreed at once and actually was the one to give him the name of Richard Armstrong and a British identity. He looks as British as I resemble Chu Chin Chau. Nevertheless the original arrangement was to take him with me as my assistant to Baghdad, via Paris. At the last minute I was instructed by 'Ivri' [one of the leaders of the Mossad in Paris]: "Be in touch with Shlomo Hillel, and tell him that we are not leaving from Paris but from Amsterdam." The reason for this was that the Mossad was very concerned about the security problem.

I was sure that Hillel didn't think I was Jewish. The instructions given to me were: "Be in touch with him but from a distance; don't reveal everything to him."

Later I took him to Baghdad: Our relations were amicable. I think it was Abd-El-Rahman Raouf waiting for us at the airport; he had close contacts with Defense personnel. There were no problems when I passed him off as my assistant and went on to stay at the Sindbad Hotel. If you ask me to whom gratitude is owing, I would say to Sofer and Eitan Shamash, we must also give acclaim to the very important contribution offered by Mordechai Ben-Porat, or as he was sometimes called "Zaki" or "Dror."

Rony Barnett was an adventurer. He was never a Yeshiva student but had admirable courage. He managed to conceal his Jewishness and knew well how to utilize his British identity. I will not conceal the fact that I had heard rumours, that Barnett also dealt with the smuggling of gold and diamonds, but without this ability, it is doubtful whether he could have fulfilled the vital job in hand. With time, he showed unity and attachment to our cause, very similar to that of any loyal Israeli.

Once I sat with Rony Barnett and Jim Wouton in Sofer's house. "Look Mordechai," Wouton told me, "we know that you are facing a new phase in your life. You are to be married and will surely need money…"

"So what?" I answered.

They were about to give me details when I cut them short. I told them under what conditions Israel was founded and what a great many people had sacrificed for her sake, which was something very precious to us. "My mission in Iraq," I continued, "isn't different from any other. At this moment emissaries working on behalf of Israel in many other places are offering their services free." There was a confused silence and I didn't hear another word on this subject again.

Following the conversation, Iraq Tours presented an official letter to the community leaders, informing them of their readiness to transfer Jews in four-engine planes to any airport, at a price of 12 Dinars per passenger, including luggage of 30 kilos each. Abd-El-Rahman, Raouf's brother, arranged for Shlomo Hillel and Rony Barnett to meet with Interior Minister Saleh Jaber. He asked them questions about fees, quantities of luggage and other conditions and mentioned that he was satisfied with the replies. He also requested that the contents of the conversation were to be given him in writing.

The following day, the letter was sent to the Minister of the Interior. We lost some time, owing to the festivities concerning the celebrations of King Faisal II's birthday anniversary, which began on 2 May 1950. A day after, on 3 May, Shlomo Hillel handed me a telegram to send to Israel: "Today Rony and I received Iraqi visas, good for three months for unlimited travel." At this stage the three of us decided to tell Cayton that he was out of the deal. This move created a big fuss. Sofer, who acted on my instructions and with the approval of Shemtob, told me of the embarrassment this engendered:

> When "Zaki" came back I received instructions from him to continue dealing with Cayton, who came to Baghdad to meet with the heads of the community and discuss the question of the transfer issue.
>
> I met Cayton in the hotel having on me a letter of introduction from Shemtob. I drove there in a private car posing as a merchant (owner of a carpet shop), who dealt with missions on behalf of the community. I took him to Baghdad-El-Jedida and told him that I had no connection with the Zionists and that I was only fulfilling orders given me by Shemtob and which dealt with English-speaking foreigners. As I was fluent in English I was always called upon to translate. I asked him how he could help me, so that the government wouldn't suspect me of dealing with foreigners, and he promised to arrange something. I told him: "Anyway, let's say

that we have known each other since 1938, when we first met at the Cumberland Hotel and have been friends ever since."

We met at Shemtob's. He was the last one to hear from Cayton of the plan we had devised and of which he approved. Shemtob asked me to smooth over the rough edges while translating. He imagined that the connection with Cayton would guarantee two things:

a) Support from the British Government and the Intelligence personnel.

b) A series of flights approved by the British Government might influence the Iraqi Government to protect the Jews on their departure.

The conditions were accepted and Cayton was asked to prepare a draft of the contract, in order to present it to the Prime Minister before the community signed it.

Cayton used to sit in my shop and type all his letters and telegrams to be sent out. In his telegrams, he arranged with Britain to disguise military planes as civil ones for the flight. After meeting with Shemtob we drove to Baghdad-El-Jedida and celebrated.

One day, from my shop I was called home where I met people I didn't know: Shlomo Hillel, Rony Barnett, Yerahmiel Assa and Jim Wouton. They asked me what I thought of the flight plan. I replied that everything had been fixed: We had a route, there was a contract for signature and there were no problems. They enquired how I was communicating with Cayton and I replied through messages from "Zaki" (Ben-Porat). Rony then told me to cancel all our arrangements as best I could.

I related all this to Shemtob and he agreed to work in conjunction with Israeli representatives. As for Cayton, I went to his hotel, where Barnett and Hillel were also staying (neither knew the other), drove him to Baghdad-El-Jedida and told him: "As a friend I have something to tell you. A new situation has cropped up and we must check it with Shemtob." He asked me if we were about to work together. I replied affirmatively.

We went to Shemtob's house. It was the Eve of Passover. Shemtob explained that planes with four engines and cheaper running costs and fares were being offered and had been accepted by the community.

Cayton was naturally furious and threatened to sue the community. It worried Shemtob and he told Cayton that any compensation required would be met by the community, but added that he couldn't believe that the British Government would sue the dejected refugees who were leaving Iraq. Cayton replied that it wasn't a matter of compensation; it concerned the prestige of the British Embassy and the British Government. Shemtob attempted to placate him saying that Prime Minister Towfik El-Suweidi had a personal interest in the scheme.

Cayton replied: "We can also alter the plans of any government," and added that he would demonstrate the superior power of Britain and the important influence she had on Iraq these days. Shemtob said that he was only President of the community and had nothing more to add.

Cayton shook hands with a promise that "we will know how to deal with this matter."

From Shemtob's house we drove to Baghdad-El-Jedida. On the way he asked what I thought of it all and I told him that it was all up to him. He asked me to help him find Ibrahim Salman (Mordechai Ben-Porat), whom he first met in Basra. I said I didn't know him and he promised that he would locate him by every means possible. I hurried, of course, to inform "Zaki" and the only thing he did was to grow a moustache! A few days later some Jews from Basra visited my shop and one of them was, I believe, called Shasha. They

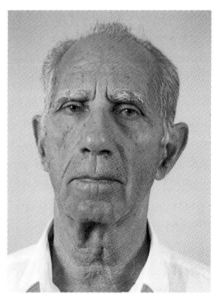

*Yitzhak David (I.D.) Sofer*

introduced themselves as friends of Cayton and said that he was in such a bad state, it could cost him his job. They asked to meet with Ibrahim Salman and promised to have just a word. I said that I didn't know him,

I didn't work with the community and didn't know anyone working there either. They left promising to try and find him themselves.

Cayton left for Cyprus and promised to return in a few days. He did so and intended to fly on to London. He asked me to report to him daily on developments and especially if I had news of Ibrahim Salman, whom he had to find. I pacified him as best I could and he returned to Basra. When he heard that I was on a plane flying to Basra, he phoned and invited me to dinner at his house in the presence of his wife and son.

I explained to him that I was only fulfilling missions for the community and I would be returning by train. He promised that the day would come when Ibrahim Salman's identity would be known to him although he had the feeling that he wasn't someone working for the community.

Cayton didn't sit idle. He probed, sent telegrams to Teheran and London and discovered the connection between Rony Barnett and the Trans Ocean Company, which was the base for Near East. The British Embassy began to suspect Richard Armstrong (Shlomo Hillel). The Head of the Secret Police, Bahjat Atia, decided to examine his passport. When Raouf was at a meeting with Sofer, he asked him to bring Hillel in to be questioned. Sofer, assuming innocence, replied that he would do so in a day or two, and Raouf mentioned that the Secret Police wanted to see him immediately. Sofer went to Barnett at his hotel in the morning and explained the situation to him.

On 5 May I wired the Mossad that "Emil" (Shlomo Hillel) will be flying to Nicosia at 11 o'clock. The telegram that Shlomo Hillel sent was: "If I don't find a place on the plane from Nicosia, I will come on Sunday." Eventually he succeeded and arrived at Lydda on the same day.

Meanwhile Rony reported to me and I transmitted the following to the Mossad on 7 May:

a) Saleh Jaber informed me that the permit has arrived and copies have been sent to the Ministry of Transport, the Prime Minister and the Community's Office. You can start with the flight arrangements immediately.

b)  On receiving the permit I will send a telegram to Near East in Rome to send us planes for the use of Iraq Tours. Near East in Rome has to advise you of this. I will take charge of the passports of flight personnel on their arrival here.

c)  The interference of Sabah El-Sa'id was still continuing. The Prime Minister and Jaber advised us to compensate him. On receipt of the permit we are considering it.

d)  Advise us on the medical steps to be taken for the immigrants. We have the means to perform medical check-ups.

e)  The approximate number of registrations in the whole of Iraq is around 47,000-4,000 are ready to leave immediately.

On 9 May, the Mossad informed us that Shlomo Hillel would be leaving on the next plane to Cyprus and would arrive in Baghdad on 11 May. That same day I sent a telegram to Israel regarding information we received from private sources; that the Interior Minister asked for the opinion of the Transport Minister, the airline office and its manager, Nouri El-Sa'id, the Head of Police and the Prime Minister. Sabah opposed giving the monopoly to Near East before the signing of a contract with Iraq Airways. Therefore, after tiresome negotiations with Sabah it was essential to sign the contract, where Rony acts as the Representative of Near East and undertakes to pay the head of the Iraqi Airlines office 30 Dinars for every plane used. The contract was sent to the American Embassy in Baghdad which was thrilled with the arrangement and requested that it be put into effect officially. They promised Rony that Saleh Jaber would accept the monopoly the following day, after getting "Sabah's" approval. I am sending a telegram to Rome to request delivery of the planes."

On 9 May, Moshe Carmil brought Sion Cohen, the representative of the Mossad in Teheran, up-to-date:

On Saturday night Shlomo Hillel came here for a short visit. The main purpose of his arrival was to delay the onset of the work which is being affected by inefficient and protracted treatment of members of the American Embassy and, also, the necessity for arranging the passage via

Cyprus. At this moment we heard details from him on the situation. We understood that the work would start immediately on receiving the permit for Cyprus. Hillel is leaving tomorrow. We approached British and American sources through the Israeli Foreign Office and hope that the permits and all necessary arrangements will be completed soon; then work can commence.

Meanwhile, it is essential to hold back the response of the Iranian Government to Iraq regarding the transfer of the Iraqi Jews.

On the same day I wired Israel the following:

a) From authorized sources we were told that Towfik El-Suweidi will inform the Arab League of the exit of Iraqi Jews, and the damage it will do to the Israeli Government in these times of financial difficulties.

b) Radical newspapermen demanded that the Government recognize the Jews of Iraq.

In a different telegram I sent that same day I wired:

In order to expedite the matter, we request the Israeli Foreign Office to inform the Cypriot Government officially of Israel's agreement to accept all Jews passing through Cyprus on their way to Lydda. Copies of this agreement must be sent to the required ministries. This is the advice of the American Embassy.

On 11 May 1950, Shlomo wired Israel:

They informed us officially from the Civil Airport that a permit is offered for one plane only. No doubt they want to check whether the plane is really flying through Cyprus and they may send an inspector to confirm this on behalf of the Government. We told them that we would obtain it on Saturday. It is obvious that we won't be able to start flying until confirmation of this is cleared up. Perhaps in the meantime you can acquire a temporary exit permit for several flights through Cyprus, despite Cayton's interference, and it is important that we start immediately.

On the same day we received the following telegram from the Mossad: "Yoel Palgui came back and informed us that Wouton will reach you tomorrow, Friday, with the permits obtained for landing in Nicosia."

On 13 May, Shlomo Hillel wired the Mossad:

a) Today we received a permit in writing for a single flight. Tomorrow we will meet with the Minister of Civil Aviation together with the Chairman of the community. We may obtain a permit for two planes.

b) It is mentioned in the permit that the flight stops at Nicosia. They will certainly send an inspector to confirm this.

c) Wouton hasn't arrived yet, and we don't know what was agreed in Nicosia.

d) Will it be possible to transfer the travellers to a different plane in Nicosia; this is desirable for the initial flights.

e) Rony will fly out and return with the first plane.

f) We will inform you and the Near East office when the first plane returns. Be prepared.

On 15 May 1950, Shlomo Hillel sent this telegram to Baghdad:

a) The situation from day to day is getting more complicated. I will have to leave as soon as possible.

b) Any hindrance may jeopardize all the work.

c) The person who will replace me will have to work full-time in this job. I don't see any possibility of his working on *Jibli* matters (meaning intelligence).

I again emphasize that I have to leave immediately, the sooner the better.

On his arrival in Israel, Shlomo Hillel sent us this telegram:

a) Wouton has arrived yesterday with the permits from the Island.

b) Meanwhile there are some delays in receiving the papers. We hope we will overcome the difficulties regarding income tax and that on Thursday we can commence the trial flight.

A letter was sent by the Immigration Department to the Mossad on 16 May 1950, which shows how far Iraqi thinking coincided with that of the Agency people; for us in Baghdad the reality looked very clear and obvious.

On 17 May, the first plane arrived in Iraq. Despite my warnings and advice, Near Eastern Overseas was marked clearly on the plane. I was afraid of trouble from the American Embassy lest they inform the authorities of the airline's connection with Israel. On 18 May, I wired Israel:

> Raouf informed "Shammai" (Hillel) that there were rumours that he is Jewish. Shemtob informed me of this through Sofer. Surveillance by the Secret Police is expected. We ceased direct contact. My opinion is that Shlomo should depart on the first plane as Inspector of the company. You must send someone to replace him immediately and to assist Barnett and Jim Wouton. I am concerned over their handling of financial expenses and am also making arrangements with Government officials. Meanwhile, I informed Rony that he has to request approval of Shemtob before arranging matters thus we will guarantee Rony's inactivity until a replacement arrives.

The Mossad replied:

> We can't send someone to replace Shlomo in the near future. We are still looking for a replacement. Well, if Shlomo is really in danger, we agree that he flies on the first plane as you suggest. We agree with your conclusion and advice regarding Rony. Give him strict instructions from us that every serious transaction as well as those to do with financial

expenses, must come to us for initial approval. For more urgent matters he must also have your approval.

While waiting for the permits we had to organize a team to do the work; that meant to direct the registration and to deal with those who registered prior to their exit from the airport.

We, in the background, feared reaction from the Opposition in Iraq. Their radical spokesmen didn't hide their feelings and expressed their determined objection to the exit of the Jews. We didn't know how the Opposition Party would react to the emigration itself. Would they encourage bad feeling and incite a mob in the streets? We decided not to take the risk and we arranged for minibuses with police protection for the travellers, to attend the first planeloads. We were using those two flights as a test and were not prepared to fail.

# Chapter 10    FLYING TO FREEDOM

On Friday, 19 May 1950, at exactly 14.00 o'clock, nine years after the bloody pogrom of Rashid Ali El-Kaylani and 2,531 years after the seizure of Zion when 42,360 people left Jerusalem for exile, a remarkable event took place: A Skymaster plane with eighty-six Jewish immigrants on board, accompanied by an Iraqi police officer, prepared for take off on the runway of Baghdad airport, and headed for Nicosia, on the island of Cyprus. It touched down at exactly 15.50 on the island and after a brief stop, took off again for Lydda airport in Israel. At 18.00 o'clock, six hours after leaving Baghdad, the wheels of the plane touched down on the runway of Lydda airport. An hour later another plane landed on the same runway with eighty-nine immigrants.

One hundred and seventy-five travellers weighed down with bundles – the elderly, anxious adults, excited teenagers and many young children were directed haphazardly towards the two planes at the far end of the airport in Baghdad. Sweating activists were stacking the luggage while others darted here and there checking that all was in order. These people had been uprooted from their homes, jobs, friends, schools, associates in the neighbourhood, environments they knew well, familiar sounds of their native tongue and headed for a voyage into the unknown, a land that occasionally filled their dreams but of which they knew very little.

Shlomo Hillel boarded the first plane accompanied by an Iraqi police captain, in a well-pressed flamboyant uniform, who seemed to be more excited than the travellers themselves, and yet he admitted he had flown before. His job was to oversee the operation and ensure that all conditions were met, particularly that the plane landing in Nicosia. Although that was the plan, the leaders of the operation had other intentions. They didn't want to upset the travellers, transfer them from one plane to another, unload and reload their luggage onto planes arriving from Israel. It was decided to treat the captain to a majestic tour of the Island and while he was absorbing the delights of Nicosia, the planes, after a brief stop, continued on to Israel, released the immigrants in Lydda and returned to Nicosia. And that is exactly as it happened.

The travellers arrived at Lydda just before sunset. The media had a field day; the radio and the newspapers hummed with excitement. In fact, the news were printed even before the planes landed in Israel. In "Maariv" of Friday, 19 May 1950, an article was contributed by the correspondent of the French News Agency in Nicosia under the headline "Immigrants from Iraq arrive today in Cyprus": "This morning the transfer of the Iraqi Jews who registered for emigration has begun. They will fly to Cyprus with permits given by the authorities in Baghdad. The immigration authorities will be employing Skymaster planes. Baghdad announced that among the 100,000 Jewish citizens, 47,000 had already registered for emigration. However, the exit of a large number of Jews will be held back, due to the fact that the question of their assets has not yet been settled. The Iraqis are hoping to use the emigration as an excuse to profit from Jewish possessions at bargain prices. A certain Arab organization has distributed a circular advising citizens 'not to buy anything from the Jews as it would all be theirs in the end'."

On Sunday 21 May, the newspapers in Israel published, in full, the fact that a large number of emigrants from Iraq have attained their freedom. The editors of the newspapers rivaled each other in enthusiasm and grandiose statements. "Maariv" also reported, among other things, that a "fire took place in one of the immigrants plane; parts of a wing went up in flames when the ground crew were topping up the fuel tank. The crew of the Skymaster succeeded in letting out all the travellers and no one was hurt. The damage was repaired during the night and the plane left to Teheran in the morning to fetch more immigrants."

On 23 May, "Maariv" published an article with the following headline: "The Ezra and Nehemia Operation is being realized," and it added: "In Lydda they waited all day and night for a third plane with Iraqi immigrants but it didn't turn up, and because of this, an extra plane took off from Lydda to Nicosia on its way to Baghdad to bring out more immigrants. The Near East personnel were apprehensive at not receiving permission for the plane to take off. The report of the arrival of the plane came from Nicosia, meaning one hour before its landing in Lydda. The schedule was as follows – 4,000 immigrants per month for a start and following that 8,000-10,000 per month. 52,000 out of 120,000 have already registered for departure. The immigrants are allowed to carry 30 kilos of movable property plus 50 Dinars (Glp 50), but the total value of the goods is estimated with Glp.150 Million. The first plane arrived in Nicosia escorted by an Iraqi officer. He was to ensure that Near East was really flying from Baghdad to Israel through Nicosia, according to the agreement between the Iraqi Government and the Near East."

"In the olden days, before Ezra and Nehemia, 40,000 Jews from Baghdad emigrated to Israel except that they managed to take most of their possessions and valuables with them at that time (in this instance we were mainly concerned with saving lives.) Despite everything no more suitable name could have been

*Jews preparing for emigration in the courtyard of the Mesouda Shemtob Synagogue in Baghdad.*

chosen for this campaign than that of the Ezra and Nehemia Operation, for the saving of Babylonian Jews."

This short article in "Maariv" achieved one of the important things in the operation – its title! There were some who jocularly dubbed it the "Ali Baba Operation"; Davar suggested: "the New Magic Carpet"; Moshe Sharret suggested: "Babylonian operation," and "Maariv" finally came up with the "Ezra and Nehemia Operation."

On 20 May, a day after the two first planes landed in Lydda, where in the first one Shlomo Hillel arrived, Rony Barnett told I.D. Sofer that Ali Ghaleb, the Director of the Secret Police, informed Raouf, the Director of the Iraqi Airways Company, that if Shlomo Hillel ever returned to Iraq he would be arrested on the spot. When I heard the news, I tried to verify it and in examining the file of the Secret Police, I found out that Ali Ghaleb also informed Raouf that the Secret Police had heard that Hillel was Jewish and were collecting information regarding his true identity. I sent an urgent telegram to Shlomo.

The Operation started in May and at first there were six flights from Baghdad, via Nicosia to Tel Aviv:

*Iraqi immigrants landing at Lydda.*

19.5.50  –  Two planes with 137 adults, 25 children and 13 babies, amounting to 175 passengers.

24.5.50  –  two planes with 134 adults, 81 children and 12 babies, amounting to 227 passengers.

31.5.50  –  two planes with 144 adults, 60 children and 8 babies, amounting to 212 passengers.

The total amount of emigrants from Baghdad in May 1950 was 614 people.

When the flights started a special office in Baghdad was required for the operation, and that was to be a problem particularly with regard to working conditions for all concerned. Most of the personnel, and those required to organize the emigration operation, were from the Movement. People who were used to acting under secrecy and who were also the object of the attention of the Secret Police were given public jobs; they worked with the cooperation of the emigration police and openly contacted the customs people and the Secret Police. In the community's offices a team consisting of Shemtob's son and two of the ex-officers of the Shura was formed. As we had secret funds, which we couldn't openly declare, we kept two ledgers, one for general inspection, intended for the head of the community and the authorities, and a secret one which was meant for Israeli use.

The difficulty of the organizing and the coordinating of the Operation was tremendous: On one side stood the Iraqi Government with its various departments dealing with Emigration, Customs, Secret Police, Defense and even the local Mukhtars who were there to certify the affidavits of the registered emigrants; secondly there was the Jewish community which, despite all its difficulties, was pressed into the registration work, and thirdly there was the Halutz Movement, whose members were subject to undercover rules and received instructions from the Mossad emissaries, supervised the finance and wireless operations, reported regularly to Israel and received guidance for the Mission. All those factors had to work together in harmony so as to manage the exodus satisfactorily.

Not one of these groups knew exactly what was required of them. There was nothing in writing and no documents detailing expertise. During the mission there was a great deal of friction between the different factors, which added to their grievances and problems, made work cumbersome and affected its efficiency. The various Iraqi Government departments took charge of the Revocation of Citizenship Act, but they disagreed as to the interpretation of its spirit and aim. Consequently, at first, they did their best to disrupt its implementation. Even the most docile of civil servants showed a sad lack of efficiency, and all they managed to do was to issue several scores of travel documents each day, for some of the thousands of Jews queuing daily to apply for emigration.

The itinerary was as follows: The emigrant with his family had to be present at one of the synagogues where we established centres for registration. The father of the family was required to state his name, age, address and the names of family members. According to these registrations the timetable of flights was fixed and those who registered were called in turn to present themselves at the Meir Tweig Synagogue in Baghdad (which is still standing and has recently been renovated by the Iraqi authorities to serve the remnant of the Jewish community). In the main office, the head of the family answered questions to prove that there was no known impediment to his leaving, as regards income tax or money owed to other government departments. He produced his photo and those of his family and paid one Dinar for stamp duty and various other governmental expenses. Iraqi citizenship was then revoked and travel documents prepared.

At this stage certain other difficulties cropped up. For instance, a Moslem who was in love with the daughter of a Jewish neighbour heard that she was leaving and went to the police asking for an injunction on the family, claiming that the father owed him money. We found ourselves caught up in a sort of devil's dance, running here and there to try to convince the emigration authorities to cancel the bans.

Some of our people had good relations with Iraqi officers and clerks and were also skilled in all these procedures; they would "marry off" couples and set up new "families" in the travel documents, by changing the names of the youngsters who were wanted by the Secret Police.

The local Mukhtars also played an important part. Their job was to check items in all the documents. Lots of them took advantage of the distress of the

Jews and asked for bribes in exchange for certified documents. We were forced to reach to an arrangement to pay them a monthly salary to leave our people be.

After delays and difficulties the name of the would-be emigrant was submitted to the Iraqi Government, for the revoking of his citizenship and in exchange the travel documents were signed and transferred to the Mesouda Shemtob Synagogue, which had been converted into an exit camp. All the activities that took place in the airline offices were also handled there. On its outer walls we would advertise the flight schedules with the names of the travellers listed for each plane and tell them to prepare themselves. The synagogue street was humming with people: Families preparing for travel, companions and relatives bidding them farewell and several curious bystanders coming to pry. The crowd drew many peddlers selling food, drinks and knick-knacks.

When the traveller's name was announced he would present himself with his luggage before the Treasury Committee which would investigate his financial situation and fix the cost of his flight ticket. The committee consisted of two respected merchants and a representative from the personnel of the emigration department. At first no free flights were offered. Needy members were kept back until a solution for financing their journey could be found. Efforts were made to collect money from the community, but this met with little success.

When the various registration procedures were completed, we would weigh the luggage of each traveller so as to prevent abuse and humiliation at the customs check-point later on. There were occasions when travel documents had to be left in the synagogue because their owners were not ready to leave. These documents were then returned to the police. Those who were prepared for departure waited in the synagogue for the plane. They were given sandwiches and drinks, but there were times when the plane was delayed and the travellers were forced to sleep in the synagogue. Hundreds of people were huddled together and, having no other option, we were obliged to convert the synagogue into a real camp with gates, sleeping areas, kitchen, showers, clinic and a store. All the departments required many workers and these amounted to more than 40. I would visit there occasionally but only those in authority knew who I was.

We would meet every evening in order to summarize the working day and plan for the next.

One of the reasons for conflict within the community was the result of notes received from the leaders asking us to hasten the departure of someone, or to fly needy families for free. This the Movement personnel resisted fearing anger would erupt in the community. We kept the queue in order as best we could and only the Halutz members and their families and former prisoners received priority. We did this for two reasons:

a) We assumed that owing to the risks of working for the underground movement and considering the danger of their possible arrests by the Secret Police, we had to get them out of the country as soon as we could. After the crisis of 1951 it became clear that we had acted wisely.

b) We wanted to create in Israel a nucleus of Hebrew-speaking, trained activists who had enlarged their knowledge on Israel and its institutes so that they could be of help in the absorption of immigrants into Israeli life. This reasoning was certainly justified; they assisted the absorption staff at the airport and in the camps, and many of them were eventually retained in the Israeli defense and intelligence services. But, the priority given to Movement members infuriated the other emigrants and some members of the community.

When the news of the arrival of a plane was announced, we would transfer the travellers straight to the airport. The customs people would receive them, check their luggage and occasionally they were made to strip, and searched for hidden valuables. The emigrants was allowed to keep a wedding ring, watch and a cherished bracelet only. The customs authorities even slashed into their suitcases probing for any forbidden objects. Khaki clothes and prohibited objects were removed and dumped onto a pile for delivery to the synagogue, where the relatives of the emigrant would come and collect them. We stored these in a special room which contained a table and upon which rested a

Pentateuch. Everyone who came to claim something had to swear on the Pentateuch that he was truly a relative.

The emigrant was allowed to take with him a cheque of 50 Dinars, each Dinar being worth 4 dollars, amounting to 200 dollars. The rest of his possessions he would have to sell at a great loss. Lots of them smuggled money abroad, and it happened occasionally that this was stolen from them and the families left destitute. There were those who smuggled their money through the Halutz Movement and received it on their arrival in Israel. Some of them bribed a policeman or a customs officer to help them smuggle out packs of gold and diamonds. As the examination of the suitcases became more vigilant, we decided to bribe the customs people and the police. We began to offer them money which superseded government pay. Each officer was given 60 Dinars a month, and when new ones were appointed they would demand 500 Dinars per month and that was twenty times greater than his original salary. But we had no other choice but to think of the welfare of the travellers and to shield them from abuse.

This wasn't all. We received telegrams from Israel that many of the immigrants couldn't find their suitcases on arrival. We secretly followed the bus that transported them to the airport and found out that porters would eject their suitcases (tied to the roof of the bus) onto the street and these would be collected by their accomplices. We soon stopped the theft.

After crossing the custom's check-point the emigrants had to wait, sometimes for hours – under Baghdad's scorching sun – until the plane was ready to embark. We supplied them with sandwiches and drinks but it wasn't sufficient for their needs. I gave instructions for the purchase of a large tent, which cost 400 Dinars, to shelter the waiting emigrants. I was remiss in not consulting beforehand with the treasurer of the Mossad Le-Aliya, Edik Gur, a member of Kibbutz Merhavia, who was really a very fine and warmhearted man, but had no idea of the terrible conditions in Baghdad. The tent I purchased made him furious and he sent me a telegram, critical and reprimanding. I told him, among other things, to: "Take a glass of cold water and pour it over your head," and this made him so angry that Moshe Carmil had to interfere, calm him down and explain the difficult conditions with which we were faced.

After all these vexations, the emigrants, about a hundred people for each flight, boarded the plane completely exhausted and flew off to Cyprus. The flight schedules weren't under our control. They were handled by Rony Barnett, who represented the company, and I appointed I.D. Sofer to be our contact man. A staff technicians was selected to maintain our planes at Baghdad airport.

Each planeload carried an Iraqi police officer, whose job was to ensure that the planes didn't continue on to Lydda. The officer was persuaded to enjoy tempting diversions in Nicosia, and while doing so and unknown to him, the plane would take off for Israel and return to Nicosia soon after. Only in the final stages of the Operation were direct flights from Baghdad to Israel permitted.

Upon their arrival, the immigrants were received by, among others, the Movement activists, who were among the first to be sent out at the start of the Operation.

# Chapter 11

# POLITICAL MANEUVERINGS

The Halutz Movement in Iraq consisted of three branches. The first was the Movement, which dealt with youth indoctrination and training headed by an emissary from the Middle East Department of the Jewish Agency; he was in fact appointed on behalf of Kibbutz Meuhad. The second was the Shura (Hagana), headed by an emissary from the same department of the Jewish Agency, who was also working on behalf of Kibbutz Meuhad, but professionally subordinate to Yigal Alon, the man in charge of the Hagana in Middle Eastern countries. And the third was the Immigration Committee, which was controlled by emissaries of Mossad Aliya Bet, most of whom were members of the Mapai Party. Although the political party affiliation of the emissaries did not intrude on activities in the Movement, its effect was certainly obvious in talks between the indoctrination emissaries and the senior instructors, that mainly centred around ideological problems.

The emissaries of Mossad Aliya Bet, who worked for the emigration campaign, tried to concentrate on the mission for the sake of which they came to Baghdad, and refrained from spreading an ideology among the activists. I also thought that I had come to Iraq to deal with Jewish emigration only and not with political activities, but when I arrived in Baghdad I found out that I was linked to set opinions regarding my affiliation to Mapai (the local instructors didn't know that I was a member of the Halutz). The heavy transgression which lay on my shoulders was my participation in the Youth Mapai Seminar, which was held in

Beit Hakerem in Jerusalem in 1947 and directed by Haim Ben-Asher, a member of the Jewish Brigade, one of the founders of Kibbutz Givat Brenner and a Member of the First Knesset. Even though my mission in Iraq only started in 1949 and although my assignment there had no connection whatsoever with that Seminar, it became clear to me, much to my surprise, that I was the subject of an extensive exchange of letters in Israel among the senior instructors of the Halutz Movement who, after emigrating to Israel, turned into fanatic supporters of Ahdut Ha'avoda, true to the notorious spirit of fanaticism of those days.

For the sake of consideration only, I bring before you a paragraph of a letter from Gideon Golani, who is today a well-known professor in town planning and currently lives in the United States. This letter was sent on 18 June 1947:

> Two members of the Movement who participated in the Seminar of the Mapai are: Abraham Shamash and Mordechai Kazaz (my previous name) who are to be sent to Baghdad soon. They are only waiting for our blessing. It is quite clear that these two will cause the Movement such aggravation as we have not previously experienced and which is an unnecessary irritant. I, myself, cannot bear to think of it, and if ever this matter is followed up, I will use my influence and friendship in all the branches over there to put thing right and explain our moves in writing after we determine our future attitude with the Halutz Committee.

> ...Can we keep this quiet?

This item was written by a young, over-enthusiastic instructor who immigrated to Israel and joined Kibbutz Ashdot Yaacov. His behaviour gave me lots of aggravation while fulfilling my duties in Iraq. In all my time there, my activities were attended by agitation and incitement against me by old instructors of the Movement and the Shura, and perhaps with the encouragement of the emissaries of Kibbutz Hameuhad. After the crisis of 1949 the status of the emissaries diminished in the eyes of the instructors. Every suggestion the emissaries made was met with lots of dissension from local instructors. I was a thorn in their flesh as I headed the immigration operation, and they, who for years founded and supported the Halutz Movement, weren't among those who took decisions and managed the campaign. This matter is propounded, for instance, in a letter which the chief instructors in the Movement sent to the Mossad Aliya on 10 June 1950:

Dear Friends,

The situation of our emissaries has always been known to you: their lack of orientation, the lack of coordination in their various jobs, and insufficient maturity in taking decisions regarding priorities. All these have had an influence on the course of their work and the Jewish attitude towards the Movement. We know, that the main responsibility in directing this Judaic influence imposed on us, and because of it we don't have the authority to take decisions on matters dealing with our work.

From our experience in the Movement we learned that it is prohibited for any person to make decisions or take control of any matters. This method has proved a failure and has caused great damage. For instance, here, the emigration of most of the instructors in times of crisis was decided by two emissaries who were on the spot at the time. We know that this decision nearly damaged the fabric of the Movement [...]

From previous experience in times of crisis we learnt to fight for our participation in debates and decisions [...] it is obvious that we can't be responsible for what others decide. We feel that some of these emissaries lack complete devotion and their work is far from competent.

In order to grapple with these matters we met with the emissaries several times and asked them to change their attitude, but some of them utterly refused [...] because of this position, we detect signs of internal crisis and conflict between the emissaries and the members, a fact that would endanger all our lives and also affect the problem of mass emigration.

We are hereby giving, in general, a description of each emissary:

"Zaki" [Ben-Porat]: seems full of energy in his work, but his method is arbitrary and dictatorial. He doesn't consult us or any other emissary and decides everything on his own. He considers himself the only responsible person there is and the only one who has the right to make decisions in matters relating to emigration. Because of this, the project will suffer and we have lots of arguments with him.

"Jamil" [Raphael Sourani]: We don't know exactly what he does, but we can say that he is unable to shoulder responsibility as he ought to do. He acts indifferently to various issues and is weak in times of crisis. He is one of the reasons why "Zaki" took over. It may be said that he doesn't make plans and hasn't a fixed line of thinking.

"Uziel": His co-workers suffer from his churlish behaviour and inattention to the seriousness of his work.

"Kamal" [Yoav Goral]: He came to us a few weeks ago, but has quickly learned the ropes regarding his indoctrination work. He showed signs of energy and dedication. We cannot understand, nor can we grasp, how the others can be satisfied with inexperienced and unskillful emissaries like these, and put them in charge of the destiny of the Movement and the Jewish people at such an historical turning point and to oversee the massive emigration taking place [...] We plead especially with the Department of Middle Eastern Affairs, the Halutz and Youth Department, the General Secretariat of Kibbutz Hameuhad, the Office of Babylonian Relations and the veterans of the Movement in Israel to put an end to this unsatisfactory situation soon.

Yours faithfully,
United Institutions of Tnua and Shura

One does not have to be a famous commentator to realize that in that letter, the instructors clearly described the deteriorating situation afflicting their relations with the emissaries from Israel.

As for their relationship with the community, from my first day in Iraq I was warned, and also tried as best I could to refrain from any confrontation and to cooperate with them in order to obtain assistance from them in time of need. This attitude was mingled with anxiety and objection from the Halutz Movement Institutions, but I didn't let it influence my work. I felt it was important to have a contact between the Movement and the community so as to preserve the interests of Israel and any benefit I may receive from the community. Later on I found out how difficult it was going to be to fulfil this objective.

I started to build up the emigration office in this climate. I recruited activists from the members of the Movement and outsiders, and there were also among them those who, like Eitan Shamash and Gourgey Shasha, kept away from the Movement because of tensions within it; after much effort on my part I succeeded in recruiting them.

Naturally, the community leaders who were involved in obtaining concessions from the Iraqi Government would also try to direct the emigration themselves. Yousif, the son of Yehezkel Shemtob, together with two ex-officers of the Shura, David Shukur and Salim Khalifa, started on their own to organize the campaign ignoring us, the emigration emissaries, and Shemtob gave them a free hand (by the way, his second son Jamil supported us). They tried to fix the emigration schedule without using our facilities, such as the secret wireless centre, through which the campaign was coordinated; flights and finances were handled by them to provide cash for the various projects and to arrange flights for the poorer people. In my reports to Israel, I dubbed Shukur and Khalifa the "troublemakers" – and today I wouldn't even use this nickname – who incited Shemtob with all sorts of rumours and slanders against me and the rest of the emigration activists, with whom I had built up an office and organized the campaign.

After the first two flights a delay of the execution of our plans took place. On 1 June 1950, around two weeks after those two flights, I sent a telegram to Israel informing them that the delays came from a small Iraqi Government department which still didn't approve of the project. Among them were the civil servants who were being influenced by the British Embassy: "We are involved with complications in every move we make, fighting bitterly against the authorities. We recruited all the friends we have to ease the formalities in the various departments. The delays are emerging really from the financial departments. About forty officers and sergeants and twenty customs personnel are striving to execute the Law and are also dealing with the exodus. Thirty-five members of the Movement are working with the authorities on a volunteer basis with stops only for lunch and dinner."

On 7 June I reported to Mossad Aliya Bet on the damage they were doing to our activities following their efforts to create conflict between us and the community leaders. I also reported that Rony Barnett and myself met with Shemtob in order to warn him of the results of not dealing with the needy people waiting for emigration. We told him that we had the means to advance the emigration, but because of secrecy in our work we couldn't let others handle this assignment. Saying this, I emphasized the good connections I had with Shemtob, who was still acting in place of Hakham Sasson Khadourie. "I can't describe the support he gives us," I wrote, "as I would need reams of papers to do so. We have succeeded in keeping him away from the conservative attitude of the community and involving him in our more enlightened outlook. This didn't sit well with most of the people in the Executive of the Movement, and several of them began to oppose him. We are always trying to gain support for him by our people. We fostered his belief that he was the only one who works for our people and the community, being careful not to create an abyss between him and the Executive."

On 28 June Rony Barnett sent a very detailed report from Baghdad, which gave a full description of the climate surrounding the campaign. Herein are some sections of it:

> On Thursday, 15.6.50, Members of Parliament passed a motion stating that the bill permitting the Jews to leave Iraq ought to be annulled. This bill has been passed by a majority, which showed the change in attitude of many of the citizens towards the Jews.
>
> Parliament was assembled on Sunday, and the Prime Minister, who was then in Cairo together with Saleh Jaber, sent word through his representative, that the Government would discuss this bill if the public would offer the Jews full citizens' rights, a response that kept them quiet until Thursday, 22 June. On that day, voices of the Opposition raised the question of "the Jews only selecting highly-qualified technicians, chemists, engineers and nurses for departure," in short the most able youngsters who might eventually carry weapons against them, whilst on the other hand, they prevented the untrained ones who were absolutely not needed in Iraq from going. These defiant statements were denounced

when the Prime Minister and Jaber returned. Nevertheless both of them were bothered by those remarks: On the other hand the Prime Minister argued that if they wanted to accelerate the exit operation, they had to support and expand it to a point where enough Jews would leave each day in order to complete the operation within a year. He emphasized that he had no intention whatsoever of bringing the matter up before Parliament again; if those people didn't leave within a year then the exodus could be halted right away. Harsh criticism came from Minister of the Interior Saleh Jaber, who was responsible for the Customs, Emigration and the Police. The Arabic newspapers warned that "a delay in completing the emigration program would give Israel time to chose the most desirable immigrants and leave the rest as a burden for Iraq." Because of the pressure on him, and personal considerations, Jaber finally agreed to take action.

A special committee was formed with the approval of the Prime Minister. Five out of sixteen senior clerks in Baghdad were appointed to take on their new jobs – preparing documents for the emigrating Jews.

The Regent came back from his vacation in Mosul on 19 June and immediately revoked the citizenship of 2,000 people by having their 850 passports stamped. Another time the Council of Ministers refused to authorize the handling of 5,000 passports, explaining that they couldn't risk revoking the citizenship of such a large number of Jews at one time, which would bring the emigration from Iraq to a standstill. The Regent has left for Amman with Saleh Jaber and will be back on 4 July. Until then we must stop issuing flight documents; it seems that there will be delays of two or three days without passengers. [...]

As for our progress regarding direct flights to Israel: On my return to Baghdad on 15 June, I immediately called Kassem, the man in touch with the Minister of the Interior, in order to clarify the reaction of Jaber to my offer of paying 1,250 Dinars per month if we managed a hundred flights, and 3,500 Dinars if the flights went directly to Israel. He informed us that Jaber showed very little interest in the scheme. I couldn't call him personally as he was at that time in Cairo. When he came back I met him privately, just the two of us, and made the following suggestions:

1.  We need to fly straight to Israel and we are ready to pay a poll tax, a Dinar on every passport to the Iraqi Government for this privilege.

2.  The Iraqi Government has lots of land which is not being used and its development is held in abeyance as there is a shortage of workers and money for equipment, investments, etc. Many competent farmers, who can be selected, are to be found among the Palestinian refugees in the Gaza Strip. I made an offer to a group of wealthy entrepreneurs and also to the Iraqi Government to pay a premium of 15 dollars for any worker they accepted from the Gaza Strip. It is a doubly profitable deal for them – money offered for the Jews emigrating and for the Arabs entering the country. In addition to this, I promised that I would get enough money from the Palestinian Refugee Committee, or from the International Bank, to finance this plan [...]

Two hours later I had a visit from Yehya Kassem, who was the special adviser to Jaber, in order to discuss with me, in minute detail, the possibilities of this novel suggestion. He said that His Excellency was very interested in anything that would contribute to the progress of Iraq. And better still, a private company could act far quicker than the Government, as it would have more freedom; besides that, the Government needed money for its current activities.

I persuaded Shemtob to be in touch with Jaber and Kassem in order to minimize Kassem's participation as a broker. Shemtob said openly that his influence on Jaber was very slight and, in his opinion, Jaber might be more interested in doing business with American participation rather than the British. He then said that Jaber offered to try.

Meanwhile, Shemtob got the consent of the Prime Minister over all the suggestions or alternatively, to anyone Jaber would support. For four days they showed great enthusiasm for the agricultural scheme. They called five representatives sent by Iraqi Sheiks regarding the two thousand Palestinian refugees, but on behalf of their people they

absolutely refused to discuss the matter of granting them Iraqi
nationality. This was a hard blow. Meanwhile they called Cairo and
received an absolutely negative reply regarding the acceptance of planes
with passengers on the way to Lydda [...]

After his second meeting with Jaber, Shemtob recommended that we
should try and raise 50,000 Dinars for distribution to different parties:
nearly one third for the Prime Minister, a third to Jaber and a third to be
shared between two or three important Ministers chosen from a group of
seven attending Nouri El-Sa'id.

We are of the opinion that if we find a way to deal with El-Sa'id, all
our problems will be solved. I haven't been able to contact him as he is
now in London. I informed Shemtob that 50,000 Dinars is out of the
question; the maximum I could obtain is 10,000 Dinars, and also that I
would not pay until the promises had been fulfilled. Shemtob came over
the next day and said that he would need at least 20,000 Dinars and
that he would be responsible to refund the money if the promises weren't
realized.

The Prime Minister is ready to permit direct flights to Israel, if only
we can arrange a representative from Iran, Greece, Italy or Jordan to sign
on the records of the manifestos that the passengers were delayed
somehow in one of those countries. It didn't matter what was written in
the flight records; the important thing was to record it in the manifestos.
Two hours later, Kassem came to see me and said that Jaber was leaving
for Amman with the Regent ("if the matter could be arranged while His
Excellency was abroad, he wouldn't mind"). Shemtob also said that with
the absence of Jaber, he would urge the Prime Minister to submit a bill to
permit us to fly directly to Israel, in exchange for compensation paid to
the Iraqi Government. This bill may prove to be very popular, as people
usually think that apart from the Government, everyone is receiving
money for the departure of the Jews, while the Government, on the other
hand, is in such bad shape that it cannot even cover its current expenses
[...]

While the community leaders were trying to increase their influence and persuade the Iraqi leaders to obtain permits for direct flights to Israel, we continued with the field work. On 30 June, I sent the following telegram to Israel: "From the day I arrived and even in my first report, I asked you to try and straighten out relations between the Movement and the community by increasing the meetings and drawing their leaders together. With that I could have acquired the confidence of the wealthy and important people of the community, and besides, I could have resolved many problems that threatened the emigration policy and the security of the Movement and its members. The Movement establishment and its members want to poke their noses into everything the community does. Businessmen, who up till now were indifferent to the Movement, are cooperating today, thanks to such contacts. The Movement requested two weeks ago that I contact its members before every meeting I have with community leaders and Shemtob, Abraham El-Kabir etc. They declared that as I am an emissary of the Movement and acting on its behalf, I had to get the opinion of its members even though it was against my understanding…"

The members of the Movement establishment wished to be involved with the registration of all the emigrants, receive the lists of all those who served us in various fields and even those who were supported by the Movement members. The situation has become insupportable. I had to work incessantly to settle disagreements between the members of Mossad Le Aliya and of the Movement, or between the individuals of the Mossad, and the most difficult of all, between them and community leaders. In Basra, a bitter dispute has erupted between the emissary Uziel Levy and community leaders. The tension has reached such a pitch that the president, Yaacov Khemara, threatened to disclose the identity of the Movement and its members to the police. I invited him to Baghdad and met him in the presence of I.D. Sofer and, fearing that he would carry out his threat, we filmed him without his knowledge. We finally reached an understanding and, in order to remove all obstacles, I left for Basra, assembled the community leaders together with Uziel Levy and the members of the Movement of the Basra branch, and at last we came to a joint decision to advance the registration and the emigration. But this didn't last long and after

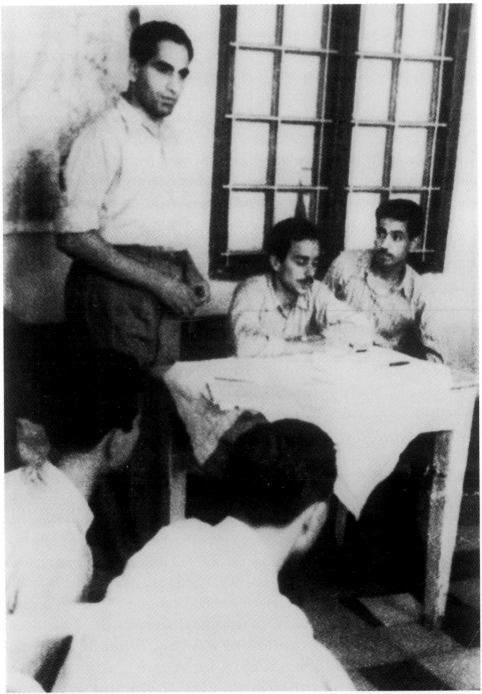

*Mordechai Ben-Porat giving a lecture to the Shura instructors in Baghdad.*

awhile the community leaders in Basra informed us that they would stop their dealings with Uziel Levy, as the authorities were watching him closely.

We had a problem in Basra concerning the members of the emigration committee who had completed their jobs. As they were wanted by the police and we couldn't fly them out legally, I insisted on smuggling them through Iran. We met together to conclude the matter at the house of someone who dealt with the smuggling of emigrants, and after few minutes of talks we heard a suspicious noise outside the house. It seemed that someone had informed on the landlord, and the police barged in. They began to look for smuggled merchandise. A police officer, with a scowling face, stood by the door and arrested every one who entered. An Arab driver who dropped in, to return some money he owed the landlord, was also arrested. The number of people arrested, apart from family members, came to twelve. I was among them.

I was examined and identified myself as Nissim Moshe Mandelawy, whose name I had already adopted after living in Baghdad with his family. I claimed that I came to Basra on behalf of the community in Baghdad in order to raise money for the poor people who wished to emigrate and, as it was Ramadan, when it is forbidden to eat or smoke in public, I entered the house to have a smoke. My testimony was supported by Shemtob. Also for the rest of the prisoners, testimonies had been coordinated. After an arrest of one week I was released on bail of one hundred and fifty Dinars. I returned to Baghdad, and there I was told that Shemtob was fed up with the members of the Halutz and also of his friends in the Executive and decided to resign. I pleaded with him not to do so. The Mossad in Tel Aviv understood that procedures in Iraq were not that simple, that the community leaders were not making it any easier for us and we, the emissaries, had to bribe the Iraqi people with whom we worked; nevertheless, they asked bureaucratic questions all over again. When they understood from my reply that they had pulled the rope too tightly and that I would ask for a release from my job in Baghdad and return to Israel, they tried to humour me by offering to bring my girlfriend Rivca to Iraq. On 13 July 1950 I sent word to Rivca not to come to Baghdad due to the instability of the political situation.

Among the complicated problems that were handed to us, a new one was created: One evening in July, when Yitzhak Eliash remained at the airport to deal

*Naim Moshe Mandelawy (Mostash).*

*Ishak Eliash.*

with preparations for the flight of the emigrants, Sofer called from the Mesouda Shemtob Synagogue to the airport office and told Eliash these words, in code: "Your uncle is sick and needs a doctor. I will send you a taxi and Edward Shahrabani will replace you."

Eliash went straight to Sofer, and together they came to meet me. I took out of my sock a tattered copy of a letter signed by the Prime Minister Nouri El-Sa'id and forwarded to the Minister of Defense, Shaker El-Wadi. He ordered him to start resuscitating the National Service Law on the Jews. I said that I feared that this would delay thousands of families from emigrating as they would never think of leaving without their sons.

Eliash was optimistic and asked to let him try and have this bad decree lifted. He said that every Friday Colonel Moukhlutz, Commander General of Mobilization, was invited to the house of Sasson Abed, who was Chairman of the Public Emigration Committee, and he would attempt to see him there and ask for his assistance.

On Thursday, Eliash called Abed and told him everything and he agreed that the next day, Eliash would visit at 11:00 o'clock when Colonel Moukhlutz was present. Eliash arrived and was introduced to the Colonel as a community worker dealing with the emigration of the Jews. The Colonel was interested in the registration and tempo of the flight traffic, and Eliash answered his questions. During the conversation, he mentioned the mobilization order that came from "police sources." The Colonel corroborated it and Eliash remarked that this act wasn't for the benefit of the country; that young Jews would be trained with weapons in Iraq and then would later leave for Palestine and might become involved in conflicts with Iraqi soldiers.

Colonel Moukhlutz thought it over and acknowledged the wisdom of the person to whom he was speaking. Eliash suggested that when Moukhlutz met with the Minister of the Defense he should propose appointing a committee consisting of himself, the General Manager of the Interior Office and the Director of Police to discuss the matter and present a report to the Minister of Defense.

At the same time Eliash assembled details on the background of Colonel Moukhlutz's family. It seemed that he was married without children, lived in El-Athamia and kept a Jewish mistress living in Ghazi Street. He also bought a car recently and was still owing 400 Dinars on it. This information was enough for Eliash. He took care to cover the loan and rented a house for him where he could visit his mistress.

A few days later, Eliash called Moukhlutz, gave the agreed code and was asked to come to his office. Moukhlutz gave him the good news, that the Committee had a meeting regarding the decree and decided to give the Jews an exemption. On 14 July I reported to the Mossad: "This comes from the Ministry of Defense. The Government decided not to delay the mobilization of the Jews, although there will be no official pronouncement on the matter."

On 19 July, Rony Barnett wrote down his personal views in a letter to Moshe Carmil:

> I am sure some sort of crisis will develop here if the policy of the deceleration of the flights continues. Although I value very much the reasons put forward for this step, the outcome of this is that the situation is becoming untenable. I am receiving complaints from all sides. All the time we have been pressing them to collect more people, and now, when they are ready, we are not supplying planes to take them.

Threats have been received that if we don't send enough planes they will find other planes to carry out the flights, which is a clear signal, that for you the flights will cease. They are preparing 150 documents a day [...] 2,500 travel documents will soon be ready [...] 386 people are waiting, parked on their suitcases in Khanakin and hoping for an immediate exit the minute they hear that the planes are ready. We may lose control over all matters if the number of planes were to be reduced drastically. What will happen if an interruption occurs – I hate to think about it.

Two weeks later Rony Barnett wrote again:

I returned this afternoon and found the situation even worse than I thought. This isn't just an "alarm." It is a fact and should be accepted and dealt with with the utmost urgency. If we don't double our flights and complete at least three flights a day – two from Baghdad and one from Basra – flight control will be taken out of our hands and we will be in serious trouble. Upon my arrival at the airport, senior clerks reprimanded me. They, together with the manager of the civil airport, warned me for the last time that if we don't take the waiting passengers out, they will cancel all our planes and rights and will get other companies to do the job. They are convinced the reason is shortage of planes. The General Supervisor of Customs handed over the instructions they received from the Council of Ministers to arrange to fly 400-500 Jews a day. Similar instructions were also given to Major Abd-El-Aziz, Head of the Passport Department dealing with the emigrating Jews. The latter, with whom I have friendly relations, has warned me confidentially that a decision has been taken to cancel the flights if we don't take all the passengers who are ready [...] Rumours are spreading that Israel is reducing the air traffic. In Mesouda Shemtob Synagogue, where they are preparing the Jews for exit, things are becoming unmanageable. Six hundred people are crammed together. Four hundred of them were removed from Arbil by the authorities. The situation has become so bad that we were forced to call the police. Local Jews tell me that the Government fears anti-Jewish riots if this continues. I think I have a

powerful reason now to continue the negotiations with the Government
and to ask for direct flights.

As time went by, the discussions deteriorated between the members of the
Shura Movement and the emissaries dealing with the emigration and also the
tension between us and Shemtob. The crisis reached its peak when the workers
from Mossad Hameuhad of the Movement and the Shura ordered members of
the Movement who dealt with the emigration campaign to resign, and this they
did. One bright day we found out that most of the Movement activists simply
didn't turn up for work.

Officers of the Iraqi police who were working with us were astonished and
remarked sarcastically: "What has happened? Where are the people from the
Movement?"

We answered with embarrassment that they had a party the night before, ate
tainted meat which brought on stomach ache and diarrhea. But it was obvious
that they didn't believe us.

I immediately decided to print an advertisement among our people seeking
qualified clerks suitable for the job to work for us on a salary basis. The replies
were gratifying, and we succeeded in overcoming the difficulties and were then
able to carry on with the work. But those incidents, and especially the shaky
relations with Shemtob, made me conclude that certain steps had to be taken in
order to stem the tide. It was clear to me that Shemtob wasn't sure, because of
slanders on one side and a need for secrecy and divisions on the other, that I was
the one qualified to handle the campaign on behalf of the Israeli Government.

On 17 July 1950, I approached the Mossad, described the incidents and
requested that they stop the flights for a few days. The following reply was
immediate:

a) You know that we are supporting your position to implement the
surveillance and complexities of the emigration, its organization and
all its financial matters.

b) You have to make genuine efforts to explain everything to Shemtob
with understanding and tact. You have to stop participating in

financing the emigration and its costs since you have to explain how the money is being spent: Without your active supervision and control of these matters you must not allow yourselves to take on any form of liability.

c) Work hard to keep Shemtob away from the troublemakers and try to win him over.

d) Threatening is easy, but one should consider what will happen if we are forced to make threats; how will it influence matters, who will suffer and what are the benefits?

e) Is it worth it to write him a letter?

f) Tell him once again that we want him to meet us without delay, in Cyprus or some other destination.

On 18 July I sent a telegram to the Mossad:

We thank you for your support.

a) Bear in mind that our relations with Shemtob are excellent and the man is very dear to us, but his sudden change of attitude leaves us with no hope. We are behaving with the utmost restraint. We explained everything to him.

b) We are dealing with paragraph C with full energy. We may succeed.

c) We thought at first to delay the plane and its passengers in Cyprus, but now we prefer you not to send a plane for few days, in order to show him your support for us. This will be a lesson to all the people in charge and those who may take on the duties after him. This is the only weapon we have left to us.

d) Yes, it is worthwhile sending him a letter with an official Israeli address and to thank him for his work, and also to tell him that he has to cooperate with us as representatives of the Mossad.

e) Regarding your request to see him in Cyprus, we shall call him today, but we are doubtful he will agree.

All of a sudden the flights were halted. I was sure that they were stopped as I requested, and on 18 July I thanked the Mossad for their support, but on the next day, on Wednesday, 19 July, I received a telegram stating: "We are very sorry that despite our orders, a plane was sent to you yesterday." The flights were stopped for three days and then renewed on Saturday evening, 21 July 1950. Only after awhile was I informed that the reason for the stoppage was technical failure, and that was what was told to Shemtob; whether this was the truth or an attempt to appease him, I had no way of knowing.

On 19 July, Rony Barnett and myself met with Shemtob in order to inform him about the Mossad's request to meet him. When I explained to him the unfortunate results that were likely to occur with an extension of the conflict, I was shocked to hear him say:

"Six million Jews have gone; let another hundred thousand go."

"If this is your answer, then you ought to resign!" I said rudely and with fury.

He snatched his *sidara* from his head and dashed it furiously to the floor.

We left the place shocked and fuming.

The next telegram that I sent to the Mossad on 20 July was written, following the harsh dialogue we had with Shemtob.

a) There is no hope that Shemtob will cooperate with us again. Barnett, who was with me at the meeting yesterday, expressed his views after we left, that the man was not quite normal and rather a fanatic.

b) We appointed an eminent person to replace him – Moshe Shohet, Deputy General of the Railway Stations. He has significant contacts with Saleh Jaber and others, and also with the British. He is respected by all the community. We are watching developments re our relations with him.

c) It is clear to us if Shemtob agrees to fully cooperate in management and control, we will work with him, but we have to show our annoyance.

d) Shemtob has mentioned several times that he is afraid to cooperate with us, especially now, as there are rumours of the resignation from the government of his friend Towfik El-Suweidi. He claims that if they accuse him of supporting the Zionists, he will lose his influence with the Government.

In another telegram on the same day, I explained that the troublemakers surrounding Shemtob told him many times that they could contact Israel directly regarding financial matters and could bring in their own clerks to do the job. I also explained that he was doubtful whether we were really qualified representatives of the Mossad and because of that we advised you to stop the planes for two days, in order to prove to him and the community that without us the work could not be accomplished. In another telegram, which I sent a day later, I explained the necessity of a meeting between Shemtob and leaders of the Mossad Le Aliya, and on 27 July I wrote:

a)  The connection with Shemtob has been discontinued.

b)  Walter [James Wouton, owner of the Alaskan Airlines, which flew the Yemenite Jews to Israel in 1948-1949, and who consequently founded the Near East Overseas Airlines with El Al and Zim as partners] did not contribute to healthy relations between Shemtob and ourselves, possibly due to my refusal to cooperate with him and take his bribes, and promised Shemtob that I would be replaced, which planted many delusions in his breast. This same man was asked by me to talk to Shemtob, and try to persuade him to meet with the Mossad's agents.

c)  Despite my hope that things would straighten out, Abraham El-Kabir and Moshe Shohet informed me this morning that there is no hope whatsoever that Shemtob would cooperate with us and that he must be replaced.

d)  The lists of the members of the Movement have been completed five weeks ago: We have no control over them.

e)  I have to clarify our requests to Shemtob:
    1.  To give us priority to manage the suggested lists for the Revocation of Citizenship every week.

2. To allow each week a 4% quota for families of the members of the Movement and ex-prisoners.

3. To establish an overall supervising committee to discuss every matter, with our participation, and we will accept their judgment.

4. To dismiss the troublemakers.

These requests are supported by: Senator Ezra Menahem Daniel, Abraham El-Kabir, Moshe Shohet, Yaacov Shlomo and Sasson Abed. They are prominent members of the community.

In the meantime Shemtob hoped to hear from Wooten about my replacement, who could then give him overall responsibility, but when the planes were stopped he understood the message, realized his mistake and sent a delegation to inform us of his agreement to accept our conditions in order to end the conflict. Meanwhile, his good friend, Senator Daniel, asked him to resign. He did so and a committee was appointed, composed of Moshe Shohet, Meir Basri, Abdallah Shina and Naim Shamash. This committee took over all responsibilities for the community. On 1 August I sent a telegram which ended with these words: "We are worried by the replacement of Shemtob. I, with my own hands, built up good relations with him. It wasn't easy to achieve this. I did not stand on my dignity and sometimes I disregarded my prestige for the benefit of the cause."

The relations with the community leaders in general and with Shemtob in particular, were the main topics in my letter to Moshe Carmil, sent on 6 August 1950, which I think it right to quote here in full:

...From the beginning of June an edginess crept in between Shemtob and ourselves when we asked him nicely:

a) To dismiss the troublemakers and especially the two senior instructors of the Shura [Shukur and Khalifa], who after finishing their job and two days before their emigration were rehired by Shemtob.

b) To give us the privilege of participating in the supervision of the weekly list in order to prevent bribery and favouritism.

These two conditions were well understood by the emissaries and the Movement, but Shemtob then asked to delay adopting them for a week. I agreed to his request in order not to annoy him, and also explained my reasons to the Mossad, who then requested we handle him firmly. I explained that I was not allowed to play with the fate of the emigrants and the Jewish people, without serious reasons […] We have to strengthen ties as much as possible with the community and all its eminent people in order that they stand by us in time of crisis […] This was met with intense disapproval from the Movement and especially the emissaries, but later on, after understanding the situation they followed me step by step.

In middle of June, manifestos of the Movement were published [where they attacked community institutes], and Shemtob claimed that I was the one to blame and that I was losing control (because he had no idea at all what the emissaries were required to do and also from which office I was sent), as we always appeared before him myself and the community leaders as one solid figure. Shemtob refused to meet us again. I phoned him at home and explained that we were playing with fire and asked him to meet us in two hours time to clear up the misunderstandings. He asked if he might bring Doron (Rony Barnett) with him.

We met at Sofer's house and after a two hour conversation we established the following:

a) The manifesto had been circulated without my knowledge and I promised him that I would investigate the matter, and until then we asked him to keep quiet on this.

b) To receive the weekly report of the Movement.

c) To replace one of the officers in the synagogue, who is a member of the Movement and who had several disputes with the community clerks.

d) To dismiss the troublemakers; he told me, however, that he couldn't do it himself for private reasons and handed the job to me.

I immediately called the two and told them clearly that they were harming our cause and that they had to leave the office quietly for their own good. They requested an extension of a week to prove to us their remorse and said that although they might outwardly appear to be against us, nevertheless they would act according to our instructions.

I agreed naively to this plea and their request for an extension (anyway I had no other choice, as I didn't want to dismiss them brusquely, not wanting to upset Shemtob).

I then met Abraham El-Kabir. This was the first time that an emissary ever met him. The man listened carefully, was very cordial and promised to try and settle the dispute with Shemtob. He met with several people in order to apply pressure on Shemtob. As a result, a meeting was fixed between Shemtob and myself in the presence of Moshe Shohet and Salman Shahrabani. I told Shemtob that I was ready to hear all his claims and promised, in front of the two, that I would immediately repair any mistakes they came across. He claimed: "Your organization is not good and your people are accepting money." I asked him to bring me evidence that some people, by offering bribes, had priority in the queue of the weekly rota, and suggested that he appoint a committee consisting of three people to supervise daily, in the synagogue, the manner in which the Revocation of Citizenship lists were being handled, and in addition to appoint together a joint committee to supervise the lists in his office.

The outcome was very logical and was approved by the two people present, but he did not agree at all and said that he intended to change the whole system of work. I said that I would accept this on condition that the work did not suffer and the network that was built up by the sweat of our brows would not be damaged. Secondly, the new clerks must work under the same conditions as ours; and as I was accountable to Israel for the finances – I wasn't ready to pay people who were not appointed by me.

Upon hearing this he jumped up from his seat and informed us that he would be responsible for all the emigration and finances and he didn't need us anymore. I asked him if he really wanted to take on all the responsibility and, he said "yes." One of the two present interrupted and warned him: "You cannot play with the fate of the Jewish people in this way; you have to discuss it with higher authority [meaning Senator Daniel]."

At this stage I told them that I had nothing to stay for and asked to leave. The two let me go and asked my forgiveness for the upset caused.

After the meeting it was decided between us that the three emissaries in Baghdad ought to meet with the community leaders and explain to them the dangers that might occur because of that decision. Senator Daniel requested that we let Shemtob work on his own for a week and then "he would be in ruins" and eventually accept the conditions. I didn't agree, claiming that I was not ready to take back a system in ruins. In addition to that, the police and the authorities would feel that something was wrong and would be surprised at the sudden replacement of the staff; and then if there was any suspicion that the staff were members of the Movement, they would now be certain and would take them all to prison. Therefore, I added, we must keep the jobs, and put pressure on Shemtob:

a) To stop helping the needy people for the time being.

b) If this didn't help, we would be forced to stop the planes for a short time as Israel couldn't accept immigrants without knowing their background. And, as representatives of Israel here and responsible for financial and emigration matters, I would never accept any responsibility regarding the emigration without full control over it.

The campaign to spread information continued for a week and the Institute explained it to all the prominent people, each one in turn, until we received the approval of all of them who promised to back us up until the dispute was settled.

During the debates there were frequent consultations between the emissaries and myself and the usual ones with the Movement. I informed them that I was sent on behalf of the Mossad Le Aliya; I only knew the emissaries who were sent from Israel and through them I usually got the opinion of the members of the Movement. They requested that we appoint someone to be their representative, to be present at all meetings. Apart from it being impractical and lacking relevance, I agreed to the suggestion for fear of a deep split my objection would incur. Shemtob sent four of his staff to undertake the job in the synagogue and as I was still hoping that things would settle down, I gave clear orders to those responsible to accept the workers and explain their duties to them, but I told the treasurer that no one other than Shemtob was to inspect the accounts.

The next day, Doron (Rony Barnett) called and informed us that he succeeded in fixing a meeting with Shemtob in his office. At the meeting, Doron, the translator, was also present. As Shemtob wasn't proficient in English and only Rony Barnett spoke English, he asked us to bring a translator on his behalf who turned out to be one of Shemtob's 'troublemakers'.

After the meeting, which lasted two and a half hours, where all the previous complaints were discussed again as was the manifesto of the Movement Institute, I declared once more that I was ready to do anything I could in order to resume the operation and thereby increase mutual understanding between us.

Shemtob informed us at the end of the meeting that he was going to resign and that we could continue with the work. Doron (Barnett) was very angry and left the meeting.

I asked Shemtob the following question: "I would like to know officially who is a dependable person in the community and with whom I can discuss the emigration matters that need immediate attention?"

He told me in an insolent manner that I wasn't the one and that I had to approach those leaders who were in the know […]

A day before renewing the flight activities, the leaders informed us that they could force Shemtob to resign and transfer the matters to a committee which would be represented by us, a committee that would accept our conditions retrospectively. We were very sorry for the change but we had no other choice. After the promise of the leaders that everything would be settled, we decided upon the renewal of the flights.

On the previous Friday, 4 August 1950, Senator Daniel sat together with Murad Jouri and Abraham Haim Akerib for the first time to resolve the problem of the community. After three weeks of talks exonerating the Movement and its assistants, they requested Shemtob to go back on his decision to resign (he was really keen to stay) and came to the conclusion that:

a) He had to accept our conditions;

b) He had to meet me and settle all misunderstandings.

c) He had to appoint a committee that would act under his management.

Abraham El-Kabir was sent to us officially to inform us of the results of the meeting, and my meeting with Shemtob was fixed for the next day, but he didn't appear. The meeting was postponed until Monday and again he didn't show up. We are now waiting to see what will happen.

We were informed today that Shemtob opposed our representative in the Committee and asked for his replacement. We agreed to this and we hope that the committee will now start to function once more.

The disagreements continued, although the planes were on their way, at an unsatisfactory pace. On 5 August, on flight No. 4, a very joyful incident was reported: A baby was born. On 6 January 1994, when the Babylonian Jewry Heritage Centre organized an evening of tribute to the pilots who helped to evacuate the Iraqi Jews, we found out that the baby had been a boy, named Israel David Cohen. The General Manager of El Al, Rafi Harlap, granted him a free ticket for life in the company.

Rony Barnett wrote to Moshe Carmil from Nicosia on 10 August 1950:

I arrived here from the "chaos," early in the morning. Thank God matters have settled down since I came back, but the tension is still there and the situation is far from improving. Everyday, the police are cramming thousands of Jews into Baghdad from the provincial cities. These people are huddled together in the big synagogues and other centres. Believe me, Zaki (Mordechai) is working like a real hero and is doing a great job under nearly impossible conditions and with very little support.

When I was in Baghdad I had a long talk with him and naturally Shemtob was the main topic. He spoke of the many difficulties that were placed in his way by him, that he refused to cooperate and even tried to prejudice the minds of influential people against him. I went to see Shemtob, hoping to invite him to meet our people in Europe as early as possible. After a two minute conversation I found out that he cared little about the serious situation regarding the emigration of our people; he was only interested in "when would Zaki be dismissed?" No reference whatsoever to the seriousness of the situation which ought to have taken priority over personal and legitimate complaints, none could alter his attitude. "Promise me," he said, "that Zaki (Mordechai) will be dismissed from here within ten days. As long as my request is not granted I will see no one."

As you know, he was influenced by others in the past. Though this stubborn stand now appears inexcusable, it is better that he stew for a while before we meet him. We have to show him clearly and decisively that Zaki has authority and he is completely supported (whether he is absolutely right or sometimes makes mistakes) by all the leaders of Israel. Otherwise, you can be equally justified in bringing him home and letting the local Iraqis manage their own affairs. However after watching him at work for the last four months it is inconceivable.

We go back to poor Zaki – and he is really resolute – he works until he is dead tired. I feel that he is developing an inferiority complex at this moment as he is not sure if he has the full support and acceptance of the leaders of Israel. He wants to meet you very much in Nicosia or Baghdad. What is needed, and I request you to do it, is to send him a very forthright telegram, where you stress that every leader in Israel backs him up one hundred per cent. It doesn't matter how many similar telegrams have been sent before; send him another encouraging one. This will cheer him up and his influence will then be much stronger than you think.

Now regarding your trip, if you ever decide to go to Baghdad this can be arranged. I am of the opinion that the legal way is the best.

The Foreign Affairs Ministry in Israel sent a telegram on 13 August to the Mossad and reported the conversation with Mr. M. Farid, the Labour Attaché at the American Embassy in Tel Aviv, regarding the restrictions put on the emigration in Baghdad. According to the report, Farid approached the Ministry for Foreign Affairs on 1 August and claimed that information had reached him from a reliable source on a resolution passed by the Government, or the Coordination Institute to stop the emigration from Iraq, or to curtail it. He made a remark that if there really was such a decision, it might cause serious complications in Iraq when it was revealed there. He asked for reliable information in order to transfer it as soon as possible to their Embassy in Baghdad.

Two weeks later, on 13 August, Farid again called at the Foreign Affairs Ministry and explained that the people in the American Embassy in Baghdad were very worried and feared for a new refugee problem in Iraq if the emigration of the Jews was ever stopped, especially since between 15,000 and 20,000 emigrants were in the process of liquidating their businesses and preparing to leave. It was explained to him that because of the international situation it was decided to give first priority to the immigration from Eastern Europe and therefore the monthly quota of immigrants from Iraq, North Africa, Turkey, etc. was curtailed, but there was no resolve at all to stop the emigration.

On the same day, Moshe Carmil brought Reuben Shiloah up-to-date; he was Director of the Bureau of Special Assignments in the Prime Minister's Office. The emissaries in Iraq informed him that the American Embassy was greatly worried about the exit of Jews in such large numbers, and a proposal was sent to Washington to curtail the Revocation of Citizenship. According to the present situation, the citizenship of one hundred and twenty Jews was to be revoked within three months. Carmil added that he asked the emissaries if such information had been checked, and their replies were: "The first sentence was spoken by Allen in the American Embassy in the presence of Jack Shaul, Editor of Iraq Times. And the last sentence – according to impressions received."

On the morning of 14 August, Shemtob left for Rome accompanied by his daughter. His mood was very bad due to the opposition of the influential people of the community towards him, including his friend, Senator Daniel. Shemtob hoped that after this voyage he would have me replaced. I asked the Mossad to let me come urgently to Israel, in one of our planes, to explain the situation and discuss it.

While waiting for an answer, the Executive of the community assembled to choose a President alongside Shemtob, who was also Chairman of the Committee. The community leaders asked for our intervention, but since the troublemakers and the Movement Institute were involved in the conflicts and fearing to complicate matters, we decided not to interfere.

Shemtob, while still in Rome, received a telegram from Baghdad stating that I was assisting in the election of a new leader. The Mossad in Paris asked the Mossad in Tel Aviv to send me an urgent telegram ordering me not to interfere. "This is our moral duty and promise given to Shemtob." The Mossad in Tel Aviv wired Shlomo Hillel, who was supposed to meet Shemtob, requesting him "to check Wouton's promise to dismiss Dror (Ben-Porat)."

Due to the complications within the Movement and with Shemtob, which upset me and also didn't permit me to act as I should, I approached the Mossad once again requesting an immediate private meeting anywhere they chose. I suggested flying to Israel in one of the planes taking the emigrants. Their reply, which only arrived on 18 August, was: "We have considered your intended arrival and we are of opinion that a visit to Israel cannot be kept a secret. Despite all the precautions, your visit will be known, and this will no doubt be broadcast in Berman [Baghdad] and the continuation of your work will be affected. Therefore, we have decided that the meeting should take place in Goldman [Teheran] as soon as possible. Make sure to keep your visit there a secret, even from those close to you. You may spread a rumour that you are sick, or that you are going on vacation or to the North. Inform us when you will be able to meet Michael [Moshe Carmil]. We will try to bring Rivca. Whom do you think can take your place in your absence? Shammai is leaving to meet Shemtob. No decisions will be taken until our meeting with you,"

On 19 August 1950, I.D. Sofer who was the contact man between the public committee and the Near East Airlines and in fact was working for emigration, wrote the following:

> I mentioned in my last letter that four stations have been opened for the emigrants waiting for transport. Their number has increased sevenfold

and they are living under terrible conditions. Two babies have died [...] there are incidents of typhus; most of the children and adults suffer from fever and I fear that we are on the verge of an epidemic. Sewage is overflowing in most of the depots, and the stench and pollution are unbearable, causing disease to spread. If the Government hears about these conditions they will close the stations and people will be wandering about the streets. Only yesterday a hundred emigrants from Mosul County have arrived; they have been waiting for some time for transport. They forced their way into our main station where six hundred people were waiting for departure, demanding flight arrangements, and at the end they succeeded in breaking down the door of the synagogue and pushing their way in. An alarm was created among the inhabitants of the building. Some of our workers were injured while trying to remove them. Seeing that we couldn't take control of the situation I called the police [...] It is a pity that your plane was grounded for three days, waiting for an engine [...] regarding your airport technicians I wouldn't want to be in their place.

On 21 August I informed Israel that Raouf was called by Hamid Rif'at, Director of the Interior Ministry, who told him that the Minister of the Interior wasn't pleased with the number of planes arriving. The company wasn't fulfilling its obligation to fly five hundred Jews a day; therefore it was decided that if the number of planes were not increased in the next few days, he would be forced to delay the plane at the airport or cancel the contract. Rif'at said that the Government was using the Revocation of Citizenship Act in a very systematic, organized way, in accordance with territorial and economical considerations. The Cabinet was revoking the citizenship of the inhabitants in provincial towns faster than those in the capital. "We are tired of asking for more planes. I am explaining the situation to you so that you can draw your own conclusions," Rif'at added.

The deceleration of the planes coming in forced the emigrants to look for new ways of escape through Basra, and therefore the authorities increased their supervision there. It was rumoured that the stress by the Interior Ministry was put on the staff of Near East airlines a result of the increase of attempts made to leave by illegal means.

Moshe Carmil wrote thus to Yitzhak Raphael (Head of Aliya Department of the Jewish Agency) on 25 August: "The restrictions put on the emigration from Iraq creates a dangerous situation. It is extremely important to increase the quota in a hurry. Do not hinder the outcome – lest we be too late."

On 28 August, Rony Barnett met with Jaber, the Interior Minister. The latter complained of the number of planes arriving and said that there were people in the Government who suggested our crossing through Jordan, to allow our people to traverse in convoys and to take them to the Israeli border by force.

Ever since our involvement, or lack of it, this topic became the central and a most controversial one in Baghdad, Tel Aviv and Paris. I thought that the time had come to clarify matters in order to prevent further misunderstandings. On 22 August, I wrote to the Mossad:

a) After several meetings within the Movement Institutions, and with the participation of Uziel Levy and Yoav Gorel, some decisions were finally reached to cooperate in the future, mainly on matters of emigration.

b) It was agreed that we stand together and take no part in the present elections of the President of the community.

c) It was agreed that the representative of the Movement should join me in meetings with the community regarding internal matters of emigration.

d) It was agreed to consider the administration of the workers and to reach a joint decision on that question.

e) It is forbidden to organize meetings with the workers Council without my presence or knowledge.

f) The instructions to the employees must only be given by reliable people, without the interference of the instructors, as it has been until now.

I sent out further information on the same day: "We did not cooperate with those who opposed Shemtob. Until the last moment they asked for our approval to alter his role, but we clearly informed them that we intended to stay neutral. As a result of that the elections were postponed."

On 24 October, Shlomo Hillel sent a telegram to the Mossad after his meeting with Shemtob in Paris: "Nothing had been promised to Shemtob, but we think any new development in Baghdad will complicate the situation. Shemtob claims that Shohet presented his candidacy for the President of the community due to Dror's (Ben-Porat) promise that the Movement and Israel would stand by him and against Shemtob."

Not long ago, when I was in the throes of writing this book, I met David Shukur, one of the two who stood behind Shemtob, and learned from him that Shemtob hoped to meet the Israeli Minister of Foreign Affairs, Moshe Sharett, in Paris, and was disappointed when he saw Shlomo Hillel instead. So it was interesting to read Shlomo Hillel's words to Moshe Carmil; they were written in Paris on 25 August regarding his meeting with Shemtob. They explained Shemtob's position from the point of view of the writer, who was out of Iraq and knew well the circle and the people working within it:

> The moment I arrived I met with Shemtob for a four to five hour conversation, which was barely enough for him to state his views. By the way, he already knew all the details about me. Rony and Wouton told him exactly who I was, the name of my family, etc. [and it seems they revealed it to other people as well!]. The truth is I don't understand why they gave him all that information especially as I would occasionally inform them that I might be going back there again, and they knew that. Was it only out of foolishness?
>
> In due time, he already knew that the limitations on emigration that occurred lately weren't due to pressure from Dror, but a story on its own. So that this double edged sword – Dror's (Ben-Porat) threat to limit or stop emigration – instead of being a pressure factor, was used against Dror himself. This immediately put me in an awkward position. While talking to him, the first complaint was made in a surly mood: This infamous rogue (Dror), when he knew that they had to slow down the

emigration, instead of coming to discuss it with me and cooperating, he wanted to stir the people up against me. All that may have ended in real bloodshed... He claimed that Dror sent needy people to him after telling them that they couldn't emigrate because of Shemtob's conclusion that Israel wasn't able to support them. To others he said that the emigration will be halted and again because of Shemtob's behaviour [...]

The dispute was a personal one, and Shemtob doesn't bother to hide it. He lives with the belief that he has actually accomplished everything himself. He arranged the emigration, his word is accepted by the chairman of the community, and any person, whether Jew or Gentile, listens to him without question, and here comes this "uncivilized" person who thinks that Shemtob ought to be his obedient servant... This is how he sees it. It is obvious that this has placed Dror in a very difficult and awkward situation... extremely difficult and awkward.

According to him, the dispute began with the manifestos and especially when he found out that Dror's people, together with a police officer took bribes in order to fix the list for emigration, and in drawing up the list a huge profiteering business was established. Shemtob asked him to fire two of the workers, and Dror refused, so Shemtob requested that we fire all the personnel. Dror informed him that he wasn't ready to pay salaries to any new employees (there was an offer to pay salaries to three) and this blew everything.

I must say that I very much doubt Shemtob's word, because during his conversation a clear tendency to control matters occasionally reared its head [...]

When I tried to explain that we couldn't replace Dror and we wouldn't be able to find someone in his place, he burst out: "And what does Dror do on the whole? I do it all by myself. His main job is to administer your treasury. This can be given to other emissaries – and that would be an end to it. And if you can't trust other emissaries – I can appoint my sons to take care it." [...]

Well, it is obvious that one cannot in fact always find a way to distribute work to everyone's satisfaction, especially when there are so many dancers in this party and each one dancing to a different tune. I asked Wouton if he really promised to replace Dror. He claimed (and Shemtob certified it) that he only promised Shemtob that he "would get satisfaction" within ten days. One way or another, there is no doubt that Rony, Wooton and the others are talking too much to Shemtob. A bit too much....

The fact is that we still need him. The minute we need someone, we have to find a way of dealing with him... It is not always easy, and not always possible, but this is the duty of the emissary, to know when to pull the rope and when to let go.

I don't know how things became so complicated with regard to the resignation of Shemtob, managing elections and so forth. Shemtob claims that Dror pointedly asked him to "resign!" and he isn't a person likely to accept this lightly. Dror approached the community leaders and influenced them (this whole idea is a myth). They are mostly people who have a few personal accounts to settle with Shemtob (and vice versa). He didn't see their approach to him as the sincere act of partners sharing responsibility in solving problems, but a way of taking revenge on him. So we found ourselves in a very difficult position with regard to this matter. Shemtob's plan, in this case, is a cunning one and we would be wise to tread very cautiously. He declared his willingness to hold elections for the presidency of the Jewish community. If he were proposed, he would surely win, and if not, then Shohet would be chosen; others would help him to see to it that Shohet is made to resign, whereas Shohet and his voters would be taught a lesson and wouldn't dare to raise their heads again! That is why I advise against holding elections until we know for sure what we intend to do.

Shemtob claimed that the Movement's plan to hold elections would not have existed, were it not for Dror who began it all. He insists that Dror must not poke his nose into any matter concerning the community.

There are two possible ways to solve the problem:

a)  To try and make peace between Shemtob and Dror. This is too far fetched, because there is no doubt that Shemtob, while he is here in Paris, has received a great deal of moral support and there is no chance whatsoever that he will agree to meet with Dror. All the people in "Berman" know that he came here in order to solve the problem, and if he reconciles with Dror when he goes back to Baghdad – it will be construed as a surrender by the public, and this is crucial to him. On the eve of his journey the situation was so bad that he insisted on Dror's dismissal. According to him, Dror claimed that Shemtob ought to be dismissed if he didn't submit to his demands. It is irrelevant and insignificant whether he did so or not: that is how he sees the picture.

b)   To give way to Shemtob, to put everything under his control, as he requested, and Dror either leaves "Berman" or stays there. If he surrenders unconditionally I can in no way agree to this kind of solution. It is unfair and will have a negative effect on the matter.

C)   To support Dror completely. Although I will try to mollify Shemtob and reach some sort of compromise with him, I don't believe that any solution can be reached. If we decide to support his demands, it will be interpreted as a declaration of war on Shemtob. There can be no problem or compromise. My assessment of the problem is that the time is not yet ripe, especially as we are now in a very uncomfortable situation regarding the "Berman" authorities and the community itself, who feel that we are slowing down the emigration and about to create a catastrophe.

The opinion of "Sammy" is also very interesting. He is Advocate Shmuel Moreh who was involved with the smuggling of Jewish fugitives into Iran, had very good connections with the smugglers, and contributed a lot to the security services in having connections with Arab agents. On 30 August, Sammy wrote the following to Hillel:

Firstly I would like to remind you that we have only heard Shemtob's claims, and nothing from Dror himself; we have no right whatsoever to make decisions before we do.

In my opinion the first mistake was that those in authority told Shemtob many things which weren't supposed to be mentioned, such as the curtailing of the immigration… This gave Shemtob a weapon against Dror. We must wholly support Dror, otherwise we will always be dependent on one man – Shemtob, as slanders are being uttered against Dror; tomorrow they may find someone else to attack.

There is no justification in choosing someone else to be the contact man between Dror and the others, as he will only minimize Dror's prestige and agree with Shemtob's opinion of him. If we really want to show Shemtob that Dror is all right, there is no chance at all. In case the right man for "Berman" is found, he can only replace Dror but never stand as his superior.

Also, as you mentioned in your letter, if Dror was involved personally – I don't know how any other emissary would have acted in such a situation. You have to admit that the situation wasn't easy at all for him or anyone with his advantages and defects.

You surely understand that Shemtob's offer to put the treasury in the hands of his people is to take control of the entire emigration matter – it is absurd. My opinion is that this thought must be utterly uprooted from his mind lest he feel too superior.

Regarding the committee and your warning of this devilish plan of Shemtob's, I must mention that these men who are on the committee have strong personal standings with the authorities as well, especially Shohet:

1.  *Shohet* – he was the Deputy General Manager of the railways in Iraq and the only one in charge of him was British. So he has a lot of connections with the authorities: he is still in touch with them. On 15 May 1948, the Iraqi authorities offered him the use of a diplomatic passport to be able to leave Iraq and stay abroad until things simmer down. There are very close ties between him and Jaber.

2. *Sasson Abed* – He was the President of the community in Basra during Jaber's Government. He is very friendly with Jaber. He also has good connections with the Iraqi authorities.

I presume from the above portrayals, that the emigration operation can very well succeed if these people were in charge and not Shemtob...

The police thoroughly investigated those who organized the demonstration. Abraham El-Kabir, Moshe Shohet and Meir Basri were summoned by Minister of the Interior Saleh Jaber, who told them that he wasn't pleased with the situation and felt that the reinstatement of Sasson Khadourie would be undesirable and that he wouldn't support Shemtob, but would be partial to Moshe Shohet in case the community Council decided to vote for him. Jaber gave instructions to organize a committee that would work separately on behalf of the emigration and also to be involved with it. He appointed Sasson Abed as chairman and Abraham El-Kabir, Sasson Nawi, Moshe Shohet and David Salman temporarily as members, and Naim Yitzhak Shamash, who was the Manager of the Ottoman Bank, was appointed as contact man between the committee and the registration personnel. He then expressed readiness to help them in all they did and also to prevent any interference in their work.

The members of the committee got in touch with me and expressed their willingness to cooperate. I arranged a meeting with them and decided to try and make Shemtob join them, although I was sure that he was an impatient man and not capable of working with committees. Meanwhile, Jaber visited Senator Daniel in his house and told him that he knew that the sons of Shemtob and others had organized the demonstrations, and as Shemtob was involved with it, he would not press charges against him.

I met with all the members together with Eliezer, the representative of the Movement Institution, but our efforts to placate Shemtob failed utterly. They threatened to resign if we insisted. Jaber also threatened that if the committee resigned he would appoint another one with Moslem representatives only. However, we discussed the principles of the work with complete accord. The members also visited the registration and accommodation centre and were very impressed.

On 28 August I informed the Mossad that it was very important for us to send at least two planes a day for a week, in order to encourage the committee and also to prevent the interference of the authorities. This was our last chance to settle the problems regarding emigration.

As my request to return to Israel for consultation wasn't approved, I decided to plan a trip across the borders to Iran. I informed the members of the public committee that I was going on vacation for a few days. I travelled to Basra and intended to cross the Shatt-El-Arab waterway. The emigration activists in Basra found a smuggler from a distinguished family to guide me to the borders with five other boys from the Halutz Movement (Sasson, Dan Meir and three others). We left from a street in Basra and drove for half an hour. A policeman tried to stop the car for an inspection. The smuggler, who was calm and self-assured, refused to stop. "This policeman really wants a bribe," he explained. We drove on and after a while, he transferred us to a different car and a new driver. The latter took us to the shores of Shatt-El-Arab, at the crossing point. He housed us in a place surrounded by an orange grove where we were served tea.

We didn't have enough time to enjoy our drink before the police surrounded the house and arrested us. We were taken to the police station in Basra. We made a prepared statement and declared that we were going to visit the tomb of the Prophet Ezra Hasofer. The prison conditions were bearable. The members of the Movement did their utmost to make things easier for us. Two angels, Nazima Khemara and Hela Sarraf, supplied us with food. One day a police officer arrived. He was angry with the smuggler, El-Sa'doon, scolded him and even spat at him. Another day, we were transferred to some other police station for an identification parade to identify the driver. As is customary with the Movement, we showed no recognition.

We were kept in detention for twelve days and on 19 September 1950, I was released on bail of 150 Dinars in cash. Three days later, when I was back in Baghdad, I brought the Mossad up-to-date, that I had to appear before a court at the end of the month. I added that efforts were made to come to an arrangement with the judge to dismiss my case with a symbolic fine of 25 Dinars. As is customary, they would revoke my citizenship and although I was supposed to leave within a month on one of the planes, it was also possible to arrange that I would be delayed for several months.

On 30 September, I informed the Mossad that I intended to arrive in Israel on a regular plane and return by ship via Asloug (Abadan). After several weeks, on 5 October 1950, I received the following letter from the Mossad:

> During Shemtob's stay in Paris, he was met with representatives of the Mossad, other Government Departments and the Joint. He was assured that they would do all that was necessary to increase the emigration quota. They emphasized the necessity of increasing the community's participation in the travelling expenses of the poorer Jews and other costs incurred by the emigration work itself, at local levels, and the need for concentrated activities at the community and personal levels to ensure the safe transfer of emigrants assets through the channels authorized by the Israeli Government.

I replied to them on 9 October:

> Friends, I already know Shemtob very well. I praised him highly when I stood before the community and the Movement so as to protect him. But during the increased pressure of work (he) seemed to be influenced by the troublemakers. We don't blame Shemtob alone, but the Movement, Wooton and the two troublemakers who work with him. We are still ready to cooperate with him. If he changes his mind, we cannot convince the new committee to deal with him. At the time I informed Shemtob, that we were going to register him in the Golden Book, therefore I request that you do so and send us the certificate to give to him...

Meanwhile the date for my trial approached, and I informed the Mossad that the court case ended and I was fined 50 Dinars and a personal bail of 70 Dinars, to ensure my stay in Iraq until the revoking of my citizenship. The formality in such cases, as I mentioned, is that I was to leave Iraq within a month or one more week thereafter. In fact I stayed there a further eight months.

On my return to Baghdad I wrote to the Mossad that Sabah, the son of Nouri El-Sa'id, met with Moshe Shohet and offered to help him with his plan to fly the Jews to Israel in Iraqi planes. He wanted to sign a contract for three flights a week, with twenty-two passengers on each flight, at the normal price. I claimed that this could only benefit the prosperous Jews who wouldn't be a burden on the Iraqi people; secondly, we would decide who would leave on this route; thirdly, could an arrangement be made to link this company with Israel? fourthly, with this arrangement we could have Sabah on our side (he is the favourite son of Nouri El-Sa'id), and finally, we can draw Nouri El-Sa'id closer to us now that he is back in the Government.

In another letter I wrote to the Mossad:

> We are put in a degrading situation regarding the Jewish people and the community. Everything that concerns us is in ruins. They look upon us as impostors. We know that you are the only source that we can turn to for our justified demands. We never believed that this source would work against our best interests and in such a manner as to foster the belief among our people here that Israel doesn't want them... If a representative on behalf of the Government and the Institute were present, I am sure we could have reached entirely different decisions [...] We see in this that we have to close shop and return home. Why do we have to stay here and watch the slow demise of the Jewish captives, whom we, with our own hands, have gathered here? We shouldn't miss this opportunity, otherwise we will bitterly regret it later on. Every slight neglect will cost us a great deal in the future. I do hope that this time your answer will not only be messages of regret...

I didn't abandon the idea of having contact with Nouri El-Sa'id through his son. "Sabah wishes to be in Cyprus on Wednesday [meaning in three days time] in order to discuss the matter with the Israeli representative there." The next day I informed them that Nouri El-Sa'id summoned Shohet for a meeting and told him that he approved of the emigration of our people and would do his best to further the project. He understood that the delay in emigration didn't come from the airways companies themselves but from Israel, as all the shares of these companies were in Israeli hands. If the matter stayed this way, he felt he couldn't bear to watch the sufferings of our people; he himself would arrange to have them taken to the borders.

He also thought of the idea of flying the Jews to Cyprus in Iraqi planes. The conclusion was that Shohet and Sabah would not leave for the time being, but wait for a reply from the manager of the Iraqi Airways Company, Colonel Moustard, who was to leave for Cyprus for initial checks, and a final decision could then be reached. Nouri El-Sa'id emphasized that if the matter could be satisfactorily arranged it may gain momentum and lead to bigger things.

But he was not satisfied with handing us carrots only; he had to use a stick. Rony Barnett related that he received a letter from the Iraqi Government and in it was a quote from the words of El-Sa'id: "It is obvious that Israel doesn't want these people. There is another reason why we want them out [...] lately Israel deported five thousand of our people by force across the Egyptian borders, and many thousands more were expelled through other frontiers. Our standpoint is obvious: We, the people of the Arab countries, have to recompense them measure for measure. If these Jews won't leave this country sooner – we will make our own arrangements! We don't need planes. It is much easier for us to deport them across the borders of Jordan, ten times the number that are being expelled, and we will do this unless your company hastens to deal with the matter," and Rony Barnett added that "this gentleman gave us an ultimatum to accelerate the flights by the end of the month or leave."

Not only our sources warned that time was running short, but so felt the American Ambassador in Iraq. On 29 September he reported to his State Department: "During my formal visit with Nouri El-Sa'id, he mentioned that he was very worried about the Iraqi Jews hanging around who have revoked their citizenship and are ready to emigrate to Israel. Nouri informed us that although 9,000 to 10,000 Jews have already left Iraq, there are still some 27,000 whose credentials could be arranged within two weeks, and another 31,000, within three weeks. He emphasized, that according to Iraqi Law, emigrants whose citizenship has been revoked, are required to leave the country within twenty days. He also told me," the Ambassador continued, "that his representative was sent to Tel Aviv in order to accelerate the emigration to Israel, but after a week of futile discussions with various officials, the man returned yesterday empty-handed. Nouri commented dryly, that according to Israeli Law [meaning the Law of Return], those refugees are entitled to enter Israel, and if the authorities are concerned over their large numbers, or for any other reasons, this isn't Iraq's business. The Prime Minister has openly declared that he is also of the opinion to let these people go as soon as possible, and he is ready to give orders to the Iraqi airplane company to fly them to Cyprus or Beirut, and to continue on their journey, or straight to Lydda, if the Israelis agree. If this matter is not settled, he will send them by bus to Jordan or Beirut, and from there they will have to cross the borders into Israel. He has admitted that he hasn't yet contacted the Lebanese or the Jordan Governments, but he is ready to do so in a short while."

On 3 October, the American State Department circulated a statement to their embassies in Baghdad, London, Beirut and Amman: "The State Department supports the observations of the American Ambassador regarding Prime Minister Nouri El-Sa'id's concern, as they are realistic and humanitarian points, to make the Jewish emigrants leave in a reasonable orderly rate and not in a mass exit compelled by higher authorities [...] the State Department is of the opinion that the Iraqi Government has to discuss the new suggestions of El-Sa'id with the Israeli Authorities, in the form it was made previously. It doesn't make sense that other Arab countries which are interested in this matter would permit the emigrants to cross their lands. The State Department is also dubious about the wisdom of this plan in view of the perpetual dangers inherent within [...] The State Department appreciates El-Sa'id's suggestion of direct flights, Iraq-Israel and is inclined to support it. As he hasn't mentioned anything about Near East Air Transport (NEAT), which can be authorized to operate such direct flights, the State Department is interested in verifying whether this nonreference was intentional and whether to lend any credence to the fact that El-Sa'id only mentioned "Iraqi Airlines."

So much for the American State Department's directive. El-Sa'id's words about sending an envoy to Israel were incomprehensible to me. I could not guess whether he was referring to Col. Moustard, or some other undercover envoy about whom I knew nothing. Somehow Israel missed, in my opinion, a golden opportunity to establish relations with Iraq. El-Sa'id took various steps in an endeavour to establish a connection with Israel. His indecision regarding relations with Israel was unwarranted but, I believe, Israel herself didn't act decisively enough to meet him halfway. The Israeli or American archives may contain documents which could throw some light on it or provide some answers to this question.

On 1 November 1950 I wrote to the Mossad: "We have been informed by the passport officials that their manager, who is responsible for the revoking of citizenship and flying our people out, is leaving tomorrow for Amman to complete the arrangements for driving them by bus to the Israeli borders. In addition to that, we have heard from a conversation between the passport officials that a new customs station will be put in location H3. We will try to confirm this from other sources."

Three days later, I again reported: "With the progress being made on the Amman route and the possibility of a mass emigration from that direction, we have to prepare our people for this experiment. Therefore, it is absolutely necessary to know your opinion as soon as possible, whether to instruct our people to refuse this possibility, or to allow them to agree with the authorities? The same thing concerns the revoking of citizenship. Shall we delay our people from having it revoked?

Meanwhile Israeli Intelligence brought Moshe Carmil up to date that on 29 or 30 October, the Jordanian Minister of Foreign Affairs invited the Iraqi Ambassador and told him that King Abdallah discussed with El-Sa'id the matter of the Iraqi Jews and wished to know how the Iraqis were planning this operation. He also asked that a special person should be sent to Amman with all the necessary information. The Research Department of the Foreign Office added that the King agreed to the request of the Iraqis to permit the Jews to cross via Jordan into Israel. The transfer would be accomplished by Iraqi Airways planes (which the Iraqis were willing to expand) to Amman and from there by car to Israel. The King's agreement was made known to the British Ambassador in Baghdad.

On 11 November, the Iraqi Prime Minister, accompanied by Minister of Transport Wadi Ja'far, visited Amman on his way to converse with the Arab League. The Arab News Institute reported, that they coordinated viewpoints with King Abdallah and his Prime Minister, Samir El-Rifa'i. Nouri El-Sa'id wanted Jordan to agree to the crossing of the Iraqi Jews through her territories in exchange for 2 Dinars a visa and 20 Dinars for transport fees, and also Iraq would undertake to supply Jordan with the amount of wheat needed by the Iraqi Jews. Jordan refused the offer.

The confirmation of this report was acquired from another source; the American Embassy in Baghdad reported on 24 January 1951: "...Jordan refused in its entirety the proposal of Nouri El-Sa'id to permit 75,000 Iraqi Jews who had had their citizenship revoked, to cross through Jordan on their way to Israel. El-Sa'id's offer held the additional prospect of financial rewards if Jordan permitted these Jews to cross through its territory. According to authorized sources, he offered Jordan 20,000 tons of wheat and in addition she would receive 2 Dinars a visa and a gain of 20 Dinars for transportation fees on every Jew. However these considerations didn't motivate the Jordanian Government to change its position. Clarifying his decision on the matter, the Jordanian Prime Minister said that incidents of disastrous consequences could take place if Jews were to cross through Jordan, watched by the Arab refugees from Palestine. There would be an understandable resentment that they were crossing into Israel to take possession of lands and buildings which belonged to the Arabs before they were dispossessed. We were informed that, in reply to this remark, El-Sa'id suggested that Iraqi Jews should travel through Jordan in columns protected by armed Iraqi soldiers. To this surprising offer, Samir Pasha El-Rifa'i said that "under such circumstances it is conceivable that Palestinian Arabs might attack the Iraqi escorts, and that it is very difficult to envisage Iraqi Arabs and Palestinian Arabs exchanging blows to ensure the security of a collection of Jews.

This perplexing situation had an influence on El-Sa'id and he began to search for other routes to accommodate the exit of the Jews. Perhaps that propelled them to agree eventually to direct flights. Meanwhile the planes continued to arrive at a slow rate which didn't satisfy the needs of the people. The distress increased, and things reached such a point, that on 13 January 1951 two hundred and ten Jews from Basra sent the following telegram to the Iraqi authorities and to Iraq Tours:

> We, the Jewish citizens of Basra, Kal'at Saleh and El-Azar, are putting our plea before you just as Moshe asked mercy from God, and hereby approach you to ask for your sympathy as Arabs to save us from our distress and suffering.

Five months have passed since we left our homes and our situation is very sad. We and our children are facing disaster. The planes are continuing to fly from Baghdad but we cannot understand the reason for refusing flights from Basra. Please, look upon us with sympathy and generosity. Save us from hunger and misery, in fact, from death. Our lives rest in your generous hands. Rescue us from this injustice. We are putting all our faith in you.

This telegram didn't represent the situation in Basra only. I saw this from the perspective of an organizer and detailed the general situation in a report which I prepared for Sasson Abed's Committee, whose members were supposed to meet with Prime Minister El-Sa'id. On 17 January 1951, I sent a copy of this report to the Mossad:

### 1. The Committee in Basra:

The situation in Basra has reached such a difficult impasse that has never been seen in all the provincial towns and not even in the capital. Khemara, with his secretary, and with the participation of Banda from the Underground, were directing the emigration affairs, collecting money from the emigrants before they revoked their citizenship and spending an unauthorized 200 Dinars per flight apart from the daily expenses which amounted to 100 Dinars [...] He always collected an advance payment from the emigrants in order to cover the deficit caused by those who had already left.

We still need to send thirty planes to Basra. We calculate that Khemara can pay (from money collected from the emigrants) for another 20 or 22 people, and the rest we will have to pay after four or five months. Under the control of Khemara there are community funds amounting to more than 8,000 Dinars. This money he uses, without supervision, as the committee has been dismissed by him and he has refused to appoint another one, going on now for three months. To press him to pay, we held back the planes this time until he elects a new committee to take care of the emigrants needs. In this way we can ensure supervision on his income and avoid paying around 10,000 Dinars later, and at a time when we can afford to apply pressure on him through the indigent people and thus begin to collect part of the assets.

In the last two months he threatened us in various ways such as calling in the Secret Police. He sent requests to the Prime Minister, met with the Minister of the Interior in order to hire different planes, and all of them, after making arrangements, sent him to a committee whose job it is to supervise the distribution of planes in Iraq. He knows no one in this committee. Lately he seems to have relented and has agreed to choose a committee.

## 2. Orphans:

This problem came up when the government refused to revoke the citizenship of orphans under the age of eighteen, claiming that these orphans must stay in Iraq until they are eighteen. We have in our charge eight orphans, boys and girls, and we are unable to have them released. The problem is not only a human, but a religious one as well, and we fear that the Government want to put them in Moslem institutions.

We decided eventually to create families without children to "adopt" these youngsters in order to save them.

## 3. Those subject to conscription:

This edict arose from the Ministry of Defense, with the approval of El-Sa'id; it will get worse when the number of young emigrants reaches 9,000. It now stands at 7,300. 9,000 are permitted to emigrate without restriction and over that number those who are between 18 and 28 will not be permitted to leave.

## 4. The prohibition put on the emigrants a week before their leave, or even an hour before boarding the plane:

Every Jew is not sure of his departure until the very last minute, as there is always a chance of receiving a letter forbidding him to emigrate. The prohibition can come from various Government offices, from private citizens, etc. Anyone can make charges against a Jew claiming that the latter owes him money. There are unscrupulous guarantors who are making money out of it, and every Jew who is prohibited to leave has to face the complainant and request that he give evidence that he isn't a debtor. This request sometimes costs him 20 Dinars. There are lawyers who are extorting around 30 Dinars a day in this way.

### 5. The airport:

The airport has become a target for any government employee who wishes to create publicity for himself. Any employee who hits an emigrant at the airport is considered a great patriot. Imagine, every day around thirty new louts arrive at the airport, and we have to use all our influence – whether it be pressure of the Committee on the various employees or cash bribes – to restrain the blows directed at the emigrants and their luggage. These days, the situation is slightly better, following the election of Moshe Shohet, a member of the Supreme Committee, which discusses every complaint made at the airport. We succeeded lately in supplying two plates and a blanket to each emigrant, a primus stove for every family and all the used clothes they might need.

### 6. The sick:

A committee has been formed to establish the truth of the claim of some emigrants that they have to leave immediately because of illness [...] We have around thirty patients who are requesting priority in the queue. The matter is being discussed with the Government. We, of course, don't really wish to support it.

### 7. The personnel dealing with emigration:

We have been trying for over a month and a half to revoke their citizenship quickly and fly them out without queuing, and in regular planes. If this can be achieved, it will solve us a lot of trouble and we won't need to smuggle a large number out through Goldman (Teheran).

### 8. Those who work on Friday:

Lately emigrating Jews are prohibited to fly out on Friday (the Moslem Sabbath) in case forbidden objects are slipped through without checking and when most of the employees of the airport are on their weekend vacation. The other prohibition is not to let the Jews depart if the second plane doesn't land before 15:00 Greenwich Mean Time. On these days only one plane takes off per day, as the plane doesn't have time to return before the appointed hour.

A few days later, on 23 January, I sent the following telegram:

1.  The customs employees at the airport are requesting payment for extra hours of work. When Doron was here he wanted me to pay them then and I refused. A decision must be reached about who is liable to pay, as the employees are insistent. You must decide.

2.  They are also pressing for a large shed at the airport to check the emigrants and their luggage; we have already informed you, that this will cost around 600 Dinars. We have convinced them, for the time being, to erect at the airport a military hospital tent. This tent with all the equipment will cost around 350 Dinars. Decide on that as well. I have to make clear that the committee's treasury cannot support these expenses due to the many demands made on them last month for handing out bribes at the airport, mobilization, etc.

The next day the Mossad sent the following telegram:

a)  The committee met with Omar Nadhmi, Acting Minister of the Interior. Lots of problems were discussed. The problem of mobilization is solved, and instructions have already been given to the police in writing, to register every Jew who wants to revoke his citizenship without stating his age. As for the candidates, between 9,000 and 31,000 of them, whose ages are between 18 and 38, and who are waiting for a permit from the Cabinet, no instructions in writing have been given. A request by the committee for changes among the customs staff have also been approved.

b)  The committee met this morning with Saleh Jaber as he requested. It lasted for two hours and the situation was discussed. The committee expressed its bitterness at the negative attitude of the Government, the emigration trouble and the internal security of the Jews. He agreed with them and criticized many personalities who on gaining power, amended their attitudes and promises. The committee understood from Jaber that if he took a new initiative, he may once more attain power.

On 31 January, Rony Barnett sent the following letter to the Iraqi Minister of the Interior, Omar Nadhmi:

I have the honour to approach you regarding our conversation this morning, when we discussed matters of accelerating the flights of Jews from Iraq.

This company [Near East] has been handling the flights since May last year under many and prolonged difficulties, of which you are surely aware. I am pleased to inform you of the latest developments which have eased the difficult situation regarding all parties concerned, about deporting these people from Iraq as soon as possible.

The instructions your Highness gave to the police and the customs employees at the airport, to provide services for twenty-four hours, will surely help in accelerating the movement. We have supplied more planes for this campaign, and we are ready to bring in even more if we find that all the matters concerning their exit are fulfilled. If everything goes well we presume that we can fly between 600 and 700 passengers a day.

On the other hand, taking into consideration the large number of people who have to leave Iraq, it would seem that the current situation is far from satisfactory, inasmuch as the time factor is concerned. If authorization be given to our planes to fly along the route Baghdad-Lydda-Nicosia-Baghdad, we can undertake the obligation to double and even triple the current number of flights, thus making it possible for these people to leave in a hurry.

With due respect, if I may mention that now and then the planes of companies like BOAC, KLM and Cyprus Airways fly and are still flying to Israel and to Iraq at the same time. This is a well-known fact. But it was mentioned officially that this is unimportant as long as the flights don't leave directly from Israel.

Therefore we presume that all official requests will be completed if every plane, after releasing its passengers, flies to Nicosia in Cyprus, and from there takes off for Iraq. We feel that this arrangement will be for the best for all concerned in this matter and will also fulfil all the official requests, and within few months we will be able to fly these people directly from Iraq.

Please be sure that such flights will only be achieved with your knowledge and your permission in advance.

In case the question of flight information from Lydda is raised, I suggest that there is no need for such information and that the planes themselves can disclose their flight plan when they are in the air; this will prevent direct contact between Iraq and Israel.

We would very much appreciate it if these suggestions are studied as soon as possible by the official department concerned. I am at your disposal for any clarification needed for the subject under discussion.

Incidentally, the pilots who landed in Lydda reported that their take-off was from Nicosia, therefore fulfilling the conditions of no direct flights between Iraq and Israel.

In Israel, the problem of landing planes on Saturday was raised. The Head of the Immigration Department of the Institute, Yitzhak Raphael, approached the Chief Rabbis of Israel, Rabbi Herzog and Rabbi Uziel, in order to obtain their opinion. They answered that, considering the special situation of the Iraqi Jews and the need to save them within a limited time, it is permitted in times of necessity and having no other choice, to take off with emigrants from Baghdad on Saturday, but to direct the landing of the planes in Lydda at the end of the Sabbath.

Meanwhile, the question of my replacement was raised once more. In a telegram on 2 February 1951 that was sent from the Mossad to Sion Cohen, the emissary of the Mossad in Teheran, it was written: "Dror's replacement is ready to leave and must be accomplished with the utmost urgency. Inform us immediately how many days it will take you to effect the transfer. In the next post, a letter will arrive from Malkin requesting a Goldman 'seedling' (Iranian visa) for Dror's replacement. Cancel the name in the letter and send a 'seedling' immediately in the name of Shmuel Green for an Israeli travel document. What chance of his landing at your end without a 'seedling'?"

The more time passed the more I and my colleagues, the emissaries and activists felt that we, in the field, had no one in Israel to listen to us and no one there to give an opinion on the distress and the difficulties with which we were working. We had, however, the help of the dedicated Moshe Carmil.

In my telegram of 5 April, I tried to transfer my feelings to Israel and hoped that the message would reach the listeners, but I was apparently too naive. I found matters to be very different on the surface; for instance on 10 April two parcels arrived in Baghdad containing 162 letters from Teheran to be forwarded to Israel. I had no idea whether it was a mistake or not, but it worried me, as such letters would normally be referred immediately to the Secret Police and then returned to their source. This time luck was with us. A fugitive in the name of Mounir Hafeth, who worked during the Mandate in the post office in Jerusalem and was sent to work in Baghdad under the supervision of Haim Shamash (Eitan's father), quietly sent these letters back to Teheran. There was another incident: In a circular sent to the emissaries of the Middle Eastern Jewish Department (Journal No. 5 from March 1951) I found lots of news on Iraq, which were exact copies of our memos from the 12 till 14 of that month, where names of ministers and of the Jewish connection with whom we were linked were inscribed. I immediately sent a furious telegram to the Mossad and demanded to know who was responsible for this blunder and who released that information. I ended my telegram with the words; "We request you to stop any publicity regarding our emissaries and activists who risk their lives. We are warning you that if no action is taken, we will be forced to desist from sending you any political information."

It happened that the Ezra and Nehemiah Operation continued until January 1952. Twenty months to be exact. 110,618 Jews from Iraq arrived in Israel by air on 900 flights (38,000 via Cyprus and 72,618 direct to Lydda Airport). 9,352 Jewish fugitives were smuggled from Iraq to Iran and on to Israel. All in all, 119,970 immigrants from Iraq, from a community of 138,000 people, arrived in Israel, and were thrust into a new reality – living under appalling conditions, in tents or huts, in transit camps, with rationed food, sickness and infection, a new language, new customs and a different set of traditions from those they knew. And yet, despite the difficulties, the immigrants succeeded in putting down roots and establishing themselves in Israel. The proof is evident today in all spheres of life here and throughout the business world. And if this isn't success then I don't know what success is.

*Iraqi immigrants dwelling in tents in transit camps (Ma'abarah) in Israel.*

## Contents of the twenty-second meeting of the Iraqi Cabinet on 10 February 1951 where a decision was taken on direct flights

*Translated from Arabic*

During the twenty-second meeting of the Cabinet, which was held on 10 February 1951, a letter, No. S/238 issued on 6 February 1951, was read out. It suggested taking the necessary steps to expedite the deportation of the Jews who had their Iraqi citizenship revoked (as detailed in your ministry's letter). Attached to the letter was a note from the Near East Transportation Company. The Cabinet listened to a clarification of the subject given by H.E. the Minister of the Interior and noted his decision, which was taken at the Ministry's meeting held on 27 May 1950. After close scrutiny and discussion, it was found that the Cabinet, at its above mentioned meeting, agreed to authorize the Near East Company to transfer the Jews in accordance with the Company's conditions as stated in the Company's offer, which was sent to the Council of Ministers, and which is included in your letter No. S/876 dated 8 May 1950. One of the conditions was that the airplane carrying the Jews who wished to leave Iraq, must not land in any country which has no diplomatic relations with Iraq, as stated in paragraph No.5 in this letter, and that the Council of Ministers agreed to authorize the Company to transfer the Jews within the framework of conditions stated in this letter (included in the above- mentioned paragraph No.5). And since it was found that this condition, as stated in the letter sent by the Company's Assistant Director and submitted to your Ministry, impedes the transfer of Jews at the required rate, and since public interest dictates that the transfer operation be implemented with the utmost speed, and since the company clarified in its latest letter, attached to this above letter, as mentioned in the introduction to this decision, that it was ready to transfer between 600 and 700 people daily; and since allowing a large number of the Jews who have already revoked their citizenship to stay behind, and all these oppose the public interest, the Council of Ministers decided to agree to your Ministry's suggestion that: "The above-mentioned Company will continue to fly the Jews out without being committed to land them in a specific location, and to be satisfied if its airplanes arrive in Iraq directly from Nicosia, and that the above mentioned decision be thus emended."

This decision was approved by the August Parliamentary Council.

في جلسة مجلس الوزراء الثانية والعشرين والمنعقدة بتاريخ ١٠ / ٢ / ١٩٥١ تلي كتاب وزارة الداخلية المرقم س/ ٢٣٨ والمؤرخ ١٩٥١/٢/٦ والمقترح فيه اتخاذ التدابير للاسراع في تسفير اليهود الذين سقطت عنهم الجنسية العراقية – حسبما فصلته وزارتكم في الكتاب – ولوحظ مرفقة كتاب مساعد شركة الشرق الادنى للنقل . واستمع المجلس الى الايضاحات التي ادلى بها معالي الوزير المختص ولاحظ المجلس قراره المتخذ في جلسته المنعقدة بتاريخ ١٩٥٠/٥/٢٧ وبعد التدقيق ولدى المذاكرة تبين ان مجلس الوزراء في جلسته المذكورة وافق على السماح لشركة الشرق الادنى بنقل اليهود وفقا للشرائط المبينة في عريضة الشركة الواردة الى مجلس الوزراء ضمن كتابكم المرقم س/٨٧٦ والمؤرخ ١٩٥٠/٥/٨ وكان من جملة الشروط ( بان لا تهبط الطيارة التي تحمل اليهود الذين يغادرون العراق في بلاد التي ليس للعراق فيها علاقة دبلوماسية ) مما ورد في الفقرة الخامسة من هذا الكتاب وان مجلس الوزراء وافق على منح الشركة تسفير اليهود ضمن الشروط الواردة في الكتاب ومن جملتها الفقرة الخامسة المذكورة . وحيث قد تبين من كتاب معاون مدير الشركة الموجه الى وزارتكم اخيرا ان هذا الشرط يعيق الشركة عن تسفير اليهود بالسرعة المطلوبة ولما كانت المصلحة تقضي بانجاز عملية التسفير باسرع وقت وحيث ان الشركة بينت في كتابها الاخير المربوط بكتابكم المشار اليه في صدر هذا القرار انها على استعداد لتسفير (٦٠٠ – ٧٠٠ ) شخص يوميا ومن حيث ان بقاء زمرة كبيرة من اليهود الذين اسقطت عنهم الجنسية يخالف المصلحة لهذا قرر المجلس الموافقة على اقتراح وزارتكم وذلك (ان تستمر الشركة المذكورة على تسفير اليهود بدون الزامها بانزالهم في محل معين والاكتفاء بان يكون قد وم الطائرة الى العراق من نيقوسيا مباشرة) وتعديل القرار المذكور من هذه الناحية على هذا الوجه .

لقد اقترن هذا القرار بموافقة هيئة النيابة الجليلة.

بغداد ١٩٥١/٢/١٢

# Chapter 12

# BOMBS IN THE STREETS OF BAGHDAD

With all the important activities of the Zionist Movement in Iraq especially during the years of 1950 and 1951, and despite all the dedicated work done by the activists, who risked their lives and helped to bring over one hundred thousand Jews to live in Israel – a dark shadow hovered like a black cloud over the whole campaign – the accusation of throwing bombs to achieve a purpose, which took thirty years to clear up; after which the Movement and its activists were completely vindicated of this despicable accusation. In my eyes, as one who headed the Ezra and Nehemiah Operation, the slander accusing the Israeli emissaries of throwing bombs in the heart of Baghdad, so as to create alarm among the Jews and fuel fear and a desire to flee to Israel, is almost like a blood libel.

This false Baghdadi charge was conceived in the Iraqi police headquarters and supported by enemies of Israel, and with the passing of time gathered many adherents. In 1954 the story once again received some credence, when Israeli agents planted bombs in some buildings in Cairo. Anyone comparing the two incidents, that of Baghdad and of Cairo, found a few similarities: For example, in both incidents bombs were also set off at an American Center. Henceforth the conclusion was reached that in both cases, the planning and execution were the work of emissaries of the same state – Israel. The bombers in Egypt were caught and confessed that they were sent by and acted on behalf of Israeli Intelligence, and this, without doubt, supported the conclusion that the perpetrators in Iraq, a few years before, were also emissaries of Israel.

It is understandable that world opinion was ready to connect Israel with the explosions in Baghdad and later in Cairo. Even in Israel there were certain circles, close to the Israeli Labour Party and David Ben-Gurion, who supported this theory and publicly endorsed it, thereby giving it authenticity and lending legitimacy to various researchers whose aim was to discredit Zionism and present Israel as a state that would stop at nothing to realize its aims.

As far as I can remember, during the Lavon Affair, in 1963, when the discussions in the Mapai Party Convention reached its peak, I held a meeting at my house in Or Yehuda with the participation of Pinhas Sapir. He asked to appear in front the Mapai's activists, to persuade them that there was no need for this investigation after all these years, and added: "How can we investigate the tragedy now? Anyhow, we all know what happened in Baghdad..."

At the end of the evening, when I escorted him to his car, I asked him: "Perhaps you can tell me what happened in Baghdad?" and he answered defensively, that he had no details on the matter. His reply made me angry, and the next morning I sent him a letter asking him to present facts on what occurred in Iraq, or else apologize in public for his irresponsible statement. I added a postscript to the effect that he must understand that he was facing a question of defamation. But he replied evasively and gave me no pretext for a court case.

The use of weapons and bombs in private disputes was common practice in the Arab countries, including Iraq. And even if the relationship between Jews and Moslems in Iraq was correct and normal, attacks on Jews, damaging their property and causing bodily harm were accepted norms and they often occurred, due to business competition, religious or nationalistic fervour. During the Second World War several Jewish moneylenders were murdered and dumped into the river in sacks tied with ropes. On 17 September 1936, during the declaration of Palestine Day in Iraq, several Jewish passersby were killed by a bomb.

In 1948, Yacov Azachi, a dentist, had a clinic in a two-storey building adjoining the El-Amana Suk in Baghdad. The first floor was occupied by shops and the second, by various workshops. Azachi was the only Jew occupying a place in the building. They were anxious times: The city was still ruled by martial law. Shafik Adas was hanged in Basra on a false charge of selling surplus arms to the British Army in Israel. The Iraqi Army that headed for the Palestine borders was beaten on the battlefield in combat with Israel, and anger towards Israel and the Jews increased.

Yacov Azachi was at work in his clinic when suddenly a tailor's apprentice burst into the room to inform him that a bomb had been found on the roof of the building. Azachi sent his son to check this, and when he confirmed it, Azachi rushed off to inform a Moslem friend who had good connections with the police. The police soon arrived and dismantled the bomb. They also succeeded in catching those who were from the national Istiklal Party, a party that held extremist views regarding Israel and the Jews.

On 8 April 1950, a bomb was thrown at a coffee-house, the El-Beidha Casino in Abu Nawas Street on the shores of the Tigris River in Baghdad, a place frequented by Jews. This time the bomb did its work.

A day later I reported in a telegram to Israel that the bomb had been thrown by a group who sent three youngsters to do the job, and six Jews had been injured. One of them was in a critical state. I added that after the bomb incident there were other provocations and throwing of stones at Jewish citizens in various parts of the capital. I emphasized that it was very difficult to draw conclusions based on these incidents and that we began a series of consultation with prominent members of the community to decide on what our reactions ought to be. I suggested that should these incidents recur, immediate resistance must be instigated; for example, to train groups in hand-to-hand fighting and organize foot patrols in the streets in order to respond to every incident, but without the use of firearms.

The Mesouda Shemtob Synagogue was the next target chosen by the bomb throwers, the centre where all the travellers who completed their formalities for departure, assembled, and it was the last stop before driving to the airport. The synagogue was a two-storey building; the first floor contained the prayer halls and offices and the emigration organizers were stationed on the second floor. A courtyard was built around the building; it was always noisy, filled with worshippers, travellers, drivers, members of the Movement, employees and community leaders.

*The Meir Tweig Synagogue, where many Jews were preparing for emigration;*
*on the left: Moslem houses.*

On 14 January 1951, a grenade was lobbed at the synagogue; three people were killed – two boys, Saleh Shaba and Sasson Yitzhak, and an adult, Moshe Baghnou from Irbil City (he succumbed to his injuries a day later). Six were seriously wounded and nineteen had light injuries. The emigrants and the employees weren't hurt; all the wounded people were to be found among the crowd who were standing outside the synagogue where the grenade fell. If it had fallen in the yard, where hundreds of people were gathered, the tragedy would have been far more serious.

Leah Cohen, who was near the bus that took the emigrants to the airport, was holding the hand of her five-year-old son, Eli, when she heard a deafening explosion. She grabbed her son and fled, then noticed that his hands were bleeding. At home, she called her aunt and they went to a local Moslem doctor, who attended to the boy, removed a splinter from his hand and cursed the Moslems who performed this criminal act.

At the time of the explosion, I was present at the home of Flora and Haim Shamash, parents of Eitan (Saleh) Shamash, who was one of the leading organizers of the emigration campaign; hearing of the disaster I rushed over there. The street, usually well-lit, was in darkness. Later I was informed that the grenade (a British Mills) had short-circuited the electric cables in the street.

This attack on the synagogue, where all the activities were centred, bothered us a lot. I got in touch with Sasson Abed, head of the Public Committee for Emigration Affairs, and met him at his house in order to inform him of the incident: Moshe Baghnou, who was critically injured, had seen the bomb-thrower. He was a Moslem dressed in khaki, who stood on the balcony of an Arab house facing the synagogue. It was confirmed that all the Moslem pedlars, who would have been selling their merchandise in the street, mysteriously vanished just a short while before the grenade was thrown.

Here is the affidavit of Yitzhak Eliash, who was then responsible for airport matters.

Every day, between 3 and 4 p.m., I used to go to the synagogue to pick up the travel documents of the emigrants so as to give them to the airport police officer, Abd-El-Jabar. On my way I often bought tasty bagels

from a vendor who sold them there. On the day the bomb was thrown, I arrived there as usual, but found the street blocked by the police.

The bagel vendor was not to be found. The following day I asked him the reason of his absence. At first he hesitated and then answered in a friendly manner: *"Wallah ami shagoullak?"* (Well, sir, what can I tell you?). He continued to say that a day before the bomb incident, a gentleman came to him and asked if he traded there regularly. He confirmed it – This was his living. The gentleman advised him not to turn up the next day (on 14 January 1951), lest evil should befall him. The vendor enquired: *"Kheir shu yezir?"* (What is likely to happen?). The man

*Eitan Shamash.*

refused to give details and repeated his warning. Eliash asked for the gentleman's description and whether he thought he was Jewish, Christian or Moslem. The vendor replied that he appeared to be a Moslem.

We requested Sasson Abed to persuade an examining magistrate to take evidence from Baghnou in hospital. Abed approached the police, but was told not to interfere as the matter was "sensitive."

The condition of the injured Baghnou became worse and as I realized that his evidence was vital, I asked some of our activists to join us at the hospital, to donate blood. We all made our contribution, but to our dismay it didn't help. He died at eight o'clock the next morning, and only then did the magistrate arrive.

An inquest followed but the government didn't appear to take the matter seriously. Attempts were made to ascertain the identities of the bomb throwers. Some thought that it was an attempt by the Istiklal Party to revenge themselves on the government, for persecuting them and closing down their newspaper. A day or two later, another view was expressed, that it was the work of the Government itself, who wished to find an excuse to declare martial law because of the opposition of the Istiklal and the start of Shiite activities during the rule of Saleh Jaber, the Shiite.

On 17 January 1951, I reported to the Mossad that on that very day Abraham El-Kabir, Moshe Shohet, Sasson Abed and Yehya Kassim met with Mustafa El-Umari, the Deputy Prime Minister, in order to state their opinions regarding the way the investigation was continuing. At the same time we succeeded in obtaining a copy of a report written by an Iraqi Army sabotage specialist. It was stamped "Top Secret," dated 14 January, and stated the following:

> As ordered by the Commander of the military police, I arrived at the police directorate in the Area of Baghdad on 14 January 1951 at 19:00, and then proceeded to the site of the bomb explosion adjacent to Meir Tweig (a mistake: it should have been the Mesouda Shemtob) Synagogue at the Bab El-Shargui Quarter.
>
> After inspecting the site of the explosion and the shrapnel pieces which were collected, it was proved that the explosive device was a

highly-charged hand grenade No. 36. This type of grenade is a British Army issue and is in use by the Iraqi police army. It is a modern type of weapon: Twenty-five men and one woman suffered various injuries in the explosion, and one child died from a damaged electricity cable. All the injured were taken to hospital. Six were released after receiving first aid, and the rest stayed on for further treatment. After finding the priming device and the nail [used as safety pin] my investigations lead me to conclude that the grenade was thrown by an unknown person standing between the explosion site and the eastern side of the street. Anyhow it cannot be disproved that the grenade-thrower wasn't far from the alley leading to Ghazi Park.

On 22 January 1951, I sent the following telegram to the Mossad:

a.  In spite of the committee's findings and its influence on the police and the Government, we were unable to arrive at any conclusion or agreement regarding the identity of the grenade-thrower. It is now evident that the government was negligent in its method of conducting the investigation.

b.  No official statements were issued regarding the above incident after the El-Istiklal editor released a long list of suspects in an editorial, accusing the Jews of exploding the device on Israel's orders.

c.  Regarding the progress of emigration no official statement has been made except that the Deputy Prime Minister refuted, before committee members, the news broadcast and printed in London, that emigration is expected to cease in March. Police sources cannot confirm that the registration of candidates and the revoking of citizenship will stop on 9 March. However, for those whose citizenship has been revoked, emigration will continue as planned.

The bomb, aimed at the synagogue, was one of a series of similar incidents. On 19 March 1951 a bomb was planted at the American Information Center in Baghdad, situated in a building on El-Rashid street. The "El-Shaab" newspaper described the incident in these words: "Yesterday, before eleven o'clock in the morning, a deafening explosion was heard near Imam Taha Square. Later, it was discovered that the bomb exploded at the American Information Office in Baghdad and caused the injury of a few people. Four wounded people were taken to hospital. Two of them, Naim Nahum and Abd El-Wahab Muhamed, stayed behind for further treatment."

On 10 May another bomb was set off – this time in a Jewish shop, Bet Lawee, which was situated in El-Rashid Street and was the centre for several car import companies. Luckily, there were no casualties.

A few weeks later another bomb exploded near the Rafidain Bank, opposite the Telegraph and Post Office. It was on 6 June. Two nearby cars were set alight and several Jews whose citizenship had been revoked, were arrested, but were released a short while later. On the night of 9 June 1951, a bomb was thrown at the Jewish shop of Stanley Shashou. This time the building was damaged, but there were no casualties.

On 9 July at 10:00 a.m., a letter bomb exploded in the house of Advocate Jamal Baban. According to the servant's report, someone handed him a letter and asked him to give it to the landlord. The furniture was beyond repair.

On 10 August, the "El-Yaktha" newspaper reported (according to the newspapers of Basra) that two bombs exploded while firemen were at a training course. The paper wanted to know if this was a continuation of the acts of the Jewish "octopus" in Basra, and wondered how the authorities were not able to trace the source of the Jewish arsenal.

As mentioned, the false charge was created at police headquarters in Baghdad and in due course gained credence in other countries; and to my regret, in Israel as well. The assumptions that the Zionists threw the bombs in order to create alarm among the Iraqi Jews, to force them to leave their wealth and the Iraqi Garden of Eden and to emigrate to Israel. But whoever believed, or continued to believe this charge forgets, or doesn't know, or wishes to ignore the basic fact, that a large number of Jews left Iraq for Israel before the mass emigration took place. They escaped through Syria, Turkey, Jordan and especially Iran, and weren't influenced by the dangers. The Halutz Movement was flooded with requests by Jews wanting to leave Iraq, and there were

Jews who had to wait two years in order to arrive at the date set for their departure.

The Iraqi authorities couldn't ignore the outbreak and yet were powerless to stop it. My estimation is that around 12,000 Jews had escaped via Iran, that is around ten per cent of all the Jews in Iraq.

What made so many Jews leave? The logical reply would be that the escape had two motives: the constant pressure the Iraqi Government used on the Jews and their Zionist beliefs, meaning their yearning to emigrate to the Land of their Fathers, and their vision of Jerusalem.

Anyone persistent enough to study the political events in Iraq during the end of the forties and the beginning of the fifties will find that, more relevant than the existence of a connection between the dates when the bombs exploded and the period of high tide of the emigration of our people, there is a remarkable similarity between the dates of bomb explosions and other political events in Iraq. Iraqi Jews registered for emigration at such a rapid pace that no elements whatsoever, and certainly not the Zionist Movement, or Israel, had any reason to accelerate emigration by reverting to such inane acts as that of using explosives.

The Revocation of Citizenship Bill was ratified by the Iraqi Government on 3 March 1950. In the beginning, as long as there was no sure way of escape, the Movement resisted the registration. We, the activists, who were appointed to oversee the emigration, applied heavy pressure on Shemtob to influence the Prime Minister Towfik El-Suweidi to direct the emigration westward, not eastward via Iran. We were aware of the dangers of the eastward path and that is why we opposed it. We sent the activists of the Movement to the synagogue to try and persuade those who wanted to register, to wait awhile. But when the law was ratified in Parliament on 5 March, it was too late to stop the registration.

On 13 March 1950, I reported to the Mossad: "Yesterday, instructions to register were given by the Government. Today, a Government committee began the registration. We advised our members not to register and explained our opposition: It would last as long as the Government had not yet selected the exit route.

However, until 8 April 1950, the day when the explosive charge was put down at El-Beidha Casino, 220 people have already registered, in spite of our opposition. In deliberations conducted at Mossad headquarters on 9 April, fear was expressed that if we didn't agree to registration, it would dilute our influence on the people's will to emigrate. For lack of an alternative I acceded: We decided to encourage it. The following day this change of policy was announced in the synagogues. We were interested to know how many Jews would use this right to register. Heads of the Iraqi Administration reasoned that the number of those registering would be about 10,000 to 14,000 people. Salman Dabby, an Iraqi Jewish police officer, was asked by Alwan Hussein, Commander of the Police Department in charge of Revocation of Citizenship to investigate, before the bill was ratified, the general opinion of the Jewish community. Dabby issued a report claiming that if government oppression of our people continued, the pace of registration would quicken. He didn't give statistics but I anticipated that the number would comprise a third of the Jewish community, meaning 40,000 out of 140,000 – and true to my prediction, 47,000 Jews had registered by the 7 May 1950, far more than the expected estimates.

Eleven days after the explosion of the bomb in Mesouda Shemtob Synagogue, that is until 25 January 1951, the number reached 96,000 people, and on 13 March 1951, the day when the Iraqi Cabinet approved the entire list of people whose citizenship was revoked, that list numbered 103,866 people.

As previously related, on 19 March 1951, an explosive charge was planted in the American Information Center and, three days later, on 22 of the month, the Bill confiscating Jewish property was ratified. On 10 May, a bomb exploded in Bet Lawee and on 22 of that month we, the emissaries of the intelligence unit, Yehuda Tajer and myself were arrested. Within two days Rodney was also arrested. On 6 June, a bomb exploded in the Rafidain Bank building, and on that same day Salim Mouallem, Deputy Director of the Rafidain Bank, was arrested. On the next day, I was released on bail and arrested again because of a car accident. On 9 June, a bomb exploded in Stanley Shashou's shop and, on the next day, Yousif Basri and Shalom Saleh were caught. Within a month of their arrest, on 9 July, a letter bomb was delivered to the office of Advocate Jamal Baban, who acted as my attorney and arranged bail for me after the car accident. On 10 August, when the emigration campaign was almost over, two bombs exploded in the city of Basra.

In their baseless claim, those who believed in the "libel" pounced on the short cessation of flights in July 1950, right in the middle of the miserable dispute that occurred between Shemtob and myself, as proof of a conspiracy. As previously mentioned, in order to prove to Shemtob that we were acting in full coordination with Israel and on her behalf, which he could never grasp, I asked the Mossad to temporarily cease the flights for a few days. The flights stopped and were renewed again. This interruption of flights gave the "pro-conspiracy" people the proof they wanted.

When the slanderous gossip increased among the emigrants, an investigating committee including Shlomo Hillel, one of its members, was appointed in the early fifties. The committee interviewed many witnesses but was unable to positively confirm or refute these rumours. The committee therefore recommended that after the prisoners who were at that time in Iraq, served their prison sentences and were released, a new investigating committee would be appointed, which held hearings for the prisoners and tried to arrive at new conclusions.

In the sixties, after the release of the prisoners from Iraq, Yehuda Tajer among them, and following the "mishap" in Egypt, it was decided at the Israeli Prime Minister's office to appoint a second investigating committee, to ascertain if similar instructions were also given in Iraq. On 16 November 1960, this committee was appointed by Issar Harel, who was then in charge of the secret services, but its findings were kept under wraps until now. When I found out that the misinformation was accepted by a larger public than expected and even among historians, I approached the Prime Minister, David Ben-Gurion, and asked him to let me have the results of his findings. On 13 June 1966, attached to the commemoration ceremonies for the executed Yousif Basri and Shalom Saleh, Haim Israeli, the devoted assistant of all the Ministers of the Defence until today, gave me the report with a letter attached from David Ben-Gurion. In the enclosed appendices in this book I enclose a letter from Ben-Gurion and the full report of the investigating committee, and I hope, that at long last, the final curtain has come down on this false Baghdadi charge.

## The bombs in Baghdad and the development of the emigration campaign

| | |
|---|---|
| 1948 | A bomb was laid on the roof of Yacov Azachi's clinic in El-Amana Suk. |
| 4.4.1950 | The Movement opposed the registration for emigration so long as no fixed exit route had been advised; members of the Movement visited all the synagogues to explain the reasons for their opposition. |
| 8.4.1950 | A bomb was thrown in El-Beidha Casino in Abu Nawas Street. Six Jews were injured. |
| | The Movement's objection to the registration continued, but the pressure of the Jews who wished to register was getting greater. |
| 9.4.1950 | Mordechai Ben-Porat informed the Mossad in Israel that it had been decided to permit the registration; members of the Movement informed the people in all the synagogues. |
| 10.4.1950 | The registration began. |
| 12.4.1950 | 3,400 people registered |
| 14.6.1950 | 60,000 people registered |
| 19.10.1950 | Nouri El-Sa'id reported that 84,000 Jews had registered whereas the government reckoned on between 10,000 and 12,000 only; Ben-Porat's estimate was 40,000. |
| 14.1.1951 | A bomb was aimed at the Mesouda Shemtob Synagogue where the exit to the airport was centred. A bus full of passengers stood by the gate on its way to the airport. Two children and an adult were killed and 25 were injured. All the Moslem pedlars had vanished from the scene before the explosion. |
| 22.1.1951 | Ben-Porat reported to Israel: "Despite all our efforts [...] and our connections with the government and police, we couldn't reach any conclusion regarding the bomb throwers." |
| 19.3.1951 | A bomb was planted in the American Information Center in Baghdad. 4 people were injured. |

| | |
|---|---|
| 10.5.1951 | A bomb was thrown at a Jewish shop Bet Lawee which was an agency centre for importing cars; no casualties. |
| 22.5.1951 | Yehuda Tajer and Mordechai Ben-Porat were arrested by the Secret Police. |
| 6.6.1951 | A bomb exploded near the Rafidain Bank. |
| 9-10.6.1951 | A bomb was thrown at the shop of a Jew, Stanley Shashou. |
| 14.6.1951 | Mordechai Ben-Porat succeeded in escaping from Baghdad. |
| 9.7.1951 | A letter bomb exploded in the office of Advocate Jamal Baban; no one was hurt. |
| | Most of the Jews had already left for Israel, and around 15,000 awaited their flights. |
| 10.8.1951 | Two bombs exploded in Basra, A newspaper demanded: "Is this a follow-up of the activities of the Jewish 'octopus' in Basra?..." |

# Chapter 13

# THE PRISONERS

When I read the following telegram on 24 June 1949, before I left for Iraq I was desolate. It was a brief one: "the condition of our prisoners is worsening daily [...] In our opinion we must apply pressure on the United Nations and the International Red Cross and demand that they visit the prisoners and examine their conditions [...] We contacted the prison warden and did our best to alleviate the criminal injustice to which they are being subjected. The warden admitted that he could do nothing about it..."

A further cable dated 28 August 1949 drew an even harsher picture: "The condition of the Prisoners of Zion goes from bad to worse. Lately they were being subjected to hard labour without cause. Seven of our comrades from Karkuk, who were apprehended a year ago and released on bail, were recently sentenced to various prison terms of one to three years [...] The prison warden transferred some of them to Badra [a remote prison camp used mainly for Communist prisoners], which makes it difficult for us to visit them [...] Our prisoners in Iraq are begging us to present their case to our institutions in Israel and the United Nations in order to rescue them from their plight."

Among the telegrams, I found a short letter written by an instructor in the Movement, who was arrested in April 1948 for receiving a letter from his brother in Israel; he was released only after paying a bribe of 1,000 Dinars to the Ministry of Defence. In his letter, the man described how the judges asked him only six questions about this letter and within three minutes the court declared him "a Jew with connections to the Zionists in Israel," and sent him to gaol. As I pondered over these letters, I realized that the problems related to the prisoners would be one of the most urgent and sensitive issues I would have to deal with in Baghdad.

The imprisonment of the Movement operators in Iraq came in two main stages. The first occurred during the crisis which the Movement suffered in 1945 and the second came four years later during the 1949 crisis.

In 1945, a Jewish truck driver, Daoud Jardoon, was arrested while driving on his regular route; he was carrying letters and circulars of the Movement containing sensitive information. Jardoon, grossly negligent, stowed the forbidden material between the legitimate sacks of goods he was carrying. He couldn't foresee that his wife, who was involved in a quarrel with him, would bring disaster on him. She tipped off the authorities; they searched the truck and he was arrested. The papers were discovered and shortly afterwards a wave of arrests of the Movement officers followed.

Albert Shamash, who served in the Movement as an expert forger of passports (he handled the passports of my family's emigration in 1944) and had good relations with the Secret Police, tried to have the truck driver released or at least to retrieve the incriminating material, but failed. He managed to see the driver who was arrested in Ramadi Prison and assured him that if he kept silent the Movement would look after him. But the driver was unable to keep his promise. Fortunately, Jardoon was only superficially acquainted with two members of the Movement, Raphael Sourani and Ezra Kadoorie (Tsuri) his case officer, and only knew them by their first names.

Meanwhile the material discovered in the truck was analyzed and sent to Baghdad. Based on its contents, the authorities drew up a list of seventy suspects. The affair snowballed into exaggerated proportions: It was said that the printed matter became a shipment of artillery, Tsuri was sent by the British Secret Service in Palestine to trap the Movement members in Iraq and the Chief Rabbi of Baghdad was summoned by the British Consul, and falsely accused of accepting 3,000 Dinars and that ended the episode.

The authorities, however, didn't just engage in rumours and stories but conducted an energetic chase to hunt down the suspects. No effort was spared to collect additional intelligence, especially about the leaders of the Movement.

The Interior Minister took personal charge of the investigating team and demanded daily reports of all developments.

Aryeh Eshel, an emissary of the Hagana who was in charge of the Shura, turned to the British in an effort to conclude the episode. In a meeting with a high-ranking British civil servant, Eshel handed him a letter from Eliahu Epstein (Eilat) of Jerusalem, a friend of the British functionary. However, a few days later the British official replied: "I have approached the authorities who claim that the Jews are making a big commotion over it, so how can you expect the affair to simmer down?"

The community Committee, who approached many people seeking to use their influence, formally decided not to interfere, as the affair had taken on a political (Zionist) complexion. However, informally, the Committee members did what they could to keep the investigation from becoming harsh and explosive.

The authorities would not call off the investigation. The driver Jardoon, accompanied by Government agents, roamed the streets in search of members of the Movement. They followed a female member for two days, after which she was seen to enter the residence of her liaison officer, Marguelite Shashou. On the third day, they searched her house in her absence and found a lot of printed matter belonging to the Movement, in Hebrew and Arabic. Marguelite herself had to go underground just as other Movement members had done.

The Movement dispensed with a generous fortune and received a list of the suspects, thus making it possible to smuggle some of them away and rid themselves of incriminating evidence. Among them was the emissary of the Mossad, Ezra Kadoorie, instructor Raphael Sourani, his brother Shmuel, Louise, daughter of a retired judge, Yehezkel Murad and a young lady named Ilana. Four of these escaped to Israel posing as young married couples and using false passports. It was decided that Kadoorie should leave for Israel and his colleague, emissary Yehoshua Givoni, escape to northern Iraq. The large library of the Movement was shifted from one area to another in search of safe hiding places.

The police were particularly anxious to find Albert Shamash, the man who went to Ramadi to save the printed matter. Shamash managed to get away. Police searched his house and found no incriminating evidence. Frustrated and angry they smashed his furniture and arrested some members of his family, as they did with others.

Albert Babai (Uri), a local instructor of the Movement who also escaped, was told that the police were seeking to question him, promising not to arrest him. He surrendered, but contrary to police assurances he was arrested, interrogated and even brought before the driver Jardoon for identification as the "Albert" they were seeking. Jardoon didn't identify him and so he was released. When the rumour that Albert Shamash was being sought, lots of people began to panic. Police officers who were engaged in the business of smuggling Jews, fearing exposure, offered to help smuggle him out of Iraq. But his activist, the emissary of Aliya, Aryeh Abramovsky, refused to release him.

At last the storm abated. The fugitives came out of hiding and resumed their activities; community leaders now stood in awe of the Zionist "virus." Prominent members of the community who wouldn't publicly identify with Zionism, now helped the Movement as best they could. The Movement passed its first difficult test successfully.

Four years later, in 1949, the second crisis cropped up. The Iraqi regime decided to crush all elements of political opposition such as the Communist Movement and the Zionist Underground. Two activists who were working for the emigration project and an emigrant whose name had been disclosed in the city of Khanakin were immediately sent to Baghdad. In retaliation, the police arrested the aging community leader, together with other prominent members and charged them with smuggling and conspiracy to smuggle Jews out. A few dignitaries were arrested in the city of Hilla. Jews were arrested in Mosul and blamed for smuggling money into Israel and, in Amara, policemen encircled the synagogue on Yom Kippur and arrested ten worshippers including the chairman of the community. They were searching everywhere for would-be emigrants.

In the beginning of September 1949, four hundred and fifty Jews were serving time in various prisons all over Iraq. They had been sentenced from three to ten years, some of them to hard labour. They were found guilty of corresponding with Israel, sending money to Israel, Zionist activities, Communist activities and the like. Another one hundred and fifty detainees were awaiting trial.

On 8 October 1949, the last day of Succoth, four cadets of the Young Halutz were arrested as they were walking in the streets. Apparently a 17 year old, who was arrested on charges of Communist activities and was a member of the

Young Halutz when still a boy, knew some of its members and instructors and agreed to collaborate with the police, hoping for a reduced sentence. The news spread like wildfire even though, at that time, no one credited it with much significance. It was assumed that as in many previous arrests, all four would be released after posting adequate bail.

When Yitzhak Shamash (Boaz), a Movement instructor and Shura commander was arrested, the event took on a different aspect. He went to the police station to enquire about his brother's arrest and was immediately taken in himself. When the young collaborator pointed him out – it was enough to render him a suspect as a Movement leader. Itshak David Sofer, a Movement supporter with good connections with the Iraqi police, was sent to enquire about the reasons for the arrests. The superintendent said frankly: "Had you not been one of our acquaintances, you wouldn't have left these police headquarters a free man."

This was more than a hint that the arrests were made on government orders. Sofer barely had time to advise his superiors about the situation when another instructor was arrested in his office at the Electric Company. This was Aziz Kashi (Aryeh), a member of the editorial staff of the Movement's Underground newspaper, who knew the location of the caches, where their typed and printed material was deposited and also the typewriters and the mimeograph machines were kept. At the time, the library of the Movement, consisting of about 3,000 books, was concealed in his basement and an arms cache was hidden in his backyard.

That was in mid-October 1949. The Movement declared a state of emergency. Its institutions and those of the Shura were dismantled and replaced by a new establishment – "the Institution for the State of Emergency." Under this new body, emissaries held meetings, intelligence information was collected and instructions and orders were issued. A committee was also nominated and included the instructors Naim Bekhor, David Shukur and Selim Khalifa, who were in charge of exploiting their connections with Jews and Moslems and approaching them when required. All the printed material and equipment were hidden in secret caches and decisions were made about new ways of establishing contact between members and instructors.

The detainees confessed under torture to belonging to the Movement and even gave names of their co-members and instructors. Money was paid to acquire the "wanted" list which grew longer by the day. At night, when the arresting team broke into the houses of suspects, they couldn't be found, and so they seized family members, leaving chaos in their homes. The Institution for the State of Emergency instructed people not to open their doors to the police, in order to slow down the arrests. It didn't help. They would simply shoot the locks off the doors.

Instructors and activists abandoned their homes and went into hiding. Documents containing lists of members were destroyed. The chase continued at full speed and no end was in sight. The steady increase of pressure brought with it a decrease in the number of places of refuge, which were considered safe, and this gave way to the alternative of escaping to Iran. Departure of the Movement leaders meant a certain erosion of its infrastructure, and the Zionist sympathizers argued among themselves as to what came first, the people or the Movement and the cause. Some argued that instructors and activists need not be smuggled out unless in mortal danger.

The Mossad Le Aliya Bet in Israel issued this directive: "Whenever possible transfer wanted instructors to Iran." This laconic statement was open to interpretation. It didn't say this should be done only when they were in mortal danger, neither did it explain whether the fugitives should stay temporarily in Iran and return after things had calmed down, or continue on from there to Israel.

On 30 December 1949, five weeks after my arrival in Iraq, I sent a letter to the Mossad, and among other things, I wrote the following:

> The relations between the Movement on one hand and the Government and Secret Police on the other were so weak that when the first five were arrested, there wasn't anyone who could get close enough to the Secret Police to be able to offer bribes and obtain their release [...] Regarding the disbanding of the instructors, the prevailing opinion here is that it was unnecessary, and those who already went into hiding can now return [...] Disbanding the instructors of the Shura and the Movement left a bad impression here on the people who are questioning "if not

now, when is the instructor ever going to stand up for his cause?" The Movement had such tense relations with the leaders of the community, so much so that during the crisis, when the Movement asked them to cooperate and apply pressure on the Government, they turned their backs on it and barely responded to the Movement's request to ease the strike and the fasting [...] Not many were appointed deputies to the responsible members inside the Movement, Shura and the Aliya, so that after the instructors were disbanded, the emissaries stood alone, helpless.

In this letter I suggested some points outlining our conduct in times of an expected crisis that was bound to crop up:

To establish good relations with the Secret Police, to pay salaries, to bribe people, even those who are without immediate usefulness to us [...] To act with caution when disbanding instructors; to make it clear to the instructors that they must be the last to leave, and only after all members have departed; after which disbanded instructors must go into hiding in Baghdad itself, temporarily, and only until things return to normal [...] We must immediately start mending our fences with the community leaders and establish good relations with them and cooperate with them whenever possible [...] In my opinion, an emissary should act as emissary to the Agency as well to the Jewish people. Emissaries must reach out to the congregation, detached from the Movement, and meet with the dignitaries even though they could not possibly become Movement members. The emissary must initiate such meetings and try to win them over (of course only to ascertain limitations and providing he does not jeopardize his own safety). Not to underestimate the rich and the influential. Not to be concerned purely with the interests of the Movement. All the time we must go back to the public from our secret places – this will gain us the cooperation of the community dignitaries who have influence in government circles, those same people who during the last crisis wouldn't lift a finger to help us, claiming that they could not act as the Movement's friends only in times of crises. They needed perpetual cooperation.

Although this long letter didn't change their attitude, it gave them food for thought. Meanwhile in Iraq, a most remarkable thing happened: Within six weeks, fifty-six instructors and commanders were smuggled away to Iran.

The continuing wave of arrests inflicted increasing pressure on the community and especially among families of the detainees. They appealed to the chairman of the community, Sasson Khadourie, who had his own way of avoiding them. The Institution for the State of Emergency held a rowdy meeting where feelings ran high and some even suggested that the Shura ought to perform some headline-catching sabotage against the Iraqi Secret Police and the chairman of the community. On 21 October 1949, a short while prior to my arrival in Baghdad, the following telegram was sent to Israel: "The members of the Movement and Shura have reached the threshold of despair. They demand action, even to using weapons against some of the Government and the community hierarchy. Some members are threatening to use our hidden weapons, against our orders."

The Mossad's reply received the next day, was: "The Government of Israel is making every effort to stop the persecutions. Do everything to persuade the members that the use of weapons at this point can only aggravate the situation and bring to a stop all possible actions against the Iraqi Government."

At the Institution for the State of Emergency it was decided to appeal to the community leaders, at least those who could still openly influence Government circles, to act. Raphael Sourani was sent to appear before the community leaders to persuade them that the time had come for them to intervene since the persecutions were operated against all members of the Jewish community and not only against the members of the Movement. He warned that if the searches were to continue, the hidden weapons would eventually be found. But they wouldn't listen to him. One of them said to Sourani: "When you established the Movement and bought weapons, you did not consult with us. Why do you come to us now? If you are really concerned about the safety of the community – give yourselves up and hand over your weapons."

The Institution for the State of Emergency decided to organize a demonstration that would send a clear message to the Chairman of the community and the Iraqi Government and support the Israeli Government in its struggle through diplomatic channels. The demonstration was planned to take place in front of the offices of the chairman of the community at the old quarters. On the night of 22 October, the news was circulated and on the next day thousands of demonstrators gathered in front of the community offices. Hundreds of women, fearful for the fate of family members, called out, pleading with Khadourie to come forward. He locked himself in his room and refused to meet with the demonstrators. The situation turned nasty and a group of women broke into his room, attacked and dragged him out into the street in order to force him to see the Prime Minister. In the heat of the moment they took off his headdress and dashed it to the floor.

Shocked and dismayed, he tried to calm them down, promised to help and demanded that they all return quietly to their homes. The women demonstrators, having broken the furniture in his room, turned into the central street in Baghdad, El-Rashid, and walked towards the Regent's office. When they reached Amin Square, they were surrounded by policemen. The police arrested many men and women; fifteen of them (13 men and 2 women) were charged on 12 November and sentenced from two to three years hard labour. It was later discovered that an assistant in Khadourie's office tipped off the police, since he couldn't bear to witness his master's humiliation.

On 23 October 1949, when the Institution for the State of Emergency demanded from the community's committee to declare a day of prayer and fasting to protest the wave of arrests and torture, Khadourie agreed. He finally got the message. The 25 October was declared by the leaders as a day of rest, fasting and prayer for the whole community. The Jewish establishments were closed and the synagogues were packed with worshippers. The Moslems were astounded and the local press was crying out that Tel Aviv was behind the actions of the Jews of Baghdad. A member of Parliament, Yaacov Battat, and the Interior Minister, Omar Nadhmi, complained about the atrocious measures used against the detainees. The Minister's reply was extremely harsh: "All these measures are necessary to deal with the situation. We have made up our minds to persist in our investigations despite the demonstrations." Khadourie acted quietly behind the scenes, but his endeavours went unnoticed by the laymen of the community and consequently they decided to continue their struggle. In the beginning of November, they introduced the meat boycott, previously mentioned. Khadourie couldn't silence this protest; the tax on meat (*Gabella*) was the community's main source of revenue. Under pressure Khadourie resigned on 10 November 1949. His resignation was accepted and Yehezkel Shemtob was elected to replace him as deputy. The boycott ended and in the meantime arrests and searches diminished until they petered out by the end of November.

During the six weeks of the second crisis about seven hundred people were arrested, most of them relatives of wanted suspects. Sixty were court-martialled and charged with having some kind of connection with the Movement and the rest were released. Those court-martials were divided into three categories, in

*Some of the individuals imprisoned in Iraq for their Zionist activities in 1948, from right to left: Salman Shamash, Ezra David, Abraham Yehezkel, the then Chief of Staff Major-General Moshe Levy, Menashe Babila, the late Kadoorie Nissan Abed, Fouad Abraham, Yehezkel Habba.*

accordance with the seriousness of their offenses. They were collectively punished with prison sentences from two to five years.

On my arrival in Baghdad on 23 November 1949, I was deeply absorbed in dealing with the problem of the prisoners. I wanted to visit them to give them moral support. I threw caution to the winds and went to see them in their prison cells, accompanied by the emissary of the Movement, Yerahmiel Assa, who came to Baghdad for a short stay. The prisoners didn't know me and probably thought I was, like them, a prisoner. Only our liaison man, Naim Barzilay knew my real identity.

By 15 February 1950, we were able to accumulate a comprehensive list of prisoners and the prisons that held them and sent it the Mossad in Israel. In addition to the prisoners, we were also anxious about their families, who in some cases lost their bread winners when a father or son was taken away.

In an effort to improve their conditions or try to obtain their release, we had to use the only means that could influence the wardens – bribery. By 21 November 1950, we had an estimate of the amount of money required for bribes. In order to release fifty-three prisoners, sentenced between a year and a half to seven years, we had to pay 180 Dinars (equivalent then to $720) per prisoner, amounting to a total of 9,540 Dinars. We contacted the Mossad requesting the above sum and a month later, on 20 December 1950, we received the following: "The Jewish Agency has allotted 5,000 Israeli Pounds for the release of prisoners; you have to raise the remaining amount from the community and the prisoners' families. Keep us posted of the situation and chances of release, in order to obtain the money from the Agency." On the following day we replied: "Sorry, but the sum barely covers half the expenses, and we anticipate defeat. The chances of release, according to the broker are excellent. We will contact him again today and raise the matter, but understand, that one of the conditions is that the money be deposited with a well-known neutral person who, in case of failure, will return it; we are in need of all of the 5,000 Dinars immediately."

Before closing the deal, we obtained a copy of a secret official letter, dated 7 January 1951, addressed to the Revocation of Citizenship Bureau. Attached was a list of 175 Jewish prisoners whose citizenship the Bureau was instructed to cancel immediately.

On 1 May, we sent a telegram to the Mossad suggesting that one of the families who had a son in prison should, on arrival in Israel, petition the Red Cross, the American and British Embassies in Israel to intervene on our behalf. No reply was received.

The attitude of the Israeli establishments was very frustrating. Two weeks later, Yoav Goral, the emissary of the Movement in charge of indoctrination, informed the Middle East Department that he had finished his job in Iraq and transferred the responsibility of dealing with the problem of the prisoners to the Intelligence emissary, Yehuda Tajer. The latter was staying behind in Baghdad on behalf of the office for special operations in the Ministry of Foreign Affairs. In order to influence Iraqi public opinion, we planned a publicity campaign using opposition newspapers to publish editorials demanding the release of the Zionist prisoners and thus saving the Iraqi people the expense of keeping them in prison. On 21 May 1951, a day before Yehuda Tajer and myself were arrested, I sent a cable to the Mossad reporting that "El-Hawadith," the evening paper had already published such an editorial, demanding that the Government should deport the prisoners after their release from prison. Three similar editorials were to be published in three opposition papers, and this would have been followed by Diwan El-Thiban, a member of Parliament presenting a motion to hold a session on the subject.

The problem of the prisoners gave me no peace and even after I went back to Israel, I kept trying to interest various establishments to act on their behalf.

# Chapter 14

# THE INTELLIGENCE NETWORK COLLAPSES

May 1951 seemed full of promise. The planes continued to carry Iraqi Jews to their longed-for destination, and the campaign's officers effectively controlled almost everything. Their liaison with the Secret Police and Emigration officers was a close one. My relations with the committee members, presided over by Sasson Abed, who was chosen by the Minister of Interior, went well and with mutual understanding. My activities were not restricted; I visited the Meir Tweig Synagogue anonymously, where registration and issue of documents were managed and the Mesouda Shemtob Synagogue, where the main procedures for preparing the "Olim" (immigrants) for immigration was conducted. The Iraqi Cabinet accepted the surrender of nationality of its 103,866 Jews, and in May 1951 about 80% of the Jews who had registered for immigration had already arrived in Israel.

My longing for home increased. I missed my family, my mother Regina who said to me when I left Israel, "I entrust you into the hands of God and he will send you back," my faithful companion Rivca and above all, my homeland, Israel. Twenty-two months passed since I left Israel. I began to put pressure on the Mossad Aliya Bet to send someone to replace me and did not cease badgering them until I incensed even Moshe Carmil, who was known for his easy-going temperament. Eventually he sent me the following message: "For the tenth time, please believe me, we are looking for a replacement, and I am quite sure we will find someone soon. Do not despair. See you soon."

One day Mohammed arrived at Naim Moshe Mandelawy's house, where I was staying with his family. He was the driver who ran errands for us between Baghdad and our people in Teheran. He said to my host: "I brought you your 'cousin'." Before he turned to go, he mentioned that he was worried about the health of the traveller he had introduced, as he had eaten more than a kilo of pistachio nuts throughout the journey! Mandelawy hastened to inform me that my replacement had at last arrived. The news made me very happy; to my regret my expectations were short-lived.

The emissary who was sent to replace me was Yacov Frank. He had served as a Lt. Colonel in the Israeli Air Force and was full of good humour and the will to fulfil his mission as well, but in no way was he equipped for the assignment. His appearance was foreign to the Iraqis: He was a redhead and he spoke with a Palestinian accent. He held an Iranian passport and possessed a document claiming he was an Iranian merchant. This would have been useless to him in his job. Now the question was, what kind of work should he seek, and how to prepare him for awkward situations such as queries from nosy people or the police.

No Jewish families would invite such a person into their home; it would have spelt great danger for them. We had no choice but to find him a room in the Semiramis Hotel, where foreigners and tourists liked to stay. Several days later, Naim Moshe Mandelawy told me that he spoke privately with Frank and advised him to return to Israel, in order to avoid bringing trouble on himself and danger to the Aliya campaign. Frank did not react; he was too stunned to reply.

The next day in Eitan's (Saleh Shamash) house, I introduced Yacov Frank to I.D. Sofer, George Shasha and Yitzhak Elias. Shocked as they were, they understood and accepted my decision to return to Israel but they thought this would bring about a catastrophe. They said: "Frank may be a very talented person, but he is not the right man for this job." Yitzhak Elias, who was our contact with the Secret Police, added: "To the best of my knowledge, the Secret Police are looking for such a man – a fair-skinned foreigner, who may well be a Russian spy. Frank would definitely interest them and this would cause us great concern."

We discussed this with Frank and decided unanimously to send him back to Israel. According to Iraqi rules, all foreigners who arrived in Iraq had to register with the police within two weeks in order to obtain a three-month visa. To avoid doing so, it was agreed that Frank should leave immediately. On 27 April 1951, a flight to Turkey was arranged, and after a few days he arrived safely in Israel. On the same day, I sent the following cable:

a.  Ger (Yacov Frank's nickname) flew to Turkey this morning via Beirut… The conclusion that he cannot remain "black" [illegal] was drawn in the light of circumstances here. There is at present no Jewish family able to host an Israeli emissary, even one who is dark-skinned and speaks the local dialect. We are still having difficulties deciding what to do. You gave us no time to consult you, since he had to go to a hotel immediately, otherwise suspicion may have arisen as to his method of departure.

b.  After he registered, I took him on a tour and explained the work to him. He met frequently with his co-workers and members of the Committee and became acquainted with all manner of action here. The decision to give him an exit and travel permission was made without my knowledge. I asked him to stay for at least another week.

c.  At all times I made sure that he felt like a fifth wheel, that his usefulness or activities were limited. However, he himself arrived at the same conclusion and decided to go.

d.  If you want him to stay on at the end of the operation, you can recall him by the end of May, as I told him, to enable me to leave early.

e.  I regret that during my conversation with Doron an impression was formed that his early departure and the fact that we did not consult you, were planned in advance; of course this impression, if it were so, came as a hard blow to us, but we hope that Ger himself will explain the situation to you and that he was the one responsible for it.

Later, as Chairman of the Workshop's Union, Frank became a candidate for the Eighth Knesset as a member of the Leftist Party, the Ma'arach, and in mid-term he became a Member of the Knesset in place of Pinhas Sapir. He used to point me out and tell Knesset members and those of the press: "Thanks to this man, Mordechai Ben-Porat, my head is still on my shoulders." He bore me no grudge; he understood that what we had done for him was the right thing.

On 4 May 1951 I travelled by car to meet with Chris (the code name for stewardess Ilana Marcus) at the home of my uncle, Abdel El-Aziz (Aboudy Shmueli). She was required to hand me sensitive documents from the Mossad and letters from my girlfriend, while I gave her intelligence information and lists of passengers on the various flights. Suddenly a drunk, speeding on a bicycle, wheeled out of a side street and collided with my car.

I walked over to investigate the matter and an imposing, well-dressed man thrust himself forward and began inciting the crowd against me. I replied angrily. No one seemed to suspect my Jewish identity. With the help of two volunteers, I carried the injured man into my car, never for a moment forgetting the sensitive documents meant for Chris. Being close to my uncle's house, I stopped a moment to leave the documents there and continued on to the police station. The station commander, who was on our payroll, gave the injured person a dressing-down for careless riding. I then took him on to the hospital.

Meanwhile news of the accident reached our people. Yousif Basri, who had good connections with the high echelons in the government, had already used his influence with the hospital staff, who were told to play down the importance of the incident. He was examined and given four days sick leave.

Later on, in court, I was surprised to see the man who tried to inflame the crowd against me. He was in the Courthouse wearing the army uniform of a captain and had arrived to give evidence.

When Yacov Frank left, I began counting the days in anticipation of the arrival of my replacement. One day, Mohammed, the driver, showed up at Naim Mandelawy's house accompanied by a traveller from Iran, Ismail Salhoon, holder of an Iranian passport. He was Yehuda (Youdkeh) Tajer, who was sent to replace me as the liaison officer of the Intelligence network.

While I was working in the Foreign Office in Israel, I dealt with Intelligence material concerning Iraq. I was assigned, in Iraq, among other things, to send through my officers-in-charge in the Mossad Aliya Bet various reports of this nature to the Foreign Office. Apart from what I provided, I would receive from the Foreign Office, from time to time, lists of political questions, which I did my best to answer and transmit to Israel. Here is a typical telegram I received: "In agreement with the army you are to continue your work for us according to instructions. Regarding military matters, you have to coordinate with Moussa (meaning Uri Babay who acted in Iran for military Intelligence and the Foreign Office)."

The source of my intelligence information was Yousif El-Kabir (Abraham's brother), a well-known lawyer and adviser to several British commercial companies. The Iraqi authorities were often in need of his advice, as were Jewish firms who had links with the authorities. I would prepare the answers and send them to the Foreign Office in Israel, and continued to do so until Uri Babay succeeded in mobilizing Iraqi Jews who could manage Intelligence networks to be subject to his authority. Among them was my childhood friend, Yousif Basri (Abratz), who came to Teheran on his way to Israel. After recruiting him, I used to meet him together with his colleagues in Baghdad at the request of Uri Babay, mainly for the purpose of coordination and resolving various conflicts. From time to time, I was also asked to transfer money to them for their work, although I did not participate in it.

On his arrival in Baghdad, Yehuda Tajer helped me a lot and took quite a burden off my shoulders. In this way I was able to devote more time to the Aliya (immigration) matter, which was coming to an end. I found out that he was more experienced and qualified than I was to carry out Intelligence activities, and this is what led me to believe that, unlike myself, he had undergone a thorough professional training before he was sent to Iraq.

When Tajer asked me to recruit an Intelligence officer who could oversee the contacts between the various agents, I reasoned that such a person ought to come from among the existing instructors of the Movement. So I invited Yousif Khabbaza (Beit Halahmi), an officer in the Shura, to join us. I did not hasten to introduce him to Tajer until I could be certain of his competence and ability.

He started working and, after a period of time, he himself recruited Salim Mouallem, Deputy Director of the Rafidain Bank. After recruiting Yousif Khabbaza and introducing him to Yehuda Tajer, I relinquished all my Intelligence activities, and so the ultimate separation between my Intelligence work and that of Aliya took place. The only connection I had with Yehuda Tajer was to provide him with finance and telegraphic services.

After the incident of the bicycle rider and the meeting with Yehuda Tajer, tired and very homesick, I sent the following telegram, on 10 May 1951, to Israel: "I have come to the conclusion that it is vital that I should conclude my work at the end of this month. You have to appoint my successor immediately. If I do not hear from you, I will transfer my work to the chief members of the staff, under the supervision of Yehuda Tajer or Rony Barnett."

Shortly before that, I heard rumours about a stranger living in Baghdad who hosted top-rank individuals from the Iraqi hierarchy at his parties. I mentioned it in a telegram but did not attach great importance to it. Meanwhile I heard through Tajer that he was in touch with someone else by the name of Peter Heinz Yaniv, alias "Robert Rodney," a British businessman living in Baghdad. He was born in Hamburg in 1922 and when the Nazis came to power, he escaped to England with his family and there he studied Semitic languages. In the Second World War he served in the British army and achieved the rank of Major in the Intelligence Service. He had served in India and Palestine. Just before the founding of the State of Israel he was released from the army, emigrated to the country and lived in Jerusalem with his Jewish wife. He then studied at the university and worked for the Information Service of the Haganah Defense Organization and in the political department of the Jewish Agency. Rodney arrived in Baghdad before Tajer. He thought that with his abilities and talents, he would be able to reorganize the Intelligence network, but when Tajer arrived and explained to him that he would work under him, Rodney was disappointed. He kept house with a belly dancer whom he had met in Iran, in a rented villa in the El-Karrada area, south of Baghdad, and continued to host dignitaries there from the upper classes of Iraqi society.

Rodney sent me several messages asking me to meet him. I refused, as I wanted to keep a complete distance between the Intelligence network and immigration activities. It was quite suitable for me to be in touch with him through an agent, Abraham Towfik (Ben Mordechai), who started off as our chief wireless operator and had then been relieved of this duty. I also used to send money to Rodney according to instructions I received from Israel. I was lucky that I did not accede to his request to meet him, as this saved my life later on when I faced him at the police station after we were both caught. One day, after they arrested me, I was taken to the detention centre. A judicial interrogator was sitting there with a group of officers. When I was led into the room, he pointed at me and asked a man sitting on a sofa: "Is this the one?" The man said no. It was Rodney.

My relation with Tajer was different. We used to meet once a week in the evening in a conventional meeting place, and from there we'd drive to a lonely spot. We frequently parked in Baghdad-El-Jedida an area which was developed mainly by Jews. During these meetings I would bring him up to date regarding the Aliya operation and the general atmosphere in Iraq and receive Intelligence material from him, which I'd then transfer to the wireless operators for transmission to Israel. During these meetings and feeling very home-sick I'd often find myself singing Israeli songs and he enjoyed accompanying me.

Once, in the second half of the month of May 1951, Tajer asked me to accompany him to a well-known department store, Orosdi Bak, in order to buy a belt and some stationery. Unlike my cautious self and feeling over-confident that day I accepted. Actually this was the first time I met Tajer in public in broad daylight. Early on Tuesday 22 May 1951, I drove Tajer from our meeting place in my black Citroen car: Neither of us knew where the other lived. We drove

*Orosdi Bak Square in El-Rashid Street in Baghdad.*

towards the store in El-Rashid, the main street in Baghdad. Being wary, I parked the car about twenty meters away from the store and continued on foot. We entered the store and walked up to the second floor. Tajer did not find what he wanted so we turned back and made for the exit. We went out together and after a distance of twenty meters, I noticed three men approaching us.

"Youdkeh, we are doomed!" I muttered in Hebrew.

I did not look at Tajer, so as not to give the three, who appeared to be detectives, any clue as to our relationship. I seemed to recognize one of them. We studied together in elementary school, where he sat beside me in class and would pester me and cheat from my work in exams; in the end I'd always be the one to take the blame.

They stopped us, hailed a taxi and asked us to get in. The man I recognized sat in front, with Tajer between him and the driver, while I sat in the back between the other two. I slid my hand into one of my pockets and felt for a piece of paper. It was an article from a local newspaper which we had instigated. It attacked the Government on the problem of the Zionist prisoners. I was eager to get rid of it, so I shoved my handkerchief into my pocket and brought it out with the cutting concealed within. I then pressed it into the back of my seat. I was unable to know how Tajer felt. From where I was, with detectives to my left and right, I couldn't move freely, and focussed on the back of his head.

As the car drove on, the detectives spoke quietly between them in coded language, and I heard one say the word: *"Balkat,"* meaning "hope." From this I concluded that they were looking for someone in particular and thought they had found him.

We arrived at the police station in Baghdad-El-Jedida. They separated us. After a short while, they came to me and without asking my name or address, they fired questions at me:

"From where do you know him?"

"I don't know him," I swiftly replied.

"What is your name?"

"Nissim Moshe," I answered. I carried an identity card in the name of Nissim Moshe Mandelawy, a brother of Naim Moshe Mandelawy. The owner was now in Israel, but like him I had a dark skin, dark, frizzy hair and could easily pass for any young Iraqi. During my lengthy stay in Iraq I used different pseudonyms according to the missions with which I was involved. When I travelled to northern Iraq, I had a genuine identity card, which was issued by the Chamber of Commerce in Baghdad; in Basra, in the south, I carried the identity of a lawyer; with Jewish acquaintances I would use various names, one for each centre where I worked: Zaki, Habib, Nissim, Salman, Nouri, etc. I was Nissim Moshe to the detectives and in the two instances when I was caught, in Basra and now, I carried the same identity. Later I was informed that Tajer gave his name as Ismail Salhoon and produced his Iranian passport. When they spoke to him in Farsi, he could not answer them and this aroused their suspicions.

Yitzhak Elias, an Aliya agent, who was on his way to the Mesouda Shemtob Synagogue, spotted my Citroen car parked near the square in the centre of town, and became suspicious. He called I.D. Sofer and George Shasha, and when the wireless operators informed them that I hadn't arrived as scheduled to pick up a telegram, they were alarmed. *"El dast aswad,"* agreed Sofer and Shasha, meaning, "It looks very black."

As they were trying to fathom the reason for my absence, another blow followed. Abraham Towfik, the oldest of wireless operators, who was employed by Tajer in the network, phoned his boss and an unfamiliar voice came through. They now knew that Yehuda Tajer was also in trouble. So our network members began to dispose of several account books, which were slated for delivery to Israel. That day several strangers appeared in the synagogue with a search warrant and made for the safe in the office in order to check financial statements. One of them, who knew Yitzhak Elias well, took him aside and asked him if he had heard of Nissim Moshe. Yitzhak said he did and pointed to a room on the second floor saying: "That's his room; he is a clerk, like me." Another detective parked himself by the phone in order to trace incoming calls.

The detectives then accompanied employees to their homes, which were thoroughly searched, but luckily nothing was found. In one of the houses they came across a metal suitcase, securely locked, containing hundreds of Land Ownership Deeds belonging to Iraqi Jews who had acquired land in Palestine, brokered by Aharon Sasson Ben Eliahu, known as the "Teacher," who was Chairman of the Zionist Federation until 1925. In Iraq extensive Zionistic activity existed until 1935. The Teacher spread the idea of the Zionist shekel and sold lands in Palestine to Jews through the Land Development Company. The suitcase containing the deeds proved too difficult to open and the detectives gave up and left it behind.

After a short interrogation I was driven to the police station El-Sarai in the centre of Baghdad, not far from my father's shop. I was hustled into a narrow room, adjacent to that of the investigator's, where an overhead light shone cruelly for twenty-four hours. I was mentally and physically tired. I covered my eyes and tried to sleep, but sleep evaded me.

I decided to make a pretense of it but kept my ears open for what was being said in the adjoining room. I was anxious to transfer the information I heard, mainly names of wanted people, through one of the workers at the station to our colleagues outside, so as to help those on the list to escape before they were arrested. Compared to what I went through later, this brief arrest in El-Sarai was a joyride, especially as the policemen, at least those with whom I was involved, were a hopeless lot. Take for example the policeman who was requested to type the names of the participants in a Communist demonstration. He asked me, although I was still in detention, to read out the names for him as he typed. An officer who was passing by saw us collaborating and reprimanded the simple policeman and dismissed him.

On 22 May, the agents reported to Israel: "Dror and his second-in-command vanished before noon. Their car was found deserted in the main street. The police entered the immigrant's camp, Mesouda Shemtob, and arrested seven important agents and searched their homes. The police were also looking for three more agents, apart from Dror; they remained there and prevented us from using the telephone. We can only presume that Dror has been taken."

A few hours later, our people stealthily approached the Citroen car, checked that no one was following them and turned on the engine. Here was proof that Tajer and I hadn't been followed before entering the department store.

The next day the emissaries wired Israel: "Dror and his aide are imprisoned in two separate cells in the offices of the Secret Police. It was discovered that they were taken by the police, who must have followed them to the department store. The seven workers who were arrested were released yesterday on bail, on condition that they report the next day. The interrogation is continuing. Also five clerks from the department store were also taken for questioning. In a separate telegram the emissaries informed them that they had not succeeded in meeting the prisoners and added: "Dror told them that he was a clerk in the Immigration Office. At three o'clock in the afternoon, Dror was seen manacled and taken by car to the Dora police station with a heavy police guard. It is known that a police officer, Salem Jasem, notorious for his skill in torture methods, was present at this station." In another telegram on the same day, the names of the imprisoned people were mentioned: Naim Moshe Mandelawy, Saleh Yona, Yitzhak Elias, Meir Elias, Saleh Yamen and Ezra Yamen. The agents made sure to inform Rodney about those arrested, left a message to the air stewardess not to come into town and also informed Yousif Basri and others to cease all activities. Also they informed the Aliya foundation that the police had been to the home of my uncle, Aboudy Abd-El-Aziz (Shmueli), and arrested him and his son.

I had no idea how the agents received the information so quickly. I was transferred to the Dora Station after being in El-Sarai for several hours. It was late afternoon. I was put in a stable, where iron chains hung from the walls; these were originally used to tether the horses. They chained my two legs and one hand together. Around midnight, a man dressed in civilian clothes came in and tried to make me talk: He wanted information about Tajer and the significance of our acquaintance. I said that I didn't know him. He began beating me cruelly until he was weary. The same thing happened the next day, only they freed my legs. Evening came and it began all over again. Then I heard a shrill whistling sound in my ears and felt that they were about to explode. The investigator was livid:

"Ihchi! Goul! Al akall subni!" – "Speak! Talk! At least curse me!"

I remained silent.

He gnashed his teeth, clenched his fist and started to beat me again.

Spitting blood I soon realized that I had lost two teeth. I shouted for a doctor but all I got were more blows, kicks and butting with his head. The torture went on for four days and a half, a series of tortures and intermissions.

On 27 May they released me. I was left in a cell with six other criminals. Against all reasoning, my cellmates greeted me with sympathy and admiration for the way I had endured the interrogation. At night they heard the shouting and were very impressed with my self-control and silence. We were partners in destiny. They served me tea and food and each one related the reason for his imprisonment – theft, murder and so on.

One day, on 28 May, they released my chains. I was transferred to a solitary cell. On the concrete floor lay a mat and on the ceiling a bulb shone mercilessly for twenty-four hours. I removed my shoes, put them under my head and fell asleep. From time to time high-ranking individuals would come to visit, and the jailers would guide them to the peep-hole of my cell door – I was the star attraction of that gaol.

Six days later, a gaoler came to my cell and handed me some shaving accessories. I had neither shaved nor washed since the day I was arrested. Spruced up and presentable, I was transferred back to the El-Sarai Police Station in Baghdad. On the way I saw some buses driving immigrants to the airport; this gave me a great deal of satisfaction and relief. "I may have been arrested," I thought, "but at least the immigration operation in which I took part continues to function." At the station I was taken into a room where my "brother," Naim Moshe Mandelawy, sat waiting for me, as under these circumstances he had to fulfil the job of a "brother" until the end; he accomplished this with complete devotion and subject to great danger. He brought me food, but although famished, I was unable to eat. I was exhausted, weak and depressed. Years later, sitting with Naim and recalling the past, I heard things from him that I couldn't recall, as if memory had taken flight.

He told me that the policeman tossed me from his jeep into the cell as if I were a sack of potatoes. I was bent over like a foetus, battered and swollen all over. When he approached me, he heard me say: "Are the birds still flying?" He didn't understand my question but replied in the affirmative. When I recovered a bit, I urged him to press for my release as I was beginning to feel quite desperate. He didn't need urging. He and Gourgey Shasha met with Yousif Fattal, a lawyer who was not connected with the Movement in any way, but had good relations with Moslem lawyers. Later that night, while they were all visiting at

*Advocate Yousif Fattal.*

Shalom's house (the pharmacist) they told him that Zaki was caught. He was shocked; he did not know who Zaki (myself) was, but had heard of his existence. After asking a few questions about the circumstances leading to my arrest, he said that it might be possible to solve the problem at a modest level of litigation by engaging the services of a prominent Moslem lawyer.

On 25 May our agents wired the Mossad: "Dror was badly beaten during interrogation. The police searched the house of the Hindu (Rodney). The results are unknown. We were informed that the police discovered that Youdkeh is not really Iranian and is holding a false passport. We informed Mizrahi not to leave his new quarters. Then from Israel the Mossad wired the following instructions to its branch in Paris: "The situation of our comrades in Babylon is very bad. It is important to ban any publicity or information on the matter, also within our circles."

The following day an extra telegram was transmitted to Israel: "The inspection of the house of Dror's uncle, and also that of the Hindu, took place after their telephone numbers were found in Youdkeh's diary. From this, we can deduce that the two were not followed before the incident. The lawyer Baban, who took it upon himself to deal with the matter of Dror, has not yet met him. We hope they will meet today. They are shuttling Dror from one place to another. We have no news of Youdkeh."

On 27 May, on inquiry from the Mossad Aliya Bet regarding any plans we may have for Youdkeh, our agents replied: "We are unable to deal with the matter. An outsider must take care of that. We were informed that his denunciation came from the Iraqi legates in Iran. Dror gave power-of-attorney to the lawyer Baban. He promised to get him released on bail within two days."

Later on they reported they were able to reach Dror and give him food and bedding. "He is feeling fine and sends his regards to his friends. This was made possible after paying a bribe. We will soon let you have further details..."

About a week after my arrest, and during a session of interrogation and torture, I was taken to the detention room to issue a warrant for my arrest. There I met Tajer for the first time: he was sweating from the heat and asked for water with salt to drink.

"From where do you know Ismail Salhoon?" the judicial investigator asked me.

"I don't know him. We simply met by chance," I replied and spoke as slowly as I could so that Tajer could follow my Iraqi dialect. "I was in the Concert Hall that is next to the Ministry of Defense, when this man sat beside me," I said and pointing at Tajer. "He asked me if I knew any Jews in Baghdad and I answered: 'Yes, I myself am Jewish.' He then requested me to come with him to buy some articles and I agreed. That's all I can tell you."

The interrogator then pressed Tajer to relate his version of the story. He asked to give his evidence in English. However, the translation into Arabic was a problem. Until today it is a puzzle to me how, among all those who were present no one could be found to accomplish the translation into Arabic, leaving me to deal with it. Being wary of any sort of trap, I did my best to be true to Tajer's testimony, smoothing out evidence where possible.

I was later sent back to the Dora Police Station, far from all these events. Meanwhile the lawyer Fattal prepared the document applying for my bail. Lawyer Baban signed it and submitted it to the Court of Criminal Appeal. After a short while he came out with an order for my release on bail for 500 Dinars.

The court phoned the police station and asked them to prepare the prisoner for bail. Fattal went to the police station to meet me, and saw me for the first time, sitting on a bench. The problem was, who could be found to bail me out! It was a Saturday. They tried to call the synagogue, but no help came from there. Fattal was racking his brains trying to think of someone who would agree to stand surety, and then thought of one of his partners, Muhammed Sacran, a member of the Trade Bureau. He told him about the arrest of Naim Moshe Mandelawy's brother and asked for his help. Sacran immediately agreed: "I am ready to do so," he said. And he did.

The Secret Police gnashed their teeth, but continued to try and trap me. They offered me some "friendly advice"; that if I wished to help the prisoners, I must find the man known as Habib or Zaki. They were, as you know, my pseudonyms.

In the files of the Secret Police, my registered home address was the synagogue, so I went straight there. On the same day, 3 June 1951, I met Yousif Khabbaza (Beit Halahmi) who was active in the intelligence network. I told him to warn Salim Mouallem and Yousif Basri to leave Baghdad, or at least to stay in hiding. A few days earlier, on 29 May, Yoav Goral, the last emissary remaining in

Baghdad, sent a telegram to the Mediterranean Section of the Jewish Agency, informing them that we had no support left in the Jewish community after the Aliya had slowed down. As to the members of the Movement and the Shura we mustn't delay in bringing out all the stateless emissaries left: "I can find no way of leaving for Israel except in the way Uziel Levy did (meaning with a *laissez passer*), and considering my new situation it is imperative that I leave immediately. At the moment I am in hiding and secretly moving from one house to another, having no capability of operating at all. I request immediate permission to leave. Details of the urgency of the situation can be received from the Mossad. Request immediate reply."

I also reached the conclusion that Yoav should leave immediately, as his staying over brought us no benefit except to endanger himself. The Aliya was continuing, thanks to a skeleton staff headed by I.D. Sofer, Gourgey Shasha and Meir Elias. The number of Jews still waiting for a flight numbered 20,169.

While staying in the synagogue I was called to court, presided over by Judge Salman El-Bayat, with regard to the traffic accident in which I was involved. The same Iraqi officer who was a witness to the accident was present. He mentioned in his testimony that I had deposited some papers in a certain house.

"How many days were you kept in detention on account of the accident?" the Judge asked.

"I wasn't detained, as the case was a straightforward one," I answered.

"See how the Jews are dominating your country?" the Judge remarked to the officer.

"Two weeks imprisonment!" the Judge ruled.

I was taken to prison and the barber, who could not be persuaded by any financial inducement not to shave my head, did so. In prison, I met some of the Movement prisoners, among them I.D. Sofer and Rony Mizrahi (who until today insists that he lent me 20 Dinars in prison). The ever-attentive Fattal went to Advocate Baban and told him how the police imprisoned me again on the pretext of my involvement in an accident. Baban, known for his hot temper, promised to show them "what is what." Fattal prepared an appeal to the Supreme Court, Baban signed it, and five days later I was out, a free man.

Meanwhile, the interrogation of Yehuda Tajer continued. His examiners searched his pockets and found documents, which helped the police trace

Rodney and arrest him on 24 May. Luckily Rodney hadn't met any local agents or emissaries. He mentioned two of my pseudonyms, but he couldn't describe me, as we had never met. Another agent, whom the police traced, was Latif Ephraim, an intelligence network agent. He was the pharmaceutical salesman in a company owned by Advocate Shlomo Horesh and Yaacov Battat, a member of Parliament. On arresting Latif the police searched his office and one of the officers, Salem El-Koreishi, noticed a letter written by a clerk in the company, a Moslem, addressed to "My brother Abu Yaagoub," which means Yousif.

During the meeting of the agents, after the arrest of Latif Ephraim, which took place in the evening, Yousif Fattal and Shlomo Horesh, who witnessed the inspection of the office, reported that the police were looking for someone by the name of Yousif. "How many Yousifs are there?" was the question tossed at us. There was Yousif Khabbaza from the Intelligence network and Yousif Basri, who was not involved with us in any way. The outcome was to hastily remove Yousif Basri from the area and take Yousif Khabbaza out of the country. Khabbaza was ready to leave on 6 June and Yousif Basri hid himself at the home of a relative, Sasson Sadik. In order to prevent further capture I also requested Khabbaza to persuade Salim Mouallem, of the Rafidain Bank, to "get lost" and prepare to escape. Salim, who read in the newspapers that two Israeli spies were captured, was convinced that they were Yehuda Tajer and Rodney. He took it calmly since, by agreement with Khabbaza, the material he gave him should not have remained in Baghdad for more than twenty-four hours. He didn't know that among the papers and documents found on Tajer there was material that he had given him three months earlier. Tajer later explained that on leaving for Rome on the Eve of Passover, he took the material with him in order to read it through and, not having had the time to do so, he took it back with him to Baghdad.

On 5 June, Salim Mouallem worked in the bank until late in the evening, and then went out with friends to the movies. He returned home after midnight. Yousif Khabbaza called him and told him to leave the house at once. Salim left for the appointed meeting place and noticed two cars, one occupied by Shalom Saleh and another by Khabbaza. "The situation is critical and dangerous," he told him, "You have to hide and preferably leave Iraq!"

"I am ready to hide," Mouallem answered.

"Do you have a place in mind?"

"I think at this hour of the night there is no sense in doing anything. I am sure the capture of Latif will not affect me. I am going back and tomorrow I will go to the bank as usual. I shall then leave the bank without my coat in order to allay suspicion, take the car which will be waiting for me and escape."

When Salim returned to his house, he was stunned to find several policemen, Latif Ephraim among them, waiting for him there.

"Are you Salim Mouallem?" the police asked.

On confirming this he was immediately arrested. At the police station, he appeared unaware of the reason for his arrest. Ephraim had been his student at the university and their acquaintance was minimal. Until his capture he was unaware that the documents were found with Yehuda Tajer.

The examiners did not mention the documents or espionage; instead they questioned him on the bomb that was thrown at the Rafidain Bank.

That very night a bomb had been thrown between the government-owned bank and the store of Stanley Shashou, a Jew. All questions centred on the bomb. Salim denied any irregular activity and any connection with the bomb. His interrogators then showed him the documents connecting him with Yehuda Tajer. If you recall, they had already captured Latif Ephraim, Mamdouh Zaki, Sammy Bassoon and Maki Abd-El-Razak and they all worked with Tajer and had connections with Salim: One can well imagine how deeply involved he was and how vulnerable.

As Yehuda Tajer was also questioned about the bombing, it appeared that the police were looking for someone to connect to the bomb-throwing incident. All this occurred before the arrest of Yousif Basri and Shalom Saleh. Even when Rodney was caught he was also questioned about the bomb and not espionage matters.

Whenever the interrogators of Salim Mouallem heard his repeated denials regarding the bombings, they then switched tactics and referred to the question of espionage. "Salhoon" (Tajer) they said, "has already confessed. You are mentioned in documents as an economist and you are connected with Mamdouh Zaki, who has already revealed a joint operation." His interrogators put pressure on him and showed him the documents, which he recognized and believed to be safely out of the country.

Mouallem was not fazed. He knew that Khabbaza was supposed to travel the following day and presumed that Shalom Saleh had also departed. Therefore his answers were vague and clueless; he wished to give the other two a chance to leave the country as well. He used various pretexts such as giving names of Jews who had already left Iraq.

Yousif Ajmi, one of the partners of the taxi company Miami, whose services we used, related that the police came to the offices of the company and searched for a black Austin car. They arrested and interrogated a taxi driver in the name of Abraham Zingi. He told them about the movements of the network agents, the trips of Yousif Khabbaza and his meetings with Yousif Basri.

Formerly Basri lived with his sister Nazima, and when she immigrated to Israel, he hid in the house of relatives, Sasson and Simha Sadik in southern Baghdad. Shimshon Houbeba and Reuben Elias would visit him there and bring him up-to-date on the subject of arrests and interrogations. While the taxi driver was in the hands of the police, he showed them the house of Sasson Sadik, to which he would drive Yousif Khabbaza, and where Basri was staying.

According to the affidavit of Simha Sadik, on Saturday 9 June, late in the evening, the Secret Police arrived at their home in six cars, together with the taxi driver of the Miami company. Yousif Basri hastily concealed himself behind a cupboard in the corner of the room which was used by Sadik's daughter Emilia (Aviva). Simha was watching.

"Where is Yousif Khabbaza?" The police asked her.

"There is no such person here. I don't know to whom you are referring," she answered. In the absence of the landlord, the Secret Police did not dare search the house, so they waited for him in the garden. Sasson arrived three and a half hours later. Simha went into the garden, slipped purposely into a water canal nearby and, soaking wet, asked the Secret Police to let her into the house to change her clothes. When the police agreed she went straight to Emilia's room and told Basri: "I am about to short-circuit the electric system so that you can jump out of the window and escape over the garden fence." Yousif refused.

"Get out. Leave me alone," he said with impatience.

When Sasson came home the Secret Police asked him where Yousif Khabbaza was, he shrugged his shoulders and denied knowing any such person. They searched all the rooms. They were on their way out when they heard a noise behind a cupboard. They found Yousif Basri and began questioning him. Receiving no adequate replies and no reason why he chose to hide himself, they took him together with Sasson Sadik to the police station. They didn't bother anyone else in the house. The next day they came for Simha Sadik and questioned her need to take frequent rides with her daughters in her Mercedes car alongside the Tigris River. They accused her of being a Zionist agent fulfilling missions under the guise of these frequent trips. Simha denied all this. The interrogation went on for nine months. Once they took her to see Yousif Basri in the detention room, where he was hanging by his feet from the ceiling, his eyes bulging from their sockets and his mouth dripping with blood.

Simha and Sasson Sadik employed a Christian maid and the Secret Police decided to use her to apply pressure on the Sadik family. They accused her of complicity and threatened her with arrest unless she cooperated. They persuaded her to use a mine detector in order to search for hidden arms. When Simha Sadik got wind of this she took fright, as there was a cache of six pistols and hundreds of bullets belonging to the Haganah in the house. So she took a large basket and hid the arms under loaves of bread, vegetables and a pan of cooked food and left the house. She took a taxi to her husband's shop in Suk-El-Sfafir (market of copper hammering). There she handed it to a trusty Kurdish guard.

Arriving home she found members of the Secret Police already there with a mine detector, conducting a thorough search. They apologized for damaging her hot water tank although they found nothing. Then they questioned her at length at the police station. She later told us when she last saw Yousif Basri, he seemed very optimistic about his chances to escape.

But Yousif Basri was unable to do so, and efforts made far and wide to set him free were to no avail. Haim Sarid (Peter), of the Mossad, met with Yehya Kassem in London, an Iraqi journalist who had close connections with the authorities, and offered him 10,000 Dinars to try and have the death sentences canceled; prisoners like Yousif Basri and Shalom Saleh were doomed. Within twenty-four hours Kassem made a positive decision about the foreign agents; regarding the natives he could promise nothing.

Simha was desperate. She burst into the chambers of Camil Shahin, the magistrate in charge, when he was at a meeting with Salim El-Koreishi, one of the investigators. She asked the judge to send the officer out and when he left the room she told him: "I will not die alone. I will incriminate you too. You took bribes and have effected the release of others."

"Go home and leave me to take care of this matter," he retorted angrily. Her husband, who was under arrest, was released close to the moment Basri was hanged.

Sometime prior to his hanging, Simha Sadik met with Yousif Basri in prison. He apologized for the suffering he caused her husband and herself and added: "I served Israel and in return I am to lose my life. Please see to it that my remains are taken to Israel."

Shalom Saleh was a shoemaker. His job in the Shura was to prepare arms caches. In the Ezra and Nehemiah Operation he worked in the kitchen and was nicknamed Shalom Matbah (Shalom Kitchen). After my release and while I was staying with Yousif Fattal at his home, we dug a hole in his garden and buried a damaged radio in it. The next day, on the Feast of Shavuoth 1951, Yousif Fattal, Yacov Battat, Shlomo Horesh, Naim Moshe Mandelawy, Shalom Saleh and myself sat down to eat the traditional pastry of the Shavuoth festival – "Kahi." At the end of the meal I told Shalom Saleh to go to Israel as his mission was complete. He did not tell me that Menashe Ben Hayim, one of our two wireless operators, had asked him to prepare an arms cache for him before leaving.

The overall responsibility for the arms caches in the Jewish quarter was with Uri (Ephraim Dror). After my release from prison, I was told that the man was suffering from a nervous breakdown. Aware of his extensive knowledge of the existing arms caches, I was alarmed. I suggested to Maatook Dori, one of our senior officers in the Shura, that we hospitalize Dori in a psychiatric hospital, where the owner, a Dr. Jack Abboud, was Jewish. I visited him in hospital in order to examine the level of his recuperation and cool-headedness. To my surprise, it became clear that his condition blurred his memory and he was quite confused. Once, when I asked him a question regarding the arms caches, he contradicted himself and asked me to identify myself.

Maatook, who was a very careful fellow, did not rely on this memory failure and did his best to try to find all the arms caches and transfer them to other places. One of them was in the house of Reuben Elias and was transferred to the Hakham Hezkiel Synagogue. The job of preparing the ground in the synagogue was left to Shalom Saleh, together with another agent, alias Abraham. Maatook appointed Abraham to keep track of the synagogue beadle so that, when needed, he could unlatch the doors from the inside.

Shalom Saleh and Reuben Elias went down to the cache and removed the weapons: They were in prime condition – Tommy-guns, Stens and grenades.

The weapons were then packed and sturdy Kurdish carriers were hired to carry the heavy load. Shortly afterwards, the group arrived at the synagogue. The agreed signals were given and Abraham opened the door and let the weapons-carriers enter. The basement floor was rock-hard. Volunteers worked for half a day in order to prepare the cache and hide the arms. Similarly, other caches were transferred to other locations. Shalom Saleh took part in every operation and knew all the hidden spots. These incidents occurred before Shalom Saleh and myself dug the arms cache in Yousif Fattal's house.

On 10 June, the day of the Feast of Shavuoth, policemen came to the synagogue inquiring after someone called Shalom Saleh and explained that they were told that he owned a sports shop and they needed to purchase some equipment. They were told that Shalom worked in the kitchen and he was not there at the moment. The policemen waited for him and arrested him. Whoever was acquainted with Shalom Saleh knew how naive he was. The police used all kinds of torture on him and succeeded in breaking him to such an extent he could no longer distinguish between facts and the lies they told him. He signed whatever they prepared for him. They even tried to force him and Yousif Basri to write down that Salim Mouallem, Yehuda Tajer and Rodney were bomb throwers. The inquisitors tried, without success, to make every prisoner sign a statement that he or others he knew exploded bombs.

Shalom Saleh claimed in court that he signed the statement under torture. Maatook Dori remembered that one day while he was at the synagogue, assisting with the transport of the immigrants, he saw Shalom Saleh brought there by the Secret Police. They went straight for his suitcase. "We who knew him," Dori related, "pretended that we were waiting for a flight." Marks of torture were visible on his body: He was all puffy and red. He glanced at us and turned away. The police exploited his fear and pressed him to sign the statement they prepared for him, promising to release him later on."

When he was brought to the synagogue and the arms dump discovered, I.D. Sofer and Gourgey Shasha were there. "Did either of these men, or one of them, help you to hide the weapons?" The police asked him. Shalom shook his head. "I don't know these men, and those who assisted me have already left the country."

At the moment the arms cache was discovered in the Hakham Hezkiel Synagogue, the police located other caches, such as the one in the house of Eliahu Gourgey Abed (Evron). In Eliahu's house there were actually three caches: one contained weapons and bombs belonging to the Shura, and the other two held material belonging to Yousif Khabbaza – list of names of the Movement's members, the location of the Hagana posts in the Jewish quarter and maps showing the locations of the caches. In addition, there was a case containing material that belonged to Yousif Basri. Hearing about the arrest of Yousif Basri, Eliahu Gourgey hastened to burn all the material relating to the matter. When Eliahu was arrested, while he was with the brothers Selim and Yousif Khabbaza at their home, they questioned him and searched the house, but found nothing, and he was released on personal bail.

After his release, Eliahu heard about the arrest of Shalom Saleh, and for fear of his telling his interrogators about the caches in his house, he hid himself in his uncle's house. There he heard that a huge military force and police had surrounded his house and removed the contents of the caches they found there. As his uncle was very frightened, Eliahu found a different hiding place with some friends. He remained hidden for a month, waiting for the atmosphere to calm down. Then his friends prepared new identity papers for him and planned an escape route.

He travelled by train to the city of Khanekin in the north of Iraq. On the train a schoolmate who had become a police officer recognized him and arrested him. He was taken back to Baghdad in handcuffs. A series of interrogations followed. He fainted. At dawn during a respite from torture, they demanded that he sign a statement, naming the man who exploded the bombs. They questioned him about the weapons found in his house and about other members of the network. He stuck to his story: "I joined the Movement in order to study Hebrew as I intend to leave for Israel." As for the weapons, he said he had no knowledge of them and that he had only rented a room to Yousif Khabbaza."

He was transferred to Dora Police Station, where he was tortured once more. He was made to dig a hole and threatened with death, then brought before a judicial interrogator, but did not change his story. He stayed in prison for two months until the trial began. The sentence was fifteen years in jail. He was released after eight.

Eliahu Gourgey Abed believed that Nouri El-Sa'id was eager to stage public trials, in order to give the Iraqi people a topic with which to occupy themselves and to distract them from the oil deals he had contracted with the British. The fact that the oil contract was signed on the very day Yousif Basri and Shalom Saleh were hanged seems to prove this theory.

On 3 July 1951, a whole series of messages reached the Mossad: "The situation has deteriorated. Five Jewish girls have been arrested. They must have talked too much, and said that Rony Barnett paid them visits." Another message stated that the Iraqis claimed the capture of a wireless, and in a third one, "The situation of the two (Yousif Basri and Shalom Saleh) is very bad. They were beaten and it is reasonable to assume that they talked. The Iraqis have began a manhunt for Dror. All the Secret Police members were given his photograph and are looking for him. Rony Barnett is not able to contact local people any more."

Individual agents, who did not run away or hide, took over all the dangerous activities that needed to be dealt with. Mahmoud, whose job was to keep a check on the Secret Police who were on our tails, provided us with very valuable information. He gave us a list of wanted suspects which needed frequent updating and, thanks to his reports, many active agents, wanted men, were quickly smuggled out of Iraq. Nearly one hundred agents were saved: Yousif Khabbaza was one of them. The activist Yousif Dalah, who was our liaison with the police in the Meir Tweig Synagogue, recalls: "When they came to me and warned me that Yousif Khabbaza ought to emigrate at once, I arranged for the necessary papers to be intermingled with those of other passengers. I then applied to Abd-El-Razak for his signature. He signed. Yousif Khabbaza was quickly transferred to the airport. After the plane took off, the Secret Police rushed to the airport and asked Yitzhak Elias to see the passenger list. Since Yousif had flown under a false identity, they were unable to find his name mentioned on the list. They went into a huddle and considered recalling the plane but it seemed it was beyond their capability, and Yousif escaped.

Yousif Khabbaza arrived in Israel a free man. I was also rescued and taken back to Israel. In Iraq, Yehuda Tajer was imprisoned for many years in an Iraqi gaol and Yousif Basri and Shalom Saleh paid with their lives for their services in the Israeli Defence Force.

# Chapter 15

# MAINTAINING CONTACT

With the arrival of the first emissaries in Iraq, it was obvious that they could not do their work competently without regular and dependable wireless contacts between them and their superiors in Israel. Someone had to receive reports from them on the situation in Iraq and also to send them instructions or confirmation. Because of this need, a contact was made through the efforts of a Jewish wireless operator who served in the British Army in Baghdad – Nahman Bornstein from Haifa, the ISLD man (Inter-Service Liaison Department). The story of how he was recruited is very interesting. In 1942, during a vacation in Israel, when talking to friends of the experiences he had during his service in Iraq, Hagana men were present; he revealed that he made contact in Baghdad with an anonymous station whose transmission drew his attention. He suspected that it might belong to the Hagana in Israel.

After saying this, things began to happen very quickly. Since the reception was so clear, the Hagana men concluded with me that their wireless station in Israel could be used to broadcast information, employing a specific code, to the emissaries of the Movement in Iraq, via the wireless station of the British Army where he worked. It was also reckoned that he could transmit, from his station in Baghdad, the information that Enzo Sereni would need to send to Israel, to the Hagana centre.

On his return to Baghdad, Nahman Bornstein did as he was asked; he received transmissions from Israel and passed them on to Sireni. But the messages that the emissaries wanted to send to Israel somehow didn't reach their destination. This one-way contact was not acceptable and there were people in the Hagana who blamed Bornstein for not fulfilling his agreement.

A few months after these unsuccessful trials, those in Israel abandoned the idea of using Jewish wireless operators serving in the British Army. It was evident to the emissaries, as well as their superiors, that it was ridiculous to rely on favours, or the good-will of either this Jewish soldier or some others, as regular contact was a vital element in their work.

In December 1942, during the visit of Shaul Avigur (Meirov) in Baghdad, it was decided to establish a wireless station there belonging to the Mossad Le Aliya Bet. It was Munia Meridor who brought the transmitter to Baghdad and after a while, in April 1943, they sent across Malka Rofeh, a wireless operator in the guise of a soldier; she was a member of Kibbutz Maoz Hayim. It took her several months to operate the station successfully. The first transmission was made in July 1943 but after a short while the service was discontinued, the apparatus concealed and she returned to Israel.

An idea was suggested that a local person who was a member of the Halutz ought to be sent to Israel for training as a wireless operator and eventually take over this responsibility in Baghdad. And so it was. The man chosen was Towfik Murad (Abraham Ben-Mordechai), a young lawyer who also studied engineering for two years in Kushta. In the middle of 1944, he was trained in Israel to handle the transmitter and returned to Iraq to reconstruct the centre. The apparatus was removed from its hiding place, practically undamaged. Towfik decided to put it in working order himself, proving he possessed golden hands. But he only succeeded in partially working the machine: He managed to transmit messages but not to receive them. For months, the emissaries sent telegrams to Israel but couldn't receive them at all. Only in June 1945 the apparatus was satisfactorily repaired and then constant and steady communication was made possible between Iraq and Israel.

Three years later, in 1949, a new and improved apparatus was sent to Baghdad, disguised as a radio of the K.B. type. The old transmitter was sent to Iran and wireless contact was established between the emissaries in Iraq and their representatives in Iran. During the summer of 1949, when the transmission between Iran and Israel was constantly being disrupted, the

Baghdad station became a centre, directing wireless traffic between Israel and Iran. The wireless operator, Yitzhak Sayegh, would receive telegrams from Israel and transmit them to Ephraim, the operator in Teheran.

In order to understand how difficult was the work of the wireless operators, one had to see them in action. They worked in a dark, sealed room, with scarcely any ventilation, minimum light and without earphones. They were always on edge lest they be discovered by the authorities. The wireless, which looked like an ordinary radio, was put on a table in the centre of the room. On removing the partition at the back, a button was revealed; with a sharp press it would convert the radio into a transmitter, for which a special code was devised. They had to be so vigilant, so alert; were the authorities to discover the location of the station, it would have spelled disaster for them. It was no wonder then that the wireless operators in Israel were permanently complaining about the unpredictable reception of the transmission from "Berman" (meaning Baghdad).

The wireless was left in the house of Menashe Shasha and later in that of Towfik Murad, a senior member of the "Gidonim" (nickname for wireless operators) who trained all those who came after him. The transmitter was then moved several times from one place to another for security reasons. The management of the job was straightforward; those responsible at the centre were emissaries for the emigration program. The wireless operator would receive reports daily from me – to deal with the text of the telegrams, coding and transmission to Israel. For five weeks until my arrival in Iraq I kept the new and complicated code in my head. I won't say that my memory was perfect and that no errors were made, but the wireless operators, headed by Yitzhak Sayegh, overcame the obstacles, and transmission began with a brand new code. Feeling that he had mastered the complexities, Sayegh transmitted the following telegram to Israel: "Happy New Year, telegram to follow."

The telegrams received from Israel were deciphered and then brought to me. I was the only one who went through them and then destroyed them myself. For the purpose of the work I had to commit a great deal of important information to memory. When I returned to Israel and went through the messages that were sent during my mission, I was astonished at the huge amount of data I had succeeded in committing to memory.

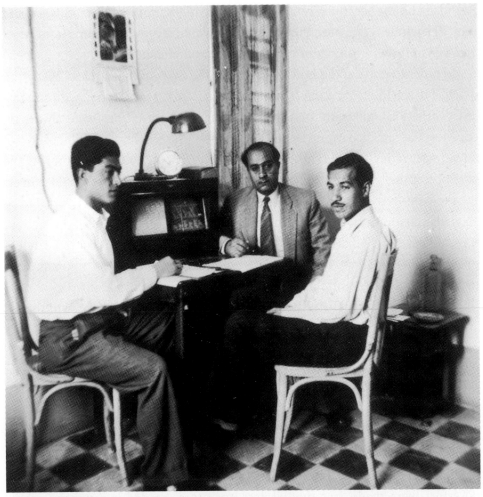

*Wireless operators beside the wireless apparatus which had been camouflaged as a regular radio, from right to left: Shimshon Hubeiba, Abraham Ben Mordechai, Yitzhak Sayegh.*

Four Gidonim worked with me during the mission: They were Towfik Murad (Abraham Ben-Mordechai), Yitzhak Sayegh, Shimshon Hubeiba and the youngest of all, Menashe Ben-Hayim. Their dedication knew no bounds. They saw their work as an important task and handled it with great concern and without complaint.

The transmitter in Baghdad was kept in strict secrecy, its whereabouts known only to the emissaries from Israel and the Gidonim themselves.

Therefore the Gidonim, who were instructors in the Movement, had occasionally to skip their regular duties. These absences were construed as negligence and infuriated their seniors and the trainees as well.

One day, Yitzhak Sayegh related some of his personal experiences: "My main job in the Movement was to teach Hebrew. Sometimes I would miss my class, because of work at the station and often I would come to class worn out after my session with the transmission shift. My seniors, who weren't aware of this secret job, and of the concentrated forces required by my work at the station, imagined I was playing truant and decided to fire me. This decision was known to all the members and the ban caused by it had a negative impact on me. I became very despondent."

Towfik Murad, the moving spirit at the centre in Baghdad, and his family moved into the house of Yehezkel, Towfik's brother, situated near Kasr El-Abyadh (the White Palace). Yehezkel was a well-known lawyer and judge. His house was spacious and as luxurious as a palace, surrounded by a large estate. It was near the Police Academy. Adjoining the wide entrance was a large garage for cars and above it, two rooms had been built. One of them was Towfik's bedroom and the other was used as our wireless station. This house, whose landlords knew nothing about the transmitter, was visited by ministers, judges and lawyers; in short, all shades of Iraqi high society.

Yitzhak Sayegh entered Murad's house one evening, as he was accustomed to do, holding sheafs of telegrams for transmission to Iran. That same evening well-known people had been invited there, among whom were Fakhri El-Jamil, ex-Chairman of the Iraqi Parliament, Towfik El-Suweidi and Jamal Baban. While they were sitting in the garden, around tables full of delectable food, Yitzhak slipped quietly into the wireless room. Towfik would then lock the door from the outside so that no one could slip in unexpectedly. When Sayegh finished transmitting at eleven o'clock at night and was about to leave, he found himself locked in. Towfik only remembered to release him very early in the morning and hurried to let him out.

Yitzhak Sayegh dashed up the street on his way home; although he was extremely tired he moved quickly. Suddenly he heard an order to "stop!"

"What are you doing in the street at such an early hour?" the policeman wanted to know.

"I am employed by a British Company and I have to see to the workers. I must really hurry," Yitzhak replied.

The policeman continued: "The house of ex-Minister, Nasrat El-Faresi was robbed a while ago and we were told to arrest any strange person found in the street." However he let him go.

"One evening," Sayegh recalled, "during the assignment of an emissary of the Aliya, David Ben-Meir (the man I replaced), I was supposed to contact Israel at 19:00 hours. Ben-Meir brought me the material and I started working on it. This was during the crisis of 1949. Several of our members of the Movement were captured, following information, given under torture, and many names were revealed. The police hunt went into full swing. I was in the centre looking out and I saw many policemen approaching us from both sides of the street. The windows of the room where I worked were covered with thick paper, to block out the flickering lights of the apparatus. I continued working but wasn't very happy. After a while I peeped out once again from the window and saw that policemen were entering the adjoining house. I wired Israel asking them to contact us at 21:00. I asked for G.R., meaning "special telegram," and transmitted it to Zick (Moshe Yerushalmi), who was at that time the officer of the stations abroad (Tahal) and responsible for contact between Berman (Baghdad) and Goldman (Teheran). I explained that our situation was difficult and we were facing danger hourly. Zick ordered us to leave the centre. Luckily, no policemen came near us."

Sayegh remembered this incident for many months afterwards. "I used to have nightmares," he said "policemen were coming at me and while running through the gardens I tried continuously to avoid shots to my head. Even when I woke up I felt pain in the right side of my head, where I imagined I had been shot."

During my mission, two persons worked intermittently on the wireless – the new recruit Shimshon Hubeiba and the experienced Yitzhak Sayegh. One day, when they were about to finish transmitting, I appeared unexpectedly in Towfik Murad's house and asked both operators not to shut off the transmitter. I fished out of my pockets several lengthy telegrams for transmission. Years later, when I sat with Yitzhak Sayegh and recalled the incident, he told me: "Until you arrived we were used to thirty or forty-word telegrams, and when there were interruptions those telegrams could take several hours to transmit. That day, when you entered the room and gave them to us, we were taken aback. They were so long. I remember once when you came in with a pile of papers and a newspaper containing the text of the bill relating to the Revocation of Citizenship. You translated the bill and added many other items. This was an especially difficult shift and went on until the next morning, but we tackled it with good humour."

The work at the wireless centre was difficult and yet very exciting. Yitzhak Sayegh said "Kol Israel" had a program for Arab listeners called *Hal Taalam* (Do you know?), which would broadcast various items on what was taking place in the Middle East. One morning they broadcast information that we, the operators, had transmitted to Israel the previous evening. This worried us greatly, in case the Iraqis, who also listened to "Kol Israel" realized that there was a wireless transmitter sending messages to Israel. One afternoon in November or December 1949 (I can't recall) I walked from Bab-El-Shargui towards El-Rashid and heard newspaper vendors hoarsely proclaiming: "*Nouri El-Sa'id yousarrih! Nouri El-Sa'id yousarrih!*" ("Nouri El-Sa'id declares! Nouri El-Sa'id declares!"). I purchased a copy of the El-Yaktha and to my shock and horror, in a news item covering a session of the Iraqi Parliament, Nouri El-Sa'id, the Prime Minister, stated that he was convinced of the existence of a wireless centre in Iraq which had been transmitting information to Israel, and this station was situated somewhere in an orange grove or a deserted house [...] I decided to discontinue transmitting that very day, at the usual hour. I also sent a wire to Israel to alter the times of transmission.

Another operator recalled that "once in the house of Yeheskel Murad, when well-known Iraqis were being entertained there, the transmitter was operating on an upper floor and we could hear it spelling out the dots and dashes of the Morse code. It took us a while to figure out the significance of the noise. One of us hurried up to the operating room and abruptly switched off the wireless. The guests relaxing on the first floor couldn't understand what those noises were and were then surprised at the sudden absence of sound."

One day, in the beginning of the fifties, when Yitzhak Sayegh was in the middle of a transmission, the wireless stopped and an odour of burning penetrated the room. Sayegh checked the apparatus and found that it was still transmitting but was not receiving. As agreed in such cases he informed the listeners in code that the apparatus was not functioning and he couldn't hear them. He told Towfik to inform me of this and began to check the lamps. Every day Towfik would take one lamp from the transmitter to a relative living in Bab-El-Shargui in order to inspect it properly. They proved to be in good shape. Meanwhile, Sayegh continued to transmit my telegrams. Towfik opened up the apparatus and set about to repair it; he asked for me to be present. "I rely on you a hundred per cent," I replied to Yitzhak. "Tell Towfik that my coming will not solve the technical difficulties." Towfik then dismantled the wireless and an acrid smell emerged from it. Yitzhak pointed to a burnt cable. When the latter was replaced all was well again.

There was another incident which scared us all: A Jew named Moshe Ben Mouallem Menashe had a dispute in 1936 with the Rabbinate regarding his divorce, and decided to become a Moslem. He changed his name to Mousa El-Nasir. Years later, in 1950, when most of the Jews had their Iraqi citizenship revoked, including his family, Mousa decided to leave Iraq. His sister Rivca, thirty years old, wanted to study Hebrew, but because of her age they refused her tuition, as only teenagers were accepted in the classes run by the Movement. Her parents (who were friends of Yitzhak Sayegh's parents) asked him to give her private Hebrew lessons, during which Rivca told Sayegh that her brother wished to speak with him. After Mousa met Sayegh he felt drawn to the Movement and asked for his help to leave Iraq. To prove that he identified with the Halutz Movement, Mousa revealed that he was recently called by the military authorities to listen to a mysterious wireless transmission, sending out signals which appeared to be in Hebrew. Mousa, now a high ranking official in charge of wireless and telegraph services over the whole of Iraq, confided to Sayegh that he rejected this suspicion out of hand. He had no idea that Sayegh was one of the people who transmitted from that station.

I also experienced an unpleasant incident regarding the wireless apparatus of the Movement in Baghdad. We used, among other things in the Halutz Movement, the services of R., a Christian driver who carried our mail to our friends in Iran and vice versa. Once we had a discussion regarding a financial request he made. R., in my opinion, quoted an inflated sum, and in refusing I said it was beyond my authority to agree and that I would have to confer with

Israel. I promised an answer within two or three weeks. He was surprised that a reply could take so long. His words caught me off guard: "By post? Remember it is I who brought you the wireless from Iran." So I had to agree to his demands. By the way, some credit is due to R., for in the crisis of 1951 he was arrested with others but didn't mention the apparatus during his interrogation.

Shimshon Hubeiba and Menashe Ben-Hayim related: "After Dror and Yehuda Tajer were arrested on 22 May 1951, we sent an agitated telegram to Israel with the information we had. The apparatus was, at that time, in one of the houses in Alwiya. As Dror used to visit the house regularly we decided to remove it to another house for safety." This move was very similar to the instructions given by the Mossad and received later, on 24 May: "If there is fear that the Gidonim and the house where the station is situated become known to the police, we advise removing the transmitter and to stop working. We will keep listening for you at the appointed time, for ten minutes each time. If there is no alarm, continue working at the same fixed hours. Don't arrange alternate hours. Transmit the important information only, regarding the detainees and offers for their release."

On 23 May 1951, Shimshon met, by chance, someone he knew who worked in real estate and asked him to find him a house. The man took out a bunch of keys on the spot and told him: "choose." Those were the keys of Jewish houses abandoned by their owners who didn't have time to sell them. Shimshon chose a one-storey house with a back garden in a far distant and quiet area. Shimshon and Menashe rented a carriage (*Arabana*) and put furniture on it consisting of a bed and a mattress, on it. Menashe placed the heavy apparatus on his knees and Shimshon, who sat near the waggoner, held the dismantled antenna. Arriving at the house the waggoner tried to persuade them to sell him the big radio to which he took a fancy. The two had to find various excuses to refuse his request.

Within less than two hours the apparatus was ready for use. The house was empty and unkempt. There was only a table, bed, mattress, the big radio and the antenna, five meters long. They decided to stay in the house only during transmission and informed Israel of their decision.

On 17 June 1951, Shimshon and Menashe were on their way to Mesouda Shemtob Synagogue, perhaps to draw some support from those who stayed behind to run things: I.D. Sofer, George Shasha and Meir Elias. Those three who refused to give up their citizenship, were considered loyal citizens and stayed behind to support the emigration effort, against all odds. They were even summoned from time to time to the Secret Police Headquarters to answer questions. Anyhow, Shimshon and Menashe observed, on their way there, crowds of people gathering near the synagogue. There were police and soldiers as well. When they asked what was going on, they were told that weapons had been found in the synagogue. The security forces had searched the synagogue in the presence of community leaders, assisted by Shalom Saleh.

One must give credit to Saleh that with all the gruelling torture he faced during his arrest, it didn't affect his wits, and when the police interrogated him on his involvement with certain activists, he kept insisting that no one of those mentioned was ever involved with Zionist activities. He acted likewise when they took him to meet Sofer, Shasha and Elias; due to his courageous behaviour he prevented the arrests of others. Shimshon and Menashe, who knew Saleh well, were told by people there that he was assisting the Iraqi policemen in the synagogue, so they decided not to take chances. They turned back to the house and stayed together with other members. After a while they returned to the synagogue, to I.D. Sofer, and told him that they wanted to emigrate. Sofer didn't know exactly what work they did, but at that stage he had already heard about the wireless and he was pleased with their decision.

"Thank God we are getting rid of you. Come into the synagogue and don't leave it again," he told them.

The two couldn't explain that they had an immediate job to transmit and also to destroy the apparatus. They asked him for a short breather to enable them to prepare for their departure and he agreed. They went back to the house where the apparatus was, sent their last message, which went as follows: "The tie is getting tighter. We may have to leave tomorrow. If you don't hear from us this means two things, either we have been caught or we are on our way to you." After the transmission they started to dismantle the apparatus. They unplugged the lamps, took the transmitter to pieces, broke up the antenna, wrapped it all with a piece of cloth and threw it into a canal by the side of the house. They then buried the transformer and headed back to the synagogue.

The plane that was to take Menashe and Shimshon was expected to arrive the next day at 12 o'clock, 18 June 1951. Shimshon's papers to revoke his citizenship were ready, but Menashe, who was supposed to stay behind to continue with the mission, was still considered an Iraqi citizen. Sofer and the other activists decided that Menashe had to leave under a false name – that of Yousif Abraham Shlomo. He was told to accustom himself to his new identity.

Sofer drove them to the airport at three o'clock in the morning. Arriving there, they passed the customs and the police post and reached the reception area. Menashe and Shimshon were wearing sombre suits. For security purposes they decided to sit apart from one another. Suddenly an officer approached Menashe and beckoned him to follow. He took him to the control tower where other officers were standing about, cursing him all the while and mouthing crude insults. Menashe was convinced that this was the end of him. A senior officer shot a question at him: "Do you dress every day in a suit like this?"

Menashe answered calmly. "As I am travelling to a foreign country I thought it better to dress correctly."

"Go, you dog and son of a dog!" the senior officer told him; another officer slapped him twice, forcefully.

Menashe didn't react. He was so stunned that they had let him go.

The policemen insulted the passengers waiting at the airport. One of the officers barked at them *"Gwawid, gumu! Gwawid, gumu!"* (pimps, get up! Pimps, get up!). This abusive language persisted until the plane approached.

Menashe and Shimshon took their seats and fastened their seat belts but they were still apprehensive. Only when the plane took to the air did they feel more relaxed and knew that a difficult period in their lives had come to a satisfactory conclusion.

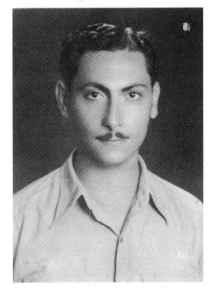

*The fourth wireless operator,*
*Menashe Ben-Hayim.*

# Chapter 16

# ANXIETY AND FREEDOM

On my release from prison, I was required, as was the custom, to report to the Secret Police Headquarters. Since I knew that the investigations had reached a critical stage and a great deal of information had already been collected, I decided not to show my face in their offices. I left the prison accompanied by an armed warden. At Agd El-Nasara (Christian Alley), I exploited the warden's momentary distraction, slipped away and made straight for the pre-designated meeting place to see Yousif Fattal, Yaacov Battat, Naim Moshe Mandelawy and Shlomo Horesh at the Cafe Brazil in El-Rashid Street. From there, I was taken to Yousif's house.

This was the first time I spoke without restraint, face to face with Yousif Fattal, Yaacov Battat and Shlomo Horesh, since we hadn't met before. It was also my first opportunity to acquire the latest news about Israel, the War of Independence and other related subjects. Yousif's mother prepared some delicious food and I felt relaxed, but I couldn't ignore the black cloud of future arrests and investigations hovering over my head. The next day, I asked Shalom Saleh to leave Iraq at once, but he first went to the synagogue and there he was arrested by the Secret Police. After he was caught we were all forced to abandon Fattal's house. I went over to hide in Naim and Naima Aboudy's house. Naim, father of six children, worked for the merchant Kamal Bekhor. Various meetings of activists were held in his house, assisted by his brother-in-law Yehezkel Yona (who had in the mean time left Iraq), and in the days of illegal emigration, it served as a transit base. Naim allowed us the use of his house gladly and freely. Later on, when he was asked by Gilad Cohen, one of the heads of the Emigration Committee, how he managed it all, surrounded by Moslem neighbours, he said that he told them that at long last, after five girls, a son was born to him and since his family and relatives were so numerous he couldn't invite them all at once to the festivities and had to host each large group separately, due to the lack of space.

At Naim's house I read all the reports in the newspapers regarding the investigations and drew satisfaction from their derisive attitude towards the Government, and especially the police who had yet to catch Habib, who must now be in Tel Aviv... The police had discovered that Naim Moshe Mandelawy wasn't my brother but an associate in undercover activities. Under the circumstances, Naim joined me in my hiding place. The Mossad sent me a message that I was to make every effort to leave Iraq and wondered if it could be arranged through lawyers and bribes? It is incredible how far from reality that idea was.

On 12 June 1951, the following telegram arrived from the Mossad:

Urgent

To: Noah Aran (meaning myself)

From: Or Ruth

a. "Boaz" (Rony Barnett) left tonight on his way to you. All is ready to implement the plan tomorrow after midnight.

b. You are required to wear dark clothes and a dark *jalabia*. Leave by car, if possible, accompanied by a young man and a young lady, on the race-course track in the direction of Habaniya, till you reach the rear of the airport. Leave the car and follow a trench along the wall to the end of the course, which is situated about thirty metres from the road. The accompanying pair must stay in the car. The plane will be parked at the end of the airport at exactly one thirty in the morning, your time, revving up its engines for ten minutes. You must approach its left side, go towards the tail end and climb a rope that will be lowered from the back hatch of the plane. You must move quickly and cautiously. Wear padded clothing, since you might brush against a barbed wire fence on the way. In case of any suspicious movement or disturbance, you must hurry back to the car and leave the place immediately. If the plane is canceled tomorrow night, we will try again on the following night, at the same time, using the same method.

c. When the signal is given denoting your approach to the arranged site, Boaz will make a phone call to Mesouda Shemtob at exactly twelve forty-five in the morning, requesting them to expedite the departure of the passengers. If the plane fails to take off, Boaz will say "all your explanations of the delay are worthless." Boaz will pass additional details through Tzuk (I.D. Sofer).

d. Tzuk must be present at Iraq Tours tomorrow at one fifteen in the afternoon.

e. In case of failure, the crew will claim that, just as they were about to take off, an individual on the ground shouted to them that he was a passenger who had been left behind. You must corroborate his story. If you think you are being observed, leave immediately.

f. The plan is well thought out and has been checked over. Boaz will be at the airport and the crew will be cooperative. Do not carry anything on you except money. After boarding the plane go directly to the cockpit.

While writing this book and sitting in the archives library of the Hagana, I found the affidavit of Menashe Ben-Hayim which throws light on the event and the effort required, from a wireless operator's point of view:

According to the plan, we were supposed to transfer him [meaning me] to the airport. The plane in question was one that carried emigrants. Because of the urgency of the matter, we were forced to give our consent immediately to Israel, so that they could organize the details of the plan and all that was connected with it. That posed a dilemma, as we ought to have checked to see if the plan was viable. One of the difficulties was that we had to go to the far end of the airport, which was out of bounds. Another problem was that the airport was situated not far from the King's Palace, and the route to the airport was the same one that the King used several times a day, therefore the security there was very tight and any strange movement alerted the suspicions of the guards. But the biggest problem was how to bring Ben-Porat to that fixed spot, a thorny area, difficult to reach and far from the road.

We took the telegram and rushed to Ben-Porat's hiding place. If we were accustomed to travel in single file, this time we went together [Menashe Ben-Hayim and Shimshon Hubeiba] with some space between us. We gave him the telegram. He was very troubled and in a poor frame of mind, but because of the telegram he perked up a bit. He studied it and read it through several times. It brought hope back into his eyes and colour to his cheeks. He studied it again and then read it aloud; in fact we all went through it in every detail. I must say the plan was an excellent one. In every detail. The planners didn't forget any item of clothing, the hour of exit, how to travel, how to get there and so on. Whatever they mentioned, couldn't be faulted and we had to make very few amendments. We collaborated with Sofer, who was much older than we were. Then we incorporated two more men, Advocate Fattal and Yaacov Battat, a Member of Parliament. After all the analyses had been completed, we decided to accept the plan. To tell the truth, there was nothing further to say – we had no alternative.

The next problem was how to take me to the airport with my head shaved, indicating that I had been in prison. An idea was formulated to recruit the grooms minding the horses near the airport, so that when I came by, I would be able to slip away and sneak into the airport area. Yaacov Battat remembered that he had a friend named Sa'id Sheik Khazaal, the son of a prince, who was involved in the dispute between Iraq and Kuweit and gave his full support to a free Kuweit. He was a man we could depend on. They decided to tell him that I was the brother of Naim Moshe Mandelawy and that the police were conspiring against me and to ask if he would drive me in his car to the airport.

At the same time Rony Barnett approached Sofer to map out the route to the airport. Sofer was supposed to come to my hiding-place, but was afraid to do so in case he was followed. He had a rule that before going to any appointed place he would first visit Gadisha, the prostitute. The agent who followed him had to wait for him outside. George Shasha declared later that the agent told him that Sofer placed him in a shameful position, as he made him wait for him in front of a well-known brothel, and passersby took him for a pimp. On his way to me, Sofer entered the brothel through the main entrance and immediately left by a side door, hopped into a car waiting for him and came to me.

We sat in a dark room by candle light. With us were the devoted wireless operators Shimshon and Menashe and my colleague in hiding, Naim Moshe Mandelawy. We discussed the plan in detail, reviewed the airport area and its access, and I studied the route. Sadly I was separated from them. Sofer told me with deep emotion that this would be the last time we'd be seeing each other. Sofer was supposed to meet Rony Barnett the following noon, in order to keep him posted of the plan, so that Barnett could direct the pilot and keep the airport Control Tower occupied.

The next morning at nine o'clock, Sofer was summoned by Abd-El-Sattar to the Secret Police station. Arriving there Abd-El-Sattar told him that this time he was going to arrest him because of information he received that Sofer, being a well-known merchant, was helping his brothers, who were in Teheran. Abd-El-Sattar advised him to call his brother, who knew Bahjat Atia, General Manager of the Police and the Secret Police, who could help him, otherwise he would spend the night in gaol. His brother Moshe did what was asked and Sofer was released at twelve-thirty. He went over to meet Rony Barnett at Iraq Tours, the Iraqi airways company which served the Near East Company. There he told Barnett of his brush with the Secret Police.

Meanwhile Yousif Fattal became very tense and worried. According to plan, Fattal was supposed to meet the prince's son in order to coordinate the hour of the drive to the airport. He called the synagogue, but Sofer wasn't there. Fattal and Shlomo Horesh decided to go there themselves. They asked about Sofer but no one knew anything. Half an hour later, policemen and soldiers entered with a mine detector. Fattal and Horesh had to hide themselves in a corner and pray for a miracle. Fattal then noticed an officer whom he knew, but the officer made out as if he didn't know him. Meanwhile, Sofer entered the synagogue and the plan went ahead. Yaacov Battat went to meet Khazaal and they sat together in a bar drinking until the hour of escape presented itself.

The car drew up, as agreed, driven by the Prince and sitting beside him the Member of Parliament, Yaacov Battat. I, with my shaven head, wearing a *sidara* and holding a bottle of drink, sat in the back seat and was driven towards the airport. Half an hour later we arrived at a man-made hill built up to protect the airport from flooding, descended and ran towards a barbed wire fence; I continued to creep along a ditch until I reached the edge of the airport perimeter. On the other side of the airport, Rony Barnett was in the Control Tower celebrating his birthday with the operators, the police and others; in this way was their attention diverted from the plane approaching the fence.

I saw the plane coming in towards me with its lights flashing as planned. It stopped, but its engines commenced revving up with a strident clatter. I approached the rope they lowered for me and thanks to my training in the Hagana and the help of the navigator, John Owen, I clambered up. I made for the cockpit, passing a load of agitated passengers who had had the experience of search and abuse by customs personnel and the police.

With the instructions I received, I was told that if the plane didn't flash its lights it meant that something had gone wrong with the plan and I mustn't go

*Gourji Shasha*

*Meir Elias*

*The wedding ceremony of Rivca and Mordechai Ben-Porat in July 1951, immediately after the author returned to Israel; standing behind them: Moshe Carmil.*

near it and that I was free to do whatever I thought best at that moment. Luckily, I didn't have to experience this alternative, which I construed to mean only one thing – the gallows.

Returning to the synagogue, I.D. Sofer saw many policemen and soldiers milling around. They let him enter and he hurried to the second floor, waiting to hear the expected password from Rony Barnett. It was a tense period at the synagogue and some workers were being arrested. As for me, no one, not even Gourgey Shasha, knew that I would be leaving that night.

Sofer was very edgy all evening. He tried to occupy himself preparing the emigrants for the flight on which I was supposed to travel. At the hour – an hour after midnight – Sofer asked Shasha to go up to the roof garden and try to locate the plane of the emigrants and see if its lights were flashing.

Shasha wasn't happy to do so in the middle of the night. Sofer kept insisting but didn't reveal his purpose.

הסוכנות היהודית לארץ־ישראל
## THE JEWISH AGENCY FOR PALESTINE

In reply please quote: : בתשובה נא להזכיר

| | |
|---|---|
| Dept. ................................ המחלקה | |
| Ref. No. ................................ המספר | |

המשרדים בתל־אביב
**TEL-AVIV OFFICES**

P.O.B. 28 .ד .ת
Telephone 1561 טלפון

TEL-AVIV ................ תל־אביב .כ׳ב חשון תשי״ב
(21.11.51)

Tel Aviv 21/11/51

To the participants and to Mr. Mordechai Ben-Porat
The Pioneers House
37 King George Street
Tel Aviv

Dear Members,

I regret I will not be able to participate in the affair to be given in honor of our colleague Mordechai Ben-Porat since I have two weeks ago undertaken to give a lecture this same evening at the club of the young members of the Party.

Please allow me to offer my heartiest congratulations to the guest of honor and the participants.

Our worthy colleague Ben-Porat has created a legend in the entire Jewish world and, especially among those who, thanks to him, were rescued during the Babylonian exile undertaking.

Very few colleagues have arisen in this generation to whom the Israeli people can honor and offer thanks like Mr. Ben-Porat.

May he have the chance to enable him to carry on his great work for the sake of the Israeli people as he has always done in the past.

With my heartiest wishes,

7th. Yousiftal

*(translated from the Hebrew)*

Shasha went up, and after fifteen minutes he came down and confirmed the flashing signal; he noticed Sofer's instant sense of relief.

"What is the matter?" Shasha asked.

When Sofer told him, Shasha fainted. An hour later Sofer enlightened him: "Someone who could have been a great danger for us has left the country. At least we are Iraqis and can continue to work."

Four hours later, at five in the morning, on Thursday, 14 June 1951, the plane landed at Lydda Airport. From the cockpit I could see the members of Mossad Le Aliya Bet waiting for me.

Leaving the plane I faced a small problem – I had no passport. It was supplied on the spot – I was given a certificate confirming my arrival in Israel. I immediately sent a telegram to Baghdad: "Warm regards to you and to all the workers. Despite your situation I believe you can soldier on until the end of the mission. Although I regret leaving you at such an hour I am sure that you will still have the last laugh."

The camaraderie and good humour that existed among the activists assisted the small group which took upon itself to care for the rest of the emigrants. I.D. Sofer, Gourgey Shasha and Meir Elias together with the wireless operators, were those who took on this responsibility despite the attendant danger. Apart from dealing with the emigrants, they also succeeded in smuggling out several people who were being hunted by the police and were forced to hide in various places. One of them was my "brother," Naim Moshe Mandelawy, who was in hiding with me at Naim Aboudy's house. In order to save him Shasha was assisted by a friend of his, Hussein Awani, Assistant General Manager of the Museum in Baghdad. He claimed that Nissim, Naim's brother had escaped and as a reprisal the police were determined to find Naim, so he asked for his help to smuggle Naim across the border. Awani, without hesitation, parked his well-known car at the border at Naim's disposal and took him out through Khanakin to freedom.

Also while in Iran, Naim continued to serve Israel. When I was sent on a mission to save the Jews in Iran during the Khomeini revolution, Naim worked with me. He and his family emigrated to Israel after the revolution.

Following my escape from Baghdad, Yousif Fattal, Yaacov Battat and Shlomo Horesh were instructed to cover my traces. Fattal revealed to Baban my method of escape. He showed no interest in it but asked me to repay a debt of 400 Dinars as well as another 200 for the appeal in the car accident case. Also, the bail problem where he deposited 500 Dinars was solved. The police released him from that with a fine of 300 Dinars. We paid him the money from the campaign fund.

The police officers were enraged on learning that I had managed to escape, and I have no doubt that it was they who put the letter bomb in Baban's office because he dealt with my case.

With this opportunity, I must mention the assistance given me by Nouri Rajwan, Sofer's brother-in-law, who was introduced to me on one of my visits to Sofer. He was also recruited to influence the examining magistrate, Kamal Shahin, so as not to oppose my release on bail, and he was successful.

Naim Moshe Mandelawy told me that on his arrival in Iran, he received an Iraqi newspaper where two court verdicts had been published: one, the death sentence against me and the other, sixteen years in prison for him. To my regret and his, a maid mistakenly discarded the paper. To my joy and his, we were saved from a dreadful punishment.

In Israel, I felt obliged to continue giving my help to the members of the Movement, and especially the activists working for the emigration who came here. I worked in the Employment Bureau, and with the kind assistance of Yisrael Carmi, David Ezra and the rest of the employees, we found various jobs for them and some were sent to the kibbutzim.

More than forty years later, to be exact, on 6 January 1994, when the Babylonian Jewry Heritage Centre organized an evening of tribute to the pilots who participated in the campaign to fly the Iraqi Jews out, I also had the opportunity of hearing the actual stories the pilots had to tell.

Arthur Lippa's description was very moving especially for me. He was the American pilot who flew the plane that rescued me from Baghdad; "It was a dark night; there was no moon; the passengers were strapped in their seats and we were supposed to take off in a short while. Of course, none of them knew what was going on. We prayed that all would go smoothly and without complications. As was usual, we informed the Control Tower that we were ready to take off. The engines were not working at full pressure so as not to cause any difficulties. We saw the runway, the lights. Between the guiding lights on the runway vague objects were visible; we thought they might be soldiers and that worried us. According to plan, that was the time to let down the rope. Jack Owen was the one who drew it up, while Mordechai handled the other end; with the help of Owen, he made it safely. Those moments seemed endless. When we saw Mordechai, we felt such a sense of relief. We immediately extinguished our lights, guided the plane onto the runway and headed out. In the air it was just another routine flight."

# Chapter 17

**THE BITTER END**

Whatever satisfaction and joy were obtained by those who had been rescued, no relief or consolation was available to those others who were still under interrogation and abuse: Their anxiety and distress continued. They were taken later on to court and sentenced within the full rigour of the law, which in this case was only subject to the malice of the judges. When I write here "they went on trial," I doubt whether we are talking about normal acceptable legal procedures. I believe that "show trial" or "cruel farce" would be more accurate.

The Iraqi court convened six times where many speeches were made by the district attorneys and the witnesses, together with the monologues of the accused who hoped to be able to alter their predictable fate. I will not quote you all the details but will give you short extracts, statements made by the condemned prisoners, which simply throw some light on the matter.

A day before Yousif Basri and Shalom Saleh were hanged, the prosecutor said, among other things:

> It seems that the Special Service Branch police of Baghdad received information that two people were arrested on 22 May 1951. One claimed that he held Iranian nationality; his name is Ismail Salhoon, and the other identified himself as Nissim Moshe Nissim [Mandelawy], who was released on bail and succeeded in escaping to Israel. It was disclosed that

he was the head of the undercover Zionist Organization in Iraq whose aliases were: "Ziv" or "Habib" and he was the man who provided Salhoon with money and information.

It seems that Israel sent the accused, Nissim Moshe Nissim, or Habib to Iraq, to carry out a dangerous mission. He contacted the escapee Yousif Khabbaza, and both acted together in order to create the undercover Zionist Organization. At the same time, Israel sent the culprits Ismail Salhoon and Rodney to assist in forming the organization and its activities. Nissim Moshe Nissim, known as Habib, provided them with funds. At one time he paid them 260 Dinars...

For long weary hours, the prosecutor continued with his venomous speech, giving evidence which was valueless.

In order to do justice to Yousif Basri and Shalom Saleh I quote the affidavits they gave in court, without adding any comments; and this is what Advocate Yousif Basri said:

On one of those hot summer days during the month of Ramadan, some interrogators came from the Special Service branch to the El-Waziriya Police Station, where they arrested me. Before having breakfast they took

*Yousif Basri (left) and Shalom Saleh, martyrs of the underground in Baghdad.*

me and strung me up in such a way that my hands were held upwards and I wasn't able to sit or hold anything. The interrogators informed me that the Deputy Police Officer, Selim El-Koureishi, would be coming to question me in the evening. I was left hanging until eight o'clock in the evening. The Deputy Officer arrived, took me down and transferred me from the cell to the Station, He ordered them to string me up again but this time my hands were held high and chained to the wall and one leg was raised about seventy centimeters from the floor. I was left in that position for an hour and when I couldn't take it anymore I started screaming and they decided to release me [...] I was unable to walk and they began to kick, abuse and curse me and called me a rogue.

El-Koureishi then ordered two policemen to take me to where the officer in charge was stationed. They lowered me into a chair and handed me a cigarette and some cold water. The Deputy then told me that the kind of torture I endured was mild and that it could be much worse, by taking off my nails, and began to show me various types of torture I had never witnessed before, so he advised me to complete the matter quickly. It was obvious that he wanted me to give him some money.

As I had been arrested for some time, I asked to have my relatives brought to visit me, and this was denied. In my situation I couldn't say anything, therefore I kept quiet. When I didn't reply, the Deputy Officer phoned someone and informed him that they had no further use for me. He put down the receiver and ordered me to strip. I was wearing only a shirt and underpants. I refused. He got up and forced me to do so. It left me completely naked. I didn't know what they had in mind. At that moment, Abood, the Sergeant at the station, entered and slapped my face, used clenched fists to hit me, cursed me, then ordered me to dress. While hitting and abusing me he asked for a gun and a whip. His colleague started to beat me with painful sharp blows. The interrogator telephoned the Special Branch department and ordered them to bring him shovels and leather straps.

Fifteen minutes later, the interrogators of the Special Service branch entered, blindfolded me with a big white handkerchief and dragged me to a car. After an hour's drive the car stopped. They removed the blindfolds, and here I found myself at a deserted place: nothing moved. They threw me to the ground, bound as I was. One of the men ordered his two colleagues to dig a grave with the shovels they had brought.

The interrogator took out his gun and said: "Make your peace with God before I shoot you."

I asked: "What is keeping you back? What do you want me to confess?"

The interrogator answered: "There are weapons hidden in several synagogues, do you know of other hiding places?"

As I knew of no others I decided to say my prayers.

One of the interrogators took me aside and threatened me: "I suggest you do some thinking before we shoot you!"

After a silence of several minutes, he continued: "There are weapons in several synagogues. Do you know of other hiding places?"

"I don't," I said.

"What does it matter if you say there are weapons in other synagogues?" he urged me.

Before I had time to answer he said to his colleagues that I had admitted that there were weapons hidden in other synagogues. Therefore the first interrogator and one of the two who dug my grave went together to Dora Police Station to inform them about developments and I couldn't tell if they wanted permission to continue with their method or to take me back to the Special Branch department. The result of it was that they "took" my so-called "evidence," but they weren't satisfied, and I was brought before the examining magistrate, who expressed himself with such vile remarks I'd hate to repeat here [...] The tortures began again and became more violent.

One day, at about one-thirty, several investigators from Special Branch came to El-Waziriya Police Station. They strung me up and said that the Deputy Officer would come in the evening to interrogate me. The evening came and went: night followed and then morning and noon; over twenty-five hours passed and I was still left hanging. Only when I reached the end of my tether and blood began to ooze from my nose and mouth did the person in charge of the station call the Special Branch department.

I understood, from one of the policemen who was present at the interview, that the person in charge informed the Special Branch department that my situation was critical and that he wasn't prepared to take responsibility for my death. Instructions were given to take me down. For two days I couldn't stand on my feet let alone walk. I was left without food and water on that day and on the following two days.

I don't wish to speak much of the incidents of torture – the suspension and the flogging. These were done in a large room, dark and sealed. That was one part of the torture, the physical aspect, the other was the mental and moral inquisition effected by the examining magistrate. When I refused to sign an affidavit to suit their purpose, he reprimanded me and said that I was like a lawyer who wished to conduct his own defence. Every time I refused to sign their fictitious affidavit, he ordered them to string me up.

Once, before closing their file on me, I was taken by the examiners of the Special Branch from the El-Waziriya Station to that of El-Sarai. It was morning; They presented me with a report saying that there were explosives of the Jelnit type in a suitcase resembling the one I had with me. They said that I had transferred explosives in this suitcase. I replied that they had taken this suitcase in which I brought some personal objects two or three days after my arrest, and since then it had been opened. When they took it they didn't seal it, therefore it was rational to say that they themselves put the explosives in the suitcase so as to incriminate me. I suffered mental torture thanks to the examining magistrate, who gave orders to hang me before nightfall.

And here is Shalom Saleh's testimony in court:

It was seven in the evening. They took me to the Special Branch department, tied me with ropes and chains; then they hung me upside down and warned: "You have to admit that you know someone who photographs military installations."

"I don't know such people," I said.

They transferred me, with my hands tied, to another police station. The Sergeant started hitting me with the butt of his pistol. He wasn't satisfied with that and wrapped an iron chain around my neck and began to tighten it, threw me to the floor, hit and kicked me. I stayed that way until 2:15 in the morning [...] Then they continued to torture me. They pulled hair from my mustache, eyebrows and eyelashes.

When I told the examining magistrate that I had done nothing he declared: "If you don't admit what we tell you to, we will torture you further!"

In order to put an end to the suffering I was forced to "confess"; I told them that someone or other threw bombs with my assistance. After the "confession" the interrogators took me to various places and instructed me to say that I threw bombs in those places. As I had no other choice I admitted this as well. I said whatever they forced me to say. This is all I have to say to the court.

Witnesses who saw Shalom Saleh with his inquisitors remarked on his swollen eyes and the bruises on his face. The last compassionate act shown towards the

*Gourgey Muallem, the last person to visit the two, sentenced to death on the eve of their execution.*

two who were condemned to death was offered by Gourgey Muallem, who was a teacher and director of the community school. He reported:

On 20 January 1952, I finished work at school and went home to rest. Fifteen minutes later the school janitor arrived and informed me that the President of the community, Yehezkel Shemtob, had phoned up requesting to see me urgently. I went immediately to the community office and found that, apart from Shemtob, many of the eminent members of the community were present.

Shemtob hurried up to me and said: "We have just received bad news. The Regent has signed the death warrant of the two men, and now we are in need of a Rabbi to attend them in prison before they are hanged. As no Rabbi is willing to go, I have decided to ask you to do so."

I was stunned and told him that I couldn't bear to see two Jewish men hanged in one day, but when I understood that the situation was irreversible and heard from him that we would disgrace ourselves in the eyes of Israel and Iraq if no Rabbi was sent the next morning, and above all, that the Government might take revenge on us, I decided to go despite the danger I might incur. I asked him to check with the Governor of the prison the hour of execution. The hanging was supposed to take place the next morning at six o'clock and the community was asked to send a Rabbi before four in the morning, with a letter.

Shemtob wrote the letter on the spot and handed it to me. He instructed a driver of Meir Elias Hospital to take me there and to wait for me.

I left the office and went home crying. I was unable to sleep. At a quarter to four the driver arrived and we drove to Bab El-Muatham, where a Moslem crowd was waiting in the execution square. The officer of police in Baghdad, his deputies and many soldiers were also present. The atmosphere was very charged. In order to protect us from the excitable mob, we were taken through another gate. The Deputy Governor of the prison stood at the entrance. After scanning the letter he took me to the Governor, asked me to take a seat and about half an hour later the judge, doctor, Sergeant, his Deputy and several officers entered.

I noticed that it was already a quarter to five. I asked the Governor of the prison to be able to visit the two men as there wasn't much time. He accompanied those present and we went to the room where the accused were held. I was appalled to see them and could barely stop myself from crying. At that moment, the Governor stood at my right, the Judge to my left, and the rest behind us. I asked the Governor if he would let me speak to them and he nodded. I asked to have the handcuffs removed from their hands and legs and to bring me water so that they could wash their faces and hands and then asked for two skull caps.

I told the two that I was sent by the President of the community in order to fulfil the religious requirements before the execution and asked them if they had any message to convey to Shemtob or to their relatives.

Yousif Basri replied: "We have nothing to say as friends have already visited us." Then he added that his request was to take their bodies to their relatives after the execution [meaning to their families in Israel].

I answered: "Of course that will be done."

The Governor confirmed this on the spot.

Then they asked if anyone could read Kaddish for them.

At that stage, I could hardly speak for the tears that almost choked me. I told them that there were lots of people who would do this for them. They also wanted me to take down their full names for the prayers.

I was about to do so when the Governor snatched the paper from my hand and said: "Let them speak and I will write."

Then Basri said: "My name is Yousif son of Ephraim Abratz and my mother's name is Gourgiya, born in 1924."

Shalom was in very bad shape and said: "My name is Shalom Saleh Shalom. My mother's name is, if I recall rightly, Hana. I was born in 1927" [His mother's name was actually Hasniya].

I told them that a man's manner of dying is ordained the moment he is born, whether by drowning, fire, the sword or by hanging, and that is every man's fate. The law of the Government is the Law and must be obeyed. All that happens in the world has been written in heaven.

Following this, I opened a prayer book, handed it to them and they proceeded to recite "Shema Yisrael" (Hear oh Israel).

All those present looked on with surprise and horror, as the name of Israel was mentioned. I explained to the Governor that this chapter was written in our Holy Bible and in the Torah which our Prophet Moshe presented, and that I was ready to translate it into Arabic. The Governor answered: "Proceed, we don't have time."

After we finished the doctor told me: "You must come and take them from the hospital at eight o'clock, because they will be kept hanging for two hours." The Governor ordered his Deputy to fetch two policemen to accompany us to the car until we reached the corner, because of the crowd gathering outside.

I went to the Hevra Kadisha (burial society) and asked them to be prepared at eight in the morning to receive the bodies from the hospital for burial. Then I went to the community office and updated Shemtob. I asked him to let me arrange seven days of mourning for them in the Zilkha Synagogue. He thanked me a lot and said: "You have saved us."

I went to the synagogue and arranged everything. Four men read the psalms, two during the day and two at night. On the seventh day I assembled, with difficulty, a number of people and we all went to the cemetery, where I eulogized them as they were erecting the tombstone.

Basri requested, as mentioned, that his remains be sent to Israel. Until I completed this book we have not been able to fulfil his last request. Anyhow, after their death, they were granted, in Israel, Officer's status and were honoured among the fallen of Israel's Defence Forces. After the *shiva*, a memorial service was held in the Big Synagogue in Tel Aviv. In 1968 a monument was unveiled in their memory in Or Yehuda, which adjoins the Babylonian Jewry Heritage Centre. I was at that time, head of the Local Council. Leaders of Israel and a large number of people participated in the ceremony. On Mount Herzl in Jerusalem, two graves were prepared for them, in hopes that the day would come when their remains could be brought to Israel. From information we received from Baghdad, Saddam Hussein demanded that the Jewish community transfer, at his particular request, the Jewish cemetery there, in order to put up an Iraqi military one on the site. The community was forced to exhume some of the graves and among them were those of Shalom Saleh and Yousif Basri.

Yehuda Tajer's destiny was a very hard one, but he was saved from the gallows. He was arrested with me, as previously mentioned, imprisoned, questioned and sentenced to nine years – at the end of which he succeeded in being released and returned to Israel a free man. On 10 October 1960, David Ben Gurion met Yehuda (Youdkeh) Tajer, and in his memoirs he recorded the meeting:

> Tajer, who was released a few days ago from an Iraqi gaol, came to see me this evening. Nine years ago, he was sentenced to life imprisonment on a charge of espionage (he was sent to Iraq by Issar and was caught). He wasn't tortured, but was told that he would be sentenced to death by hanging. They put a black coat on him and gave him a necktie and asked him who his co-conspirators were. He stuck to his statement. They then took the necktie away from him. Because of good behaviour they shortened his prison sentence to nine years. He sent several letters to Kassem – one reached him and he was taken to meet him on 23 December. Abdou and Abdul Wahab Amin (Minister of Welfare) were also present. Tajer was sure that Kassem wasn't a Communist and that he tried to keep a balance between the Left and Right. According to him, he was a very talented man and his popularity was great. He came back to Israel through Beirut and Cyprus. There are still around five thousand Jews in Baghdad. Many have become wealthy and are smuggling their assets abroad. The Sinai Operation left a great impression on the Iraqis and, since that time, they began to treat Tajer with more respect. During his first years in prison his hands and legs were chained. Later they released his hands. I don't know how this man stood up to it all. According to him, he comes from a family whose ancestors go back five hundred years in Israel, soon after the Expulsion from Spain. After that they went to Turkey and then on to Jerusalem. All the sufferings of those nine years of imprisonment left little impression on him.

One way or another, it is very interesting to read the affidavit of Yehuda Tajer, as it appears in the Commission of Inquiry held by Issar Harel (see Appendix B). Here is a section of it:

> "On the last night before the execution, I sat with both of them. I was taken there at their request at 9 in the evening. I was taken out later, but when the Governor of the prison went home they let me go in again. I sat beside Yousif; Shalom sat some distance away.
>
> I asked Yousif frankly: "Did you throw those bombs and did what you said?"
>
> He said: "I don't recall; ask Shalom."
>
> I asked Shalom (in front of Yousif) if Jews threw those bombs. I didn't exactly catch the word yes, but I had the impression it was them (after such a night I believed their words, because of what I saw later on).
>
> Q. When you had the impression that he answered affirmatively what was the reaction of Yousif?
>
> A. (silence.) He didn't say yes. My firm impression then was that it was a negative reply. Until then I doubted him but after a second or two I began to believe that it was so. Since then my explicit belief in him has not changed much.

In the memoirs of Ben-Gurion there was reference to a conversation between him and Issar Harel, where Issar reported the debates of the committee and brought a section of Tajer's affidavit to the committee.

> Tajer saw them both before they were hanged. One of them absolutely denied throwing the bomb. Shalom Saleh (the one who confessed) told Youdkeh, that he did throw a bomb. Youdkeh believes that as Shalom was at death's door he couldn't have been telling a lie. Nevertheless the Committee was of the opinion that as he had confessed in Court [Shalom Saleh denied it all in Court] it was difficult for him to deny it before his death. In my opinion it remains an enigma…

The monument erected in Or Yehuda in their memory, was unveiled on 8 December 1983. Youdkeh Tajer, who was absent from the ceremony, sent a letter written in his own handwriting as follows:

> Due to my illness I very much regret my not being able to participate in this solemn ceremony; therefore I authorize my friends to read the following message: "Lately, specific charges to do with the closure of the Israeli Intelligence Network that operated in Iraq were commented on. I wish to declare that I was not a partner to this and don't accept, nor do I believe, in this false charge. I have full admiration for all the members of the Underground, their devotion and contribution, I hereby esteem especially the great success of my friend Mordechai Ben-Porat in managing the Ezra and Nehemiah Campaign."

*A statue in commemoration of Yousif Basri and Shalom Saleh and to those killed by the bomb thrown at the Mesouda Shemtob Synagogue. It was erected beside the Babylonian Jewry Heritage Center.*

Regarding his conversation with the two condemned men, Tajer told me verbally that he had questioned Basri, who denied everything, and when he asked Saleh he didn't reply.

On 30 November 1992, Tajer added by writing to me: "...today, if I am asked I must say that I don't know the answer to the question, whether they did throw the bombs. I know that some bombs were thrown by Moslems. It is possible that one or two bombs were thrown by young Jews of their own accord, out of a desire to help us when we were caught..."

I don't intend to form a conclusion from the nuances in Tajer's report on that conversation with the two men. With this in mind, one should remember that both were under the influence of a drug that Tajer gave them to help them pass those terrible final hours before their execution. I also consider the possibility that Tajer himself wasn't in a normal frame of mind due to the court case and the interrogations, and was probably influenced by the many rumours mentioning the Jewish bomb-throwers. Most of the detainees were furious at their arrests and were ready to hold on to any report, especially those whom the police cooked up to put the blame on some of the prisoners. Therefore, and it is understandable, that after his release and return to Israel his thoughts had changed to a sincere belief that the Jews really threw those bombs.

The hanging of Yousif Basri and Shalom Saleh was an incident that exceeded all bounds beyond Iraq, and also for those diplomats who trusted Iraq, and sent statements to their governments. On 4 February 1952, a report was sent from the American Embassy in Baghdad, forwarded to the State Department in Washington, with copies to representatives in Tel Aviv, London, Paris, Amman, Basra, Beirut, Benghazi, Cairo, Damascus, Jedda and Tripoli. It runs as follows:

> Yousif Basri and Saleh Shalom, two Iraqi Jews convicted of bomb throwing, were executed in the early hours of the morning of January 21, 1952, these being the first Iraqi Jews put to death since Shafik Ades was executed in October 1948.
>
> The Embassy hopes to be able to forward in the air pouch leaving Baghdad on 2 February complete summaries of the proceedings of the trial which the Department's legal staff may wish to examine. Enclosed with this dispatch is a memorandum containing the Embassy's informal

comments on allegations of trial irregularities set forth in a document prepared by the American Jewish Committee and forwarded under cover of the Department's instruction number 15 of December 18, 1951. These comments are transmitted with the caution that it is very difficult for this Embassy discreetly to obtain accurate facts about the trials. Even telephone calls have been picked up and reported by the press.

Also enclosed is a report published in El-Yaktha of the final hours of the convicted men and photographs of the execution displayed in the same paper.

The Iraqi public has taken the affair quite calmly, and El-Yaktha was the only paper which has published the details extensively. Most of the Iraqis are convinced the trial was fair and orderly and the death sentences just.

Iraqi Jews, on the other hand, are, as could be expected, bitter in condemning it. Jack Shaul [who immigrated in 1966 with his sister Najiba] supplied us, when still in Iraq, with all kinds of information. He was the Iraqi Jewish correspondent for the Iraq Times, who, on more than one occasion, was known to defend the Iraqi Government against false allegations regarding the mistreatment of Jews. He told an Embassy representative that most of the Jews there today are nervous and as fearful as he is.

Shaul said candidly that there existed a wide Jewish undercover organization dealing with espionage. He said that most of the Jews knew of its existence and were prepared for members of this organization to pay for their acts if caught. Also, they thought that the death penalty had been too harsh, due to the evidence presented in court and were especially shocked by the stories of torture practised there. Their attitude was that apart from feeling sympathy and pity for Shalom and Basri it was certainly possible to force Jews to confess to any crimes in the world after undergoing such "intensive care."

Shaul said that he didn't think that the judges of the Appeal Court were convinced of Shalom and Basri's guilt; rather that they felt committed, due to the pressure of public opinion, to accept the verdict of the Special Tribunal. He also said that, according to information he received, one of the judges, Ibrahim Shabender, disagreed with the majority opinion in both cases. He also mentioned that after the Appeal Court allowed the death penalty, the final word was left to the Regent – and the Jewish community lost hope of saving Shalom and Basri, knowing that the Regent was too weak to stand up to public opinion and needed to expedite their punishment.

Apart from all this, Shaul reasoned that the executions would not have created massive emigration of the few Jews who were still living in Iraq. He pointed out that those who stayed behind represented a tough core, who due to old age, their deep attachment to their surroundings or their successful adaptation to it, have decided to stay on. But he also foresaw that those Jews would completely refrain from any involvement in political activities in Iraq, and that the four remaining Jewish members of Parliament would certainly not be reelected at next spring's elections.

The American Embassy would never take it upon itself to pass sentence on the tribunal. It felt that it would be extremely difficult to prove a definite miscarriage of justice. It was also impossible to say that this case and others like it, where the suspects were Jews, could have been judged without obvious political overtones.

The Embassy could say, with much more certainty, that it believed that the kind of evidence produced against Basri and Shalom did not justify the sentence being commuted to life imprisonment. In their opinion, however, there was no doubt that the Iraqi Government, in order to protect its standing in the international community, ought to have heeded our counsel and commuted the death sentences, irrespective of the prosecutions just cause.

On the other hand, the rules of the desert that permit no quarter to an enemy who surrenders still runs in the veins of all Iraqis, including the sophisticated ones. Those who encouraged and supported the Jewish Underground Movement and its espionage activities (one can never know the practical reasons for that) ought to have taken this into account.

Despite those factors responsible for the situation, it appears that their political aspirations led to the complete decline of a community of some very talented people, who once had an important and valuable influence on life in Iraq and were duly rewarded with relatively comfortable conditions for their advancement and prosperity after they made suitable adjustments to reality in this country.

Edward S. Crocker

Enclosures:

1. Memo;

2. The report published in El-Yaktha on the final hours of the two condemned to death.

## Memo

Commentary and notes affixed to the memo of the American Jewish Committee dated 11 December 1951, in order of the clauses of the original memo:

### 1. Appointment of the Court's Judicial Panel

A. The Court Panel was appointed by decision of the Justice Ministry. Formerly, people suspected of crimes against the State (since the Palestinian crisis) were tried before Military Tribunals. The special court which tried people accused of Zionist activities was a civil one that acted in accordance with the current laws of Iraq. As far as can be ascertained, that court and its panel was the first of its kind ever appointed in Iraq.

B. The presiding Judge in that special Court, Hamed Sadr-El-Din, is a former prosecuting attorney who has sat on the benches of the highest court in Iraq since 1950. The presiding Judge and the other judges are reputable and well-known and were trained to adequately dispense justice.

## 2. Behaviour of the defence lawyers

The lawyers representing the suspects were privately hired by the defendants (and not assigned by the court). It should be noted that these defence lawyers, though not famous criminal lawyers, presented a singular line of defence. Neutral observers pointed out that during the court sessions, they were fully aware of public feeling against the defendants. Both lawyers were allowed free reign to present their case before the Court, and the sessions were not conducted "in camera."

## 3. Presentation of evidence and its acceptability

A. Contrary to official claims, no eyewitnesses to the bombings were brought before the court.

B. There were several incidents of contradictory testimonies during the trial.

C. Both defendants protested that their confessions were obtained under physical torture applied by the police. The court, however, reasoned that even if the confessions were obtained by torture, the facts proved themselves and were recognized later by the Court as prima facie evidence. The confessions of the defendants led to the discovery of hidden weapon dumps.

D. As far as we know, this matches the facts.

E. All evidence presented against the defendants was circumstantial. The defendants anyway were unable to come up with an iron-clad alibi as to their whereabouts at the time of the bombings. Their defence consisted mainly of denials of the prosecution's claims. However they were unable to present any proof of their innocence, even though there was every opportunity to do so. This attitude, however, contradicts the accepted American belief that a person is innocent unless proven guilty.

4. **Other aspects of the trial**

A. The court, as far as we know, did not examine the defendants' claims, regarding the terrible torture they had undergone in police custody.

B. The objective facts in this clause seem reliable. It is worth noting that the cross-examination of witnesses in Iraqi courts does not conform with procedures in the Western World.

C. The Embassy was unable to investigate this matter [...]

### The Report of El-Yaktha

Upon my arrival in prison [the newspaperman wrote] I saw Salman El-Bayat, Judge of the Magistrate Court, Mohammed El-Samourai, Deputy Officer of the Police and Hussein Abed Ali and a senior officer. Accompanied by the officer and the prison doctor we went to see Basri and Shalom before taking them to the North Gate [in the city of Baghdad] to be hanged.

After informing Basri of the execution hour, they asked him to state his last wish. Basri wanted to see Ismail Salhoon, who was sent from Israel, and immediately Salhoon arrived, they embraced and kissed each other several times, until the Governor of the prison feared that Salhoon would slip some poison into his mouth to enable him to commit suicide. The mouths of both were examined by the doctor of the jail.

Basri requested Salhoon to give his heartfelt greetings to his sister upon his return to Israel, and after serving his sentence.

Another man by the name of Nadham Feirouz was taken to Basri and also embraced him. He cheered him up and said that "he was prepared to pay 20,000 Dinars only to save his life."

Then Sasson Sadik entered; he was the one accused as a Zionist spy and is Basri's cousin. He blessed him for the last time.

The Judge asked the two for their final wish. Shalom didn't answer but Basri said that he had with him a suit, 11 Dinars in cash, a watch, two blankets and various objects which he would like to give to his cousin Sadik. Shalom interrupted him and told the Judge: "Give my things to Ismail Salhoon, that's all I have to say."

Those were their last words.

When the El-Yaktha reporter left the room he asked the Governor of the prison if Shalom and Basri asked for anything the night before, and he replied: "When they asked Shalom and Basri what they desired to eat or drink, they asked for some fruit, coffee and cigarettes."

At 5:45 a.m. their heads were covered with black hoods and they were led into a black car, their hands and legs chained. At 5:50 a.m., they left the prison, and at 5:55 a.m. arrived at the North Gate; out there, a large crowd was waiting to watch the execution.

They were taken out of the car, and after releasing their hands and feet, they were tied with ropes and at 6:00 a.m. they were hanged. The physician on duty pronounced them dead.

At 7:30 the bodies were taken down from the gallows and sent to the Medical-Judicial Department for confirmation.

At 9:30 a messenger of the Jewish community arrived to collect the bodies.

Every Rabbi refused to fulfil this religious duty. They sent instead a junior member of the burial society.

As Basri and Shalom were put on trial on a charge of throwing bombs in Baghdad (and in court it was claimed that they had confessed), the question remained – did a Jewish hand really commit this foolish act? I would like to quote excerpts here from various discussions that took place in 1968 referring to the subject and in which certain people took part, such as activists and ex-prisoners who could throw some light on this the matter.

**Mordechai Ben-Porat** (talking to Salim Mouallem who was caught and arrested): I understand that the interrogators questioned you immediately after your arrest regarding the bombing incident. This was when Yousif Basri was still free; only after his arrest and the planting of explosives in his suitcase did they accuse him together with Shalom Saleh of throwing bombs.

**Salim Mouallem:** They didn't only question me about the bombs but Yehuda Tajer and Robert Rodney as well.

**Eitan Shamash** (talking to Salim Mouallem): Without doubt no one from the Movement or the Jewish community would have thrown a bomb between the Rafidain Bank and the Jewish store of Stanley Shashou. Don't you think it possible that the Government might have arranged it and with all of you in detention and about to be tried, looked for someone to frame?

**Salim Mouallem:** In my opinion, one of two factors might have been involved in this: Either our people hatched the plot, or the police did. When members of the Movement deny it completely, then the police are the only ones who could have done it.

**Eitan Shamash:** This is a most painful episode. As is well known, after finding the weapons in the synagogues, they invited foreign newsmen and the Manager of the YMCA, who was known to be a British spy, to watch the proceedings. At the end of the weapons display, Abd-El-Ja'far Fahmi, Commissioner of Police in Baghdad, declared that "now there is no doubt who threw bombs at the American Information Center, so as to disturb relations between America and Iraq." The fact that they had found weapons was enough for the Commissioner to arrive at these conclusions. This explains the pressure put on the police to find a culprit, whatever the outcome.

**Salim Mouallem:** In order to find a connection between events occurring in the region, one should refer back to a similar incident that took place in Egypt, and (as Pinhas Lavon pointed out) the bomb episode in Iraq. Perhaps there was a secret link between the two. He said that he heard from the police that they had known for some time about the Movement and the weapons. The question was why did they only reveal it on 5 June 1951?

**Mordechai Ben-Porat** (asking Maatouk Douri, who was in charge of Shalom Saleh and who also took part in the Shura and in preparing arms caches): You were in contact with the weapons and the arms caches. Do you think that Shalom Saleh was capable, on his own, of secreting from the caches, a bomb or an explosive device and do what he did?

**Maatook Douri:** Shalom was a modest man and lacked initiative. The weapons he used were always given to him by officers. He had no exclusive access to them at all.

**Itshak David Sofer:** I would like to reconsider the assumption that a secret link existed, apart from that of the Movement.

I was restless for a number of years. I found no satisfaction in discussing this subject at length. I was always on the look out for an opportunity to obtain a decision by a court of law. I had such an opportunity when Barukh Nadel, a former LEHI Member (Fighters for the Freedom of Israel: Underground Movement at the end of the Mandatory Regime in Palestine) and sworn enemy of the state, and especially of David Ben-Gurion, was interviewed by Maarakha, the organ of the Sephardic and Oriental Jews (Edition No. 195 of April 1977), in which he said, among other things: "regarding the matter of saving Iraqi Jews, there was an agreement that said, 'give us the people and take their assets [...]' In Iraq the agreement didn't work out: the Jews who lived in Iraq in affluence had no desire to emigrate, so the Israeli State's emissaries exploded bombs in Jewish population centres to cause a panic that lead to the flight of almost all the Iraqi Jews within six months."

Since the interview was published on the eve of the election in which I took part representing an independent party, I did not want this matter to interfere with the election campaign. So I replied to Barukh Nadel by suing him later on in August 1977. I hasten to add that Nadel made great efforts to support his claims in that interview. He initiated meetings with scores of Iraqi immigrants to collect supporting evidence. When he found out that he couldn't prove his slanderous accusations, he sent along a few mediators to effect a compromise. Not until the 3 November 1981 was a settlement reached. It stated:

The Magistrates Court

H E R Z L I Y A

Civil file 63/81

The Plaintiff:    Mordechai Ben-Porat

-versus-

The Defendant: Barukh Nadel

The two parties hereby inform the Court that they have reached an agreement, as follows:

1. The Iraqi Jewish immigration, within the framework of the Ezra and Nehemiah Operation, was accomplished due to the yearnings of the Iraqi Jews for the Holy Land and also because of the unbearable pressure put on them by the Iraqi Government which involved persecution, arrests, hangings and so on.

2. The emissaries of Israel who operated in Iraq, whether those who came from Israel or the local activists, did their work with devotion, without exception and under dangerous conditions.

3. In suggesting that the emissaries of Israel threw bombs on Jewish settlements in Iraq, in order to accelerate the exit of the Jews, Mr. Nadel was influenced by malicious journals published by the Iraqi authorities, and unsupported by any evidence.

4. When the facts were fully explained to Mr. Nadel, as conveyed to him by a Member of the Knesset, Mordechai Ben-Porat, Chairman of the Babylonian Jewry Heritage Centre, Mr. Nadel hereby withdraws his accusations against the emissaries of Israel and its activists, and apologizes for any injustice done to them due to the publications.

|  |  |
| --- | --- |
| Mordechai Ben-Porat | Barukh Nadel |
| Plaintiff | Defendant |

This agreement was presented to the Magistrates Court in Herzliya on 3 November 1981. The Judge certified it, passed judgment and instructed to have the claim deleted. I agreed to waive the court expenses. This was the end of a chapter and Nadel had no interest in discussing it further.

# Chapter 18

# PROPERTY –
# AND LIVES

I t appears that whenever one meets up with an Iraqi Jew, one gets the image of someone closely connected to banking, finance, accountancy and real estate in general.

Iraq, which is but a part of ancient Mesopotamia, has been one of the most prolific regions in the world, with plenty of water, which enabled it to have a flourishing agriculture, an abundance of oil latent in its soil, an ideal location between the East and the Western world, its proximity to the Persian Gulf, all this has made it a country replete with economic and commercial potential.

The Jews who arrived in Iraq due to the Yehukhin Exile and the destruction of the First Temple in the year 586 B.C. lived there as a minority for more than two thousand five hundred years. Moslems are in the majority in modern Iraq, and apart from their engagement in conventional areas of agriculture, handicraft and local trade, they also fill military, police and governmental positions. The Jews knew that they would not be accepted into their public institutions. Therefore, similar to what happened in various periods of exile, they turned their energy to other trades such as import and export, and managing companies and finance. The Jews who emigrated from Iraq to other countries continued to have trade relations with the mother country and with the communities there.

They soon reached prominent positions in the trade circles of Iraq, at the beginning of the Eighteenth Century. Jews of Baghdad and Basra began to have intensive trade relations with the Ottoman Empire – Turkey, Syria, Iran, India, Yemen and others. Up until the Second World War, there were many established Iraqi Communities in countries such as Israel, India, Malaya, Singapore, Hong Kong and China, and of course England. The success of Jews in international trade, although it invited the antagonism of the Moslems, gave Iraq new opportunities and contributed a lot to its economy.

The British influence in Iraq, from 1917 until 1921, and later their occupation of the country continued until 1932 and was an era of prosperity and great success, and an example to other more modern forms of government and economies. The Jews played a significant part in this economy. Import, which until then, ranged from food and various manufacturing materials, was enlarged to include building materials, agricultural equipment and machines, clothes, shoes and so on. British rule helped to change Iraq's attitude towards the Jews and they began to be accepted in interim jobs and senior positions in public spheres. In this environment and at that time, certain people distinguished themselves, such as Advocate David Samra, who filled a series of jobs and reached his peak as Vice President of the Magistrate's Court; Salim Darzi, Manager of the Post and Telegraph Services, Moshe Shohet, Deputy General Manager of the Railways; Ezra Lwaya, Assistant to the Economic Controller; Abraham El-Kabir, General Manager of the Finance Office, Yehezkel Sasson, the first Minister of Finance in independent Iraq and who also designed the framework for the administration of Iraqi finance.

Sasson, Minister of Finance in the Iraqi Government in the twenties, was the one who arranged the foundation for the Government budget and who secured, in 1925, the royalties from the British Oil Company, which later merged into the Iraqi Oil Company, so that it should be paid on the basis of the gold standard rate and not Pounds Sterling. As requested by the company, a decision was made that contributed, without doubt, to saving Iraq from economical collapse during the Second World War when Sterling fell and gold went sky-high. Abraham El-Kabir was brought in by Sasson to be the Comptroller of Finance: He was a successful man in that field and received the Two Rivers Royal Medal. He was a representative for the Iraqi Government in negotiations that took place in October 1924 to settle Iraq's debts to the Ottoman Empire, and it was he who presided over the complicated operation to regulate the Iraqi economy and the

Dinar, which became stronger than Sterling. Abraham El-Kabir was elected along with three committee members to found the Rafidain Bank in 1941, and had considerable influence on that bank's decisions. In 1948, he was the only Jew among the nine members of the Board of Directors of the Iraqi Central Bank which was then established.

In 1937-1938, 56.3 percent of the exporters were Jews, and Jewish merchandise importers constituted 54.7 percent. In the years 1938-1939, among the list of members of the first rank in the Chamber of Commerce (people who had a turnover of between 22,500 and 75,000 Dinars) Jewish firms held a very distinguished place: Adas (merchants, car agents and insurance), Rajwan (tea merchant), Haim Nathaniel (transportation and travel agency), Eastern Bank, Khadourie Aboudy Zelkha (merchant and money-changers), Khadourie Ezra and Meir Lawee (car agents), Shamash brothers (tea merchants), Sion Shlomo Aboody (money-changers) and others.

During and after the Second World War a conspicuous decline took place among some Jews in foreign trade: from 10 per cent before the war to 2 per cent after it. During the War of Independence and the establishment of the State of Israel, there was a change in Moslem relations towards the Jews. Anti-Jewish feeling, in fact one can call it anti-Zionist, came to the fore. The support for the Palestinians increased and, owing to that, some prominent merchants were arrested, including the distinguished Shafik Adas. He was close to the Regent, had powerful connections and was quite influential among the higher echelons in the Government, and yet he was executed in 1948. Two other Jewish merchants, Stanley Shashou and Salem Shamoon, were also put on trial.

Among some Jews, however, whose feelings were influenced by a strong attachment to Iraq, considered her their Motherland and to whom they remained loyal despite the cruel vicissitudes of time. This pragmatic attitude was influenced by the needs of the community to prove to their Moslem brothers that, despite the Balfour Declaration, they would remain loyal citizens. At the same time, they also demonstrated a clearly anti-Zionist attitude. Most prominent of those who raised this banner was Yehezkel Sasson, who, at a meeting with Abraham El-Kabir in 1921, tried to persuade him to enter public office and said: "...Circumstances have now altered. We no longer serve strangers in a corrupt administration facing ruin and annihilation. We will be serving our Motherland who has a glorious past and a promising future, a land blessed with fertile soil and an abundance of water resources, whose people aspire to march forward to rebirth after laying in ruins, dormant and neglected for so many generations [...] Our role is that of pioneers [...] Come and join forces with us in the creation of a developing nation that will remind the world of the past splendours of ancient Iraq." This was quoted by El-Kabir in his book *My Life in Public Service,* and he added: "This was a turning point in my life [...] I have always been an idealist. I was spellbound by the chance of contributing towards the creation of a powerful state. My co-religionists had lived in this land for 2,500 years. Many contributed a great deal to its progress in science, finance, literature and even politics, and I saw no reason why we, the Jews of this generation, could not resume what our ancestors did." (The original manuscript of *My Life in Public Service* was handed to me by Abraham El-Kabir and I have placed it at the Centre for safe keeping).

Menahem Saleh Daniel, one of the more distinguished leaders of the Iraqi Jewish community and one of the first subscribers to Iraqi renascence, worked wonders and in September 1922, sent a letter to the Zionist Organization in London, where he made it clear that he was inclined to ignore the Zionist activities in Iraq. "All the Iraqi Jews without exception must show devotion to their country, which is trying its best at present to build a future of its own, and Jews should take part in it." They had suspicions, and yet had difficulty accepting, that they were sitting on a barrel of explosives. Inasmuch as the agitation against the Jews increased, it became clear to them that things would never be the same again. Wealthy family members, faithful to the Iraqi tradition, such as the Daniel family, El-Kabir, Dangoor, Sawdayee, Khalastchi, Shemtob and Basri, began to think of emigrating, even if it was a temporary measure. But living in luxury and hoping that the troubles gathering were but a wind that would blow away caused some hesitation. Eventually when they emigrated to England, Canada, America, France and other places they were forced to leave behind huge assets – land, property, factories, money, gold, jewellery, etc. During my activities in Iraq I found out about the extent of that wealth and understood its significance in the eyes of its owners. So I began to draw the attention of the Iraqi Government to these assets:

**Funds:** The Jews deposited, in the various banks in Iraq, a fabulous amount of money acquired during the upsurge in the economy. The question was how to transfer this money to foreign countries, including Israel, with the minimum of danger and commission. The Movement had lots of chances to transfer large amounts of money to Israel, but the transfer had one drawback – the commission charged. The Israeli Treasury demonstrated an abysmal lack of foresight, and instead of seeing these funds as a contribution to the development for economic and industrial growth, it demanded a 20% commission – an amount that no one in the world would accept – whilst on the other hand, transferring money to England, for example, took only 5%. It is obvious that because of the Israeli Treasury's shortsightedness, the capitalists who succeeded in transferring their money abroad chose other channels.

On 6 December 1949, a short while after my arrival in Iraq, I sent a telegram to Israel where I strongly protested the Treasury's demand and implored them: "In our opinion, it is very important that you show interest in saving this Jewish capital, with practical charges." Two weeks later, on 5 February 1950, I pressed them further and cautioned: "I have the impression that Israel doesn't realize the importance of this problem. There are hundreds of thousand of Dinars, and maybe millions, in cash, that their owners want to transfer to Israel. Friends who are close to the Movement and trust it are ready to transfer the money at not more that 10% commission, as they feel that their transfer would be in safe hands."

All transfers of money done through the Movement were completed to the entire satisfaction of the capitalists. But those transfers were comparatively few owing to the attitude of the Treasury. I sent another telegram where I warned them again of the danger that Jewish capital may suffer. I quoted articles in Iraqi newspapers for requests to freeze all Jewish assets and yet despite this mounting pressure Jews were forced to change their money and gold at usurious rates. I still had no response.

**Land:** Many Iraqi Jews bought land in Israel in the thirties and forties through the representative of the Zionist Organization, Ahron Sasson Ben Eliahu Nahum (the Teacher). Those who bought property presented the Movement with hundreds of Tabu certificates, which we transferred to Israel asking them what we must do to claim our rights. On 10 January 1950, we received the following answer: "The Government will give its full assistance to the landowners in Israel, who were absent for war reasons, and will not increase their taxes specifically for their benefit [...] After completing a small procedure they may use their properties as they wish." It was obvious that this general answer didn't give any satisfaction to the landowners.

**Investment in Israel:** The Iraqi Jews were also interested in this. It appears that the next example I give here will clarify the matter in the best way. On 13 March 1950, I sent a telegram to Israel: "A merchant named Sasson Shmuel Sasson who owns two hundred and fifty thousand Pounds (the bulk of which is spread abroad) is ready to invest in Israel and is interested in offers. He is a textile merchant [...] Can you send a financial expert here, who is skilled in economics, to give him suggestions and information on various opportunities open to him. We will take care to see that he is able to enter Iraq." This telegram, to my regret, had no response. Sasson Shmuel Sasson invested his money elsewhere.

I decided to offer practical suggestions to Government officials:

As Palestinian refugees left houses behind in Israel, I suggested, on 6 March 1950, that an exchange arrangement could be made with them. The Palestinians would then receive Jewish homes in Iraq and the Jews, upon immigration, would take over Palestinian homes in Israel. However, in Israel, they weren't enthusiastic about my proposals regarding capital, and certainly not any of my other suggestions: On 10 March 1950 the Treasury instructed the Mossad: "You have to warn Dror, firmly, not to promise any compensation to Jews who are leaving their homes in Berman [Baghdad] and no exchanges are to be made with the refugees. An incautious arrangement from our side will invite claims and difficulties in Israel. Ask for confirmation of this instruction."

On 18 March 1950 I made another suggestion, that "Jewish capital be transferred to the Prime Minister and Interior Minister as an inducement to facilitate the handling of exit permits, and that the owners of capital receive compensation in Israel." This suggestion also created antagonism against me in Israel.

When the subject was brought before David Ben-Gurion, he was much more attentive and open than the Mossad over which he presided. In his memoirs written on 22 March 1950, Ben-Gurion stated: "I support the idea of establishing a special organization to deal with the assets of the Iraqi Jews, and possibly with the exchange mentioned." Later on he mentioned his opposition to the hold-up taking place in emigration

On 16 April 1950, Moshe Carmil wrote the following letter to Ben-Gurion: "From a stack of information received between 26.3.50 until 15.4.50 it is obvious that the time has come for a mass emigration from Babylon. Problems of the liquidation of the assets and its transfer to Israel require extensive and firm support in Israel, and especially abroad. The matters are complicated and need serious attention and authority. The Government and the Agency must select, without delay, the right person to take over this responsibility and management."

An appreciation of the situation in Iraq, as confirmed on 27 February 1950 by the Counseling Bureau for Special Matters in the Israeli Foreign Office, was: "Our people approached Washington and London and asked them to press Iraq to permit every emigrant to take out 250 Dinars in place of the 50 Dinars now permitted. [There is an inaccuracy here that must be corrected: in fact, the Iraqi Government allowed every emigrant up to ten years of age to take out 20 Dinars, and up till twenty years old, 30 Dinars, and any emigrant over and above that age, the sum of 50 Dinars]. The first reaction was positive, but when this was addressed to the American Embassy in Baghdad, it refused to handle the request, claiming that it feared that its interference would be rejected, as the quota of 50 Dinars had been fixed in Iraq for years; also that the Iraqi Government was taking into account the fact that Jews have been smuggling their money out anyway."

The report described the general situation in Iraq: "When Towfik El-Suweidi rejoined the Government, as Deputy to Nouri El-Sa'id, an atmosphere of moderation was introduced into the Cabinet regarding the Jews. A few ministers were inclined to permit Jews to remain in Iraq. They claimed, though, that as long as Nouri El-Sa'id was Prime Minister, it was impossible to change his tough stance, especially when considering public opinion and the attitude of the media, who were still not ready to accept any change in their resentful attitude towards the Jews. A few newspapers demanded that the 'treacherous' Jews be kept in special concentration camps until their departure from Iraq. On the other hand, the tremendous damage affecting the economy was aggravated when the Jews left Iraq. The administration itself and the large banks (mostly British) were especially stricken due to the resignation of key Jewish figures. In retaliation, the Government issued restraining orders against some of its Jewish functionaries. The cessation of activities by Jewish importers caused widespread shortages in vital materials usually supplied by foreign exporters, especially since no one in the local markets was able to replace the experienced Jewish importers. As a result, the public pointed an accusing finger at the British who, they said, were the guilty ones and responsible for the massive Jewish exodus and by their actions intended to weaken Iraq and direct the people's anger towards the Jews at the same time."

A group was formed to locate and rescue the assets and register them. Naim Yitzhak Shamash was the liaison man between myself and the Public Committee, headed by Sasson Abed, which provided us with various services. I was introduced by him to two engineers, Salim Gahtan and Naji Ephraim Shashou, who were experts in the field of assets, investments and their worth in 1948-1949, and charged them to study and estimate the value of these assets. The two, assisted by Naim Yitzhak Shamash, presented me with the report I requested, and on 7 March 1951 I sent the Mossad and the Treasury the following letter with the enclosure of a first-hand report on some of the private and public assets belonging to Iraqi Jews. In the report it mentioned, among other things that: "a) The statistics regarding the private and public Jewish assets existing in Iraq approach the official figures by as much as 90%. We will try our utmost to look for further details on the assets, which are not included in the enclosed booklet. b) Despite the great work invested in obtaining this material, we are trying our best to get copies of the official community book. c) We are also trying to get material, concerning the assets existing within various other communities in Iraq."

On Friday, 9 March 1951, one year after the bill of Revocation of Citizenship, the Iraqi Cabinet approved the certificates for 103,866 Jews. The next day, on Saturday, an urgent meeting was held in the Iraqi Parliament, where the Government presented a bill to freeze the assets of all Jews whose citizenship had been revoked. This bill (which was kept a secret even from some of the Ministers) provoked a great debate in Parliament. Saleh Jaber, a Shiite Moslem, who was the Minister of the Interior in Towfik El-Suweidi's Government and during whose tenure the bill of Revocation of citizenship was passed, left the session sullen and displeased. Ezra Menahem Daniel, a Jew and a member of Parliament, said some harsh things and blamed Nouri El-Sa'id for the plight of the Iraqi Jews. El-Sa'id replied sarcastically that all Jews were Zionists and had assisted in the founding of the State of Israel.

After passing the bill, and in the absence of the Regent, it was also confirmed by a special committee, whose members were Jamil El-Madfaee, President of Parliament, and Muhammed Sharif Hussein, brother-in-law of the Regent. This committee added a decree appointing Hamid Rafaat, who was General Manager of the Foreign Office and known as an honourable man, to be a trustee over the assets. Many employees were hired immediately in the Trustee Office to administer the frozen assets. The Minister of Finance ordered the banks to be closed for a day and then another day, meaning until Monday, and the Iraqi radio station repeated details of the bill several times. The Jews who had their cash deposited in the banks were in great distress. Naim Yitzhak Shamash, Manager of the Ottoman Bank, endangered himself by disregarding the order to close and left the bank open until the last depositor had withdrawn his money.

In Israel, the authorities acted hesitantly and even impotently, although in Iraq they took action with vigour. The authorities decided to increase control over the Jews. The police arrested and searched every Jew they found walking in the streets with a suitcase or parcel in his hand. Jewish shopkeepers, including food and meat shop owners, weren't allowed to open their shops. The police, striving to discharge the law, began to put a ban on Jewish shops whether they belonged to citizens who had had their citizenship revoked or not and sealed them with the State seal. Jews were forced to buy food, especially meat, from shops belonging to Arabs.

On 11 March 1951, I wrote the following to the Mossad: "This bill is causing hardship for tens of thousands of Jews who haven't liquidated their businesses. Enormous amounts of money have been frozen in the banks. There is a great fear that the frozen assets will be distributed among the personnel, and because of this we are of the opinion to direct every effort into sending an international committee to supervise this problem."

Nouri El-Sa'id was in a joyful mood. The newspapers, contrary to the hostile attitude formerly adopted against him before the new bill was passed, showered him with praise and lauded his actions. He met three times with the Regency Committee and demanded that all Jews whose citizenship had been revoked be rounded up and held in a concentration camp. Fortunately, the committee refused to grant his request. Saleh Jaber was incensed. In a meeting with members of the Jewish committee appointed to direct the emigration, he promised to bring up the subject before the Regent. He called El-Sa'id a criminal. Jews who registered for emigration and temporarily deposited their money in the banks found themselves penniless and in want of food. They visited the synagogues and caused an outcry demanding that their emigration be expedited. News came from the city of Kut that Moslems had broken into Jewish homes. Meanwhile the emigration continued. Yaacov Battat, a member of Parliament, met with two Ministers, Zia Jaafar and Abdel Wahab Farhan, and offered to resign together with the rest of Jewish members of Parliament. Both Ministers promised that the situation would improve and that the Government was about to issue a permit allowing every Jew whose assets were frozen to withdraw 50 Dinars.

The economic situation became worse. The Government hastened to issue certificates to those Jews whose citizenship had not been revoked so that they could continue working. The newspapers went on writing about the terrible situation and urged the Trustees to issue certificates to those Jews. In describing the situation, the Israeli broadcasting station and the Middle East station forced the Government to increase the supervision on the police and to assist the Jews. This was felt at the airport – less searching and more courtesy in removing obstacles. Senator Ezra Menahem Daniel and Abraham El-Kabir met with the Regent, Abd El-Ilah, and put before him the situation of the Jewish people who were staying on in Iraq.

In another telegram, on 12 March 1951, I mentioned the subject once more and asked the Foreign Office: "It is better that you start questioning all the immigrants and listing their frozen assets."

I cannot conclude this matter without presenting an updated one, or an image of recent circumstances. Years later, on the basis of the persistent claims of the Palestinians regarding their assets which they left behind in Israel, I took the initiative and established WOJAC – World Organization of Jews from Arab Countries – who among its founders were Oved Ben-Ozer, Haim Goshen, the late Matilda Gaz, Menahem Yadid, David Pettel, the late Avigdor Rokah and Shaul Ben-Simhon. Two men were appointed to head the organization: the late Leon Taman of London and myself. Until my resignation in 1988, we held four international conferences, in Paris, London and Washington. Advocate Shlomo Toussia-Cohen (who replaced me), Taman and Ben-Ozer held two conferences in Israel. In the Fourth National Conference of WOJAC, on 16 December 1993, it was agreed in a statement that among other things:

> WOJAC was the first to draw the world's attention to the reality of an "exchange of population," which began between the Arab refugees who left behind their property during the founding of the State of Israel, and the Jews who hurried to leave the Arab countries due to persecution, deportations and arrests, as a basis for a future settlement between Israel and the Palestinians [...]
>
> WOJAC represented an international organization of Jews from Arab countries in Israel and worldwide, with a delegation from Arab countries, some of whom were chosen from the committees who dealt with the refugees and the multilateral committees. It may have been useful and would have brought positive results to all sides thanks to the complete information we had on Jews who were uprooted from their communities and forced to leave their homes, and also thanks to their knowledge of the language, the understanding of their mentality and familiarity with Arab culture.
>
> The management of WOJAC is of the opinion that the constant and direct cooperation of their representatives in every political negotiation and with the peace process in progress would bring about a better understanding between us and our Arab neighbours. We have no doubt that the bridge, now in construction, between Israel and the Arabs, will

be that much stronger with the full support of WOJAC representatives in all stages of negotiations.

The last official Population Census before the Ezra and Nehemiah Operation was held in Iraq in 1947, when Jews numbered 130,000. It is reasonable to assume that until the flights started three years later, in May 1950, the Jewish population increased by several thousands, due to natural increase and immigration from neighbouring countries which came to 137,000 souls. Until the end of the operation, in January 1952, 110,618 people emigrated from Iraq to Israel, and another 17,352 Iraqi Jews escaped to Iran or were Iranian Jews who returned from Iraq. Those who stayed behind numbered around 7,000 people (see chart).

Those who remained were probably the ones who didn't want to, or couldn't, leave Iraq and emigrate to Israel and didn't even want to leave for other countries. Each one of them surely had a good and justified reason to stay, but it seems to me that one can determine in general that the main excuse which was common to most of them was economical – they didn't want to leave the huge assets they had accumulated, mainly in real estate, and exchange them for an unfamiliar environment and insecurity in another country. Among the emigrants, however, there were many who succeeded in taking money and valuables out of the country. There were others who were afraid to take a gamble, not wanting to lose part of their wealth in paying rapacious brokers, and there were also those who didn't want to sell their assets at a great loss. Extremist factors in Iraq instructed the Moslems not to purchase the estates of Jews, as "in a short while all their assets will eventually fall into our hands." This advice had its effect, and was another important consideration that stopped the Jews from pulling up their roots and leaving. There were many among the Iraqi Jews who integrated well into Iraqi society, held good positions and had difficulty in giving it all up. They seemed to feel completely safe and secure, and even those warning signals didn't have any effect on them.

## Iraqi Jews who arrived in Israel from 1949 to 1952

| Month | 1950 | 1951 | 1952 | total |
|---|---|---|---|---|
| January | 1,145 | 4,448 | 53 | |
| February | 1,159 | 6,346 | | |
| March | 1,444 | 15,018 | | |
| April | 1,128 | 21,651 | | |
| May | 1,133 | 18,094 | | |
| June | 2,739 | 14,889 | 200 | |
| July | 3,999 | 5,757 | 29 | |
| August | 3,942 | 1,298 | | |
| September | 2,875 | 415 | | |
| October | 4,449 | 94 | | |
| November | 3,773 | 97 | | |
| December | 3,841 | 54 | | |
| | 31,627 | 88,161 | 282 | 120,070 |

## Comments

Towfik El-Suweidi, the Prime Minister of Iraq, said that in the census of 1947 there were in Iraq 130,000 Jews:

| | |
|---|---|
| 115,000 | Jews from Iraq |
| 10,000 | Jews from Iran |
| 5,000 | Jews who didn't register |
| 130,000 | |
| 7,000 | Jews who were registered because of natural increase and immigration between the time of the census taken until 1950 |
| 137,000 | total number of Jews in Iraq in 1950 |

They were subdivided as follows:

110,618    flew to Israel (38,000 via Cyprus; 72,618 direct to Israel)

   9,352   Refugees who escaped from Iraq to Iran and then to Israel.

   8,000   Jews of Iranian origin, who flew to Iran and from there to Israel

   9,030   Jews who stayed in Iraq after the mass emigration

137,000

The depletion of the Jewish community did not go unnoticed by officers of the Iraqi administration and economy. In a session of Parliament held on 2 January 1952, Farouk Samerai, a member of the Istiklal Party, proposed a motion to discuss the subject of Jewish representation in Parliament: "since for years there were six seats reserved for Jews – three representing the Jews of Baghdad, two for Basra and one for Mosul* – isn't it about time to restrict the number of Jewish seats, especially in light of the mass exodus of Iraqi Jews? Isn't it absurd and overdoing things to reserve seats for members of a turncoat community, who abandons the country that has treated them so benevolently?" he added. Samerai proposed that until they leave Iraq all Jews requesting emigration should be confined to a concentration camp and that they be divested of their rights to possess this inflated representation in Parliament. The rowdy discussion that followed resembled a shouting match and was an indication that the situation of the Jews who chose to remain in Iraq could never be what it was before. On 29 January 1951, I reported to the Mossad Le Aliya Bet:

A. Abraham El-Kabir, member of the committee that supervised the emigration, met yesterday with the Regent. They discussed the situation of the Jews who were willing to stay in Iraq if their rights were preserved. He also went over the obstacles facing the

---

* **Ezra Menahem Daniel:** Member of Parliament. Stayed on in Iraq. He distinguished himself, with his impressive personality and appearances teaching Jewish law. **Yaacov Battat:** Left Iraq in January 1952. Assisted the Halutz Movement in its difficult hours. **Sasson Tsemah:** Representative of northern Iraq who had his citizenship revoked because of demonstrations and emigrated to Israel in July 1951. Two of his sons are judges in Israel: Yaacov and Rahamin Tzemah. **Salman Shina:** Left Iraq for Turkey in July 1951 and from there he offered his resignation to the Iraqi Parliament. He was a very distinguished man and very close to the Iraqi Government. **Abdallah Mouallem:** Stayed on in Iraq. **Naim Saleh Shamash:** Stayed on in Iraq.

committee, who were helping those Jews whose citizenship had been revoked.

B. Abraham El-Kabir's impression was a positive one. He says that the Regent had changed his attitude completely and promised him that when El-Sa'id returns, the Jews will be aware of a significant improvement in their conditions, whether they were emigrants or those who wished to stay.

Among the emissaries in Baghdad and their colleagues in the provincial cities, there was a feeling that time was pressing on. The first of March was the last date set aside for registration. Meanwhile, whoever had registered found himself with his back to the wall: He was jobless and under various restrictions including the freezing of his assets. The assets were worth hundreds of millions of Dinars.

On 12 March, a second law was passed in which "all the assets of Iraqi Jews who were living abroad and hadn't returned within two months would be frozen." This law had its impact. Apart from this, secret and intensive activities appeared to minimize the damage and troubles occurring to the Jews who were staying behind. In a report I sent to the Mossad in Tel Aviv on 2 April, I wrote:

A. The meeting with the Treasury hasn't yet been fixed by the Palace. Ezra Menahem Daniel and Abraham El-Kabir will attend this meeting and will present a memo explaining the situation of those Jews who are staying behind, together with an inquiry into their background, and asking to improve conditions as was promised before the last Bills were put forward.

B. The effect of the Revocation of citizenship Law on those who are staying behind was discussed at a meeting of the community leaders: The outcome was not acceptable. The committee had requested, through Daniel, to meet with Shemtob and to stand as one before the Government and explain the severity of their situation. Shemtob has refused to cooperate and has stated that the community isn't permitted to involve itself in political matters.

C. The committee, with the cooperation of Daniel, has initiated an information drive supported by important Iraqis such as Saleh Jaber, Mezahem El-Pachechi, Jamal Madfaee, Abd El-Mahdi, El-Sadr, etc. They have all said that El-Sa'id has enacted those laws following the failure of his policies to appease his people. Pachechi says that pressure from the West is being put on El-Sa'id, to force him to declare that the Jews who are staying behind are Iraqis, with full rights, as long as they acknowledge Iraq as their homeland.

D. The news of the coming resignation of the Government is still a rumour. The prospective candidates are Madfaee and Jaber. I and the circles to which I am connected doubt whether any change will take place in the near future.

E. No reports of physical abuse were evident. The police commander published a statement requesting Jews to lodge complaints directly to him should there be any offence or reports of irregular behaviour committed by the police. The financial situation of the Jews is becoming worse every day. The Trustee office is working intermittently. The stalemate reflects the financial impasse. The Minister of Education declares that he will introduce evening classes in economics, so as to prepare young people to fill the space that Jews have left behind, in business and Government offices.

The anxiety increased due to the unsettled situation and rumours emanated from various sources. On 28 April 1951, the following was transmitted to the Mossad from Iraq:

A. There are strong rumours that regular passports are being offered to Jews. They say that the passport will be valid for three months and for one destination only. If the passport holder doesn't return to Iraq within a limited time, his citizenship will be revoked and his assets frozen.

B. If the rumours are accurate, which country do you suggest we chose? We are of the opinion that the British Government should be asked to grant visas for Cyprus in order to enable an easy transit flight to Israel.

C.  Those who have received passports are Jews who have chosen to stay in Iraq, and most of them are wealthy.

These passports were supposed to be given out according to the following conditions: Everyone who receives a passport must state the name of the country to which he wishes to travel; they must report the length of time they will be absent from Iraq; they must guarantee not to sell their assets through their family or agents during their absence from Iraq. The reason for this was that all the assets of the Jews – whether belonging to those whose citizenship had been revoked or of those who wished to stay – would be entered into an official record, and every Jew who didn't return within the fixed period of time would lose his nationality. The Iraqi Government thought that this method would permit a greater number of Jews to leave without the need to renew the Revocation of Citizenship Bill which was valid until 9 March.

Foreign diplomats in Baghdad followed developments in the country with great interest. Report No. 2085 of 9 May, signed by Edward S. Crocker, a Member of the American Embassy in Baghdad and forwarded to the State Department in Washington, mentioned that the Ministry of the Interior published new regulations re the issue of passports, subject to four conditions:

1.  Medical care: Each person who presents an official medical report, certifying that he is sick and in need of medical care abroad, will be permitted to stay beyond the Iraqi borders during the appointed period of time mentioned in the report, with an additional thirty days for emergency cases. This extension will be granted according to his needs, and depending on medical certificates stamped by the Iraqi Consul. The sick person can be accompanied by a member of his family to care for him, if the report approves it.

2.  Students: A passport will be issued to any student who wishes to study for a first or second degree abroad, on condition that the Ministry of Education certifies the fact. He will be permitted to stay

abroad during the period of his studies with three extra months in case of emergency.

3. Business trip: A merchant who is a member of the Chamber of Commerce will be given a passport valid for three months, on condition that he presents certificates proving his trip is for business reasons.

4. Recreation: A passport valid for three months will be issued to people who want to take their vacation abroad, after checking their financial status and other circumstances.

This order was published by the Iraqi Minister of the Defence and following that, further explanations and steps were taken:

1. To make every person wanting a permit to travel abroad for medical care present himself before an official committee to prove the validity of his requirement.

2. For those who wish to travel for the purpose of study are required to present certificates approved by the Ministry of Education; also certificates from the Iraqi Diplomatic Corps abroad proving that they have really been accepted by the universities there.

3. Each person who leaves the Iraqi border has to deposit a large sum of money, in order to prevent them from any wrong-doing during their stay abroad, as this would harm the public interest. We wish to take suitable steps to solve this problem once and for all so as not to cause us harm in the future. We were told that some Jews were performing unlawful acts such as incitement, sabotage and the placing of bombs in Arab countries and this always poses a threat that may lead to further destructive ideas; its purpose is to wreck security and invite disorder.

This was the official stand taken by the Iraqi Government towards the Jews who decided to give up the idea of leaving Iraq.

I cannot conclude without the addition of these few sincere remarks:

*Members of the crew who helped the Jews to board the plane at the airport in Baghdad.*

Since I climbed that rope into the plane at Baghdad Airport, on the night of 14 June 1951 on my way back to Israel, I sometimes find myself thinking about the city I abandoned and the people I left behind; I miss the side streets that I knew so intimately, the odours and scenery that I cherished. I feel for the people who stayed behind, some of whom I knew so well, an affection mingled with compassion. I couldn't accept their reasons for staying, but understood them. Deep inside, I knew they were destined for hard times and accompanied by distress and dangers. Of course, today, I know that I made no mistake. On the contrary, everything proved to be more daunting than I had anticipated. Iraq underwent several bloody military overthrows, dictators came to power and fell by the use of brute force, and those who rose to positions of power every once in awhile adopted harsh and cruel policies against their citizens, mercilessly accomplished, mass-murdering many, arresting thousands and throwing them into gaol for unlimited periods.

Since I was rescued from Baghdad I have followed the Iraqi news and have been updated on the life of the Jews there. The final blow came in 1969, when young men were hanged in the square in Baghdad, who committed no crime, and tens or maybe hundreds were kidnapped or imprisoned and disappeared. No one can remain impassive, learning of the fate of the entire Kashkoush family who were brutally murdered one day.

The situation of the Iraqi Jews still occupies the minds of Israel's Leaders. The Government acted in two ways: giving information and taking action. Shlomo Hillel, who was a Deputy Director General of the Foreign Office, activated committees for human rights in various capitals all over the world, hoping that the cry for help from those who stayed behind would be heard. In one of the meetings, which was held in Paris and in which I participated, some disturbing reports were received. Israeli agents sent emissaries to Baghdad and assisted around 4,000 Jews to escape, via Iran, to Israel. David Fattal (Petel) welcomed them in Teheran and he dealt with those who chose to emigrate to Israel. I also had the opportunity in the last few years, with the assistance of the Israeli Foreign Office and also of England and Holland, to help facilitate the departure of eighty people from Baghdad. To my regret, many of them chose to settle in Holland and England.

In writing this book during 1997, around sixty Jews are still in Baghdad, most of them elderly. Their lives centre around the Meir Tweig Synagogue. Apart

*The Israeli stewardess Ilana Marcus (Lilian Nada).*

from those aging people the ancient Jewish community left behind other important items: The tombs of the Prophets Yehezkel and Yona, the tombs of Ezra Hasofer and Prophet Nahum Alkosh, and also the tombs of many of the great Rabbis of the Babylonian era. Then, too, there were those who were killed in the pogroms of 1941, the bodies of the two who were executed, Yousif Basri and Shalom Saleh, and those who were hanged in the seventies; they are all buried there. There is also a great deal of material of Judaic interest, which is priceless, such as the Scrolls of Law and hand-written material of a hundred years past.

I watch and hope that the day will come when we can reach an understanding with the Iraqi rulers, so that we will be able to take the living and the dead out of Iraq as well as the Judaic treasures, whose place is here. Only then will the last curtain fall on the Babylonian exodus of a community – the most ancient in the Diaspora.

*An evening of tribute to the American pilots who participated in the 'Ezra and Nehemiah'*
*operation. It was held in January 1994 at the Babylonian Jewry Heritage Center.*
*Left to right: Mordechai Ben-Porat, Bob Steffes, Shlomo Hillel, Ilana Markus,*
*Arthur Lippa, Milton Lang, Philip Marmelstein.*

# APPENDICES

A. Letters of David Ben-Gurion and Yitzhak Hofi

B. Report of the Investigating Committee

C. Ezra and Nehemiah Campaign – a sketch of its formation

D. Functional Departments in the Synagogues – a sketch

E. List of the Immigration Activists

F. Contents of the 22nd meeting of the Cabinet on 10.2.1951 where a decision was taken on direct flights

# Appendix A

## Letters of David Ben-Gurion and Yitzhak Hofi

N° 24

[Handwritten Hebrew letter]

1.4.69

[Handwritten Hebrew text]

*Ben-Gurion visits the Ben-Porat family in 1969, from left to right: my late wife Rivca, Ben-Gurion, Mordechai and daughters Tamar, Michal and Edit.*

13.6.66

Sdeh Boker

To the Public Committee in commemoration of the Iraqi Jews who were condemned to death.

Shalom and greetings

I hereby send you a report on the investigation carried out regarding the Iraqi Jews who were condemned to death, as per my request as Prime Minister and Minister of Defence, on 16.11.60.
You may publish this with the declaration on the last page but without the two and a half lines that were deleted by me on page two.

With best regards,
Yours sincerely,
D. Ben-Gurion

**Department of Intelligence and Special Operations**

Top Secret
Personal

4 June 1980
lrm/237

Mr. Mordechai Ben-Porat
Chairman
The Babylonian Jewry Heritage Centre

Dear Mordechai,

In reply to your letter of 17 April regarding the report of the investigating committee, I have decided that the report can be presented in court, but its publication should be delayed until after the court case.

Sincerely,

Y. Hofi, General
Head of the Mossad

# Appendix B

# Report of the Investigating Committee

Top Secret

State of Israel

The Prime Minister's Office

Committee of Heads of Intelligence and Security Services

8 December 1960

242/04

To the Prime Minister and the Minister of Defence

Enclosed please find the report of the investigating committee appointed by me on 16.11.60 for the purpose of checking the incidents that took place in the years 1950 and 1951, during which time Jews and Israelis were condemned for sabotage.

Sincerely,

A. Harel

Head of the General Mossad

of the Intelligence and Security

**State of Israel**
**The Prime Minister's Office**
**The General Mossad of Intelligence and Security**

Top Secret
Personal

16.11.60

H. Yaari – The Mossad
Y. Karoz – The Mossad
S. Moreh – General Security Services

Ref.: Investigating Committee – Nomination

A. The background

1.  Five incidents occurred in Baghdad during the years 1950 and 1951 when five bombs were thrown, which caused damage to property and the loss of lives. Of those five incidents, four were directed against Jewish property and one against the American Information Center.

2.  When the Jewish arms caches in Iraq were discovered, extensive arrests were made from among the local Jews. The prisoners were accused of throwing bombs, were put up for trial and sentence was passed. All the accused, apart from one, denied the accusations. The one who confessed during interrogation claimed in court that he did so under pressure from torture.

3.  At the same time, information was given out that the bombs were thrown by either Arab gangs or by the Iraqi Authorities, and that Jews were not involved in it.

4.  Meanwhile, those who were imprisoned for various periods of time had been released and most of them immigrated to Israel. There is a chance that they will be able to contribute some information towards clarifying this matter.

B. Members of the Committee

The undersigned are hereby appointed committee members to deal with the investigation:

H. Yaari – Chairman

Y. Karoz – Member

S. Moreh – Member

C. Reasons for the investigation:

To study and form some conclusions to the following questions:

1.  Were all or some of the bombs thrown by Jews?

2.  If this is so, was the act done by instruction from Israel or was it a local initiative?

3.  If the act was done following a request from Israel, who was responsible for the order, how was it given and for what purpose?

D. The method

1.  The Committee will conclude its job as soon as possible and will present me with its conclusions.

2.  The investigation will be conducted in secret and will make sure that it follows up every line of questioning

Sincerely,

A. Harel

Head of the General Mossad

of the Intelligence and Security

7 December 1960

To the Prime Minister

Re: Investigating Committee

Affair of bomb-throwing in Iraq

The Committee was appointed to investigate and draw conclusions on the following questions:

1.  Were all or some of the bombs thrown by Jews?

2.  If the answer is in the affirmative, was the act done according to instructions from Israel or was it due to a local initiative.

3.  If the act was done as a request from Israel, who was the one responsible and who gave the instructions, in what manner and for what purpose?

The Committee questioned twelve witnesses, three Israeli emissaries and nine local activists. Besides that, the Committee received written affidavits from two other men. The Committee also went through a great deal of written material that has accumulated in this affair.

They have reached the following conclusions:

1. Regarding the first question:

**Were all or some of the bombs thrown by Jews?**

a) The Committee found no proof that the bombs were thrown by an organization or any Jewish individual. The Committee also did not find any logical reason for directing a group or individual Jews to throw bombs in order to improve their lot or to promote local Jewish interests.

b)  The Committee was surprised to hear from most witnesses certain suspicions of baseless accusations that those bombs were thrown by Jews. Several witnesses, who once held the view that the bombs had not been thrown by Jews, now claim that they are unsure of their fact. They arrived at their latest beliefs in ways unclear to the Committee. One of the witnesses came to this conclusion after hearing that some Jews had exploded bombs in Egypt in 1954.

The Committee tried to investigate the reasons for such a view. The following are some of the causes which the Committee found to be rational:

1.  The influence of Iraqi propaganda on Jewish public opinion.

2.  The purely coincidental timing of the first explosion and the ebb and flow of Jewish emigration.

3.  Shalom Saleh's behaviour during his trial and interrogation, and especially his ambiguous denials uttered before his fellow prisoners, created the impression that the confessions extracted under torture were actually true.

Nevertheless, the Committee finds it difficult to accept this account and is inclined to believe the version that no bombs were delivered by Jewish hands.

2. Regarding the second question:

**If it is affirmative, was the act done as per instructions, in any way, from Israel or due to a local initiative?**

A)  The Committee is convinced that no instructions were given from Israel to perform this outrage.

B)  Even if there is a grain of truth in the witnesses' opinions, quoted in the above paragraph 1.B, it is absolutely clear to the Committee that the instructions for performing such acts were neither given by an Israeli organization nor a local one.

3. Regarding the third question:

**If the act was done as a request from Israel, who was the one responsible to give the instructions, in what manner and for what purpose?**

As the Committee is convinced that no such instructions were given by any factor in Israel, it finds itself released from answering it.

<table>
<tr><td>_____</td><td>_____</td><td>_____</td></tr>
<tr><td>H. Yaari</td><td>S. Moreh</td><td>Y. Karoz</td></tr>
</table>

## Affidavit

I, the undersigned, hereby give the affidavit:

A. I was responsible for the wireless station of the Underground organization in Iraq since 1943 and until my departure from Iraq in June 1951.

B. During the time that I was responsible for the Berman (Baghdad) station, which was linked to Israel and Teheran, I was aware of every telegram coming in or going out.

C. I can state with certainty that while I was held responsible for the above station, I neither received nor transferred any telegrams concerning the use of bombs or explosives for the purpose of sabotage.

Abraham Ben-Mordechai
Before "Towfik Mordechai"
(Mizrahi)

5.2.60

## Affidavit

I hereby declare that during my time in Teheran, as representative of the Intelligence Branch in the years 1950-51, I did not receive from any Israeli factor, and didn't transfer to Baghdad, any instruction regarding the use of bombs or explosives for espionage.

Segan-Aluf (Colonel)
Ehud Rapaport

The full report was published in the first Hebrew edition of this book which extends to a hundred pages. I do believe that the full publication of the testimonies in English are not of great significance to our readers here; therefore I have selected important sections only for your inspection. Any researcher who wishes to go through the original manuscript is welcome to visit the Babylonian Jewry Heritage Centre in Or Yehuda in Israel, where the original manuscript is kept.

**The testimonies are as follows:**

7.12.1960

**Mr. Eliahu Gourgey**

Mr. Gourgey was imprisoned in 1951 for fifteen years. He was released in 1959 as the result of an amnesty. He observed that every member of the Movement who joined the Shura (Hagana) was trained to use weapons, kept a store of them in his house. He joined the Movement in 1949. Those who were allowed to open the store were: Dan the Officer; Yousif Bet Halahmi and Shalom Saleh.

He was arrested on account of his visit to Salim Khabbaza (Bet Hallahmi), brother of Yousif Khabbaza, on 7 June 1951. After interrogation he was released with the assistance of his cousin, tried to escape via Iran but was apprehended. Meanwhile, the police found the arms cache in his house. They came across guns, bombs, bullets and grenades there. He had heard that some Jews had thrown bombs. When he was asked for the source of his information his reply was "everyone knows about it" and when he was asked to give his own opinion, without referring to others, he replied: "I can't really tell you…"

22.11.60

**Mr. George Shasha**

In 1942 he joined the Halutz Movement, but in 1945 he entered into business and left the Shura (Hagana). When the emigration started he volunteered again and participated in its activities. He was in Shemtob Synagogue on the evening when the bomb was thrown. It was dark outside. There were people killed and injured. One of the porters testified that "someone wearing blue working clothes was standing on the roof garden of a Moslem house in the vicinity and appeared to hurl something…" The porter at the synagogue was seriously injured and died in hospital and didn't have time to give his testimony. He added that ten minutes after the explosion, he saw Yousif Basri entering the synagogue wearing his usual elegant suit. When George was asked for his opinion, he replied "that only Moslems could act in this way"; then he described the arrival of the police to search for weapons in the synagogue. When he was told that "Shalom, during his trial, said that what he told the police regarding the bombs was given under torture..." he agreed and said that he was made to say what he did in order to end the torture, which he couldn't stand any longer. The night before the execution, Shalom asked for a Rabbi to visit him. I heard from that man that Shalom said out loud: "If they are to hang me for what I am supposed to have done, I am resigned, but you are accusing me of things I haven't done."

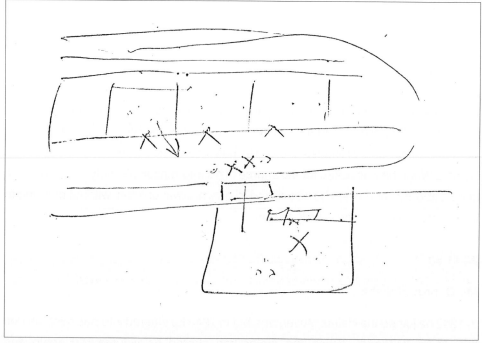

*From testimony of Gourji Shasha, the graph of the bomb.*

## Mr. Yehuda Tajer

He relates that the bomb thrown on the Mesouda Shemtob Synagogue was dispatched a short time before his arrival in Iraq. He approached Habib (Ben-Porat) and Rodney on that. Habib denied completely that it was the act of Jews, and Rodney said that an Iraqi military officer who was on pension threw the bomb... When he was asked if Habib and Rodney were acquaintances of his he replied negatively. Tajer spoke of his meetings with Basri and Saleh in prison and he was convinced that Basri didn't throw the bombs but that some other Jews did. He added that "he couldn't give us facts." On the night of the execution, he was sitting with Basri and asked him if he had done it. Basri used these words "I don't know, ask Shalom." When I asked Shalom if Jews threw the bombs, he didn't say the word "yes." But the impression was a positive one. Tajer was asked "when you had the impression that he answered in the affirmative, what was Basri's reaction?" Tajer replied that there was a silence. He didn't say yes, and at that time Tajer believed him, but years later when he spoke to Eliahu Gourgey in prison, he said that the balance kept changing from the positive side to the negative side, Tajer's impressions were confirmed:

"A.  When Habib (Ben-Porat) said "no" – I believed him

B.  When Yousif said that he didn't throw a bomb – I was sure that he didn't.

C.  I didn't say that Jews didn't have a hand in it. In a way I was convinced they had, because of what I heard and also because Shalom didn't deny it."

## Mr. Salim Mouallem

He said that he heard of the bombing incident when he arrived at the police station on 5 June. The police questioned him about it and asked whether the Jews had done it. Mouallem was arrested, and accused of giving financial aid to Tajer. He said that when he arrived in Israel he felt that the Iraqi Jews in Israel were convinced that it was done by their own people. He thought that this was the result of rumours they heard; as if someone had convinced them to emigrate. This was exactly how he felt. He was asked "If Jews didn't do it, who then was responsible?" He replied "it could only be the Istiklal." He was also asked "if Jews had done it what would they have gained by it?" He replied "that this had to be investigated at source, whether such instructions had been given. There may have been some definite instructions given out but there were no records of it…" He was asked whether he believed Shalom's testimony, and replied: "From the start I felt that Shalom's statement shouldn't be taken seriously. First of all, he had a very basic education, he was never in touch with the people; it looked as though he was a broken man, seemed very confused and didn't trust anyone." Then he was asked "You've been in prison and suffered severe interrogation; do you accept that after undergoing torture for five days and nights a person can break down?" He answered: "When it comes to education and responsibility I separate the matters. If they had continued to torture me, I knew (and told the police) after what they did to me I would have confessed to anything…"

4.12.60

## Mr. Mordechai Ben-Porat

I am really glad that this wretched affair has been brought to life again but I regret that it has come so late. Five years ago I asked Shlomo Hillel to bring this matter up in court, so as to clear the names of those two who were hanged for a crime they didn't commit. I tried my best to find out who could have done this deed and why. Even before the bombs were thrown I knew that there was great activity in the Istiklal Party; they were being organized and trained in Judo and close combat, and they were against Nouri El-Sa'id. Then we heard about the bomb affair. At the beginning I didn't pay much attention, until the occurrence at the synagogue. I went there at once and groped through the darkness, and was aware of the pandemonium around me. I decided not to stay, out of caution, but I immediately called some friends who told me that one of the injured men saw the man who threw the bomb. It came from the top of a house opposite the synagogue entrance and he was wearing khaki. This detail was of interest to me and I wanted the injured man to give his testimony to the police. I went directly to Sasson Abed's house, and remember that we sat by the telephone as Sasson tried to locate an investigating magistrate to come and take evidence. Two or three hours passed and we couldn't reach him. I arranged for several members of our Movement to donate blood for this man. He barely stayed alive until the next morning. Sasson finally located the examining magistrate, but he arrived an hour after the injured man passed away. In my opinion we had lost a very important witness. The bomb had been thrown and there was no evidence that someone other than a member of the Istiklal Party had done the deed. So when the trials began, torture was part of it, and I presume that Shalom had a weaker spirit than Basri. When they felt that someone was about to crack under force they would use greater pressure on him. At the time when they tortured me for various reasons, without success, I am sure that had I said anything they would have continued to pressure me and tried to break my spirit. I presume Basri was the stronger one and didn't give in, and that he told the truth. I am positive that our people didn't do it. I had no doubts with regard to those of the Movement. I was involved with them (after Rodney left) and I knew their views. The newspapers didn't stop reporting it and accused the two men and I think this influenced Jewish opinion. Only a small percentage of Babylonian Jewry believed that it wasn't our doing (that is, the work of the Movement), under orders from the Israeli authorities. It was most infuriating. If I had thrown a bomb I would have seen it as my duty to explain why we had done it. When the bombs were thrown, over sixty thousand people had already registered for emigration and here in Israel they said they were unable to absorb so many. So why the pressure? Whenever someone from Israel sent a letter to Iraq complaining of their plight, they said that in Iraq it wouldn't have had any effect. There was no need to force the rate of emigration. And yet, who could have done it? How could those men, whom I knew and who were in contact with me, have done it? They weren't trained professionally nor had they the expertise. As far as I knew, this wasn't a ready-made grenade but an explosive that was put together. I can only point a finger at the Istiklal Party, and say that Nouri El-Sa'id needed two Jewish victims in order to keep a tight hold on the community.

**Q.** If you accuse the Istiklal Party and El-Sa'id's Government, what was the purpose of throwing a bomb in Jewish centres? And secondly, if we accept that Sa'id's Government was a party to it (that his opponents were behind the bombs) wouldn't he have wanted to expose them, in order to break and destroy the Opposition?

**A.** Regarding the first question: I think that those who threw the bombs wanted to create an uneasy atmosphere in the country. As for the second: You may be right. And yet, perhaps, El-Sa'id wanted to blur events. He may well have imprisoned those from the opposition without publicizing it and making heroes out of them; and he accused the Jews in order to create a situation and an atmosphere that he was still in control and able to mete out punishment.

**Q.** What was the situation of the Communist Party in Iraq at that time?

**A.** They were very depressed. Most of them were in gaol. They took care of their own internal problems and had no interest in other matters.

**Q.** Do you know if, apart from these five bombs thrown, the Istiklal Party ever used any firearms or had thrown bombs before?

**A.** No.

**Q.** If such a party wanted to use this method, wouldn't it have continued do so? Wouldn't they have continued to use weapons later on?

**A.** The fact that they didn't use weapons before or after this doesn't mean that they were prophets on that score. A party could decide to use such methods for a period of time and, if it got them nowhere, cease to do so.

**Q.** Regarding the type of bombs, are you of the opinion that they made them themselves? From police reports and such activists as Gourgey Shasha, who was in the synagogue at the time, they identified the bomb as a Mills type. The problem was whether we, in the Hagana, had ever used the same Mills 36 that the police identified or not.

**A.** Regarding this primitive weapon, I came to the following conclusions on two counts: When I visited Sasson Abed at Lawee's store and he showed me the damage created by the explosion; and two – I remember what had been written in the newspapers about it at that time. If a Mills bomb had been used the resultant damage would have been far greater than the injuring of two people.

**Q.** Your explanation is logical, as this street was always crowded with people and the fact that our people could have identified the kind of bomb used from the fragments collected.

**A.** Did anyone else examine the fragments or was it the result of Shasha's testimony alone?

**Q.** His and that of the Iraqi police. The investigating team at that time had difficulty in determining the type of bomb, whether it was similar to that used by the Hagana.

**A.** I cannot really say that they didn't use a Mills, I am not absolutely sure. Here you are giving me details of these facts, but until today I think the effect of a Mills would have been much more severe. It happened on a main road and the only damage was a shattered window and their entrance door and no one was injured at Lawee's store.

**Q.** There's a rule here that in their testimonies, members should implicate those who had already left Iraq, and put the blame on them. Salim Mouallem was caught on the fifth of June. Two days later Shalom was taken because of him; according to the testimonies Shalom didn't say anything until the fifteenth of the month when he denied everything; at the same time, on the tenth of June, Basri was arrested. Shalom saw Basri when he was arrested; Khabbaza managed to escape. I would have been satisfied if Shalom had put all the blame on Khabbaza, but why did he have to include Basri in the same trap? What was the point of that?

**A.** The logic was to blame the outgoing travelers: It is logical that everyone ought to have reached this conclusion without being told. Firstly, I think there was no contact between Shalom and Basri, for better or worse. When Shalom was caught, did anyone know that he would be caught before the others, so that they had time to tell him what to say? How was Shalom caught? The police went to the synagogue and started speaking nicely to him. Shalom had made a phone call there, and the officer took over the receiver and spoke in such a wily manner, luring him to the synagogue where he was arrested on the spot. Until the last minute, he hadn't the faintest idea that he might be caught and no one imagined that the chain of the events would end up like this; therefore he wasn't prepared. I believe that if he had known that Khabbaza had already escaped, it would have been obvious to put the blame on him. I am sure they said to him – what do you lose, say this or that….

**Q.** Then why did he involve Basri as well?

**A.** I will tell you why; I feel that it was the result of his weak character. It seems that they may have come and told him: "Your passport is ready, and the certificate as well, say what we tell you, what do you have to lose?"

**Q.** Are you presuming it or is it something you have heard?

**A.** I am presuming it (judging by what they did to me). I didn't hear it from anyone else.

**Q.** We said that until the fifteenth of June, Shalom was tortured and said nothing, and then he said what he did. In court he denied everything and claimed that he was forced to say it through torture. Youdkeh stayed with them on the night of the execution and asked Basri in the presence of Shalom: Did you both throw bombs? Basri denied it. Youdkeh then turned to Shalom and he didn't deny it.

**A.** What did he say?

**Q.** It was taken to be "yes." He didn't give the same answer as Basri – "no." He didn't deny it and one can only assume it as a "yes." This was in the presence of Basri. And another thing, when Youdkeh asked Basri (even before that night): "Were you really involved with this?" He said: "Ask them and those others" and waved his hands about.

**A.** It is simple to explain. All the time I believed in what Basri said, as he had a strong character. I again link the misfortune to the weak character of Shalom. He lived with the idea that he had thrown it (or was told he did). If he didn't, I can't imagine who else could have done it. Maybe he was afraid of Youdkeh.

**Q.** He knew that he was about to be hanged?

**A.** It may seem astonishing, but I don't find myself thinking about it now.

**Q.** In respect of facts, how do you analyze this?

**A.** If you were to tell me that, during the trial, or even before it he had said so, I can accept it; but on the night he was hanged, it seems incredible. I really can't tell you.

**Q.** You said that you believed in Basri.

**A.** I believe, and now I am convinced, that both of them were not involved. I believe it because he refused to give up. I knew Basri from school days. When I immigrated to Israel and then returned, four years had passed; I met him a few times and relations between us were amicable. However, changes may have occurred in his personality; I cannot say for sure. But he did have a very strong character and he proved that during his interrogation. If you were to tell me that during the investigation he said this or that, I wouldn't be able to explain it.

**Q.** Basri was a lawyer, much more intellectual than Shalom. In this case, he knew exactly where the questions were leading, and he chose this method of response.

**Q.** When they asked him about the gun they found in his house and he denied knowledge of it – would you have believed him then?

**A.** Yes. I would also have said the same thing in order to deny all the facts. I would justify him.

**Q.** Would you justify him or believe him?

**A.** I would justify him.

**Q.** There is a difference between believing and justifying.

**A.** True.

**Q.** It means that we justify him but not that we believe him.

**A.** Yes, that is so.

**Q.** The question is, was he an obstinate person and why he chose this method. Youdkeh asked him that on the last evening and he said "no"; he asked Shalom who didn't deny it and Basri didn't react to Shalom's words. How do you explain that?

**A.** Perhaps Basri was angry with Shalom for involving him, and during the final moments before his death he didn't want to be hard on him. In better times he might have said something else.

**Q.** What is your opinion of what Basri said (away from the presence of Shalom): "Ask them."

**A.** He wanted to say, "We didn't do it, but how can we explain it? Ask those who did." When he saw that Shalom was so certain that he did it, perhaps Basri came to the conclusion it was better to agree with him.

**Q.** In questioning Youdkeh, he said: "Basri said: Those who threw it (he waved his hand about) they threw here, they threw there (he waved his hand towards the other room) I didn't throw it" (this is from Yehuda Tajer's testimony on 25.11.60, page No. 2). What do you think of this? About all this he claims it is only an impression.

**A.** In the Underground Movement, where Basri himself didn't know what was going on around him, it is very likely, after seeing the man sitting before him, a person who dealt with arms caches, he may have also started to think like him and said: "ask them." This is logical. I conclude with one thought only, that they weren't present under normal conditions, in detention after torture. Perhaps Basri saw the effect it had on the way they were speaking and all this caused such a reaction. You cannot have expected him to be lucid on the night of the execution.

**Q.** Regarding the weapon stores that were found; let us take the one that was at Eliahu Gourgey's house. We tried to find out who had access to the three caches. Firstly the two, Shalom Saleh and Khabbaza and also Dan Shamash, the instructor, had free access. This means that there was access to the weapons store.

**A.** I support this. I presume that Shalom did have the knowledge and access, being familiar with the structure of the arms caches and the care of the weapons. As to Khabbaza – yes, the weapons were his. There were others as well who left weapons there. So what is the meaning of access? It is better that we tread carefully here. Khabbaza had free access to his papers (maps and the like); that is so. I can't believe that he would open the caches and remove the weapons. If so, well, he also took an interest in the arms caches in the synagogue. Maybe it was so, I don't know. I also don't know how much he knew about handling weapons.

**Q.** He was a weapons instructor and an officer in the Hagana. Eliahu Gourgey said this about the stores: "There was a big store full of weapons and only someone in authority could approach it. I also knew about it. There were two stores: One of them they told me not to touch; this was the one full of weapons. The second was for my own use, it was a small store. In the big one there were various kinds of weapons, guns for instance" (this is from the testimony of Eliahu Gourgey on 22.11.60, page No. 2).

**A.** Well, OK. If there was access (one cannot be sure), he could have taken weapons and used them.

**Q.** You said before that there wasn't anyone who knew how to use bombs.

**A.** In my opinion, throwing bombs wasn't such a problem, but the technique to construct them was something else.

**Q.** (Here the question was omitted)

**A.** Regarding ready-made bombs, no. The problem lies in building a bomb, explosives, etc. I can't imagine that there was a Jewish member of the Hagana, even the bravest, who would dare perform such an act without instructions from a senior. If you ask me, at such a time I would have done it myself and not given it to someone else to do.

**Q.** Did you know Khabbaza?

**A.** Not well enough.

**Q.** During the time you knew him?

**A.** The only contact between us was the connection between Youdkeh and myself. I think I met him six or seven times.

**Q.** What was his character like?

**A.** The only trait I am interested in is whether he had the guts to throw a bomb or to give instructions to do so. On this occasion I would say no. The other thing is – did he take the responsibility on his own to transmit such a thing – I don't think he could have. He used to come and ask me about many things. There is a difference between taking responsibility and irresponsible acts. I wouldn't say that an irresponsible act was in his character. That someone like Khabbaza would give such orders, or do it himself, it's not feasible.

**Q.** When did the registration for emigration reach its peak?

**A.** There was a period when it went very slowly, until it reached twenty thousand; then it spiralled upwards at a crazy speed.

**Q.** When was that?

**A.** I think at the beginning of 1951. In June-July we reached the peak of registration.

**Q.** When was the emigration at its peak?

**A.** Towards the end of 1950; September 1950 until March-April 1951.

**Q.** At the beginning there was the Revocation of Citizenship Bill (around March 1950). Do you remember the period of time when there was an uncertain atmosphere, in Israel as well and they didn't know how to handle it?

**A.** It's not clear to me. I remember that the bill was passed and people began to register. We sent emissaries to the synagogue to prevent our people from doing so; and in Israel they asked why we were doing this, and we replied that as long as we didn't know how to direct them out of Iraq we wouldn't let them register. Later on, the committee of the Movement had a meeting and informed them to leave directly for Israel (and not via Iran). When we stopped the exit through Iran as well as the registration, two or three weeks later a contract was signed with Near East Airlines and then we permitted the registration.

**Q.** How much time had passed?

**A.** About three weeks.

**Q.** When you decided to permit registration, how did it go?

**A.** Well. The first to go were the families of the prisoners, and then a great pressure built up.

**Q.** Between the bill and the beginning of the registration three weeks had passed. And when Parliament passed the bill was there registration?

**A.** No, none at all. We prevented it.

**Q.** You stopped the registration in the synagogues and later came the announcement to register – was there a great surge of people?

**A.** Yes, a big crowd. We accepted the families of the prisoners first.

**Q.** And the public?

**A.** Yes. After two or three weeks of hesitation they began to register.

**Q.** What was your reaction then, during those two weeks of hesitation?

**A.** None at all. We were busy with the question of routing them. We didn't even think of accelerating the registration; on the contrary, the slow motion was good, because there weren't enough planes. This was a preparation period and we didn't have time to increase the emigration.

**Q.** We turn again to the Istiklal. When the bomb was thrown at the coffee-house, it became known that this was an Arab coffee-house where Jews would also meet, and besides that, there were some Jewish coffee-houses frequented mainly by Jews both day and night.

**A.** In this coffee-house there were many Jews present.

**Q.** Did any of the witnesses try to find out whether this coffee-house was a place where Jews would often meet?

**A.** The upper-class Jews would use this coffee-house.

**Q.** What was the attitude of the aristocracy towards the emigration?

**A.** Their employees registered but the wealthy people no. However, we couldn't say then that there was an indifference by our people towards emigration.

**Q.** When the wealthier classes didn't register, was there any talk among you?

**A.** No gossip. We didn't pay attention to the rich. On the contrary, we didn't need them. Israel asked for people from the provincial cities and not the kind that dealt in black market.

**Q.** It was said that instructors or officers in the Hagana expressed their opinion against these dealers who hadn't had their citizenship revoked. "Oren himself denounced them in front of his uncle, saying that 'he would like to sweep them all away with a broom" (from testimony of Rahamim Sayegh, page no. 1). What do you say to that?

**A.** Perhaps you ought to ask him what he meant by it. There were no such feelings at all. It's all rubbish. On the contrary, the Hagana people felt indifferent towards the emigration, but not once did they create obstacles to prevent it. I cannot believe that an officer of the Hagana was that interested in increasing emigration, not even Oren himself.

**Q.** There was a time when instruction was given not to prepare more than three thousand at one go, as there weren't enough planes. There was a report from the north about incidents of murder and robbery and a pressure to emigrate in masses.

**A.** If so, then maybe it was in January or February 1951, but we never reached such a stage. We requested planes and there was always pressure on Israel. It is true. There were periods like that.

**Q.** Was there a time when you organized something like a demonstration at the airport? Does this mean that you were interested in putting pressure on Israel?

**A.** I directed and asked for that. Because there was hesitation whether to receive, or not, the emigrants from Iraq and they pressed us not to keep sending more. This was perhaps in July or August, I don't remember exactly.

**Q.** The question is why was it so necessary to pressure people to the point of using violence?

**A.** This would have had no effect on Israel.

**Q.** From the point of view of local people?

**A.** If they had asked me to do something like this to accelerate the emigration, I would have told them that I was going back. In my opinion, the idea of using bombs wasn't meant to accelerate or influence Israeli thinking.

**Q.** Don't you think that the bombs influenced our people to look for a faster exit?

**A.** I don't think so. I don't think that those bombs had any effect on the Jews to make them leave, and neither such incidents as this or even murder would have stemmed their desire to go to Israel. To their credit, one can say that they always yearned for Israel. This, of course, added bitterness and a greater stimulus. Whatever it was, it didn't create any panic.

**Q.** Mesouda Shemtob?

**A.** In that case as well, I think the answer is "no."

**Q.** This didn't affect the numbers desiring emigration?

**A.** I can't tell you exactly. At that time (January 1951) we were sent as many as twelve to fifteen planes a day; we couldn't cope with any more.

**Q.** In conclusion I would like to ask another question: To those groups which had branches and representations in Iraq (the Mossad Le Aliya, the Middle Eastern Jewry Department, the Agency, the Movement) the contact lines were shared. A shared wireless station, sharing the services of the air hostess [Ilana Marcus]. What wasn't shared was the connecting links between Teheran and Baghdad. All the joint lines reached you. A) Did any instruction whatsoever come from Israel, from any source to perform such acts, through the contact lines that you know of and that were under your control? B) If any such instruction did reach you through those contact lines, is it possible that an order slipped in without your knowledge?

**A.** This is an interesting point. The telegrams went like this: The boys would come to me, usually at noon, and I would discuss the activities of the day and most of the time the emissaries were also in attendance. If there was something urgent I'd send messages at night as well. There was an incident when Sourani wanted to send his telegrams direct and I was strongly against it and gave instructions that all telegrams should only go through me. I received nearly all the telegrams sent from Israel. Now I wish to add two things: There was an incident when one of the wireless operators (Yitzhak) had had a nervous breakdown at the end of 1950. He wanted to transfer gold to Israel and we never handled gold. Cash yes, but not gold. I explained this to him and he went very quiet. Our relations were generally good. Later I heard that he was very angry and would have liked to have stormed the synagogue and killed someone. The matter then became very critical in respect of the wireless job and our relationship. I had a talk with him and calmed him down. During the crisis between us and the Movement we found in the post a book that was destined for Turkey (Saleh's father worked in the post office and assisted us). It was hollow inside and a small gun could have been hidden in it. He showed it to me. When I enquired who was the sender they told me it was Eliezer. I immediately went to his home and he started to stammer. I came to the conclusion that he meant to transfer articles by post without my knowledge. Those were the only incidents I can remember. Perhaps one should investigate this matter further.

**Q.** To whom was the book sent?

**A.** I don't know, someone in Turkey.

**Q.** Perhaps it had to do with smuggling.

**A.** He had no connection at all with smuggling.

**Q.** You didn't yet give us an answer whether any such instructions came over the wireless for the activists.

**A.** There weren't any. It couldn't have come without my knowledge. Perhaps the operators may have received instructions and didn't pass them on to me, but it's very unlikely.

**Q.** How would you react if you had heard of an officer of the Hagana, from the main office here, who did some smuggling or dealt with a personal smuggling matter using your wireless. What would be your opinion of him?

**A.** Most negative.

**Q.** Would such a person, in your opinion, have reached a point of using weapons and bombs?

**A.** I think one had to be an ideologist to throw bombs.

**Q.** I don't mean Johnny. An officer of the Hagana, who had access to the arms caches and weapons; would he be able to do such a thing?

**A.** It's difficult to compare the smuggling of gold and the ideology of throwing bombs.

**Q.** Was this matter also used for his own purposes?

**A.** Very possibly. To bomb a coffee-house or to kill a partner – perhaps so, but I wouldn't have connected the two things together.

4.12.1960

**Mr. Yoav Goral**

**Q.** Do you believe that Jews threw all those bombs or only a few of them? If so, what was the reason for it and who was behind it?

**A.** As far as I can remember, the bomb that made the greatest impact was the one thrown at the synagogue. I wasn't in Baghdad; I was up north at the time working for the Movement. When I returned the next morning I heard about the explosion. We were continually hearing from our people that the Movement was doing this to encourage emigration. There were strong rumours all the time. I didn't attach great importance to the first explosion, but after hearing so many reports, I began to study the matter, either there or here in Israel. Perhaps it was true. I remember many had wanted to know why, previous to the explosion, they came to us and warned off the street pedlars.

**Q.** Who warned them?

**A.** I don't know, some people did. I received this information from an instructor.

**Q.** Perhaps Arabs came to warn the pedlars

**A.** No. The pedlars were Jews.

**Q.** Some say they were Arabs.

**A.** This I can't say for sure. I went around the synagogue. I tried not to go in there, for safety reasons.

**Q.** Were you becoming suspicious that there might be an element of truth in it? You were an emissary of the Movement there; and such a thing would have affected the good reputation of the Movement. Didn't you try to search and investigate?

**A.** That's a leading question. If I started to suspect someone during this very tense period and when the two emissaries had been arrested, I would have been forced to leave my house and go looking for a hiding place and I was too busy. Perhaps I didn't have free time then to even worry about it. Anyway, I don't remember why I did nothing in connection with it. Very possibly my suspicions started in Israel.

**Q.** Didn't you hear a claim that Moslems did it?

**A.** No, nothing at all like that.

**Q.** Did you discuss this with Dror (Ben-Porat)?

**A.** We never suspected that Jews might have done it.

**Q.** Didn't you ask him if he knew anything about it?

**A.** No.

**Q.** Why do you think they might have done this?

**A.** The Jews say that there were many emigrants waiting and only a few planes sent at the time. Ben-Porat explained to Israel the difficulties we were having in coping with the emigration and that there was an urgent need for Israel to send more planes.

**Q.** It is reasonable that for the sake of our people, they might have wanted to urge Israel to hasten the evacuation of those who had already registered?

**A.** Yes, to put pressure on Israel.

**Q.** Did you know Khabbaza?

**A.** Yes.

**Q.** Was he subordinate to you?

**A.** Yes, until he was removed to another post. I didn't know why, but I knew that Ben-Porat took him away to some other duty. He didn't even know how to hide the fact that he had received another job. He always came in elegantly dressed, proud, emphasizing his importance, and began to avoid the instructors' meetings and emigration matters.

Q. Did they look upon him as they would a deserter?

**A.** Yes, we didn't understand why he was so idle.

**Q.** I asked you if you thought that Oren (Khabbaza) was a courageous man?

**A.** I thought so. I presume that his courage resulted from his high aspirations to be someone of importance.

**Q.** Shahrabani spoke of the history and the split between the Movement and the Shura at that time. He said that Yoav (Goral) gave moral support to the rebellious group. Can you add to this version a single point – how deep was this split, critical or otherwise? Do you think that this disagreement was so serious, that the group may have used violence to create disturbances involving matters of emigration?

**A.** No. Not at all. You understand, they always saw themselves as inferiors then. It was as if those who represented the Movement to the Jewish man in the street were strangers from abroad, and not close to matters of importance. Members of the Movement, whose values were very dear to them, heard various complaints about finance and other things.

**Q.** You said in the protocol of the committee in 1952: "I was also concerned about the scarcity of planes. Many people wished to emigrate. In the north there were disturbances, robberies and murder on the roads and misuse of assets and people. There were many people in the capital and the quota allowed for the emigration of 3,000 a month wasn't adequate" (page 1 of Yoav Goral's testimony, 3.4.52). At that point when you saw this, weren't you obliged logically to increase consultation among the emissaries?

**A.** To request Israel to send more planes and to make her aware of the critical situation.

**Q.** Did you speak to Dror (Ben-Porat) about it?

**A.** Of course.

**Q.** Were there reactions on how to hasten the project, what to request?

**A.** After the explosion I believe Dror came and told me that they were preparing a group of young boys to fly to Israel and, with placards, to inform the public about the situation and to demonstrate their plight at the airport, to make Israel feel uneasy about the critical situation in Iraq and explain how very difficult things were. This was his aim.

I knew about it. If there were other plans I wouldn't know. Very possibly, before that, he spoke of ways that seemed right, in order to hasten the project. He always told me that we had to exaggerate our plight, in Israel, by any means we could, to pressure them to send more planes.

**Q.** In 1952 when you testified during the questioning about the one who carried out the action you said: "I don't know. There was a general opinion that those who threw the bombs were those who had done it previously – Arabs who wanted to take Jewish lives" (page 2 of Goral's testimony in 3.4.52).

**A.** Is this what I said before? I didn't reckon on Jewish complicity when I was abroad.

**Q.** (Goral's report, page 2, 3.4.52). "The Chairman: Is it conceivable that Dror (Ben-Porat) was involved with the throwing of the bomb? Yoav: Perhaps he was. Until now I hadn't given it a thought."

**A.** Very possible; I don't remember but it's very likely.

**Q.** Did we reach such a point? Why didn't some Jews want to emigrate?

**A.** There were all sorts of obstacles: They hadn't completed the sale of their homes, they hadn't liquidated their businesses and such like.

**Q.** The emigration continued, people arrived in Israel, and information of the difficulties here began to reach Iraq. Did this create alarm?

**A.** I don't remember. I don't think it was a factor. I seem to recall that an instructor, a woman, emigrated and wrote to her friend saying that food was scarce. Yes, there was also a letter written by a Jewish shop-owner from Baghdad who had emigrated and wrote to his relative in Baghdad that he regretted the black day he had had his citizenship revoked. That the situation in Israel was very difficult, and to try and stop anyone from selling his possessions and having his citizenship revoked. We took it as a bad joke and published it in the Movement leaflet.

**Q.** Was this subject brought to the attention of Dror?

**A.** Yes, he used to read the leaflets. However, I don't believe that there was any negative reaction to our departure. I remember there was a delay due to the shortage of planes; they simply felt that they still had time. It was a period of slowing down.

**Q.** You also said in your testimony of 1952:

> **Q.** Following the bomb incident I found the telegram you sent to Israel to increase emigration. Was the delay caused not by someone in Iraq but because of the shortage of planes?
>
> **A.** The police didn't want to give out further travel documents without completing the existing ones. We also wanted some sort of order.
>
> **Q.** Wasn't it logical at that time to increase the pace because of the explosion and the slowing up of emigration?
>
> **A.** I said that with sarcasm and yet it is an objective possibility.

**A.** Yes, it's from an objective point of view, he could have told one of the officers to organize a group to throw bombs. This can be true, objectively speaking.

**Q.** Did Dror (Ben-Porat) have control over the stores and the weapons, after Raphael left?

**A.** Since I wasn't involved in security matters, as I remember, (it's very possible Raphael gave us both the authority) – from a security point of view very little was done – I think I remember that Dror (Ben-Porat) took upon himself all the security and matters of authority. I don't remember any specific formality. The members knew us as emissaries and didn't acknowledge any separation of authority; therefore, whenever someone gave an order the people would accept it as a natural thing.

**Q.** Let us say he had done something like that, or if he had given such an order – would you have known about it?

**A.** No. Why should it have come to my knowledge?

**Q.** Because they looked upon you as an authorized person too.

**A.** No, secret matters were very important and guarded by us. No one would have spoken of it to anyone else on receiving an order.

**Q.** In your testimony of 1952, you said: (page 6):

"The Chairman: We didn't say that Jews might also have thrown that bomb? (meaning on Lawee).

Yoav: There was no such knowledge. Only the Jewish and Arab mob said that members of the Movement threw the bomb."

How does this sentence compare with your words?

**A.** Perhaps I understood that you meant the Movement members.

**Q.** In your testimony you said: "I discussed this a lot with our people in order to remove a bad impression they had against the Movement and persuaded them of the futility of this act" (page 6, Goral's testimony on 3.4.52).

This means that you discussed this since you were there?

**A.** I can also say now and then, since I was there.

**Q.** How was the relationship between Khabbaza and Ben-Porat?

**A.** I didn't meet them in their day-to-day affairs, therefore I have to try and remember if one of them ever told me, or anyone else, something of relevance. I don't remember any such thing.

**Q.** You arrived in Baghdad on 22 February 1950. The first bomb was actually thrown a month and a half after your arrival. How did you react to this?

**A.** What can I tell you? I knew of this even before my arrival in Baghdad, actually in Iran.

**Q.** Shalom, after torture, said, or was forced to say, that he was the bomb thrower. He re-enacted the American Information Center incident and claimed that Khabbaza and Basri also participated. What do you say to that?

**A.** I didn't know him at all. I didn't even meet him; therefore I can't judge on the state of his mind. It seems he was a simple person who received instructions to build arms caches and he did so. He didn't have any of the principal jobs; he had no attachment to the Movement.

**Q.** How do you explain the fact that others like Salim Mouallem and Youdkeh spoke up without being tortured and simple Shalom kept quiet for five days under torture until he finally gave in? And you claim that he hadn't any feelings?

**A.** I didn't say that he wasn't conscientious on behalf of the Movement. I meant that when they took him to build the arms caches, they explained to him the responsibility and dangers involved; but he wasn't a mature person.

**Q.** Do you mean that he couldn't have given an ideological speech?

**A.** Exactly.

**Q.** But emissaries from Israel did talk, and as a result of that the police discovered other sources. I want to know to what extent one can give credence to Shalom's words? Do you think, today, that he gave an accurate confession?

**A.** I have nothing to say to that. The question is if he knew both of them.

**Q.** Yes. He went around with them in a taxi, and Khabbaza told him that he was going away. He also knew that Basri had been imprisoned. You knew of the contact with Israel. You were allowed to use the wireless. If an instruction to do such an act was sent from Israel by wireless or through the dispatch box in the planes, would you have known about it?

**A.** No. If this came to us I didn't have to know about it. The two boys who used to bring the telegrams delivered them to Dror (Ben-Porat) if they were meant for him, and if they wanted to they could have told me about it, but this wasn't an order.

**Q.** If such instructions arrived, would the operator deliver it to you and Dror?

**A.** If it was destined for me – yes, if not for me – no.

**Q.** If it had arrived for Dror, would he have told you about it, due to the good relations between you?

**A.** The relations between us weren't of friends in all things, also because of the conflict (when I took up a special stand).

**Q.** Did you hear of such instructions from Israel?

**A.** No. If I had I would have thought otherwise.

4.12.60

### Edward Shahrabani (Maskil)

**Q.** What was your nickname there?

**A.** Maskil (educated).

**Q.** Who is Dan?

**A.** Dan Shamash.

**Q.** What were your duties?

**A.** I fulfilled various duties, partisan jobs on behalf of the emigration. At the same time I was an officer in charge of training and responsible for the weapons.

**Q.** During what period?

**A.** End of 1949. I was his active deputy; when he emigrated, I took over the job.

**Q.** With what weapons were you trained?

**A.** Special courses in firearms (they didn't use weapons in reality, only in theory); I trained with guns, bombs (of two kinds – dummy and live grenades)

**Q.** What type?

**A.** Mills and I think they were of Israeli manufacture. There were also dummy grenades. Those were the three types of bombs, around 12 types of guns, but we trained in Iraq with Fairblum and Toffee.

**Q.** Molotov cocktail?

**A.** Yes, just theoretically in fact, for the instructors; for the members – only how to do it; yes, heavy weapons – the Sten; special courses for the instructors; in addition to that, sub-machine guns. This was nearly all the heavy weapons we had.

**Q.** Cold steel?

**A.** Knives (we didn't instruct everyone, only the wireless people). We also taught them how to use sticks. I myself was trained with sticks. We also trained with knives and judo. These were nearly all the courses.

**Q.** Explosives?

**A.** Apart from molotov cocktails there was nothing else.

**Q.** Wrestling?

**A.** No, it wasn't my job. There was no one to teach such a thing.

**Q.** Gelignite?

**A.** No.

**Q.** Was there any in the Movement?

**A.** Yes.

**Q.** Where?

**A.** In the stores.

**Q.** Which one?

**A.** I have no idea.

**Q.** Did you see them?

**A.** Yes.

**Q.** How did they look?

**A.** Like cheese of a whitish colour.

**Q.** What were they for?

**A.** They didn't use it. They said in case they wanted to make bombs, those materials were needed.

**Q.** Did you train in explosives.

**A.** No.

**Q.** Who was your senior instructor?

**A.** Raphael Sourani.

**Q.** Didn't Raphael speak to you about training in explosives?

**A.** No. You surely want to get to the root of the bomb affair. To my knowledge, when one wants to understand something, one has to know the historic root of everything connected with it. In my opinion, this is important. I don't know how this problem arose. It wasn't my job. I will tell you the history of it. I will start from the beginning of the crisis, almost at the beginning of 1949. At that time I was an instructor in the Shura and I also used to meet with other instructors. The members of the Shura used to look to the instructor as an experienced person and from whom one had to take orders and follow them. When the crisis occurred, people melted away. One day, I received an order that everyone should abandon their stations. I found a safe place and stayed in it as the main contact between the workers and the instructors. Time passed and some of the men were sent back to Israel. The weapons remained in the arms caches. After a period of time, when the situation improved, Ben-Porat arrived. We met with him (Sasson, Somekh and myself, as far as I remember) and decided to continue with our work. We reorganized and doubled our activities. We strengthened ourselves by buying weapons. Mordechai took part in the action; he is a very qualified person. He brought people to me who were close to him and trusted him, and we started working together. Jews began to escape to Basra. This was at the end of 1949, before the bill of Revocation of Citizenship was passed. People arrived there in masses.

**Q.** Was the rush to leave for Basra due to the likelihood of a swift exit?

**A.** Yes, through Iran. We opened the way for the Movement to save people, and then we began to improve the connections. At the beginning the authorities ignored it. In addition to that, there were mountains on the north-east route of Iraq. Government and military people were also involved with this and received lots of bribes. The authorities then replaced their employees in Basra so as to halt the emigration. I was in Basra at the time. I was sent to train instructors on Stens. The emissary who directed the emigration was Uziel. I then returned from Basra. This was the situation regarding emigration and everything else. The Government in Baghdad finally decided to put a halt to it. My assumption was that the Government realized what a situation we had created and that people wanted to leave at any cost. The pressure finally did its work and the bill was enacted at Purim. Now, from the beginning, the relations between us and due to the urgency Israel indicated, we all met in my house for the first time. We realised that the situation was in such a state that we had to give orders and take the matter of emigration into our own hands. In fact there were two organizations in Baghdad – the Shura and the Halutz Movement. I would place the Shura under a different category from that of the members of the Movement. They were people of action. There were in the Shura better individuals and also people of higher positions in public affairs.

**Q.** You mean that in the Movement there were wealthier people and in the Shura better qualified people?

**A.** Right. The attitude towards the people of the Movement was different from those of the Shura. When the bill was passed, we immediately grappled with the situation and our real reason for action, was first and foremost, defence. The emissary, Ben-Porat, studied the material, correctly assessed the situation and brought us all together, members of the Shura – people to whom one can talk. At the same time we saw the emissary of the Shura – Rafi – who utilized the situation to disband it himself. We saw how he was neglecting matters and we told him that his place was not here with us. It was a very turbulent and dramatic session. Without informing us he quit through Iran. We didn't know it, but of course he informed the emissaries. Since then, formally, we were all dependant on Mordechai. This is how matters developed.

**Q.** When the split took place, what were the duties of the group that organised itself as an Underground in the Shura.

**A.** Each one stayed at his post. The organisation was concerned with emigration and not the Shura.

**Q.** Didn't you decide what targets and duties to accept outside the framework of the emigration?

**A.** No. This was only to preserve the purity and ideals for emigration needs.

**Q.** Did the emissaries, or anyone of them, know of the organization of this group, and did any of them join you?

**A.** Yoav (Goral) supported us to a certain extent, symbolically only and inconspicuously. We didn't receive any encouragement from Rafi, and we were made to keep our distance from him. At the same time I remember that I was at the airport in Baghdad (Yitzhak Elias was also with me). All of a sudden he came to me and said he had heard that a bomb had been thrown at the American Information Center.

**Q.** Can you remember approximately when that was?

**A.** 1950 – I think, between March and April.

Regarding who threw the missile, I can only give a rough guess. After we reached the point where a thousand planes had taken part, we had a party to celebrate. Information from people who had emigrated to Israel began to reach us, and the news was very bad. Those in Baghdad felt a kind of withdrawal and fear, which made them start to think how to save themselves and regain their citizenship, and they tended to defer their departure. It seems that the situation frightened some of our people. Whoever did the deed I cannot tell, but I presume that the bombs were used by people whose intention was to scare and not to kill. I base this theory on the bomb that landed on Mesouda Shemtob. The width of the road in front of the synagogue is around ten metres. Buses stood there to take the emigrants to the airport, together with their escorts and families; many curious onlookers in their hundreds assembled there as well as the emigrants inside and their escorts and the crowd outside. If a handgrenade had been thrown, across a radius of more or less sixty meters, and the intention was to deliver it on behalf of the Government or the Fascists, we would know that it wasn't a Moslem who could have done this job. This strengthens my opinion that it was a scare bomb, which was widely used by the Shura. The Iraqis didn't possess this type of bomb, that was not meant to have a lethal effect. Live grenades would have certainly caused many more casualties. At the same time the electricity cut out. Following this incident, a great wave of emigration started up. It was evident that there had been a slowing down in emigration and that the bomb had had the opposite effect and increased the numbers greatly. Who were the people responsible? When the bomb was thrown at Lawee's, I was in the area of Mesouda Shemtob and heard that Lawee was sick. Mordechai said that we ought to visit him and offer our sympathies about the incident and give prayers for his escape. The next day, or two days later, Ben-Porat said that Lawee may think that we came to visit him in order to provide an alibi for ourselves.

**Q.** What were your conclusions? You have given us guesses and assumptions. Your conclusions aren't concrete enough.

**A.** I want to ask you, what are conclusions? As a person responsible for weapons control, if there was such a campaign that originated from the Shura, I think we were quite responsible people and acquainted with such matters and we should have been involved with it. Such a thing had never happened before. We were at the same time very naive and surmised that when this happened, those who were our enemies did it, that is the Arabs.

**Q.** If I understand you correctly, I now have the feeling that you believe your people were involved.

**A.** I wanted to let you draw your own conclusions. Firstly I couldn't do it. I knew, within our code, that it was forbidden to open fire or shoot without receiving instructions from above. The emissaries and the officers also knew that; they had to receive instructions from a senior emissary. If such a thing were done without instruction I would regard it as audacious. If we talk of audacity, I know that many of our people have used bombs in a practical way. I know I am contradicting myself. But if the emigration did slow down – a bomb was thrown and emigration accelerated. As the pressure went down – another bomb was delivered and further emigration followed. And this continued for about six months. A logical person would finally reach such a conclusion. Very possibly, a group existed that was specially trained for this purpose. I don't know.

**Q.** By whom?

**A.** No one knows. Anyhow I don't think that this was done by an extremist Moslem group, because they had nothing to gain or reason for it. If they wanted to try and finish us off, well, we would have left in masses. If they wanted to keep us from leaving, well, they just caused agitation and panic for nothing.

**Q.** You emigrated six days after the last bomb. You left on eleventh of June and the bomb was thrown on the fifth. There was no problem of emigration then?

**A.** At that time all the organizations were paralyzed by the arrests of Tajer and Mordechai Ben-Porat and all those who came later. If there was an organization for such activities, well, it was justified. The people were being held and forced to sign affidavits over such acts. Most certainly the Secret Police knew what was being said. Anyway I presume so.

**Q.** Who were the members of the Mossad?

**A.** What I remember (because I don't quite recall) it was me, Eliezer, Dan...

**Q.** Shlomo Shina?

**A.** I don't think so. I don't remember.

**Q.** Naim Bekhor?

**A.** No. Naim Bekhor was overwhelmed with work.

**Q.** Do you remember if in your time there were terror activities being discussed?

**A.** No. We forbade that, even the thought of it.

**Q.** In which field were you in charge of Shalom?

**A.** Shalom was a person outside the Shura. He came to us to work, showed devotion, and we kept him on. He was hired to build arms caches. At that time he knew everything that took place. When we didn't receive a reply on what to do with the weapons, we began to transfer them from one place to another, and then we reached a stage where there weren't enough houses to store them. One day we sat down (Mordechai, myself, Dan and Aharon Abada) and decided to hide them in the synagogue (why they didn't destroy them, I don't know). We made a plan to make room in the synagogues (Mesouda and Ezra Dahood) to store the weapons there. Rooms were emptied and we had a cleaning campaign. I stayed up late with Shalom; we collected the weapons and packed them. Shalom himself did the same in all the other synagogues. Two days before he was arrested he seemed scared. He felt trapped because he had to build more arms caches. Before he was caught he asked me what to do if he were caught.

**Q.** I want to hear details of Shalom himself.

**A.** He was a very simple man.

**Q.** What do you mean by simple?

**A.** In all senses; apart from that he had deep feelings regarding emigration.

**Q.** Would you classify him as a man to be trusted?

**A.** Yes.

**Q.** Did you ever hear whether he disclosed the location of the stores to anyone else?

**A.** No, he didn't.

**Q.** Did you depend on him and trust him?

**A.** Yes.

**Q.** Was he a straight man?

**A.** Absolutely.

**Q.** Did he ever lie?

**A.** He had no need to lie. He was a man who worked for nothing, at the beginning.

**Q.** When he was arrested, was he capable of involving others or inventing lies?

**A.** This is something else. To withstand police torture that is another thing. I heard of something when I was in the Diaspora, that the man who was in charge of interrogation promised him, if he would confess to satisfy them he would be released. He, being a simple fellow, believed them and said whatever they forced him to say.

**Q.** Did he know that Basri was arrested?

**A.** Yes.

**Q.** When Shalom spoke he had already seen Basri. Can you believe that, being his superior, he was ready to betray a friend?

**A.** I rely on a conversation I had with him, which I remember very well. I met him two days before he was arrested; we talked about being caught, and he told me, "if I am caught what should I do; and if you or Mordechai confess what would be our fate?" I said that I was sure that Mordechai would never talk (I knew that he was in close contact with Mordechai). During the conversation I told him that I intended to travel within a day or two. I saw that he was really bothered by the situation. He had a strong will, but when tortured who could tell how he would have reacted.

**Q.** This question is about his strength, was he capable of betraying a friend?

**A.** Not to my way of thinking, especially him.

**Q.** If so, do you agree, in view of his character, that he spoke the truth?

**A.** Judging by his character it is possible that he spoke the truth. He was not used to lying. A simple man, in everything he did; if he promised to keep a secret and if he was involved in it, he wouldn't break his word.

**Q.** The first arms caches were, I presume, in the house of Eliahu Gourgey. Did you know that?

**A.** No, I didn't.

**Q.** Were maps found there?

**A.** Not maps, I think.

**Q.** Did you hear of a man called Eliahu?

**A.** I didn't know him but I heard of him.

**Q.** Did you know of those arms caches?

**A.** No. I didn't know all the arms caches, only those at Mesouda and Ezra.

**Q.** What kind of weapons were there?

**A.** At Mesouda – I think, three Tommy machineguns, several handguns, grenades (four or five, I don't know exactly), and Stens.

**Q.** Explosives?

**A.** No.

**Q.** Gelignite?

**A.** No. We never placed weapons with the explosives.

**Q.** Also was there any gelignite in Dahood?

**A.** No.

1.12.60

### Mr. Yousif Khabbaza (Beit-Hallahmi)

As well as I knew Shalom Saleh and Yousif Basri, I believe Basri to have been a man of integrity, responsible, and averse to dealing with affairs that were not in his line. I knew him for some time and worked together with him. There were always discussions and arguments between us, but it never occurred to me that Basri would carry out an act like this. It also seems strange that someone would instruct him to do such a thing.

You all knew his capabilities: He wanted to succeed in one special field. He was skeptical about the emigration and affairs of the Halutz, he had been a member of the Shura and the Halutz and left all this for a while, then went back to them. It seems to me that even if they had asked him to do it, he wouldn't have been ready to do things that affected his work.

I couldn't believe it of Shalom either. He was a simple man, an introvert, and I can't imagine who would use him in this way. Whenever I tried to delve deeply into the matter I was left with only one answer. For my part, I can't believe that he would perform such an act. Also, if this was our doing we would have been warned of the consequences. There were contact men and officers who could have advised us.

On the other hand, it doesn't seem to me that this was a premeditated governmental act. The various organisations and parties like the Istiklal were also incapable of doing it.

There is one presumption that this was a one-person act, by someone connected with us. I couldn't figure out which character would take it upon himself to do it. Looking back, nor can I figure out who would be able to come to such a decision. This is really a puzzle. Our people believed it was an act planned by the organisers of the emigration or by Israeli agents. It was natural for them to say that, or else they heard it from someone. Anyway, this view was given about.

**Q.** When did this belief arise – at the time of the trials?

**A.** At the time the bomb was thrown at the synagogue, there was a general belief that the Movement did this in order to accelerate the emigration of the Jews. There were all sort of differing views. The Jewish public didn't have any specific opinions. They were reached by those who sat in the coffee-houses and liked to gossip, who thought that the bomb was aimed mainly against the authorities in order for them to consent to the emigration, or else against the Jews, to induce them to leave.

**Q.** How many Jews were in Iraq at that time?

**A.** About a hundred thousand.

**Q.** Was it acknowledged by our people that there was an interest in pushing them out?

**A.** This statement came about because emigration was going on, but in very slow motion, during January.

**Q.** What was the logic behind the other incidents?

**A.** Those others were a puzzle to everyone. They didn't say that Jews were involved with those bomb-throwing incidents. No rumours were evident. The interesting thing is that at that time all the organizations were at a standstill and centred only on emigration. The community became solely an organization to prepare and direct the emigration of our people and all our members were preparing for this purpose.

I can't remember whether there were any discussions or analyses involved at the time. One of our people – Johnny – was always ready to give his opinion, with conviction, that it was done on instruction from Israel. Apart from him no responsible person or activist said the same thing. In the fields in which I participated, I can't remember if there was a common feeling about this incident.

**Q.** When they took place and were linked to the Jews – and the Jewish quarter also felt the same way – didn't you feel obliged to enquire what went on behind all this?

**A.** We asked, but we didn't succeed in reaching any conclusion. There were discussions and claims. They all asked how such a thing could occur and the discussion ended with a question mark. When we said that some were connecting this with our group – they said that it hadn't occurred to them.

**Q.** Did you hear that Moslems were blamed for throwing the bomb on the synagogue?

**A.** This was the classic version.

**Q.** When did you hear that?

**A.** I don't remember exactly, but the discussion always came up among the average Jew – relating the event to the Moslems.

**Q.** Were you among those who felt responsible for collecting information? An atmosphere of fear must have been created. Why were no efforts made to enquire after the truth? Because if it was found out that Arabs threw the bomb, self-defence groups ought to have been prepared.

**A.** I remember that there was such a discussion. The man who was responsible on behalf of the Halutz and the Shura was Ben-Porat. He said that there was nothing to argue about or steps to take. Anyhow, the Shura and the Halutz worked principally in the field of emigration. Questions arose whether to create a self-defence nucleus. I remember that it was agreed that nothing could be done and we should only concern ourselves with emigration. Johnny spoke to me against the organisations, blamed Israel and local groups, as he thought they were behind it.

**Q.** The first bomb was thrown on the seventh of May; in fact, at the same time as the revoking of citizenship started. You must have known that there was a withdrawal from registration, and that the Movement circulated memos advising everyone not to register. In Israel, too, there wasn't any clear decision made nor a clear message sent whether to encourage registration or not. There was also bitterness among the emissaries who were sent to disband the community, while Israel gave no instructions. In fact, until then, only a few Jews had registered, and when the bomb was thrown at the cinema, registration began to move ahead. A memo was then circulated favouring registration. How would an ordinary man analyse the bomb affair?

**A.** At that time there was a rumour that this was the work of our people. I remember that the Movement didn't want to let them register due to discussions between the people dealing with emigration and the Halutz and Shura. Mordechai Ben-Porat said (as he was the only one empowered to receive directions from Israel) that they were obliged to accept his instructions. The people of the Shura wished to participate in the decisions. There was an impression that, because of the discussion between the emissaries of the emigration and the institutions, no instructions were received from Israel.

**Q.** After the bomb was thrown at the coffee-house there was an upsurge in registration. Are you of the opinion that this was done to encourage our people to emigrate, or to jolt the institutions in Israel?

**A.** If I were to analyse my views as an emissary, I would have thought that everyone would be against this kind of act.

**Q.** What do you think of Mordechai Ben-Porat?

**A.** In a positive way – a man of initiative and with great ambition. In public relations – he lacks a great deal. He didn't get on with everybody. He went around with people who were loyal to him, without discrimination. He wasn't ready to discuss or reach joint decisions, but was dependent on instructions from Israel. He always spoke and proved himself a master of finance and authority. He underrated the emissaries, and instead of making them feel important, with a sense of purpose, he put them down and acted in an arbitrary manner.

**Q.** Regarding his character, are you of the opinion that he was capable of doing anything bad without consulting Israel?

**A.** He always presented himself as a man of authority. Basri dissociated himself from him and underrated him and said that one should keep one's distance from him. Johnny said that he heard evil reports of him. To me, he looked like a publicity-seeker who wanted to distinguish himself among our people. At times he was ready to speak about his adventures. I expected a lot from him. I was aware that he decided many things on his own. He was so sure of himself and thought that everything he did was right. This was the reason why everyone felt animosity towards him, except for some people who were always around him. He wished to be a leader and gather people about him.

**Q.** We heard Sammy's (Shmuel Muriah) views, regarding who would have had an interest in throwing a bomb, in order to pressure our people to register. And could it be for those same reasons that the Iraqi authorities were interested in doing likewise – to attain the exit of the Jews? Were the Iraqis interested in the emigration of the Jews?

**A.** There was such a thought but I wasn't aware of it. The regime ruled through elected figureheads and I don't believe any of those rulers acted consistently in order to arrive at such a conclusion.

**Q.** We come to 14 January 1951. Haim (Yaari) asked: Didn't you ever try to discover the truth behind it all?

**A.** No, there were only discussions among us.

**Q.** Weren't funds used in order to find out how far the Government had reached in its investigations?

**A.** Only Mordechai Ben-Porat could do that. No other person was allowed to explore it on his own. I am not sure if Ben-Porat did this. There was always a conflict between him and the institutions, therefore I cannot say.

**Q.** Two bomb-throwing incidents were similar in character and gave the impression that they were not meant to create much damage. If the Arabs had thrown the bombs, they would have chosen a time when the streets were full. And, if the Jews had done this they would have picked a moment when fewer Jews were about, in order to create a minimum of casualties. When a police officer was asked about the results of the interrogation he asked to be left out of it and not to press him. Who, then, in your opinion, was capable of doing this?

**A.** As it always happened, when emigration faltered, there was a feeling that this was a Jewish venture.

**Q.** Was Yousif in the synagogue that same evening?

**A.** Yousif never entered the synagogue for basic reasons.

**Q.** Did you have any feedback from him regarding the bomb?

**A.** There were continual discussions, but we never reached any important conclusion. He never said that he suspected anyone.

**Q.** If Ben-Porat was in the synagogue that evening – and you were always meeting each other – would he have mentioned this event?

**A.** I don't remember whether he mentioned any such experience.

**Q.** Do you think that he was used to telling you everything he did or only what suited him?

**A.** We weren't close.

**Q.** Did you know Shalom Saleh? What kind of person was he?

**A.** A simple man, devoted and disciplined. He built all the arms caches in the synagogue.

**Q.** Did he ever reveal the whereabouts of the arms caches?

**A.** He was known as the arms cache person.

**Q.** Did others also know of them? Did he ever speak of them?

**A.** I wouldn't be surprised, but I really don't know.

**Q.** Do you know what Shasha, Sofer and Gourgey thought of him?

**A.** They talked and knew that he had connections with the Movement. I don't believe they were unaware of it.

**Q.** Was he an honest person?

**A.** They relied on his honesty. He dealt with technical work. He did his job and they never found fault with him. He made no demands.

**Q.** He was a very simple man. If such a person felt that he was invaluable, could this foster an exaggerated feeling of conceit?

**A.** I am sure that it made him feel important. He felt he was a responsible person and always dreamt of going to Israel.

**Q.** Following the description of his character, do you think one can believe what he told the police and also when he re-enacted the scene?

**A.** You can't tell if they influenced him. I can't tell.

**Q.** What did you feel on learning about the testimony of a man who said that he saw you and Basri in the synagogue on the night the bomb was thrown?

**A.** I don't remember. I often went to the synagogue. When the bomb was thrown, I wasn't there. I wouldn't have forgotten that.

**Q.** Did you ever go in disguise to the synagogue with a parcel or a briefcase containing explosives?

**A.** Towards the end I used to disguise myself when I was preparing passports. Since then I have never worn disguise. I don't really remember; but I had no reason to do so, only when I travelled.

**Q.** Did you ever have a discussion with Pelah about a parcel containing certain materials?

**A.** Maybe. I didn't know that they were being sent by air. I don't remember.

**Q.** What kind of materials did they take from you when you left his house.

**A.** Badges, things like that, that couldn't be burnt.

## Mr. Eitan (Saleh) Shamash

I left Iraq at the end of August 1951, after the conclusion of the interrogations, reports about which I brought with me. Two months earlier I was fully convinced that the bombs had not been thrown by any of our people or the Movement. I drew the conclusion from two factors: politically, we had no reason whatsoever to do it and, secondly, in my opinion, the bomb which caused a fatality (the one at Mesouda Shemtob), would have endangered the emigration program much more than driving it on. I always thought that there was no reason for it to be done, and especially this bomb, and that is what I said then. If others wanted to throw the bomb they would have informed me and two other people beforehand, as this could have endangered our lives. On that specific day and time, the doors of Mesouda Shemtob were opened to let the emigrants enter the buses and we might have been injured. Among those who were the first to board and could have been killed was my wife, who went out a minute before the explosion. I am sure that if those in charge (I mean those who worked with us directly) knew about it and would have informed us. This is my opinion; the bombs were used either for political reasons or to do with emigration. This was my opinion until two months before I left Iraq.

During July and August, the interrogations were continuing and weapons were found. Of course we followed what was happening each day and what was being said during the interrogations. We then began to suspect our people. Logically we couldn't think of any reason for it. Considering the procedure of the investigations we found out that the other four sites chosen, apart from Mesouda Shemtob, were attacked in the midst of great confusion. Why? When the bomb was thrown at the synagogue I was appointed to check it out. At that time we suspected that the bomb was thrown by an official from the Istiklal Party, because we had made enquiries and we knew the reason for it. The bomb was thrown at the beginning of January. It was generally understood that the bill revoking Iraqi citizenship was about to expire on the eighth of March, meaning within a month and a half to two months. We were aware that until the beginning or middle of January those who had registered were from the middle and poorer classes. Very few wealthy people hastened to do so. The Istiklal newspapers in Iraq claimed this and kept criticizing the rich Jews, who weren't rushing to register. Therefore we suspected that their aim was to persuade those people to go ahead. We suspected them then; there was a local Arab porter in that street who used to work outside the synagogue and wasn't hired by us. He used to help us carry the suitcases from the car to the gate. We would see him working daily from dawn till midnight. On that day he didn't show up. In addition to that there were Arabs who were always there, going around selling carbonated drinks. On that day they stood at the far end of the street and not in the centre as usual. This prompted the idea that the bomb was thrown by individuals whose intention was to incite our people to leave – those from the Istiklal Party. Why did we suspect those officials? Because we often saw them sitting on the balcony of a house facing the synagogue entrance. According to the fragments of the bomb found (a Mills type) and the initial enquiries of the police and their officer-in-charge, they reckoned that it might have come from the rooftop of one of the houses inhabited by those officials… This gave us food for thought. The police officer also told either Moshe Shohet or Sasson Abed to put an end to the enquiry, as though they didn't wish us to delve any deeper. At the beginning I said that that's what made me curious about the other four bombs and not this one. During the investigation, when accusations and judgments were given, the Mesouda Shemtob bomb incident didn't seem to concern them at all. I myself said to one of the officers who was a friend of ours and who knew that we did work for Israel (Mohammed Sheet, the passport officer) – I told him that I was surprised: "You say that among the bombs thrown, the only one which caused a fatality was the one directed at the Mesouda Shemtob; if you wanted to pass a death sentence, you should have accused whoever threw that bomb, as there were no casualties in the other cases. This was why it puzzled us. Another thing that made me slightly suspicious and I could never make it out: Immediately after the bomb was thrown at Mesouda Shemtob I left the room; the main doors were closed. It was twilight. The electricity had cut out. I went over to see what happened. At that moment Yousif Basri and Khabbaza approached me. One of them said: "Don't worry, it's nothing, a bomb has been thrown." Later when the investigation started I began to wonder how those two knew, at that very moment, that a bomb had been thrown? And what were these men doing there? They used to come and work there but why were they present precisely at that moment? It made me wonder.

Also, if the police had found evidence to accuse our people, why didn't they bring it with them to court, as this incident would have proved to the Iraqis that the Jews who stayed behind were against the Movement and might have committed this act. So, if the police wanted to accuse these men of actions they didn't commit, why didn't they also accuse them of the Mesouda Shemtob affair? On the other hand, from the investigation, and especially during it, the behaviour of Shalom created a lot of suspicion, that this act was really done by our people, with instructions or without, I cannot tell. There were credible reasons for this being done without instructions from anyone – by the sudden whim of a crazy person. Shalom was a simple man, assisting his brother in making shoes, totally uneducated. He was so naive that he couldn't have said all the things they claimed he did, and when a lawyer came to speak to him, he didn't even tell him that he was forced to make a confession.

This he didn't say, nor did he to any of our people. The conversation of Shalom with the lawyer was face to face (in the presence of Mahmood, who was our man); also when he stood up for the passing of sentence he didn't tell the lawyer that he was not guilty of it. Why didn't Shalom tell the examining magistrate that the confession was forced on him?

The explosive aimed at Stanley and Lawee could never have been done for political reasons, because the bill to revoke citizenship had expired and passports were being given out freely. There is one point on which I said that I was suspicious, and this was with respect to the other bombs. There was one person who always carried those bombs on him, whether during the interrogation, the judgment or elsewhere – Khabbaza. I don't deny that I dislike Khabbaza a lot, but believe me I don't let this hatred influence what I am saying here. Why was his name always mentioned in the interrogations here and not any other? They found weapons in his house, but there were arms caches in other places also. Although he was a member of the Shura, the others who were caught by the police were organisers as well, much more important than he was. We didn't influence anyone to suspect Khabbaza as he had already left. One begins to wonder, who was this man? He was a simple person who dealt with transferring materials from one place to another; he was neither important enough nor qualified to give an opinion. There was a lot of jealousy and conflict among them, and Khabbaza was popular among those who had become bitter. At that time we contacted Israel to tell us from which emissary we had to take instructions. They told us that the one representative of Israel who could give orders and whom we had to obey was Mordechai Ben-Porat. This caused these men, headed by Khabbaza, to turn against us. Psychologically, such a man who finds that he has no distinguished place within the community and the Government, would do anything in order to make people think that he had achieved something important. My conclusions were based on his behaviour and that of Shalom's and the investigation done by the police: There is a chance that perhaps it was a joint effort – the throwing of the bombs.

**Q.** Are you sure that when the bomb was thrown at Mesouda Shemtob you saw Basri and Khabbaza together?

**A.** Even if I had the faintest doubt I would still have said that I suspect them. Here I say and say again that I am pretty sure of it. I said this when I arrived and repeat it once more.

**Q.** How much time went by after the explosion took place and seeing them?

**A.** Not more than two minutes. I was a bit frightened at that moment and because of the dark I didn't go out until a policeman came in and lit a match. From where I was sitting, up as far as the yard surrounding the synagogue, it's about twelve meters; therefore it took roughly two minutes.

**Q.** Did you hear that one of the wounded, a Jewish porter who later died in hospital, mentioned something about the bomb?

**A.** I think he said (now that you remind me of it, I am starting to remember), that he saw someone from the balcony on the rooftop of an Arab house.

**Q.** Were you aware that they tried to call the police to take a statement from the injured man?

**A.** Yes. I remember that we specially asked that they take a statement from him, and the police did their best not to come on time. At that moment it aroused our suspicions why it took so long. There was another reason for suspecting that the bomb had been thrown from the rooftop opposite; it was the way the bomb had been thrown and after further calculation, taking into consideration the distance between the houses in the vicinity, it could only have come from there.

**Q.** What was the width of the street?

**A.** Around eight metres.

**Q.** You claim that the court cases and the affidavits given by Shalom led you to suspect that something was wrong. Shalom confessed to throwing the bomb on the Library and also showed how it was done on the site – But what do you think of Basri's part in all this?

**A.** Yousif Basri, I know him as a friend with whom I studied in the Hagana, was a very calculating man, serious and I can scarcely suspect him in such matters. If he did that then it must have been under orders; I don't think they would have involved him in this, because he held a very important job.

**Q.** Do you know that he didn't confess?

**A.** Yes, I know that he told them nothing even under terrible torture.

**Q.** Are you of the opinion that if he took part in this he might have confessed?

**A.** No, he wouldn't have confessed. He was very smart, a lawyer, and was aware that as long as an affidavit of his might have led him to the gallows, he would have resisted. I cannot suspect Basri.

**Q.** Do you suppose that part of Shalom's testimony was a lie?

**A.** Yes, I think so.

**Q.** If Khabbaza had a part in the affair and they were looking for him, why didn't they replace Shalom with him (as the bomb thrower) and not vice versa?

**A.** I have a suspicion that the police brought Basri here on purpose. They knew that relations between Basri and Khabbaza were very friendly. They went out together with girls, etc. This I know very well. Such a relationship couldn't have had an influence, I mean Khabbaza wouldn't have influenced Basri.

**Q.** First the Law of Registration was issued, then Israel hesitated over joint action. The Movement published a memo not to send people out (on Purim eve). Later, the second memo was circulated, obliging them to register (at the beginning of April). What was the reaction to this memo? Did people register?

A. Very few.

Q. The first bomb was thrown on the ninth of April at the coffee-house; that is, at the same time as the Movement published the memo to register and there was no great reaction. Can you explain that?

A. My opinion is if the incident was done in order to accelerate the registration they would have done it more effectively; and those who wished to throw the bombs in a less lethal but effective manner would have done it in a place where Jews were to found in hundreds at open coffee-houses.

Q. Was it a coincidence that the bomb was thrown at a time when there was no reaction to registration?

A. I myself cannot connect this with that fact. Do you know that until mid-April there was a serious disagreement between us and the Mossad here about the number of immigrants Israel could absorb.

Q. What was the Iraqi intent regarding the emigration?

A. That the Jews should be permitted to leave, only those who so wished to do so and who were in poor financial conditions.

Q. What was their reaction when you heard that Israel wasn't ready to absorb a mass immigration?

A. Deep resentment.

Q. What was the opinion of the officials? Was it to send more people despite instructions from Israel? Wasn't there a desire to embarrass Israel?

A. Very possibly. In August 1950, we received instructions to put as much pressure on people as we could. There was a complaint in Iraq that we had overstepped the mark, so we decided between us not to interfere with the work of the emissaries as they were following orders.

Q. What was the weather like in January in Baghdad?

A. Very cold.

Q. Did the sellers of carbonated drinks go about the streets in January?

A. With hot fizzy drinks, yes. They didn't only sell fizzy drinks, but biscuits, oranges and the like as well. The people waited outside for long periods and the vendors would serve them and their escorts.

**Q.** You stated that Jews couldn't have thrown the bomb at Mesouda Shemtob. You spoke about the porter and the vendors of the fizzy drinks. How many people do you think there were out of doors at that time and place?

**A.** At least two hundred.

**Q.** If you or Sofer were outside, would you have known who else stood out there?

**A.** Of course.

**Q.** If you were standing there, would they have recognized you?

**A.** Yes, all of them.

**Q.** In what position were the gates at the time of the explosion?

**A.** Locked from the inside. The big gate and the small wooden one were closed all the time.

**Q.** Where did you see Shalom and Khabbaza?

**A.** They were standing in the building, in a corridor that opened up to four or five rooms. When I went out I saw them in the yard.

**Q.** Was there another entrance apart from the two gates?

**A.** No.

**Q.** If one of them threw the bomb from the outside couldn't he have slipped inside?

**A.** No, no way.

**Q.** Are you sure?

**A.** Quite sure. The gates were opened only when Sofer and I went out and ordered them to do so.

**Q.** How long was it before you saw Shalom?

**A.** Between a minute and a half to two minutes.

**Q.** This is the testimony of Shasha who was also on the site: "I was in the synagogue. The minute the explosion occurred there was a blackout. Outside it was still twilight. I left the room where I was standing and entered the hall when I saw the late Yousif Basri entering. He was outside and came in" (Shasha's testimony, page 1, on 23.11.60).

**A.** I met Basri near the passage door.

**Q.** What was their mood like when you met them?

**A.** I don't know. I didn't pay much attention.

**Q.** What was the pace of emigration at that time, and when the bomb was thrown at the synagogue?

**A.** There were around three planes a day, not many. This was a lot compared to previous occasions, but later on we found out that it wasn't that much.

**Q.** You said that the name of Khabbaza was always being mentioned. Who involved him? Shalom?

**A.** Not Shalom. Salim Mouallem said that Basri had sent Shalom to build an arms cache in his house. So they caught Basri and brought him in.

**Q.** So Shalom said that Khabbaza was a partner in throwing the bomb?

**A.** Shalom said later that it was the driver.

**Q.** Therefore, the first one who involved Oren (Yousif Beit-Hallahmi) with the bomb affair was Shalom?

**A.** Yes, Shalom, true.

**Q.** What is your opinion of this? Isn't it possible that Shalom used Khabbaza because he knew that he had escaped and then put all the blame on him?

**A.** If that is so, why did he speak about the arms caches in Gourgey Abed's house and from whence all the disasters took place?

**Q.** He thought perhaps they had already removed the weapons. According to the testimonies we have, until about the fifteenth of June, that is, around five or six days after Shalom was arrested, he was tortured, but disclosed nothing. Isn't it possible that he thought that since he was arrested, you had already cleaned out the arms caches?

**A.** If so, why did he involve Basri as well, when he knew that he was already in custody?

**Q.** You yourself said that Iraq had an interest in involving an important high-class individual, so they forced him to say this.

**A.** Perhaps.

**Q.** Is it possible that Shalom thought that the weapons had meanwhile been removed from the arms caches?

**A.** Of course. I would have thought so too.

**Q.** As simple as he was, could he have worked that out?

**A.** Surely.

**Q.** Don't you think that Shalom's naivete was to his credit, considering that many intelligent people who are kept in prison are apt to disclose things while he, under all that pressure and torture, kept silent for five days and nights?

**A.** I said that he was simple, because when he saw that all the evidence was against him and he had the promise of release if he agreed to say what they wanted, shouldn't he have told the examining magistrate that he was promised a release if he confessed?

**Q.** I believe that there was an understanding that if anyone was caught he should implicate those who had already left the country. He (Shalom) saw Basri since he was captured. Why did he say "Basri" and not: "I didn't do it, but I know that Khabbaza did"? We know that he was very badly tortured. The problem is did Shalom speak the truth or not?

**A.** I didn't know him so well. He was a modest man.

**Q.** Do you think if he had seen Basri in prison – and knowing that he had been tortured – was he capable of doing the act himself and yet implicating Basri?

**A.** One can never tell. It is difficult to judge. I don't think that he was capable of doing such an act, especially towards a man from his Shura, who worked together with him.

**Q.** What do you think of Basri? Was he capable of doing it?

**A.** As far as courage goes – he was capable of anything.

**Q.** On the same night when you threw out the emblems, the problem of the gun was still there.

**A.** The gun was left with him. I don't know to whom it belonged.

**Q.** But he knew that he was in danger and incriminated others. A person who is in danger tries his best not to involve others. Why did he keep the gun? What was he thinking of? He denied it and said that the gun didn't belong to him, and perhaps the police put it there. He never confessed to anything, neither during interrogation nor in the trial.

**A.** I don't know.

**Q.** As you were his good friend in the work you did, when you read his affidavit, did you believe him when he denied all knowledge of the gun?

**A.** Strange affidavit. Very possibly, from a legal defence point of view he thought that this was the best step to take. He might have been afraid if he confessed something, they would have forced him to say more.

**Q.** Was he obstinate? Would he have confessed to Youdkeh before his death, if he threw it or not? Whom would you have believed, Basri or Shalom?

**A.** I would have believed Shalom if he wasn't so confused at the time, because he wouldn't have lied to Youdkeh. If both were rational, I would have believed Shalom.

**Q.** Regarding the brain-washing. It was obvious that Shalom was severely tortured and Basri wasn't. Anyhow, Shalom said that he denied it until the very end.

**A.** It's hard to judge.

**Q.** You and Basri were together on the day of the explosion. When did you leave him?

**A.** At six. Six thirty.

**Q.** Do you know when the bomb was thrown?

**A.** No!

**Q.** Did you leave him alone?

**A.** He drove me to my house.

**Q.** The bomb that was thrown on the fifth of June (a time when no factor was needed to encourage the emigration) – what then was the purpose of throwing it?

**A.** They accused Shalom of throwing three bombs. What is your opinion, knowing Shalom's character and supposing that he was telling the truth; didn't he throw the bomb at the synagogue and the coffee-house? Why didn't they accuse him of these two acts as well?

**A.** It is difficult for me to judge whether he threw bombs that evening, or that he used gelignite.

**Q.** When did you see Shalom that evening?

**A.** I took him to the synagogue in order to arrange the arms cache affair. I don't remember what time it was.

**Q.** Did you send him off to take the car?

**A.** Yes.

**Q.** Can you remember what his mood was like?

**A.** No. I would have felt it if he were tense or somehow emotional. I also don't think he had time for that.

**Q.** How did you see Basri?

**A.** He wanted to escape at any price. He was jealous of me because I could leave. He asked to be smuggled out and that the committee should come for him.

**Q.** Why was he afraid? Was there already information that he was a wanted man?

**A.** No.

**Q.** When did you feel that he was becoming jittery?

**A.** When I left him he was silent, but when we met again he was tense when he heard about the arrests. He felt that he should run away until matters were straightened out.

**Q.** Couldn't they find a house for Basri?

**A.** I don't know. I had no connection with them.

**Q.** How were your relations with Johnny?

**A.** Good. You could never know what Johnny was thinking. I didn't do anything to go against him. I was his assistant and he didn't look on me as someone who might take his place. He already knew that I would be the contact man, etc.

**Q.** How was your relation with Salal?

**A.** I knew him but we had no relations. He knew the family. He was the contact man for Mordechai and he could give me instructions in his name.

**Q.** In the "El-Akhbar" newspaper, on 31 October 1951, details from the interrogation in court were published as follows (from Salim Mouallem's testimony): "I was imprisoned until 31 June 1951. They took from me testimonies which they forced me to declare. Whenever I was brought before the examining magistrate I used to ask him why they were torturing me. His reply was always that they would continue to do so until I said that Yousif Khabbaza was the man who threw the bombs. Therefore I was forced to give my testimony when I was brought to the Special Service Department, where they requested the names of the people who were in contact with Khabbaza."

**A.** I am speaking of the testimonies as I read them. I am aware of that.

**Q.** Do you suppose true justice existed in Iraq?

**A.** No.

**Q.** Do you think that this case was conducted fairly and justly?

**A.** All of it, no.

**Q.** Was the interrogation conducted without advance coordination?

**A.** If it was coordinated in advance, why did they not refer to the bombing of Mesouda Shemtob, which raised an outcry of accusations that it was done to annihilate the Jewish community in Iraq?

**Q.** You know Basri as a friend, with a strong character – Do you believe or think that he took part in it or not? Did he really participate or know that Shalom did it?

**A.** Basri isn't the type who would do such a thing, only if there were instructions from a superior. He wasn't so stupid as to take the initiative on his own.

**Q.** Who was qualified in Iraq at that time to give orders?

**A.** His superior; in my opinion he didn't have a specific manager, and if there was one, it was probably Youdkeh.

**Q.** Youdkeh wasn't there at the time of the bomb. Who could have given him such instructions?

**A.** The instructions could have been sent at that time by Mordechai.

**Q.** By himself or through a contact man?

**A.** Always through a contact man.

**Q.** The instructions were received by Oren, as contact officer. If anything was received when Youdkeh was absent, then it was given to Mordechai by Oren.

**A.** Either through Oren or straight from Mordechai to Basri.

**Q.** You say that Basri would never do such a thing without instructions, and if he did, this was according to instructions that were given by a qualified person, meaning, logically, that Oren might have told Basri about it, if Oren himself had initiated it.

**A.** Basri wasn't so stupid. For such important things, he would have gone to Mordechai to check.

**Q.** How were relations between Basri and Khabbaza?

**A.** Good.

**Q.** There was a division of labour between Basri and Johnny. The coordinator was Oren. He, in fact, stood by Basri. Basri testified in court and didn't confess to anything. Did you believe him?

**A.** As far as I know him, yes, I believed his testimony.

**Q.** You said that he had a very strong character and that you believed in his testimony and that he told the truth. He pleaded not guilty and kept to it all the time.

**A.** It is true that he pleaded not guilty, but this doesn't mean that somehow, there weren't certain true facts that he would have denied.

**Q.** You say that you had a feeling that the police didn't want to keep on with this investigation?

**A.** We really saw that. It wasn't just a feeling.

**Q.** Don't you think that those persistent questions of yours to the police made them insist that you leave them alone and defer the matter as they had reached a dead end?

**A.** The pressure that we put on them was according to the instructions of responsible people. That the police came to a conclusion and couldn't go on – this can be, because we really bothered them a lot.

**Q.** You all saw Basri and Khabbaza in the synagogue. You saw both. Did you see Shalom?

**A.** No.

**Q.** Suppose Shalom had something to do with it. You were involved with Khabbaza and Basri at Mesouda Shemtob. If we presume that what Shalom said after being tortured was the truth, and he didn't mention things that he didn't do, and insisted on that, the police had no other testimony. What do you say to that?

**A.** I absolutely agree with you. This is one of the reasons why I really think it was done by them.

**Q.** Did you see the fragments of the bomb delivered to Mesouda Shemtob?

**A.** Yes.

**Q.** Can you tell me for sure that you recognise them?

**A.** Yes.

**Q.** Did you know the likes of it before? of what make?

**A.** Yes I knew it to be of the Mills type.

**Q.** Were there any like those used by the Hagana?

**A.** Yes. With my own hands I trained with them. But the bomb on Mesouda Shemtob wasn't of Israeli manufacture.

**Q.** You were an officer and knew exactly what was happening there. What kind of weapons were there?

**A.** We had guns of various kinds, Israeli Stens, Tommy machine-guns, knives, Molotov cocktails, bombs (real and fake), the false ones were only Israeli and the real ones were Polish, and sticks as well. I not only remember seeing that equipment but I also worked with them. I think there were also two rifles.

**Q.** What is your opinion today? Do you really believe that these things were done by our people?

**A.** The more I think about it – no. There were also no instructions from here. If it was done by our people according to instructions from here, such as: "No one must talk: just do it," I doubt that.

**Q.** What do you mean by doubt it?

**A.** I can't say yes nor no.

**Q.** Today, do you think that these acts were not done by our people, and the testimony of Shalom was given under pressure?

**A.** Yes, under pressure; I fear that it was so, indeed.

**Q.** One can draw a few conclusions: either that it wasn't our doing; or that I really believe that our people did throw the bomb, or that it is difficult to draw any conclusions. Which is the correct one?

**A.** I am more inclined to say that it wasn't done by our people after considering all matters.

**Q.** In 1952, you said in your testimony: "I heard from various sources that if the Movement prepared the bombs, and on the other hand I knew that we had no connection whatsoever with the bomb throwing, I didn't want to say anything on this matter. I myself don't know the truth. I had no connection with the Shura at that time and I am not sure. I can't imagine that we, or someone from the Shura were responsible for using the bomb on Mesouda Shemtob" (Saleh Shamah's testimony, page 5). Is this true?

**A.** Yes.

**Q.** Do you remember this testimony?

**A.** Yes.

**Q.** Is it possible that after eight years, and after a lot of reflection on this point, that there might have been something improper, or do you still continue to believe in your conclusion of 1952?

**A.** On this point I have a very tiny suspicion now that it was done by our people.

**Q.** This is more negative than positive.

**A.** Yes.

**Q.** Do I take it that you've reached the conclusion that Shalom lied about using the bombs?

**A.** Apart from a devilish impulse, that it really could happen. What is the point of it all?

**Q.** You gave an opinion on Khabbaza's character – megalomania and such like.

**A.** This is one of the points that makes me refer to that very tiny suspicion.

**Q.** Did you know that Shalom was an arms cache builder?

**A.** Yes.

**Q.** Did he tell others?

**A.** No, he said nothing.

**Q.** If you knew him as well as this, why didn't you believe his testimony?

**A.** Because with such a person, one can show him a picture, for instance, and tell him it represented such and such, and he, simple as he was, would believe you. So, I myself am not sure about all this.

**Q.** Anyhow, at one moment in court, he denied all the testimony he gave and said that because of the severe torture he received, he was forced into it.

**A.** This was based on what they promised him and he believed them. This is what Mahmood told us. I don't think Mahmood would have lied about it.

**Q.** What brought him to this?

**A.** They promised him his freedom and to be sent to Israel.

**Q.** Did he speak the truth or not? He broke down after severe torture. He was always faithful and shy, notwithstanding what he knew. Why did he lie?

**A.** I have no answer to that. I don't know what to say.

**Q.** Regarding the emigration, you said that only the upper classes emigrated (but this wasn't true). There is here a report saying: The public all claim that Oren fulfilled his task of using the bombs. The accused claimed that he heard from people that "Oren expressed disapproval of those who didn't wish to revoke their citizenship; that he possessed a broom that could sweep away all those merchants." He said it before some of them, in the presence of his uncle (Rahamim Sayegh's testimony, page 3).

**A.** He was the type who was really capable of saying such things.

**Q.** This means that you accept it?

**A.** He may have said it and not meant it. If one thinks like that, he shouldn't have mentioned it.

**Q.** Did Khabbaza have the courage to do such a thing, or was he only a loudmouth ?

**A.** Words more than deeds.

29.12.60

## Mrs. Simha Sadik

There was no proof that Shalom and Basri threw those bombs. No one could know, not even I, what the truth is. They tortured them for several days and I heard that Shalom even vomited blood due to this; so he asked what they wanted from him. Later they told him to sign a paper and he did so as a result of all their cruelty. They wrote down what they wanted him to write (that he threw the bomb, etc.) and he signed it. It was a lie. The late Yousif Basri asked me to buy him a bag for his journey to Israel and I did. It was in my room. In the trial, they said that they found the bag and there was gelignite in it, which was the same material used for the bomb at Stanley Shashou. I said that the bag was taken from my room and was never used. So truly, there was no proof and no one knew anything.

**Q.** During the trial Yousif denied everything and Shalom confessed under torture. How do you know that Shalom signed and confessed?

**A.** He said so himself at the trial. I went to the house of Yousif's lawyer (his wife was my friend) and asked for details. He told me that he couldn't get hold of the minutes, as they warned him not to interfere.

Upon my arrival in Israel they asked my opinion whether eighty per cent of the Jews believed it to be so. I replied if eighty per cent believe it, then it must be true. In my opinion, they might have done that in order to accelerate the emigration, but I have no proof.

**Q.** Regarding the bag (a quotation from Mrs. Sadik's testimony in English, page 3): "The bag in question was similar to the one I had and I had actually bought it myself for Yousif, who had seen mine and wanted one similar. He used it, to my knowlege, for everyday shopping, etc., and it was during the trial that I had discovered about the police plant as traces of gelignite had been found in it." Who took the bag?

**A.** They did. When they conducted the investigation they took everything.

**Q.** When they searched the house? Is that when they took everything?

**A.** Yes.

**Q.** There is a story going round that after taking Yousif, the police told you that he needed various things for shaving and the like and that you should bring them in a bag, and that is how it came into their possession.

**A.** He asked for various things, but I don't remember exactly if I took them in that bag or in another one. I have really forgotten. But if at the beginning I said it, then it must be so, because when I arrived in Israel, things were still fresh in my mind, not like today.

**Q.** You related that Yousif played cards on the night of the bomb.

**A.** When they asked me I said he was with us at home.

**Q.** But you weren't at home. Why did you say that?

**A.** I wasn't at home. I was at Linda's, but I told them that. I only said it to help him. The truth is I didn't know, as I wasn't there and came back late.

**Q.** Do you remember that night? How did you hear about the bomb?

**A.** After they took him and accused him. As for the bomb I heard about it from other people.

**Q.** In your testimony you said (page 4, Mrs. Sadik's testimony in English) that: "You left him (Basri) in your house, playing cards, while you went to call on a mutual friend, Linda, daughter of the 'priest'; the house was near the scene of the explosion and it was Linda who had informed you about what had happened a short while before and you, on your return home, informed Yousif Basri of it."

**A.** I think that's how it was. The place was nearby and Linda heard about it.

**Q.** Do you remember when it occurred?

**A.** I really forget. I never thought that I would but I really can't remember. I think it was late, before eight o'clock in the evening.

**Q.** When did you come back?

**A.** I was definitely home by nine o'clock, so this happened before that.

**Q.** What do you have to say about it today?

**A.** I have no proof, but it isn't so strange as to be beyond belief.

**Q.** What do you think today?

**A.** My opinion hasn't changed, even today. It makes sense. If five or ten Jews died so that more Jews emigrated, perhaps it was worth it.

**Q.** Did you find Basri at home when you came back from Linda's, on the night of the bomb?

**A.** Yes.

**Q.** We have testimony in our hands that Basri wasn't home that night. Testimonies from people he met that day.

**A.** We ate lunch together. When I came in at nine o'clock in the evening he was there. During my absence I can't say.

**Q.** When did you buy him the bag?

**A.** I don't remember exactly.

**Q.** Long before he was arrested?

**A.** Not long. I don't remember exactly.

**Q.** Did you buy the bag at the time when he used to visit you regularly, or when he moved in with you?

**A.** I don't remember exactly.

**Q.** What did the police take?

**A.** They took a big brown suitcase containing all his clothes.

**Q.** Where was the gun that you found?

**A.** It was in the drawer.

**Q.** Did Yousif put it in the drawer or did you?

**A.** I don't remember.

**Q.** When did he bring the gun home? Who brought it?

**A.** Yousif brought it.

**Q.** When did he bring it?

**A.** I don't remember. Once Yousif said that he had to travel abroad as there were too many investigators looking for him.

**Q.** When was that?

**A.** I don't remember.

**Q.** Was it on the same day that you visited Linda or before that?

**A.** I really don't remember.

**Q.** Do you agree with me that this gun was brought to your house on the same day when you came back from Linda's?

**A.** I don't remember.

**Q.** When did you see the gun? Who put it there?

**A.** He told me where to put it, and I told him, in the drawer. I don't remember when that was, on that night or the one after.

**Q.** Did you know Gourgey Lawee?

**A.** Yes.

**Q.** Did you discuss this with him?

**A.** He came for a visit to my house but we didn't discuss this matter.

**Q.** Did you discuss it in 1952?

**A.** At that time my husband was in gaol and I couldn't have mentioned it to him. Later he escaped.

**Q.** Didn't you speak to him at all?

**A.** About this no. He might have asked me some questions that I denied, but I don't remember exactly. A few days before, he gave me a letter for Rodney and I mailed it. This I remember.

**Q.** Later you took the gun and put it in the oven. Did he tell you to do so?

**A.** When they searched they didn't find the gun at first. When they left they said they would come back with a mine detector. On that same morning I closed the house and went to visit my husband. They came and everything that was made of iron, they ruined. One of them waited for me and asked me why I locked the room. I explained to him that I had a strange woman in the house, a Christian maid. Among them was an officer who always took bribes. When he found the gun, he didn't take it straight to the police, because he knew my husband and took a bribe from me, but he advised me to put the gun in the oven and to act as if I didn't know anything about it, and that I found it there. That was how it was written in the protocol.

**Q.** When they made a search and took Basri for the first time, what did they take with them?

**A.** A big brown suitcase. They took Basri and my husband.

**Q.** Did they find other things together with the gun?

**A.** Gold.

**Q.** Other things? The bag?

**A.** I don't remember if I took the bag with me, or they took it. I really can't say.

**Q.** As a dangerous person staying at your house, it is only logical that you should know if he left the house, went out or came in. Every time he left, you, too, were in danger. Can you try to remember, how was the situation then?

**A.** After what I went through, I am not surprised if I don't recall these things.

**Q.** In the trial you said that someone by the name of Johnny visited you.

**A.** As far as I remember, he visited our house twice. Once he brought the gun. I don't remember when that was.

**Q.** When he brought the gun, did he stay long?

**A.** No, I don't think so. As far as I can remember, a car was waiting for him outside.

**Q.** When did you come back from Linda's?

**A.** I am sure that I was back home between seven and seven thirty.

**Q.** On that same night when you came back, Basri was at home and then Khabbaza came and brought the gun?

**A.** I told you that I don't remember if it was on that particular night?

**Q.** Why did he come?

**A.** I remember I told him to stay and have some juice (it was very hot outside) and he said that he had a car waiting for him outside and had no time. If this was on that same night, then I came back early.

**Q.** Were you at Linda's on that same evening, the next, or before that?

**A.** Perhaps you should go through what I said the first time when I arrived in Israel. That was exactly how it was.

(They read Mrs. Sadik's testimony again regarding her visit to Linda's, page 4)

**A.** I remember something but I am not a hundred per cent sure. When I was at Linda's they spoke of bombs. I don't really remember if they spoke of bombs or something else. She said that the night before, when they sat down to eat, all the windows shook and when they made enquiries, they understood that it was a bomb that some Jews had thrown at Stanley.

**Q.** Presuming that this was before the bomb. On that same evening, if so, you were home?

**A.** What I remember; one night Yousif went out, somebody called him and he left.

**Q.** For how long?

**A.** At least an hour. I didn't ask him, because before that he told me that he wished to travel and that it was being arranged for him. Once I questioned him when he went out, and he was furious. I told him "the very cap of the thief blazons his guilt." He said that the situation was very tense and he was planning a trip. But he always answered before I even finished asking. He went out several times.

**Q.** When he left for an hour was it on that same night?

**A.** Yes.

**Q.** On the same night that you were home and Khabbaza left later?

**A.** I really don't remember.

27.11.60

## Mr. Yitzhak David (I.D.) Sofer

He was the liaison officer between Mordechai Ben-Porat and the airways company.

(The conversation was conducted in English and Arabic alternately, and the translation in English was simultaneous.)

Mr. Sofer says that he tried his best to find out facts which could not have been based on anything but events, declarations, the character of people, etc. He has a mind of his own, exceptionally clear, and has never feared to speak out. This matter has bothered him for sometime. It was crystal clear to him that the initial investigation was conducted with a view to secrecy and certain facts were ignored in the name of state security and the like. Now he wants to get to the truth of the matter, and it was for this reason that he wrote his letter. However if one were to arrive at conclusions based on actual facts, one has to realize that it couldn't be done.

**Q.** What is your opinion today of the bomb question?

**A.** It was undoubtedly thrown by us. No question at all.

**Q.** On what do you base your opinion?

**A.** The facts taken from Shalom weren't based on truth, on absolute truth. Shalom was beaten in order to tell the truth, but what he said wasn't what the Government wanted to hear. Shalom was very naive. He was young, around eighteen years of age, without education and illiterate; Abdel Fadi promised Shalom that if he would re-enact the American Library Center incident (and this is exactly what he did) he would receive his passport and be allowed to leave for Israel. Mahmoud came one evening to Sofer and told him that he really felt very sorry for the gullibility of Shalom. After acting out the Library incident, Shalom inquired about the passport that was promised him.

The "affair" in Egypt gave Sofer a new angle to his way of thinking. He began to wonder if and whether this thing was done by us, as the public believed. The "affair" in Egypt gave him the key. On the day when the bomb was thrown on Mesouda Shemtob (he meant the day when three innocent people were killed) a car was parked on the right side of the building. In his opinion, this car belonged to Basri: As a rule neither Basri nor Oren would drive to the synagogue. When the incident occurred, no one knew what happened. It was twilight; an explosion was heard and the electricity cut out. Nobody dreamt of a bomb. They enquired what had happened and were informed that a bomb had been thrown. In the background people started rushing about.

The Government couldn't make any sense of this bomb. The bomb that was thrown was the only one of that kind that had ever been thrown in Iraq. Of course, everyone said that this bomb was the work of the Jews. The current dislike of the Jews was bad enough; therefore people could easily be led to believe that the Jews did it. Bombs weren't required to upset the public. The Government need not have blamed us. It wouldn't have gained anything from this.

How could he give solid facts? No one would venture to do so, since no one knew what they were. There were still people in Iraq, Moslems, who say that this wasn't staged, and that no testimony was taken under torture. The police claimed that they had papers and maps to prove the charge.

**Q.** When the bomb was thrown at Mesouda Shemtob a local porter was injured. Do you know what he saw and said?

**A.** No, nothing.

**Q.** Did you hear anything about the porter, what he saw and told Shasha Gourgey?

**A.** No, nothing.

**Q.** Can you tell me if Mahmoud met with others apart from you? Did he associate with many other people?

**A.** He only mixed with us. With Gourgey and myself. We were in touch with him not because he liked us but because, simple soul that he was, he enjoyed telling us stories about the prisoners and such like. He received money as well, but acted in a very naive way.

**Q.** According to your explanations, there were two people who were certainly connected with the throwing of bombs; one was Shalom and the second was Basri. If we accept the fact that Shalom spoke the truth, then he must have been involved and Basri waited for him outside in the car.

**A.** When I was arrested, the police showed me Basri's passport and asked me if I knew him. I told them that thousands of passports passed through my hands and I couldn't say. Then they told me that he was accused of throwing bombs.

**Q.** If we suppose that Basri was involved with the matter and Shalom didn't lie, how do you explain the fact that Basri, until the last minute, denied any involvement or connection with the throwing of bombs.

**A.** This can be easily explained. Surely Basri wouldn't have confessed to anything, being a lawyer.

**Q.** Well, there is a maximum resistance point for a person undergoing torture. It is only a question of time.

**A.** This is exactly what I said before. He was beaten to the limit that was required. Basri, a person who was acquainted with the law, would confess up to a point and then keep his mouth shut. If they really wanted him to make a confession they would have forced him to do so. But they didn't want that and they didn't use excessive force.

**Q.** What about Shalom? Why did he deny his statement at his trial?

**A.** To save his life at the last minute. When he found out that his passport hadn't been returned and there was no way of saving himself, he called Meir and Gourgey and told them that he didn't do it and asked for a lawyer.

**Q.** Do you know that in 1952 there were negotiations with the British regarding Iraqi oil and that the opposition used this against the El-Sa'id Government. Did you know anything about that?

**A.** No.

**Q.** Is it true that one of the main reasons for throwing the bombs, if they had been thrown by our people, was to accelerate the emigration?

**A.** No.

**Q.** If it were not so, why were they thrown?

**A.** Sick people. Simply someone wanted to see how far he could go.

**Q.** What for?

**A.** Mere criminals, that's all.

**Q.** Could it be only madness?

**A.** Don't you believe that he who gave these instructions was not mad?

**Q.** Do you know of anyone at that time who was capable of thinking that way in Iraq. Can you imagine who was that crazy person, or terrorist, as you call him?

**A.** I don't know. I don't know what to say. There were people who were sophisticated enough in crime. Babay Uri was the head of the campaign in Iran at that time; perhaps he knew about it?

**Q.** Uri wasn't in Teheran then.

**A.** I wouldn't know.

**Q.** Say we remove the emigration factor, why did they throw the bomb specifically at a Jewish synagogue?

**A.** Maybe they had a reason, so that people wouldn't regret their leaving as some did.

**Q.** If so, we must go back again to the emigration question.

**A.** There might have been people who wanted to regain their nationality, but this wasn't a reason to throw bombs. Maybe there were some who thought that killing a number of people would justify the emigration. Very possibly, if this was the reason for throwing the bomb, then it must be the way he was thinking.

**Q.** If we look at it from another angle; the three people – Khabbaza, Basri and Shalom – weren't people who dealt with emigration. What was their purpose with regard to emigration?

**A.** That's a point. As in all things there are people who deal with politics and those who carry out decisions; there are those who draw the lines and the way of action, and the operators who fulfil them – the hand that does the deed.

**Q.** Are you of the opinion that there was collusion between the two factors?

**A.** They didn't ask me to throw a bomb. They did this according to their arrangement with them.

**Q.** Who were the people responsible for the emigration?

**A.** There were lots of them who dealt with it, not only Mordechai. He was the man in authority and the responsibility was his, but not politically. The political side of the emigration wasn't under his control. Tajer and the rest were dealing with the political area for defence and emigration matters.

**Q.** If that is so, who would have given the instructions?

**A.** If Mordechai reported that the majority of the people were thinking of reclaiming their nationality, this would have been reported to his seniors.

**Q.** On that date Youdkeh wasn't in Baghdad. To whom did Mordechai report? Who was (if it were so) the man in charge?

**A.** Perhaps there was a more senior individual who could have given the instructions…

**Q.** Everything went through Mordechai.

**A.** Supposing Mordechai reported on the deceleration of the emigration, etc., and a senior authority here in Israel thought that the best solution was to create alarm among the Jews – would Mordechai know of it?

**Q.** The authority in Baghdad was Mordechai. All the telegrams, even those sent to Teheran, went through him.

**A.** Very possibly these instructions didn't go through the usual channels, through Mordechai. Is it possible?

**Q.** A thing like this couldn't have happened as long as the instructions and the contacts were transferred in their usual way. Not through fixed command channels, which were in use.

**A.** Maybe these instructions were given through other command channels.

**Q.** When were you certain that these bombs were thrown by us?

**A.** After the Egyptian affair.

**Q.** When you arrived in Israel in 1952 and gave your testimony, everything was still fresh in your mind. You didn't say then that we might have thrown the bombs.

**A.** Of course not. After a time, when a man starts to think back, he begins to question certain details and to form conclusions. You don't do that when you are being interrogated.

**Q.** How do you now feel about your previous testimony?

**A.** I reject it completely. Most certainly after the Egyptian affair.

**Q.** You came to Israel with a fixed idea. Was it only the Egyptian affair that made you change your views?

**A.** I changed my views and opinion only in connection with the bombs.

**Q.** In your testimony you said that you and Shasha were in Mesouda Shemtob when the weapons were discovered. Did you see the weapons there?

**A.** Yes, I did.

**Q.** What did they consist of?

**A.** Tommy-guns, grenades, gelignite, a few revolvers, ammunition (with dates).

**Q.** How did the gelignite appear to you?

**A.** Thin sticks, like fingers, yellow. One or two sticks.

**Q.** What was their length?

**A.** As long as a finger. They were placed one beside the other, if I am not mistaken.

**Q.** Did you speak with Shasha about the gelignite.

**A.** No.

**Q.** He also saw the same things. Didn't you speak about it?

**A.** Perhaps yes, and perhaps not. When you are put in such a situation, before cameras, you don't really remember what was said.

**Q.** In 1952, a year later, you surely remembered more than you do today. Do you agree with me?

**A.** Yes and no.

**Q.** Why so?

**A.** I wasn't interested then, and somehow I didn't think deeply enough about it.

**Q.** In your testimony in 1952 you said (Sofer's testimony, page 17): "At five o'clock the army experts came here and they began taking out our wonderful stuff, hand grenades, Tommy-guns, revolvers, bullets and a packet of cigarettes containing a green paper on which a date was written."
At that time you were questioned about the gelignite and you said that there wasn't any. How is it possible that you remember this now?

**A.** Apparently I hadn't remembered it then.

**Q.** Can you remember if there were any detonators?

**A.** I don't know. There were also some black cylinders. What was in them, I don't know.

**Q.** You said that Salim Mouallem and Youdkeh found out many things during the interrogation. The maps that were found on Youdkeh weren't maps of the weapon stores. Those were found in Gourgey's house. They didn't get to the weapons until Shalom spoke.

**A.** Of course. He spoke.

**Q.** One of the injured people who was then near Mesouda Shemtob, a local porter, said something; what was it?

**A.** This I don't know. We went to donate blood for him, and I heard them saying many things.

**Q.** What did he say?

**A.** Many things were said. I don't know. He identified someone. Gourgey hastened to say that the man wished to give an affidavit, that he saw someone. But I'm not sure.

**Q.** Did you hear the story that a grenade had been thrown from the rooftop of a house opposite the synagogue?

**A.** No. But Yousif came down from the rooftop of the synagogue. I believe people saw him coming down. He didn't come from the other side, he was inside. Saleh spoke to him. I didn't do so.

**Q.** Was Khabbaza in the synagogue?

**A.** I didn't see him. I saw Basri.

**Q.** Did you know that the next day Shasha went with other well-known people from the community to the police station and filed a complaint, that someone was injured and wanted to give an affidavit?

**A.** No. I just heard that a man was sent to take an affidavit, but I didn't hear of a delay in the investigation. It is very difficult to describe such a thing. The investigators in Iraq aren't stupid. What would they gain by delaying the investigation?

**Q.** Assuming they knew who threw the bomb.

**A.** The officer knew the culprit? Not so fast. The investigation was fairly conducted, and I don't believe that they would have done so. They arrested many people, even Moslems living on the opposite side of the road and others. Why did they arrest people if they were certain who threw the bomb?

**Q.** Isn't it a bit strange that after such a long period you begin to change your opinion in this matter?

**A.** I may have lost a lot of faith and certainty after what I saw. I began to ponder over whether such a man, responsible for all the anarchy and recklessness in Iraq, was the one accused? No one had been brought to justice. In throwing the bombs there were lives involved. Why not let the accused receive his just reward?

**Q.** Do you remember Basri's reaction at that time in the synagogue?

**A.** I didn't stay with him. I accompanied the injured to hospital. But I knew that the car parked near the synagogue, on the left side, belonged to him, and he rarely came in his car.

**Q.** The last grenade was thrown on the fifth or sixth of the month. Salim Mouallem was caught that same evening. Where is the logic in that?

**A.** I don't know. Probably for the same reason that the bomb was thrown at the American Library Center.

**Q.** Were there any present when the weapons were take out of the arms caches? Weren't you inside when the weapons were discovered?

**A.** No. We slept in the synagogue. The search went on, and when they reached the arms cache they took us to see it. Then they called various people from the police and Government departments, so that they would be present while removing the tiles that led to the store.

**Q.** Is there a possibility that they planted something in the store?

**A.** No, everything was covered up. It was all taken out with the help of experts.

**Q.** How were the weapons found, by soldiers with mine detectors?

**A.** Mine detectors. When Shalom was brought there, handcuffed, he was asked if we were involved with the matter and he said no.

**Q.** From your letter, one can presume that you were clear in your mind that our people threw the bomb. Have you concrete evidence for this?

**A.** This is my own opinion, not influenced by anyone else.

**Q.** Most of the Jews said that we did it. How long were you in Israel before you appeared before the committee?

**A.** About three months.

**Q.** Do you agree that at that time you hadn't yet been influenced by public opinion? Do you believe in psychological warfare?

**A.** Yes, of course. I had the moral guts to say that we did this. I had the guts because I put two and two together. I drew my own conclusions without any outside influence, the result of all that I had learned and considered in detail during that time.

# Appendix C

# Ezra and Nehemiah Operation 1950-1952
# Responsibility for its formation and operation

Mordechai Ben-Porat, the Operation organizer

| The Jewish Agency | | Israeli Government |

wireless

| Immigratin Department | middle Easten Department | Mossad Le-Aliya Bet Moshe Carmil |

| Prime Minister's Office | Foreign Office | Defence and Intelligence Centre | Ministry of Finance |

Zion Cohen
Iran

negotiation with the airline companies: Shlomo Hillel, Rony Barnett and Yehezkel Shemtov

Acting Chairman of the Community:
Yehezkel Shemtov

Emissaries of the Mossad Le-Aliya: David Ben-Meir, Uziel Levi and Yacov Frank

Public Emigration Community:
Sasson Abed (Chairman) Abraham El-Kabir, Moshe Shohet, Sasson Nawi, David Sala (Partlet)

Emissaries of Kibbutz Meuhad: Raphael Ben-Zur (Sourani), Yoav Goral

Emmigration Committee (Illegal) and their contact with the smugglers

Iraqi Ministry of the Interior and Police

# Appendix D

## Functional Staff in the synagogues
## Mesouda Shemtob and Meir Tweig

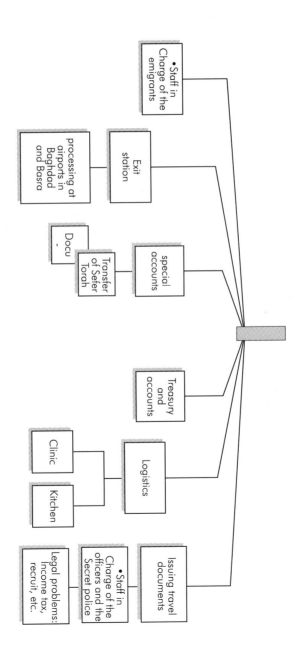

- Staff in Charge of the emigrants

processing at airports in Baghdad and Basra — Exit station

Docu - — Transfer of Sefer Torah — special accounts

Treasury and accounts

Clinic — Kitchen — Logistics

Legal problems: Income tax, recruit, etc. — •Staff in Charge of the officers and the Secret police — Issuing travel documents

# Appendix E

## The immigration activists from October 1949 and till the end of Ezra and Nehemiah operation

Abada Ahron
Abada Eli
The late Abada Sasson
The late Aboudy Naim
Abrahami Mordechai
Ajmi Eliahu
Aloni Menahem

Baba Arieh
Bahari Dr. Jack
Bar-Dayan Yousif
Bar-Nissim Yigal
Bar-Nissim Zvi
Barzilay Naim
The late Basa Akram
The late Basri yousif
The late Battat Yacov
The late Beit Halahmi (Khabbaza) Yousif
The late Bekhor Naim
The late Ben-Hai Yitzhak
The late Ben-Hayim Kadourie
Ben-Hayim Menashe
The late Ben-Mordechai Abraham
Ben-Shlomo Yehushua
The late Ben-Yair Mordechai
Ben-Yehezkel Towfik
Benyamin Josephine
Bibi Mordechai

Buba Victor

Cohen Carmella
Cohen Edward
Cohen Ezra
Cohen Gilad
Cohen Salim

Da'boul Shlomo
Dalah Yousif
The late Dalah Naji
The late Dalah Ezra
Dangoor Yonathan
Doron Uri
Dori Maatouk
Dror Ephraim
The late El-Bank Meir Yehezkel

Egozi Badri
Eliash Yitzhak
Elias Meir
Elias Reuben
Eliezer Yacov
El-Omari Aharon (Abu Shawki)
Ezer Avraham
Ezer Yuval

Fattal Ahron
Fattal Yousif
Friedman Ritchi

Gabbay Ezra
Gourgey Dr. Albert Shlomo

Hai David
Hai Yousif
Hai Dr. Yousif
Hazan David
Hazan Yehezkel
Horesh Shlomo
Hubeiba Shimshon

Jiji Edward

Kadoorie Eliahu
Khalifa Salim
Katan Daizy
Katzab Yehezkel
Khazzam Yehezkel

The late Levy Dalal
Levy Ezra
Levy Yousif

The late Mandelawy David
Mandelawy Edward
Mandelawy Naim
Mandelawy Nissim
Mayer Dan
Mayer Sasson
Menashe Simha
Mordechai Abraham
Moshe Eliahu
Mouallem Salim
Murad Dr. Latifa

Najar Shimshon
Nakar Nathan

Nawi Shlomo
Nissim Meir
The late Nouri Ezra

Obadia Zvia
Omri Aharon

The late Rajwan Nouri
The late Rami David
The late Rasouli David

Sadik Simha
The late Samra Abd-El-Nabi
The late Sarida Badri
Sarraf Hela
Sayegh Amnon
Sayegh Yitzhak
Sehayik Edmon
Shabib Moshe
Shabtai Daniel
Shahmoon (Shasha) Gourgey
The late Shahrabani Edward
Shahrabani Salman
Shahrabani Dr. William
The late Shalom Saleh
The late Shalom Rony
Shalu Yousif
Shamai Meir
The late Shamash Eitan
Shamash Naim
Shashou Abraham
Shashou Marguelite
The late Shaul Jack (journalist)
Shemtob Gamil
Shemtob Yousif

Shmueli Alfred

Shina Kamal

Shiri Eliahu

Shubi Sadika

Shukur David

Sion Ezra

Sofer David

Sofer Yitzhak David (I.D.)

Sweiri Menahem

Tweina Naim

Yadou Dr. Sasson

The late Yamen Ezra

Yamen Saleh

Yaron Eitan

Yehuda Yehezkel

Yeruham Ezra

The late Yigal Eliahu

Yona Anwar

The late Yona David

Yona Yehezkel (Austin)

Yoram Tov Anwar

Zalayet Nissim

Zakaria David

Zioni Yacov

**in the clinic**

Shamai Nazima

Shmuel Tefaha

Habiba

Juliette

# The Mossad "Aliya Bet" staff and its emissaries to Iraq (1949-1952)

The late Carmil Moshe

Adiv Dov

Itai Hanokh

The late Ben-Gur Adik

The late Barnett Rony

Gefen Ada

Hillel Shlomo

The late Cohen Sion

Melamed Shula

Markus Ilana (Lilian Nada)

The late Reis Izi

Sarid Haim

**Pilots**

Owen Jack

Lang Milton

Lippa Arthur

Lov Lenart

Marmelstein Philip

Steffes Bob

## Emissaries

Bibi Mordechai

Ben-Meir David

Ben Sur (Sourani) Raphael

Goral Yoav

Uziel Levy

The late Frank Yacov

## The Public Committee

The late Abed Sasson (Chairman)

The late El-Kabir Abraham

The late Shohet Moshe

The late Nawi Sasson

The late Sala David

# Family of Regina and  Nissim Ben-Porat

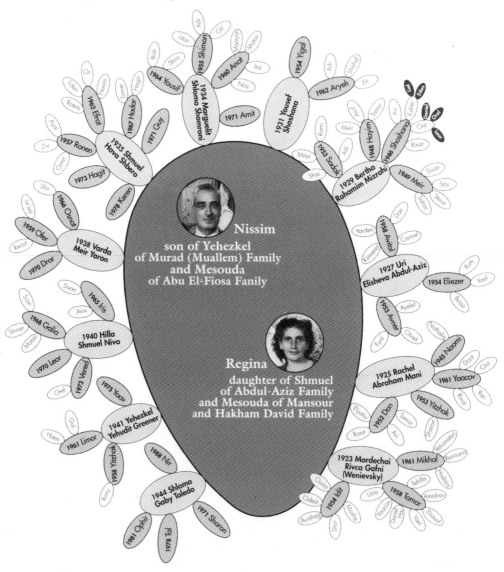

**Nissim**
son of Yehezkel
of Murad (Muallem) Family
and Mesouda
of Abu El-Fiosa Fanily

**Regina**
daughter of Shmuel
of Abdul-Aziz Family
and Mesouda of Mansour
and Hakham David Family

Sons and daughters - 11
grand-children - 40
great-grandchildren - 84
great-great-grandchildren - 5